FOOTBALL NATION

FOOTBALL NATION

Sixty Years of the Beautiful Game

ANDREW WARD
& JOHN WILLIAMS

BLOOMSBURY
LONDON · BERLIN · NEW YORK

First published in Great Britain 2009
This paperback edition published 2010

Copyright © by Andrew Ward and John Williams 2009

The moral right of the authors has been asserted

No part of this book may be used or reproduced in any manner whatsoever without written permission
from the Publisher except in the case of brief quotations embodied in critical articles or reviews

Every reasonable effort has been made to trace copyright holders of material reproduced in this book,
but if any have been inadvertently overlooked the Publishers would be glad to hear from them. For
legal purposes the list of illustrations on page 397 constitutes an extension of the copyright page

Bloomsbury Publishing Plc
36 Soho Square
London W1D 3QY

www.bloomsbury.com

Bloomsbury Publishing, London, New York and Berlin

A CIP catalogue record for this book is available from the British Library

ISBN 978 1 4088 0126 0

10 9 8 7 6 5 4 3 2 1

Typeset by Hewer Text UK Ltd, Edinburgh
Printed in Great Britain by Clays Limited, St Ives plc

For David Kynaston

Contents

INTRODUCTION

*Yet I learned from this experience that the main
components of history are not things but people.*

George Ewart Evans, *Spoken History* (1987)

O N MOST ENGLISH WEEKENDS IT is football, not cricket, that
provides the quintessential village and urban scene. Local players
commune with nature and converse in staccato shouts. On the sidelines,
substitutes warm up and chat to spectators, coaches bellow instructions,
injured players wonder when they will next be fit and a club official guards
the match balls. Onlookers talk about the weather, the developing match
and recent news items.

'Did you read about that referee who sent off his boss last Saturday?'

'No.'

'He got the sack on the Monday.'

'Is he suing for unfair dismissal?'

'I think they both are.'

If the wind direction is favourable and a top-class professional football
stadium is nearby, local players and spectators may hear a massive roar as
thousands of communal town-criers announce a home-team goal. Televised
pictures of that goal will roar louder still, reaching homes in Oshkosh,
Wisconsin, brothels in Phnom Pen, Cambodia, and all-night bars in
Melbourne, Australia. Newspapers and radio stations will report the incident,
spectators will remember it, statisticians will register it and business people
will appraise it. Thousands, maybe millions, of personal stories may erupt
from one small moment.

In the villages, and at local parks, touchlines are littered with discarded
water bottles, bicycles and old potato bags recently emptied of footballs.
Beyond the touchlines young children kick a ball to one another and
nonchalantly retrieve it from the pitch. A teenage girl in unsuitable footwear

absent-mindedly watches her new lover play. A man with a dog stops and watches the action for ten minutes until his best friend grows restless. A young woman wheels a pushchair across the corner of the pitch and leaves a track in the mud. A scout from a professional football club studies a recommended fifteen-year-old who may have slipped through the normal tracking system.

'What do you think of him?' a club official asks the scout. 'Doesn't he look like his dad?'

'Spitting image,' the scout replies. 'If only he could play like him.'

'He's a deceptive player.'

'Aye, he's deceptively slow.'

A spectator with a radio earpiece listens to a Premier League match and watches the local one. Passing motorists rubberneck the park scene for a few seconds. A double-decker bus halts at a nearby stop and briefly swells the attendance by a dozen. A father, watching his eighteen-year-old son, suddenly realises that he has seen his lad grow up through ten years of local soccer pitches. An elderly man in a flat cap talks to a complete stranger about 'Stanley Matthews' and 'proper boots' and 'them days'. A club stalwart walks round the ground with a collection box, asking for donations because the showers need replacing. The chairman talks enthusiastically about the club's mini-soccer and its ladies' and youth teams.

At the local level, teams of players gather on rectangles of grass surrounded by allotments, tennis courts, fallow cricket pitches, children's playgrounds, farmers' fields, industrial units, grassy banks, dilapidated pavilions, houses of all kinds, trees of all species, cemeteries, car parks and perhaps more football pitches. Advertising boards bear the names of local car-breakers, fish bars and Indian restaurants rather than global corporations. Inside the clubhouse, a horseracing commentary emanates from the television set as the club secretary's wife prepares an urn of tea. At half-time a substitute leaves the dressing-room in his stockinged feet to get the latest Premier League and Football League scores from the clubhouse television.

Later, five minutes before the full-time whistle, one coach walks across to his opposite number and shakes hands. 'I have to leave before the end,' he says. 'I've got to get my boy back to his mother.'

At the nearby professional stadium, supporters may have travelled hundreds of miles to be present. They may be former local residents who cannot give up their attachment to football, fans who have been attracted to the club through television or migrants whose imaginations have been gripped by the nation's star players and top clubs. Spectators enter through turnstiles operated by the latest technology, grab a coffee and a pie, and are greeted by cameras, stewards and signs ('It is a Criminal Offence to Encroach on the Pitch'). Journalists plug in their laptops in the press box. An experienced referee shuts out the crowd noise and sprints into position almost as quickly as the players. Thousands of fans in replica shirts idolise young players whom they have never met. But supporters feel they know these stars well because their heroes have revealed all in the club's programme – their favourite musical artist, their dream date, their choice of food and so on.

Such is the media influence on the modern game that a customer listening to the radio in the Original Barber's Shop in Plymouth may hear details of a goal more quickly than the man at a Premier League match whose view was blocked for the vital moment. The most experienced of football followers can be caught out by something new: a defender scores his first goal after his manager has vowed to stand naked in a shop window if it ever happens; a player scores five goals in the first forty minutes and his team leads 5–0; or a pitch-side sprinkler suddenly turns itself on during the match. The result is important but the game is about so much more.

Across England, thousands of local matches will each touch the lives of fifty or more people every week, yet fewer than fifty top professional matches will touch the lives of millions. Most players pay to play, some are paid expenses, others get match fees, some are on salaries and a select few will become full-fledged celebrities and brand names, making the national gossip magazines as well as the sporting press.

Football matches can be global, national, regional, local or neighbourhood-based. The players may be watched by hundreds of millions on television and 50,000 people at the stadium or, more likely, the players will outnumber the spectators present. On most weekends the aggregate of local players and spectators is greater than that for England's vibrant Premier League. Ultimately, though, these are simply different parts of an integrated sporting system that extends upwards and outwards, downwards and inwards, rippling like a pond receiving a pebble. The game helps to connect individuals, families, communities, different ethnic groups and, more crucially, English society.

In this book we tell short stories that feature a range of people united by a love of football. This should give you a rapid feel for the development of football and the English in the years since 1946. It is not a definitive book on post-war English football. The relationship between football and society is such a complex issue that it needs many voices to capture its rich kaleidoscope. Sports historians such as Nick Fishwick, Dick Holt, Tony Mason, Dave Russell and Matt Taylor have written excellent social histories of the game. Our aim here is merely to add to the existing literature by constructing readable tales about real football people while retaining the integrity of our original research.

PART ONE

INTRODUCTION TO PART ONE

IN THIS FIRST PART WE take up English football's story at the end of the Second World War. By 1945 the professional game had been chaotic for six years. Some club grounds had been bombed or requisitioned, several clubs had been disbanded for a year or more and many players were absent with good reason. Wartime matches were almost all friendlies played on a regional basis – even international matches were unofficial – and there was no relegation or promotion. Players were often servicemen from other clubs who happened to be stationed nearby, and they received thirty shillings (£1.50) a match.

Then, in 1945–6, came a transitional season. Matches were arranged as League North and League South. More dramatically, the national FA Cup competition was restored to the calendar in January 1946. It was arranged on a two-legged basis to ensure that every professional club had at least one home FA Cup match.

In *Football's War and Peace* Thomas Taw paints an intricate picture of the 1946–7 season. The lives of football people were dislocated and difficult as they tried to cope with a damaged infrastructure. Football equipment was substandard and travel facilities poor. The professional players' union was in dispute with the authorities, and properties were so scarce that a club could attract a top-class player by offering a vacant house. That start-up post-war season was played through a very harsh winter and, with the frequent postponements and a ban on midweek matches, the League programme was not completed until 14 June 1947.

In the late 1940s football offered hope for the general populace, a chance to restore community and belonging. Towns and cities had to rebuild and one way to do so was symbolically, through support for local football teams. Fans flocked to grounds in huge numbers, whether it be in Barrow or Banstead, Winsford or Wolverhampton. But renewed vitality brought new problems: players risked injury during matches and when travelling to fixtures; and spectators faced danger from overcrowding and crushing. Fans did their best to take care of one another in the late 1940s, but sometimes the circumstances were impossibly difficult. Stadiums were often dilapidated and the management of crowds was crude.

Spectating reached a peak in the late 1940s and then slowly declined through the 1950s and beyond. Football helped people find stability, normality and familiarity after the war, and many fans remained loyal. This was an era of relative equality within the game. Seven different clubs won the Football League Championship in the first ten years after the war. Amateur teams (or so-called amateur teams) could compete with top-class professional opposition in FA Cup ties, and works teams regularly appeared in the first round of the FA Cup. Amateur players could be selected for the England national team, top amateur matches could attract 100,000 spectators and *The Times* devoted over a third of its football coverage to the amateur game.

The British home internationals – involving England, Scotland, Northern Ireland and Wales – were more important than the fledgling World Cup (ignored by England until 1950). It was a time of expanding supporters' clubs, continuing national service and shoulder-charging goalkeepers. Overseas trips were only for the top professional clubs and organised Sunday football was an illegal activity pursued by heathens and renegades. The biggest media development during this period was the launch of hospital radio commentaries. This was the last era before television emerged as a powerful force at professional football grounds.

While the children of the day may recall the era happily, most adults of the time found it austere, drab and grey. The gloom was lifted when floodlights arrived at professional football grounds in the fifties and captured everyone's imagination and wit.

'Come on, lads,' one fan shouted. 'Pylon the pressure.'

I

DON'T MENTION THE WAR

A T THE START OF 1946 wartime experiences dominated the collective memory of football people. Men in their twenties gathered in football-club dressing-rooms in preparation for the sport's quasi-battles, and their silent twelfth man was the Second World War. The psychological trauma would remain in the communal psyche through the next generation.

Take the sad case of the Daniel family. Bobby Daniel was a fantastic schoolboy footballer who captained Wales Schoolboys and signed for Arsenal at fourteen. As a teenager he played for a Welsh XI against Western Command and scored twice in a 4–1 wartime win. But 21-year-old Flight Sergeant Bobby Daniel, an air-gunner, was killed on a mission to Prague on Christmas Eve of 1943. His bereaved father told Bobby's fifteen-year-old brother Ray, 'You have to try to take over from Bobby.' Ray Daniel was signed by Arsenal, and he went on to play for Wales, thinking that he had to be twice as good as others in case he was getting the chance to make up for brother Bobby.

Take also the fortunate example of Dennis Herod, Stoke City's regular goalkeeper in the early 1940s. Herod joined the Royal Tank Regiment in Sicily and fought through Italy before the unit was recalled to England. He was back in action the day after the Normandy landings in the summer of 1944, half expecting to be a front-line victim. Instead he escaped a blazing tank with only a fractured jawbone. Herod's war was over on medical grounds and he considered himself exceptionally lucky to be alive and back playing for Stoke City.

Or take the odd case of Henry Walters, who got his chance in the Wolverhampton Wanderers first team at sixteen because most full-time professionals had enlisted. Walters was exempt from the forces because he was serving a carpentry apprenticeship at a Yorkshire colliery. Instead he was sent to London to help repair bomb damage. On Saturday mornings he carried his boots and shin-pads in a Gladstone bag while he worked on derelict buildings. On Saturday afternoons he played as a guest for Clapton Orient. Walters saw Orient as the Cinderella club of London – he called them Clapton Ornaments – because the whole area, with its many factories, had suffered severe bombing. 'The washing facilities weren't too good,' he told people after the war. 'But there was usually a puddle somewhere.'

Sad, fortunate and odd.

In 1946 millions of sad, fortunate and odd stories were waiting to be told.

Private George Shaw spent too much of the Second World War in a Japanese prisoner-of-war camp. In the mountainous jungle he worked hard and perspired pints. As Japanese officers exerted their authority, waiting to beat the slackers and the sickly, Allied soldiers built sections of the Bangkok–Burma railway. A third of these prisoners died of torture, overwork, starvation or beriberi.

In tropical heat George Shaw and his mates swung cudgels and picks while trying to dodge the fall-out from dynamite explosions that sent debris flying at their bodies. The Japanese wore uniforms and heavy boots, but the prisoners were naked except for scraps of clothing that hid their private parts. Shaw was barefoot. With his long hair and unkempt beard he felt like a savage.

As he swung his pick, sweat dropping off his chin, Shaw spoke briefly to his nearest mate.

'Bill,' he said. 'If I'm ever lucky enough to get out of this mess, apart from seeing my family, there's one other thing I'd like to see.'

'What's that, George?' said Bill in his broad Birmingham accent.

'I'd like to see Derby County win the Cup. At Wembley.'

'I doubt it very much, George. I doubt if Derby are good enough for that.'

'But that's what I'd like to see before I die,' Shaw insisted.

He knew he had little chance of fulfilling his fantasy. Derby County had never won the FA Cup and he didn't think he'd get out of the jungle alive. But football offers scope for hope.

Quiz question: Which club won the FA Cup and retained the trophy for seven years?

Answer: Portsmouth, who surprisingly beat Wolves 4–1 in the 1939 FA Cup Final and safely stored the FA Cup until shortly before the 1946 Final. Portsmouth manager Jack Tinn probably knew more about the trophy than anyone. He knew, for instance, that it held eleven pints. He also knew that it was insured for £200, because he had dealt with the paperwork during the war years.

Tinn first put the trophy into a local bank for extra security, but the bank was hit in the blitz. The next morning, when they heard the news, anxious Portsmouth FC officials assumed the trophy had been destroyed in the blast, but Tinn had been one step ahead. Expecting an air raid, he had taken the silverware home that night and nursed it under the stairs. Thereafter the FA Cup trophy spent most of the war in the cells of Havant police station. It was finally released from police custody in February 1946.

Stanley Gliksten once said that to take over a football club you had to be a multimillionaire, a football lover and a bloody fool. He reckoned that there were some multimillionaires, a lot of people who loved football and plenty of bloody fools. But very few people had all three attributes.

In the early 1930s Stanley Gliksten and his brother Albert were chairman and vice-chairman respectively of one of the world's biggest timber merchants. Based in London, they were on Clapton Orient's advisory committee, and they knew the importance of football to their workforce. The Gliksten's employees worked five and a half days a week, left the timber yard Saturday lunchtime, grabbed a sandwich and then went to watch a Football League match, usually at Clapton Orient or West Ham United.

In 1932 the Gliksten's were approached by David Clark, the sole remaining director of Charlton Athletic FC. The brothers accepted the challenge of reviving Charlton. They negotiated with the club's creditors, raised £25,000 for new players, appointed Jimmy Seed as manager and steered the club from Football League Division Three (South) to second place in Division One. In 1937 the Gliksten's personally took over Charlton Athletic's liabilities, paid off debenture holders and met all previous losses. The bill came to £68,000.

It was tough at Charlton Athletic's ground, the Valley, during the early part of the war. The venue frequently came under enemy fire, so attendances dropped to a few hundred diehards and spectators were often forced to take cover during air raids. Matches were sometimes suspended for more than an hour and some were abandoned when delays forced players back to work. Charlton Athletic closed down for the second half of the 1940–1 season. Four bombs fell on the terraces and two on the pitch. The Gliksten's were losing money and in danger of losing fans in bombing raids.

Later in the war, however, Charlton recruited some good players. They reached two League South Cup Finals at Wembley and drew 1–1 with Aston

Villa in the 1944 national final. When the 1945–6 season began Football League clubs were forced by the government to keep jobs open for their pre-war players, even if those players were now thirty-eight and wounded. And there were other problems. Four of the six houses in Blackheath owned by Charlton Athletic and lived in by players had been requisitioned during the war.

So when Albert Brown returned to his job as a Charlton Athletic footballer he found that he had lost his pre-war home. Thirty-year-old 'Sailor' Brown had definitely not acquired his nickname from his service in the Royal Air Force. It came from the shape of his legs, bowed like those of a man experienced at coping with the ocean swell. On the football field those legs gave Sailor the balance he needed to swerve one way or the other and leave defenders guessing. He was good enough to play for England – in six wartime internationals – but had nowhere to live. So much for 'homes fit for heroes'. Sailor Brown asked for a transfer. He wanted to go where the houses were.

One of football's much-loved characters of this era was Sam Bartram, the Charlton Athletic goalkeeper. Bartram, a Burt Lancaster type from the North-East and a former coalminer, spent the war as a physical training instructor in the RAF. By 1946, though, he was back in his role as a professional entertainer. A brave goalkeeper who put his head among a flurry of flying boots, he was once asked to test protective headgear by a crash-helmet manufacturer. In safe situations Bartram might run out of his penalty area and head the ball or else dribble some distance upfield. He would even dive forward under the ball and kick it over his head with his heels. In one match in February 1946 he elected to take a penalty-kick. He ran up, hoofed the ball over the bar and faced an undignified sprint back to his goal. But Bartram also saved the team in an FA Cup game at Wolves. That win helped Charlton Athletic to qualify for the last sixteen of the 1946 FA Cup competition.

Leon Leuty was born just outside Shrewsbury in 1920, but his family moved to Derby when he was a very small boy. His folks assumed there was a French and Cornish extraction to the Leuty family. Leon was, after all, a French name and a Captain Leuty was buried in Falmouth in the sixteenth century.

In Derby, Leon Leuty's engineer father worked at Rolls-Royce, and young Leon was raised respecting the company that dominated the town's industry. A whole generation of Derby people grew up believing that the best car in the world was a Rolls-Royce and the worst was the fictional Rolls-Canardly ('It rolls down hills but canardly get up them').

Leon Leuty played football for Derby Boys for an unprecedented three seasons, the last two as captain. A chubby-faced schoolboy, smaller than most around him, he had dark hair, parted on the left, and a friendly disposition. In 1935 he played two trials for the England schoolboys' team, but the right-half place went to Whitchurch of Essex. Leuty was England's reserve.

That same year he left school at fourteen and, after trying a few jobs, started a toolmaking apprenticeship in Rolls-Royce's engineering shop. Leuty promised his mother that he would serve his apprenticeship and not do anything silly – like trying to become a professional footballer. He played amateur football for Derby Corinthians and signed amateur forms for Derby County in the 1938–9 season. Shortly before war broke out he was playing for Derby County's third team at Leicester when he damaged his right knee. When he came round from the eventual cartilage operation he realised that his mother was probably right. Football was a precarious life.

After recovering Leuty played football for Rolls-Royce. He was coming up to twenty now, taller, leaner, without the puppy fat of his schoolboy days. He couldn't play for Derby County in the early 1940s as the club didn't really exist – the military had taken over the Baseball Ground at the start of the war – but Notts County manager Frank Womack invited him for a trial. After another cartilage injury Leuty decided that his football career was over. He would be a toolmaker at Rolls-Royce, sustaining the war effort with essential work. He put away his football boots.

But Frank Womack kept in touch.

'If you ever want to give it a try, you're welcome at Notts,' the manager told Leuty.

Weeks went by.

'I need your help to keep the team going,' said Womack the next time they met. 'It's not easy getting a team together.'

One day Leuty looked out his old football boots. He found them, handled them, put them on and walked around his family home in them. Then he contacted Frank Womack and tried football again.

Wartime football was all about guest players and uncertainty. Some fans went to matches with their boots in case there was an announcement ('Are there any footballers in the crowd?'). Notts County fans watched a combination of Frank Womack's local lads and international players such as Ron Burgess (Spurs) and Tommy Lawton (Everton), who were stationed nearby. They were also lucky to see Leuty develop into one of the best centre halves in the country.

In 1942 Leuty worked nights at Rolls-Royce so as to be free on Saturday afternoons. He often arrived at the Notts County ground exhausted, then soon recovered. He gave the game everything he had; that was his style. Then, one Saturday in January 1943, when Notts County were playing some distance away and travelling was far from easy, Leuty said he was unavailable for his regular team. News of this raced around Derby. Jack Nicholas, a reserve policeman who was in charge of the regrouping Derby County players, needed a centre half that same day, so he set off for the Leutys' home in Allenton. Leuty had worked Friday night at Rolls-Royce, clocked off around 8am, eaten breakfast and was catching up on some sleep.

Nicholas woke him and asked, 'Do you fancy a game?'

Leuty set off to play for Derby County.

The club had been resurrected from a rock-bottom position of 1941 when it had no ground, no team, no fixtures, no manager and virtually no directors. Not only had the ground been taken over and hit by a bomb, but manager George Jobey and four directors had been suspended *sine die*. A joint Football League and Football Association commission had examined Derby County's pre-war accounts and found evidence of wages for fictitious groundsmen and expenses for journeys never made. Illegal bonuses and under-counter payments had been given to players.

In the latter part of the war Derby's industries provided a number of so-called reserved occupations for promising young footballers. They made hand grenades at Qualcast, concrete railway sleepers at LNER, munitions at EW Bliss and Grundy's and, of course, aircraft engines at Rolls-Royce. Two older international footballers, Sammy Crooks and Dally Duncan, were still in town, working at Coles Cranes and Derby Carriage & Wagon Works respectively. Once a man had worked in the war industries he couldn't be recruited into the forces in case he was captured and forced to divulge national secrets.

It was relatively easy to attract guest players to Derby County as the town was centrally located in England and had good rail links. The team regularly included internationals of the calibre of Peter Doherty (Manchester City) and Raich Carter (Sunderland). By the end of the unofficial 1944–5 league season, however, every regular Derby County player was either in his early twenties or his thirties. Many professional players in their late twenties were in another country.

Leuty switched permanently to Derby County in August 1943 when the Rolls-Royce night shift finally took its toll on him. He signed professional forms at twenty-three and in the next three seasons played 130 matches, more than any other Derby County player. By now he had changed physically. He was nearly six feet tall, slim, supple and striking. Off the field he could have been mistaken for an actor. His dark, crinkly hair, high forehead and dark eyebrows made an asset out of his large, pointed nose. And his friendliness was magnetic. He was growing in confidence daily – as a tradesman, as a footballer and as a man who was very attractive to women and yet decidedly one of the lads. When he smiled the world seemed a nice place again. When he laughed it was infectious. And he smiled and laughed a lot, especially when the war ended and the FA Cup competition was reintroduced. Derby County's team of players aged under twenty-six and over thirty-one now had the chance to fulfil the FA Cup Final dreams of Derby folk, including George Shaw, the ex-prisoner of war.

2

'SURELY THEY'D FAINTED'

B ERT GREGORY WAS RAISED IN the 1920s, when children played street football with a ball of twine, a pig's bladder, a tin can, a tennis ball or an old ale bag stuffed with paper. They played morning, noon and night. Bert Gregory ate, drank and slept football. There was little else to do.

He and his mates needed to avoid the local policeman, who would either clobber them, if he caught them playing in the street, or say, 'I know your father.' If the lads refused to stop playing, or gave the policeman some cheek, there would be real trouble. Bert Gregory and his pals were arrested when they were teenagers. They were taken to court and fined five shillings (25p) for playing football in the King's Highway.

Gregory's first organised football came when he played in the Bolton Sunday School League. He paid a sixpence (2½p) weekly subscription to his club and made sure he satisfied the requirement of attending Sunday School at least twice a month. In fact he went every Sunday. His mother insisted.

In 1923 Gregory skipped school to watch a Wednesday afternoon FA Cup replay between Bolton Wanderers and Huddersfield Town. That was like asking to be caned. Gregory grew accustomed to crowds of 60,000 at Bolton's Burnden Park ground, and was part of a 69,912 attendance at a 1933 FA Cup match against Manchester City. Later he was employed by Bolton Wanderers, doing odd jobs for the club, and he kept his counsel about anything he learned. The senior staff trusted him. He understood the ways of professional football. He got to know Burnden Park very well, but nothing prepared him for the events of Saturday 9 March 1946.

On this fateful Saturday large crowds of spectators made their way to Burnden Park, half a mile south of the town centre. Bolton was returning to normal. Meat and cheese were arriving from New Zealand, Hermann Goering was having to defend himself at the Nuremberg Trials and local cinemas were showing *I Know Where I'm Going* and *Confidential Agent*. Maybe the beer barrow would be back at Burnden Park for a half-time drink. A place in the FA Cup semi-finals would be worth celebrating after this destructive war, and Wanderers were 2–0 up after the first leg at Stoke City (in a season when all FA Cup ties were played over two legs).

The Railway End embankment, at the northern end of the Bolton ground, supported the LMS line that ran from Yorkshire to Bolton. The embankment was muddy, mucky and messy. There were no seats. The spectators stood on dirt with a few old stone flags for steps. Burnden Park officials reckoned that the Railway End could hold 28,435 people. That worked out at 1⅔ square feet per person. Secretary-manager Walter Rowley planned for a crowd of 50,000, having estimated 5,000 extra spectators for each of the two main stars – Ray Westwood (Bolton Wanderers) and Stanley Matthews (Stoke City).

The first spectators arrived at the ground at 8 am and turnstiles were open from 12.30. Thousands continued to arrive, the streets outside becoming choked. By 2.15 the conditions outside the turnstiles were very uncomfortable. People were packed in tight queues and some were pressed against the stadium walls. A few fell on the floor. One man gripped his eighteen pence (7½p) entrance money and said he would happily pay the ticket price just to get out of the crush. By the time he reached the turnstile he could no longer open his hand to drop the money. An old man fainted and was held upright by the crowd.

'Mind th'owd chap,' someone shouted.

The crowd was generally in good humour, even though the turnstiles seemed a long way off and the crush was severe.

'I'd be awreet if when I moved mi feet came wi'mi,' said one man.

'I wish I'd ne'er 'ad that prater pie.'

'I wish t'directors were i'this lot.'

Police Constable Lowe was one of 103 officers on duty at Burnden Park. He could see a bottleneck building up in front of him, so he went to find the head gateman. PC Lowe wanted the Railway End turnstiles closed. But the head gateman had duties all over the ground and couldn't be found.

Around 2.40, PC McDougal set off to find the head gateman. He met him near the Main Stand.

'The Bolton End could do with being closed,' said PC McDougal.

The head gateman went round the turnstiles and told the checkers to stop checking. Some had already done so. Spectators inside had been shouting that there was a problem.

By this time the turnstiles had clocked 28,137 people on to the Railway End but that figure wasn't known until later. The head gateman did not have access to the numbers and had to rely solely on how packed the crowd looked. The official attendance was 65,419, but who knows how many were really there? It was later estimated that between 85,000 and 90,000 people had arrived in Bolton wanting to watch the match.

Seeing the turnstiles closed, many fans gate-crashed the match via the adjacent railway line. They tore up the railway fence and climbed on to the Bolton–Bury line. They walked along the track to the signal-box and then dropped down to the embankment, overwhelming the seven railway policemen. Maybe 3,000 or 4,000 supporters got up on to the railway line that way. Some had a view of the pitch from behind the railway fence. Most gave up and went home.

Other fans simply climbed over the turnstiles. About 1,000 went over the entrance to the Boys & Forces enclosure without paying their ninepences (4p). A group of twenty sailors hoisted one another on to shoulders and scaled the turnstiles.

Inside the Railway End, Norman Crook decided to leave because he was worried about his twelve-year-old boy, who was feeling ill as a result of the crush. Ten minutes before kick-off Crook picked a gate lock near the Boys & Forces entrance to get out. He and his son left, but those still locked out now saw their chance.

'Come on, Charlie, we're in here,' one man shouted. About 300 spectators came through the gate before policemen forced it closed.

The incomers from the Boys & Forces entrance put more weight on the north-west corner of the Railway End, where the physical pressure was now intense.

'Stop shoving, there's children in front,' someone shouted.

A young girl was passed down over the heads of spectators.

'Go to the corner of Weston Street,' shouted the child's mother, who was trapped in the crowd.

Audrey Nicholls's father had started taking her to matches when she was five years old. That felt like a real adventure because the two of them drank coffee at the match whereas they never had coffee at home. As a teenager Audrey went regularly to football with a school pal. On the day of the Stoke City match she was standing in the Railway End.

She was a third of the way up the terrace. The view was good but she was very uncomfortable and scared. There were too many people. There was pressure from the side and pressure from the back. She felt she needed to get out. There was no point in going back towards the exit gate because that was the source of the squeeze. She wanted to get to the track, where the police were allowing smaller kids to climb the wall and sit on the cinders.

When the teams came out and the game started, the children sitting on the cinder track found it difficult to see because the track was two feet below the raised pitch. On the Railway End terrace, people craned their necks to see and pressed on shoulders in front to hold their position. Some people had their backs to the pitch, their faces to the sun, unable to turn round. Others had their arms forced into the air and were unable to get them down. There was no space to swing a rattle.

'Let us out.'

'Get us out.'

The swaying and the jostling grew worse. The pressure from gate-crashers caused a surge from the north-west corner of the embankment. People tumbled forward. Two twelve-foot-wide crush barriers near the corner flag gave way under the strain. People in the bottleneck near the front tumbled on to the floor three or four deep. Men and women were screaming. Clothes were torn from people's backs.

Seeing people in real distress, the police now broke down the wooden paling fence between the enclosure and the running track.

'Get them out any road,' the call came.

The teams had been playing for only a few minutes. The afternoon sun, after a heavy night's frost, had made the pitch black and heavy.

Long before kick-off Joe Harrison had been knocked to the floor of the enclosure. For what seemed like thirty minutes he was a human carpet, trampled from all sides. He kept his head down and managed to get one hand free to loosen his tie and collar. A policeman eventually got him out and he survived. Others were not so fortunate.

Bert Gregory sat with his wife in the Main Stand. They were three rows from the front. His wife grew agitated.

'It's only a crowd,' Gregory told her. 'They'll sort it out. There's room over there.'

He could see that the spectators were unevenly distributed in the Railway End. He assumed they would spread naturally, as crowds usually do.

'Some of them people are injured,' his wife said.

'Don't worry, it'll be all right. They're feeling a bit distressed, but they'll be all right.'

Officials brought out a body and laid it on the grass verge at the back of one of the goals.

'That woman's dead,' Gregory's wife said.

'How do you know that from here?'

'I can tell – woman's instinct.'

Someone covered the motionless woman's face.

'What are you getting excited about?' asked Gregory. 'She'll be all right.'

'No. She's dead.'

Audrey Nicholls was helped out of the crush by some men nearby. They lifted her up and passed her over the top of the spectators. She felt the hands of a score of other people as she went overhead towards the police and first-aiders on the track. It was not a dignified exit, but Audrey was glad to be out of the crowd. She stepped over the low fence at the front of the terrace and stood at the side of the pitch. That was when she saw the dead bodies laid out on the track. Their faces were a terrible colour that she had never seen before. Killed at a football match. Incredible. Football was supposed to be enjoyment and a source of pleasure, a release from the horrors of war.

Audrey's first reaction was to stare at the corpses. Her second was to leave the ground and go home.

Twelve minutes into the game, with the crowd already encroaching on to the pitch, Inspector Topping walked across and asked the referee to take the players off for a ten-minute break so that the pitch could be cleared. The referee informed the two captains, Harry Hubbick (Bolton) and Neil Franklin (Stoke).

When the players departed, the pitch quickly filled with people escaping the crush on the terrace. Dead bodies were laid out near the corner flag. Most people in the crowd thought these prone spectators were fainting cases. Bert Gregory grew more apprehensive. Maybe his wife was right. Maybe some were dead. How was it that she could tell better than him?

As they carried one body past the Main Stand, the stretcher-bearers accidentally tipped the stretcher and the lifeless body rolled on to the track. Gregory watched, disbelievingly.

One policeman wanted to open the Railway Enclosure gates from the inside but he couldn't find a key-holder. To relieve the pressure, between 1,000 and 1,400 people were shepherded out of the Railway End and into a vacant stand that had been hitherto closed and guarded because it had been occupied by the Ministry of Food during the war. About 2,000 to 2,500 spectators were brought down to the track. They spread across the touchline. A new touchline was marked with sawdust. The pitch was narrowed.

The dressing-rooms were normally a sanctuary for players and officials, but the St John Ambulance team now commandeered every vacant inch of space along the corridors under the stand. Twenty-four medical staff had reported for duty. There were two doctors, six nurses and sixteen St John volunteers. This had been increased since the previous match, when staff had been caught short by the number of flu sufferers in the crowd.

Now the casualties were brought in every few seconds. Broken limbs. Split heads. Damaged ribs. Stomach and chest bruises. Cut shins. They were carried in on makeshift stretchers. The dead were placed on wooden benches and carried to the joiner's shop, which became a mortuary. The stack of wooden benches disappeared alarmingly quickly.

'They've only fainted.'

'Let's get on with the game.'

The Bolton Chief Constable overheard comments around the ground and realised that very few people understood the extent of the tragedy. If the match were abandoned now, a rush for the exits might produce more casualties. Also, it was better to keep the spectators inside the ground so that the injured could be ferried to hospital through quiet streets.

The Chief Constable spoke with the referee, who went into the dressing-rooms and said, 'We'd better finish this match.'

After a break of twenty-six minutes the game resumed, but all the pleasure had gone out of the event. A generation of people accustomed to danger – air raids and battles – had been caught out by a strange kind of friendly fire. The dead included experienced soldiers who had survived hostile action only to be killed at a football ground. Fred Battersby had been at the evacuation of Dunkirk before serving four years in the Middle East with the Royal Artillery. His brother James Battersby, another victim, had seen five and a half years' army service.

Audrey Nicholls arrived home while the match was still taking place. Her parents were surprised to see her.

'There's been some trouble,' she told them. 'There were bodies lying on the pitch.'

'Surely they'd fainted.'

'No, no, they're dead.'

She had damaged her shoes, so her mother took her into town to buy a new pair. When she came back her father confirmed what she had said about the deaths. Audrey felt she had had a lucky escape, thanks to the men who had passed her over their heads. A fourteen-year-old schoolboy had died in the disaster.

On a Burnden Park pitch churned up by spectators and police horses, Bolton Wanderers drew 0–0 with Stoke City and progressed to the semi-finals. When Bert Gregory reached home that evening, his next-door neighbour came round.

'Hey, what about this to-do at Bolton?' the neighbour said.

'Aye, there's been a big crowd and there's been some injuries.'

'Injuries? There's a lot dead. It's in the paper.'

The final edition of the *Bolton Evening News* reported at least seventeen people killed and many more injured.

Thirty-three people died in the Bolton disaster. Around 500 were injured. A Home Office inquiry, chaired by Ronw Moelwyn Hughes KC, concluded that the pre-match crowd estimate of 50,000 was reasonable.

'The disaster was unique,' the report concluded. 'There was no collapse of a structure: it was the first example in the history of football following of serious casualties inflicted by a crowd upon itself.'

The major problem was the overall planning. There was no scientific assessment of the ground's capacity – merely the ground's previous record attendance – and no way of telling when the capacity was reached. No one was able to find keys that would have opened exit doors and relieved pressure on the crowd. Not all the turnstiles were operable. And there was no way of immediately closing turnstiles when the crowd became too large. The club officials were not readily available on the day and they left a lot to the police.

The psychology of the massed football-ground terrace was complex. People did not stand scientifically. They wanted their regular place near their mates. They wanted to be in front of a barrier. They wanted a position to suit their height and weight. No one wanted to stand where a pillar was blocking the goal or behind a six-foot-six bruiser in a trilby.

Passageways through a crowd opened and closed. The route from A to B was not the same for everyone. A full terrace had dense patches and sparsely populated areas. The dense patches could easily feel dangerous. All it needed was some extra pressure, an unpredictable sway, an exciting moment near the corner flag, a man pressing on his neighbour as he steadied himself to pee down a rolled-up newspaper, a few people heading to the refreshment bar or the exits. As spectators left the stadium at the end of the match, the meeting of two throngs could cause a crush.

The mystery of the Bolton disaster was that football crowds in this era were not more volatile. They were orderly and well-behaved. The disaster happened because of poor organisation and the lack of provision for the *possibility* of nearly 90,000 turning up. If people arrive, expectant and excited, for a crucial FA Cup tie after seven years of football famine, they will do what they can to get inside the ground, and this leaves football-club directors with a dilemma. How do we keep it safe and yet get as many people inside as possible? The problem was aggravated by football-club officials not having had to deal with these issues for seven years. For most of the Second World War stadium safety meant protection from air raids.

The lessons were there to be learned. Important matches should be all-ticket. Ground capacities should be set at safe levels. Terracing should be examined. Crush barriers should be studied for their siting, strength and type. Entrances to the ground should be safe and sensibly placed. There should be safe ways for spectators to leave the ground during play. There should be a loudspeaker system, a central control room, radio communication between police and accessible aggregate figures for each section of the ground.

The Home Office report recommended that a licensing authority (e.g. the local authority) should be appointed to issue football-ground licences and carry out periodic checks. All football grounds were at risk. They had too much timber and earth, and too little steel and concrete.

*   *   *

On the Monday after the disaster Walter Rowley sent for Bert Gregory, who was working at the ground.

'Find a rope, Bert, will you?' Rowley said. 'See the police. They'll tell you where to go.'

The police told Gregory to rope off a part of the terrace where the deaths had occurred. He found the debris of a disaster. Belts. Raincoats. Hats. Scarves. Flat caps. Shoes.

In the years that followed, Bert Gregory didn't like talking about the Bolton disaster; it meant recalling those terrible scenes of dead bodies and scattered clothing. But he knew he had to speak about it. It was a reminder of what could happen if you didn't take precautions.

3

ABIDE WITH ME

'YOU COULDN'T GET A TICKET for love nor money,' Derbyshire folk said about the 1946 FA Cup Final, and Charlton Athletic manager Jimmy Seed reckoned he could have sold 500,000 tickets. In fact Charlton Athletic and Derby County were allocated only 12,000 tickets each, even though the match was attended by 98,215 spectators. There were no supporters' clubs to aid the distribution of tickets and no voucher systems to favour regular fans. And who were the regular supporters anyway? Some had followed the clubs through the 1930s but had not watched many recent matches because they had been elsewhere in the world.

The Cup Final came at a time when the whole country was readjusting, and the Home Office investigation of the Burnden Park disaster hung over club secretaries. The staff at Derby County dispatched tickets to the public as best they could. The men at the centre of the distribution network were secretary Jack Catterall and his assistant Cyril Annable. They were very different characters.

In one publicity piece Jack Catterall was described as football's youngest administrator at the age of thirty-four. He claimed to have played cricket for Leicestershire and amateur football for the Corinthians and Manchester United. He was a flamboyant dresser with a range of colourful blazers, and he seemed to know everyone. Unfortunately his football-club administrative experience was very limited and his approach proved costly. Catterall was later suspended *sine die* for withholding players' income tax and paying excessive bonuses.

In contrast Cyril Annable, Derby County assistant secretary in 1946, was a quiet man who went about his job efficiently and effectively. He didn't seek out people but was not unfriendly when approached. At times he seemed out of place at the Baseball Ground, surrounded as he was by bantering footballers who were full of camaraderie, but he was not unusual in the world of administrators. Anyone who has dealt with hangers-on and unworthy ticket-chasers would not find Annable's liking for privacy strange. Before the 1946 Cup Final he started to receive carpets, legs of ham and other black-market products beyond the ken of rationed English folk. There were even stories of journalists giving away match tickets for a joint of meat ('forgive us our press passes'). Annable politely returned all his offerings and launched himself on a twenty-year career with his integrity intact.

At Charlton Athletic ticket applicants had their names and addresses noted and successful ones were asked to bring their identity cards when collecting tickets ('to help in the defeat of ticket racketeers'). At Derby County the ticket shortage caused a rift between players and directors. The players' wives were offered uncovered five-shilling (25p) seats, while the directors' wives were given either thirty-shilling (£1.50) or £2 seats under cover. The players weren't pleased when they heard. On the Thursday before the Final the experienced players approached the directors and demanded better tickets for their wives. The directors refused. The players issued an ultimatum.

'No tickets, no match,' said Raich Carter, a senior Derby County player and previously captain of the 1937 FA Cup-winning Sunderland team.

The directors relented. The players' wives were upgraded to covered seats.

The place of women had changed during the war and many Derby wives had been earning well in the local factories. Now the women were pushed back into the homes and the men reclaimed their masculine roles. *Daily Mirror* journalist Tom Phillips wrote some strong words on the subject: 'For organised sport, so glorified for its part in character building, makes our women suffer in health, temper and pocket. It drives the hardy from the home, turns nice, charming, sweet brides into nagging hags, and the pleasant but weak-willed into snivelling drudges.'

Peter Blake was evacuated from Dartford during the Second World War. His local football club had strong associations with Charlton Athletic. Young Dartford players went from the nursery to Charlton; old players returned to the Dartford graveyard.

In his early teens Peter Blake followed all London sports. He supported the West Ham speedway team and watched ice-hockey and professional wrestling. He joined a few hundred fans at Dartford's ground and sometimes took a special charabanc to a Dartford away match. A haircut was exciting because his barber had been a Dartford footballer. The young boy stared at the press cuttings around the walls.

The height of excitement, though, came when he mingled with thousands at Charlton Athletic. Blake had returned to London at the perfect time. Charlton were winning matches and qualifying for the FA Cup Final. On match days he caught the trolley bus from Dartford to Woolwich, and stopped in a café for a roll and a cup of tea. He then walked two miles to the Valley, past stalls selling rosettes and rattles, and arrived with an hour or more to spare. He joined the crowds on the terraces – the stands were for rich people – and was often passed down to the front over the top of the cloth caps. There was a damp smell in the air and the tension simmered. Blake assumed that every working-class kid had some football enthusiasm, an assumption that was probably true.

Charlton supporters came from the dockyards of Woolwich and Chatham, from south-east London suburbs such as Mottingham, Eltham and Blackheath, and from coastal Kent. Not all were so handily placed. Some had travelled halfway round the world to attend Wembley, calling at out-of-the-way places in North Africa, India or Japan on the way.

On Saturday 27 April 1946 groups of rival supporters met in London and the atmosphere was friendly. In the environs of Wembley's Empire Stadium, spectators mingled around rows of parked black cars. Some Charlton supporters had served with Derby supporters during the war. They looked out for them, hopelessly.

In the spring of 1946 Harold Miller was with the forces in northern Italy. On Cup Final day he was searching the local villages for a radio when a young officer caught up with him.

'What are you trying to do, Private?' the officer asked.

'I come from Derby, sir. It's the Cup Final today, and I'd like to listen to the match. Is there a radio about?'

'There's one in the Officers' Mess. I'll take you up. If anybody says anything, give them my name.'

The officer left Miller alone in a small room with no electric light. He spent the whole afternoon there, listening to the match on a wireless set that had more crackles than words. At times he bent down close to the machine or lifted it to his ears. The reception was bad but it improved a little towards extra time. Or maybe Miller had learned the set's language. Anyway he heard all the goals.

The FA Cup Final held a special place in the nation's affection. It was *the* national competition. A minute of the FA meeting of 20 July 1871 logged that it was a Challenge Cup for '*all* clubs belonging to the Football Association' (authors' italics). Attendances at FA Cup Finals grew from 2,000 in 1872 to 8,000 (1883) to 73,833 (1899) to 120,081 (1913), and an estimated 200,000 turned up for the first Wembley Final in 1923. The number of entries increased from fifteen (1871) to 548 (1922).

The FA Cup began in the 1871–2 season, seventeen years before the Football League, and its status as the nation's top football competition continued past the 1920s. It was the only reliable way to assess the relative strength of teams from different leagues. In 1901 Tottenham Hotspur won the Cup as a Southern League team. In 1920 the Football League had only seven southern clubs among its forty-four members. Forthcoming Football League clubs, such as Plymouth Argyle, Queen's Park Rangers, Southampton and Cardiff City, had to prove their worth in the FA Cup. The competition brought the country together. In 1946 that was particularly important. Once more it was an opportunity to compare teams from the South with those from the North and the Midlands. Once more it was a step towards national unification.

In Derby it was the biggest event in the history of the town. For the nation too there was something special about the 1946 Wembley Cup Final. The people had mended and made do. They had saved their waste paper, eaten their scraps and dug for victory. They had made what they could out of parsnips. And now this familiar national ritual at the Empire Stadium, Wembley, was unequivocal evidence of peace. Whatever the result, it would be a celebration of victory for both football clubs. For one afternoon it didn't matter that Britain had lost all her ships, was virtually bankrupt and had an industrial set-up that favoured munitions. And it didn't matter that people had lots of wartime secrets; they could talk about football.

Towards the end of the pre-match music Captain F. J. Harris called for number fifteen on the song-sheet. The voices entered the music, sang an extra verse and concluded with the moving chorus. Never has a hymn been sung more emotionally at Wembley than it was this day by nearly 100,000 people. Caps and hats were taken off, inhibitions were discarded and many spectators began to weep.

> Abide with me; fast falls the eventide;
> The darkness deepens; Lord with me abide!
> When other helpers fail, and comforts flee,
> Help of the helpless, O abide with me.

In the number-one dressing-room at Wembley, shortly before kick-off, radio commentator Stewart MacPherson egged on the Derby County players, and they agreed to sing for the benefit of the airwaves. But what should they sing?

Raich Carter suggested his favourite song. He had never forgotten the impact it had made on him when he scored a goal for his home-town team of Sunderland. Those Wearside voices at Roker Park conveyed power and strength and faith: their combined noise prickled the back of Raich Carter's neck and tingled his body. He knew then that his purpose was to make his supporters happy in hard times. And he knew that he could do a lot. Words could never describe what that song meant to him, what feelings it aroused, or his debt to its writer, Geordie Ridley. The Derby County players sang 'Blaydon Races'.

Over the years millions of people have been indebted to George Ridley, a Gateshead coalminer who broke a leg at the pit and took up entertaining. When he died, at the age of thirty from tuberculosis, Ridley left no wife, no children, no money, no headstone and little other legacy of his existence. Only a few songs and a rousing local anthem that Raich Carter had taught his team-mates.

'Blaydon Races' is a song about working-class people who once a year escaped their toil and were determined to enjoy their leisure. It tells of how people overcame misfortune and turmoil and enjoyed their Saturday afternoon. Although it was a song about a trip to Blaydon racetrack it could have been about the 1946 FA Cup Final.

The players left the dressing-rooms, went into the tunnel five-foot-something tall and came out, greeted by a roar, feeling like seven-foot giants. Derby's Leon Leuty came out last. His change in personality, from dressing-room to pitch-freedom, included a name change from Leon to Lee because the shorter version was more manageable for calling for the ball. He also grew more phlegmatic. The more difficult the situation, the cooler he became. On the football field he created his own time, his own mellow mood, whatever the anxieties of those around him.

Only one thing bothered him – he was worried about meeting the King.

His tension was heightened by a delay. Keyed up, desperate to kick a football, the players waited five minutes for George VI to appear on the Wembley pitch. Leon felt his knees knocking, cushioned only by the bandages that he wore to protect his damaged joints.

Finally, the King, wearing a grey overcoat, was escorted to the edge of the pitch.

'Blimey, he's been demobbed too,' said one spectator.

The band brought George VI to a halt at the touchline by playing 'God Save the King'. The crowd sang as though God had saved the country. Then the King was led forward to meet the polite and dignified players. Each footballer's hair was cropped short, in some cases as high as the top of their ears at the back. They wore their shorts long, almost down to the knees, and many boots were repaired with sticking plaster. A few weeks earlier Charlton Athletic had pleaded to fans for clothing rations in order to buy their Cup Final kit.

On Cup Final day Walter Bates returned to Derby on leave from the services. He caught the three o'clock train from Birmingham and found himself incommunicado. Bates and his fellow travellers talked the train guard into an unscheduled stop at Burton upon Trent. When the train came to a halt the passengers leaned out of the window.

'How's Derby doing?'

'I think it's still there.'

'Nah, the football team, the Cup Final.'

'Nil–nil,' somebody else said. 'Nearly half-time.'

Bates got off the train at Derby and walked towards home. The streets were deserted. No traffic. No people. The whole town had stopped to listen to the wireless. Along Regent Street Bates could hear the voice of radio commentator Raymond Glendenning in every house.

Then through the town came a roar.

Derby County had scored.

Bates was invited into one of the houses. He stayed until full-time, when the score was 1–1. Bates then made his way home to listen to extra time. Derby County scored three more goals and won 4–1. Walter Bates had the perfect leave.

In the Derby County dressing-room Leon Leuty toasted his team-mates with ginger beer. Leuty could be proud of his performance. Some journalists made him man of the match, others put him a close second. Now he sat on a bench and permitted the memories to flood back. He recalled the people who had helped him recover from two cartilage operations, especially Frank Womack, who had encouraged him back to Notts County to try again. Four years had passed since Leuty had searched for his boots, handled them, tried them on and taken the Notts County manager's offer seriously. In that time he had represented England in the Burnden Park Disaster Fund match and won an FA Cup winners' medal.

Leuty thought about his Rolls-Royce colleagues. The firm had provided his apprenticeship, his alternative security, although it had meant working months of nights in order to create the time to travel to matches. Leuty also thought of his greatest fan, his mother, who had travelled a long way to see him play.

In the dressing-room a few players considered their success in the context of wartime experiences that were still fresh and raw. Jack Howe had returned from India in March suffering from malaria. Raich Carter's hair had gone grey almost overnight when he worked for the Sunderland Fire Service. And Jack Stamps had experienced a haunting incident at the Dunkirk evacuation when he clambered aboard a small, crowded boat despite facing a British officer who was holding a revolver. 'Soldier, if you attempt to board this boat, I will shoot you,' the officer said. Stamps carried on, figuring he would get shot either way.

But most Derby County players had lived relatively routine wartime lives, especially if they became blasé about blackouts and air-raid sirens. They had worked in regular war-related jobs, played regular Saturday football and had regular entertainment. Most had lived like Leon Leuty.

In the winners' dressing-room Leuty examined his gold medal and smiled at his success. Gold took on extra significance in a country that couldn't get bananas. At one time it looked as though the players might receive savings certificates instead. The Charlton players received bronze medals (later to be replaced by gold).

'I think I'll give my medal to my mother to take home,' Leuty said to no one in particular.

4

NEVER HAVE SO MANY ATTENDED

ALBERT THOMAS WAS A 67-YEAR-OLD farm labourer from Catsclough in Cheshire. His fifty-hour working week ended at noon on Saturdays. Then, if Winsford United were at home, he walked five miles to Barton Stadium. Thomas was blind in one eye and his left leg had been lame since the 1890s, but he also walked to a few away matches. When it came to the twenty-mile trip to Macclesfield, however, he booked a seat on one of the eighty coaches carrying Winsford fans.

On Valentine's Day 1948 the small Cheshire town of Winsford (population 10,500) went football crazy. The occasion was Winsford United's second-round Cheshire Senior Cup tie at Macclesfield Town. Some fans started out very early. They carefully cleaned and oiled their bicycles, packed their holdalls and took to the Cheshire lanes for twenty miles, stopping only to eat packed lunches. The coaches left at noon. The day-trippers arrived in Macclesfield in good time. The gates opened at 1.45pm.

The match itself was a thriller. In the first minute of play over 3,000 Winsford fans let out a massive roar, but Winsford's 'goal' was disallowed for offside. Macclesfield Town then dominated and led 2–0 at half-time. During the interval at least two visiting fans let off pigeons to relay the sorry score to people back home. True to the ritual, someone shouted something extra to the flying birds: 'Tell them we've got the wind in the second half.'

Winsford were a different team after the break. They scored twice to equalise. Then, in the seventy-fifth minute, came one of those goal-mouth incidents that, according to legend, littered matches in the 1940s and 1950s. The penalty area was like Woolworth's on market day, and the ball twanged around as if in a game of bagatelle. One report said it was cleared off the home goal-line six times before the Macclesfield goalkeeper fisted it over the crossbar. But Winsford scored the winning goal a few minutes later. The only consolation for Macclesfield Town fans was that they could now identify the culpable defenders – it was the club's first season in numbered shirts.

The 9,003 attendance was astonishing for an early-round match for a local trophy, especially as five Football League matches were being played within twenty miles of Winsford and Macclesfield on that same Saturday.

Most fans walked to football matches in the late 1940s. In those heady days of huge crowds it was not unusual for a man to walk for three hours to a major football ground, arrive at midday and find the ground already full. This was particularly the case in the North-East.

Northumberland and Durham coalminers had been hardened by the 1930s depression, the Jarrow Hunger March and the Second World War. Now they were softened by the deeds of footballers like Jackie Milburn ('so fast he'd catch rabbits on the common') and Len Shackleton ('the clown prince of soccer'). In 1947–8 Newcastle United averaged 56,299 for home matches. One Yorkshire colliery found that 33 per cent of their workers missed the week's sixth shift, the Saturday shift, even though it paid a bonus.

The 1948–9 season saw a Football League aggregate attendance record (41 million for 1,848 matches). Never have so many attended. The largest aggregate for one day's League programme came on 27 December 1949 – 1,272,185 spectators for forty-four matches (an average of 28,913). The interest was spread through the four divisions. A crowd of 25,000 watched a Division Three (North) match between Doncaster Rovers and New Brighton, and 27,000 saw a 1–1 draw between Millwall and Walsall, two lowly Division Three (South) teams.

The late 1940s became known as 'football's post-war boom' or 'the golden age'. The boom was partly a consequence of people making up for lost time and enjoying the victorious spirit – young players and young spectators had lost the best years of their career to the war – but there were other contributing factors. The only alternative communal leisure activities were cinemas, dancehalls and church groups. The war had reinforced many men's loyalty to their home town, but it had also given servicemen more understanding and tolerance of other places in the country ('Where are you from then, mate?'). The forces and football had similar masculine values, and football satisfied ex-servicemen's need for family reunion and a collective external focus. Football was an extended-family pursuit. It drew brothers, fathers and sons, uncles and nephews, fathers and daughters, and sometimes husbands and wives. It was a shared community experience. If you went on your own you joined a surrogate family that offered a regular supply of cigarettes and boiled sweets.

The ritual for important FA Cup matches started a fortnight before kick-off. Fans queued from Saturday evening ready for ticket offices to open on Sunday morning. Blue with cold, they wrapped themselves in blankets and made vacuum flasks of tea last through a wintry night. They sometimes played an impromptu game of street football, or else warmed themselves next to a coke brazier borrowed from a nearby factory. In a queue outside the Southampton ground a man was overcome by brazier fumes. On a cold February night in 1948 some Manchester United fans collapsed in the ticket queue.

In Liverpool in April 1947 a queue for semi-final replay tickets began at 7.30pm on Saturday. There were 200 people at midnight, and by 9.30am, when the gates opened, an estimated 50,000 were in mile-long queues. After an hour a group of men at the rear broke ranks and rushed the gates. Thirty people received minor injuries and one man was hospitalised with crushed ribs. Mounted police restored order. The 15,000 tickets were sold in two hours.

On match days people walked or cycled. Some caught local buses, but it was risky if a succession of full buses went past. The cyclists paid a penny to store their bicycles in someone's back yard. And the very few car owners needed an essential reason for using their petrol ration.

On the terraces fans wore drab clothes – blacks, greys and browns – and waited patiently for the match to start. The long wait – sometimes a couple of hours – was filled with conversation, watching the band and drawing pieces of paper out of a flat cap to select a player for the 'first goal' sweep. Tannoy systems were still finding their voice, so gramophone records were rare, and police marshalled the crowd using loud-hailers or walkie-talkies. Child care was still the responsibility of the whole crowd.

'There was never any trouble,' fans would say years later. In fact the FA had to deal with only twenty-two cases of crowd trouble in the three peak years after the war. Eleven were missile-throwing incidents, eight actual or threatened violence against players and three pitch invasions or demonstrations.

The only space in the ground was on the field. The only people with room to move were the players. The terraces were often so crammed that spectators couldn't get cigarettes out of their pockets, and in those days most spectators smoked. Sometimes, during the match, their feet didn't touch the ground for minutes on end.

The ground was the working man's theatre and the pitch his stage. Star footballers, like top actors, played to 'packed houses' and took their audience through a range of emotions – except that footballers were exposed to the weather and they had to improvise rather than deliver a script. The special effects were just as dramatic. At clubs such as Birmingham City, Aldershot and Hull City a steam engine could create a smokescreen which blocked spectators' views and sometimes caused a match to be temporarily suspended.

The League's first-ever 80,000-plus crowd came in January 1948, when Manchester United entertained Arsenal at Manchester City's Maine Road ground. (United's Old Trafford had been bombed during the war.) Spectators were critical of the viewing facilities and hundreds left before the end. Club officials argued that the crowd huddled too closely together to protect themselves from the rain. Years later Manchester City's Eddie McMorran said, 'We played in front of some Maine Road crowds that made the grass shake.'

Given the large Football League attendances, one might think that the professional clubs became rich. More than a few players later wondered what had happened to all the money. Newcastle United spent £30,000 on ground improvements, £30,000 on houses they could rent to players, and surpluses in the transfer market. Some clubs purchased new training grounds. Most had a large staff of full-time and part-time players. Second Division Chesterfield had five teams and forty professionals, and that led to a substantial wage bill.

Fans put up with poor ground conditions because they didn't have much better at home. In the Yorkshire town of Barnsley 50 per cent of households lacked their own fixed bath, 10 per cent either shared a water supply or were without piped water and 28 per cent lacked their own toilet. In 1947–8, Barnsley, a mid-table Division Two side with a catchment area of 150,000 people, had an average attendance of 21,050 at home matches. Many men were escaping small, crowded houses with few facilities.

Some people watched matches under threat of losing their jobs. Through the late 1940s industrialists resented the absenteeism caused by afternoon midweek matches as it affected production. The matter was raised several times in the House of Commons and midweek matches were periodically banned. The 1946–7 season lasted until June because many matches were postponed during a bad winter and midweek matches were outlawed. In January 1949 five men at Birmingham's Lucas Works were sacked for attending local afternoon matches. A few employers allowed staff to clock on at 6am and finish early.

Match day was a physical effort for spectators as well as for players. After the walk or cycle ride to the ground there was no rest on the terraces. Fans shifted feet every few seconds, stretched leg muscles to gain extra height, pushed and shoved to retain their place and banged shoulders with strangers after the final whistle. They arrived home physically exhausted, especially if their team had lost and they had cycled back uphill. Most fans worked harder than the players, the more so if they'd been to work that morning.

The collective will was for peace, but the wartime influence remained. Terraces and dressing-rooms contained men who had killed the enemy, so some maladjustment and ill-temper was always likely. After a friendly in Liège, Belgium, Derby County's Steve McLachlan attacked Belgian civilians at random, simply because he felt that the Belgian Army had let down his regiment, the 51st Highland Division, during the war. It was said that in some towns 20,000 teas hit the back of the fire after a home defeat, and that wives took their new shoes back to the shop when they heard rumour of a bad result.

The legacy of war affected newspapers too. Paper was in short supply, so there were fewer pages. On the way home from the match, however, it was possible to walk down the road and watch a sea of sports papers coming towards you. On dance floors that night a man might waltz while reading a *Pink 'Un* or *Green 'Un* behind his partner's back. The football reports still contained militaristic prose. Forwards *blazed* over the crossbar, goalkeepers saved from *point-blank* range, wingers attacked *on the flanks*, defenders blocked *cannonball* shots or *howitzers*, penalty-takers *rifled* home spot-kicks, tough-tackling full backs were said to *take no prisoners* and international players were the team's *big guns*. One unimpressive forward 'didn't look like being dangerous, even if he'd had a hand grenade up his chest'.

Grassroots football adjusted slowly after the war. It wasn't until July 1946 that the Trowbridge & District Junior Football League committee read and approved the 1939 AGM minutes. In April 1948 a match between Deverill Sports and Longbridge Deverill was abandoned when a hundred Poles invaded the pitch after a Polish player and an opponent had been sent off.

Around the country there was a shortage of good-quality pitches and a dearth of referees. The Ministry of Defence still occupied many grounds, some pitches had been dug up for use as allotments, the transport system was chaotic and washing facilities might mean one sink between twenty-two players.

When the Herefordshire Football League reformed in November 1945 there were four military clubs among its ten members. By 1948–9 that league had forty-five clubs and the military influence had virtually disappeared. But clothing was still rationed. Widemarsh FC bought a set of shirts for £8 from Mordiford FC. A Widemarsh player's wife had the job of unstitching the M on the front of each shirt, turning it upside down and sewing it back on as a W.

In the professional ranks Derby County's Leon Leuty would probably have been England's regular centre half had it not been for Stoke City's Neil Franklin. Leuty won no international caps, but he captained England against Young England and was England's reserve on four occasions. He captained England B and played three times for the Football League. At the end of the 1949–50 season he was told that if he kept training he would be asked to join England's World Cup party. But he wasn't selected. That one broke his heart.

In the late 1940s Leuty was always full of fun. In one match, when Derby County led Blackburn Rovers 5–1, he played the game of his life. He was everywhere on the pitch, defending and attacking, up for corner-kicks, playing centre forward, playing centre half.

'What's up, Lee?' a team-mate asked him.

'I've got us in the sweep,' Leuty replied. 'Most goals.'

In the same match, while defending a corner-kick, Leuty crept up behind his own goalkeeper, undid the press-stud on the 'keeper's cap and pulled the cap down over his eyes. Leuty rolled around the floor in laughter.

'I've been dying to do that for two years,' he told the others.

There were lots of perks for the professional players of the 1940s. They mixed with Variety Show artists and traded free tickets with comedians and boxers. They travelled free on buses and were offered various discounts, but they had to be careful not to abuse the system. There was the story of the First Division club where the players all had free passes to a cinema but the cinema manager became suspicious when a good film attracted 222 players in one week.

Then there were the practical jokes. One time, during an injury crisis, the Derby County players took a couple of lights out of the gymnasium (to make it dark), smeared their best actor with talcum powder (to make him look pale), splattered him with tomato ketchup (to make him look bloody) and laid him on the ground before sending someone to tell the trainer that a player had run into a wall.

On another day a team-mate showed Leon Leuty a picture of two women and pointed out the one he was seeing.

'This is Marjory,' he said.

'Who's the other one?' Leuty asked.

'Her name's Wendy from Milford way.'

'I'd like to meet her.'

Leuty's reputation as a womaniser went before him, but Wendy thought she would meet him once. In fact they saw each other again, courted for two years and married in July 1950.

Football matches and weddings had much in common during football's golden age. Winsford's trip to Macclesfield, one-off FA Cup ties, routine League matches and Leon Leuty's wedding all provided memorable outings.

5

THE FLYING HORSE AT WEMBLEY

Dr Harold Thompson was an Oxford University don who represented Oxford University on the Football Association (FA) Council. On a train journey back to Oxford in the spring of 1948 Thompson outlined his plans for the next football season.

'I want to enter a combined Oxford and Cambridge eleven in the FA Amateur Cup competition,' he said.

The Oxford University soccer players listened attentively. They had just completed their season with a match in Birmingham. The only absentee from the train journey home was Tony Pawson, who had dashed off to catch a boat to Ireland for a fishing holiday. Pawson had left immediately after the match without even taking a bath.

'That's if we can get permission!' Thompson added, coughing for about five seconds as if to emphasise his point. A forty-year-old man, five feet ten inches tall and with curly fair hair, he usually spoke with a cigarette in his mouth and ash heading for his clothes. 'Won't be easy. There'll be a lot of opposition. In order to enter the FA Amateur Cup we shall need our own registered ground.'

Harold Thompson believed in true amateurism. That meant embodying the spirit and adventure of football and rejecting external rewards. The game was there to support the parts of life that really mattered, like fighting for your country, running a business, practising as a doctor or being an Oxford scientist. These values had been established by the English public schools in the nineteenth century, at a time when a healthy body meant a healthy mind, and a healthy mind meant good discipline, self-control, perseverance, courage, manliness and teamwork.

Thompson knew that most Northern League and Isthmian League amateur teams were actually illicitly *paying* players. Professional players were making snide remarks – 'There's so much money left in amateurs' boots that

they have to buy them a size too big' – so Thompson wanted to present a
better amateur model, one that countered 'this shamateurism nonsense'.

'We'd need exemption from the qualifying rounds because we have our
standing fixtures during the Michaelmas term,' he continued.

'What's the club to be called?' someone asked.

'Well,' said Thompson, after another long cough and much falling
of cigarette ash, 'my wife has thought of a name. She suggests we use the
combination of Oxford Centaur and Cambridge Falcon and call the club
Pegasus, the winged horse of classical mythology.'

Thompson paused. He sat back and gazed thoughtfully out of the window.
His plan was hatched. Amateur football's last populist adventure had begun.

Ken Shearwood, son of a Derby doctor, was educated at Shrewsbury and
played soccer and cricket for the school. As an Ordinary Seaman he served
abroad for eighteen months on two destroyers. After being commissioned
he took part in the Sicily and Italy landings and was awarded the DSC. His
Royal Navy football career was limited to one match in Messina when the
21st Flotilla played the 26th Flotilla.

After the war Shearwood worked for eighteen months as an inshore
fisherman at Mevagissey in Cornwall. In October 1946 he played his first
match for the village team in the St Austell & District Junior League. The
best feature of the sloping pitch near the top of Tregony Hill was a view
of the bay. But Shearwood's football career didn't really kick off until he
went to Oxford University at the age of twenty-six, one of many older
undergraduates during the post-war years. Partway through the first season
he found himself in the varsity team, replacing a defender who had gone
pheasant shooting. His second match was against a strong FA XI captained
by Leon Leuty, and his sixth made him an Oxford blue. At the end of that
season Harold Thompson launched his plan for Pegasus.

In February 1949 Pegasus played Bromley at home in an FA Amateur Cup
quarter-final. Extra stands were incorporated into Oxford University's Iffley
Road ground, and the crowd – just under 12,000 – was a record for a sports
event in the city. A hundred coaches brought Bromley supporters, and
Pegasus collected their own devotees from an exciting Amateur Cup run
that had seen them win four matches.

'Up the Pegs!'

'Come on the Pegs!'

Rattles swirled noisily, caps were waved and banners were unfolded.

Harold Thompson, known to most people as 'Tommy', had succeeded in getting Pegasus FA Amateur Cup exemption until November's final qualifying round. He was already a clever football administrator – he eventually became FA chairman – and had sat on two FA sub-committees.

The son of a Yorkshire colliery executive, Thompson was educated at King Edward VII School in Sheffield and Trinity College, Oxford, becoming a football blue in 1928. After a year studying gas reactions in Berlin he settled down as a fellow of St John's College, Oxford. During the Second World War he analysed enemy aviation fuels for the Ministry of Aircraft Production.

Devoted to association football, he first became treasurer of Oxford University AFC in 1931, and now added the role of Pegasus's honorary secretary. His wife Penelope – he called her 'Plop' – was a warm and loyal Classics scholar from St Hugh's, but Thompson could be very rude to women, and his bluntness upset many men too.

Thompson watched every match Pegasus and Oxford University played, and he sent the Pegasus players circulars with polite rallying calls:

'May I therefore draw your attention to some facts about Hayes.'

'Please therefore get yourself ready, before it is too late.'

'We have to do everything in our power to win this match.'

In their inaugural season Pegasus attracted lots of interest from BBC television and radio, and London-based newspapers, all of whom were staffed with Oxbridge graduates. As the Football League had banned televised football, Pegasus were better covered on TV than the top professional clubs. *The Times*'s football correspondent, Geoffrey Green (Shrewsbury and Cambridge), was also a great admirer of Tommy Thompson's enterprise.

But the first Pegasus Amateur Cup run, in 1949, ended in the quarter-finals. Bromley won 4–3 with a goal in the eighty-fifth minute.

In February 1949 Oxford had three major football clubs, and all three played *amateur* football. Oxford City played in the Isthmian League, Headington United in the Spartan League and Pegasus played friendly matches and FA Amateur Cup ties. If a footballer wanted to play professionally he had to leave Oxford. When 25-year-old goalkeeper Alf Jefferies moved from amateur Oxford City to professional Brentford in 1947, he was criticised by Oxford traditionalists who thought that professional sport was an oxymoron.

'Look at it this way,' Jefferies told one of the traditionalists. 'You were good with your hands as a bricklayer and now you're a general foreman. You've used your skills to earn your living. My skills as a goalkeeper are in my hands, too, and I've been offered the chance to earn a living with my skills. What's the difference?'

Oxford City had no floodlights at their White House Ground, so the players trained in the dark. The biggest turn-out on training evenings was when there was a full moon and it was safe enough to play with a brown leather ball. But City players had plenty of laughs. Full back Reggie Smith sometimes arrived wearing a hard bowler hat; it was the last thing he'd take off before the match and the first thing he put on after his post-match shower. These true amateurs had an air of nonchalance. There were no trophies for winning the Isthmian League – the league's Latin motto, *Honor sufficit*, meant 'honour suffice' – but City attracted crowds of over 5,000.

Oxford City considered turning professional in 1948 but the idea was quashed at the annual general meeting as the White House Ground's lease restricted its use to *amateur* football. 'Oxford people are chary of anything new,' said the *Oxford Mail*, 'and it is also true that they have a natural disinclination towards any professional sport except, perhaps, boxing.'

Headington United turned professional in the summer of 1949. They faced a much higher standard of football in the Southern League and journeys to places as far away as Colchester and Llanelli. That summer was a hectic one at United's Manor Ground. A limited company was formed and £7 shares were issued at a meeting in St Margaret's School. The first company secretary, Edmund Gibbs, joined the new directors in the Quarry Gate pub afterwards, and his briefcase, containing £1,400, sat on the floor.

Vic Morris worked at Pressed Steel. He was tired at the end of a day's work, but that didn't stop him working at the Manor Ground on weekday nights and weekends. Oxford had plenty of skilled people employed in local firms, and many worked for United for free. Bricklayers, carpenters and tilers brought their tools to the Manor Ground, builders loaned concrete-mixers and gangs of labourers queued to take over from other gangs. New dressing-rooms were built, new stands were erected and the terracing was improved with concrete slabs. Vic Morris ricked his back lifting one of these and it gave him gyp for twenty years. That was the price he paid for enjoying his club.

Jimmy Smith was in his mid-twenties when Headington United turned professional. He was a Spartan League star and well worth his place among the newly imported professionals. But Smith decided to stay an amateur. He felt he was getting on a bit and doing well in his career in hospital administration. He also realised that turning professional would prevent him from playing local football. Once you had played professionally the true amateurs considered you socially stained.

Coached by an ex-Tottenham Hotspur player called Vic Buckingham, Pegasus developed an attractive push-and-run style of football where they worked hard for one another, kept it simple and passed the ball quickly. 'I can reach their feet through their minds,' said Buckingham, a debonair man with lots of charm and an eye for the women. He wore flash coats and riding boots and was a good talker, a real contrast with Harold Thompson.

After an ordinary 1949–50 season Pegasus started their 1950–1 FA Amateur Cup run with a fortunate 4–3 win against Gosport Borough Athletic. The next tie was at Slough Town, and Tommy Thompson was worried. He sent out a circular to twenty-four players warning them to stay fit and not to underestimate the opposition:

'It may prove our crucial match. They are (according to their secretary) pretty self-confident. They have this season knocked out of the FA Cup Oxford City, Banbury Spencer and Headington United (Southern League at present 6th).'

Pegasus beat Slough Town 3–1, and could claim to be the best team in Oxford. Some Eton College boys made the short trip to Slough, and at the match they sang the 'Eton Boating Song'. Later that evening three merry Pegasus players telephoned Thompson from a public call-box.

'Swing, swing together,' they sang down the phone and waited for a response.

'Weeeell,' Thompson said, completely ignoring the singing. 'I've been giving the game a lot of thought and I don't think we're going to get much further unless we do something about our defence . . .'

The conversation continued in that manner. Thompson was focused on his plan while the three players enjoyed their singsong.

The score was 1–1 with two minutes to play in the 1951 Amateur Cup semi-final at Highbury. Pegasus centre half Ken Shearwood, one of three Pegasus players now around thirty, went to tackle Avis as the Hendon player dribbled the ball across the cloying mud into the Pegasus penalty area. Avis flicked the ball to one side and then splattered into the mud as Shearwood fouled him.

'Sorry, that's a penalty,' said referee Arthur Ellis as he passed Shearwood. 'I've no alternative.'

The Arsenal stadium contained 26,500 intrigued spectators. Pegasus goalkeeper Dr Ben Brown, a research chemist and son of a miner, prepared to face a penalty taken by Dexter Adams, the Hendon centre half and captain. Adams took his time. He cleaned the ball with his hands and placed it carefully on the penalty spot. He wiped his right boot against his sock. He walked back, turned and started his run towards goal. He hit the ball perfectly and sent it powerfully towards the target. But Brown stretched to his left and fisted the ball over the crossbar for a corner-kick.

The result was 1–1. At the final whistle Ben Brown and Dexter Adams shook hands. They had shared the final drama. In such half-seconds are hypotheses tested, stories written, memories preserved, fantasies re-evaluated, financial budgets rejigged, conclusions drawn and bets won. One of football's prime assets is its uncertainty of outcome. As Geoffrey Green of *The Times* wrote in his Hendon–Pegasus report, 'Nowadays we have so few mysteries left to us that we cannot afford to part with them easily.'

On the way to the replay the Pegasus players drove through the streets of London listening to John Snagge's radio commentary on the 1951 Oxford–Cambridge boat race. Suddenly Pegasus reverted to their natural camps – the team that day consisted of eight Oxford players and three from Cambridge – and the Cambridge men laughed uproariously when the Oxford boat sank.

The idea of two fierce rivals, Oxford and Cambridge, joining forces to form one club was amazing. What held them together was the shared amateur ethic and a strong desire to promote association football above rugby union. But there was one contentious issue – the constitution's 'one-year rule'. The Pegasus team could be selected from current students or the previous year's graduates. But Cambridge expected their recent graduates to play for Corinthian-Casuals, a rival to Pegasus. Tommy Thompson held meetings to resolve the tension.

A few weeks after Pegasus had won the Hendon replay, the 'Eton Boating Song' was heard at Wembley as 100,000 people watched Pegasus beat Bishop Auckland 2–1 in the FA Amateur Cup Final. It was a moral victory for the FA's long-running campaign against shamateurism and proof that amateur football had something to offer to all social classes. Many of the 20,000 who set off from Oxford to watch the match were members of the city's working class, and there were far more women and children at Wembley than for a professional match. These working-class people borrowed mortar-boards and gowns and posed as students for the day. One Pegasus fanatic wore an Oxford gargoyle mask, and working men made up their own lyrics for Eton's school song: 'When the game is over/Whether we win or lose/We'll go back to Oxford/And finish up on the booze.'

'They rekindled a torch,' the *Oxford Mail* said about Pegasus, 'the light of which will illumine and guide the steps of young players in the public schools and universities, where, in recent years, association football has been at second best to the rugby code.'

Two years later, in front of another 100,000 crowd, Pegasus won the FA Amateur Cup trophy again. They did not succeed in putting university football on the map, but certain schools adopted the association game at rugby's expense.

In the early 1950s there were all kinds of amateur footballers in England: amateurs who were not good enough to earn any money from football; the Jefferies-type who were ambitious to be professionals; shamateurs who took the £5 or £10 per match on offer (only a few of whom were ever punished by the FA); amateurs such as Jimmy Smith, who occasionally claimed expenses when he took the professional players in his car; amateurs who had been professionals and had obtained special permission to play (but were allowed only in certain leagues); and Ken Shearwood-type amateurs who could have earned some money but were totally committed to amateurism.

Pegasus fell away after 1955 and the club collapsed in 1963. Their short spell in the sun was a last hurrah before shamateurism became the norm for the higher echelons of the amateur game. In the early 1950s spectators were thrilled by Pegasus's intelligent pass-and-move style of play, the amateur ethic, the publicity in the quality newspapers, the high standard of the Cup matches and the atmosphere at matches. As Ken Shearwood said many years later, 'You don't fill Wembley with 100,000 people unless you have something to offer.'

6

'RUN IT OFF, SON'

IN HIS EARLY TWENTIES CENTRE forward Derek Dooley had a fine physique. He stood six foot three inches tall and weighed nearly fourteen stone. He had curly ginger hair and his pale skin reddened with exertion. On the football field he was fearless to the point of recklessness. In the 1951–2 season Dooley used his Nordic bulk and size-twelve boots to score forty-six goals in thirty League matches. His club, Sheffield Wednesday, won promotion to Division One.

Wednesday fans thought Derek Dooley was a hero, a Centurion tank of a player who compensated for lack of ball control with wholehearted enthusiasm and a belief in his own indestructibility. Some opponents felt that Dooley was crude, awkward and physically dangerous. They said he charged at defenders like a runaway bullock and injured goalkeepers. The red-haired dreadnought gave his all for Sheffield Wednesday, and some opponents gave it back to him.

Derek Dooley was born in Pitsmoor, Sheffield, in December 1929. His father was a steel worker who was unemployed for periods in the 1930s. Young Derek played in back yards and on local recreation grounds, and grew up in a world where the physical ruled. If you could fight you took charge at school. If you could take knocks your football career progressed. Dooley left school at fourteen and trained as a deaf-aid mechanic. He joined Sheffield YMCA solely to enjoy their football facilities. Then one day he was asked to play for Lincoln City Reserves at Denaby United in the Midland League. It was his first trip out of Sheffield except for holidays at Blackpool.

Dooley joined Sheffield Wednesday at seventeen. He spent a few years playing Midland League football (with the A team) and in the Central League (with the Reserves). The Midland League was a tough proving ground. Visits to local mining communities strengthened a man's resolve. The players told one another that it was a physical game and you had to look after yourself.

Dooley's professional career finally took off in October 1951, when he was nearly twenty-two. He scored four goals in a match for Wednesday Reserves one week and two for the first team the next. After Wednesday's promotion he adapted slowly to Division One. At twenty-three Dooley had a great future in the game, until a visit to Preston North End on Valentine's Day 1953.

In those days a football-club trainer's job was to supervise training, keep discipline, work on football boots with a cobbler's skill, look after equipment, treat injuries, be a confidant to the players and light their cigarettes at half-time. When Leyton Orient's Ledger Ritson suffered a compound fracture of his right leg in a match against Northampton Town in 1948, the trainer lit a fag at the side of the stretcher. 'Ritson waved cheerfully to the large crowd as he left the pitch puffing a cigarette,' wrote a local reporter.

Trainers were real characters. Harry Cooke at Everton kept mementoes of players' operations – bits of cartilage and chunks of bone – in jam jars around the treatment room. In the fifties trainers dealt with *on-the-field* casualties and physiotherapists oversaw players during the week. Trainers used a 'magic sponge' dipped in cold water for most knocks and ammonia capsules for head injuries. Physiotherapists treated bruises and sprains by alternating hot and cold water. Pulled muscles were soothed with towels soaked in hot water. Cuts, dabbed with iodine, smarted for hours. Blistered feet were soaked in potassium-permanganate baths. At Liverpool Bob Paisley studied the kinetics of racing pigeons and racehorses and extrapolated his findings to footballers' bodies. He tried out new equipment on dogs whose owners had innocently passed the Anfield stadium on their morning walk. It was evidence for the anti-football lobby, who said that footballers were little more than circus animals trained to perform lovable antics for large crowds.

Just when the boots were comfortable it was time for a new pair. A common problem when breaking in unyielding new boots was the blackened toenail, which required some drilling to release the blood pooled beneath. Players suspected that treatment methods were deliberately sadistic in order to make them wary about declaring themselves injured. At some clubs managers shunned the injured or labelled them 'injury prone' to provoke them into action. 'Run it off, son,' they told players. 'Run it off.'

Trainers had often been notoriously hard players themselves, and this could show in a dismissive attitude to injuries.

'It's me back,' the player said, walking into the treatment room. 'I've had it a long time.'

'Yeah, sure,' the trainer replied. 'I've had mine a long time too.'

Players with niggling injuries sometimes found an osteopath or a faith healer outside the club. There were also tales of surgeons taking out the wrong cartilage and players continuing to play until the second or third X-ray showed a fracture. When one player went into a nursing home for a groin operation he decided to shave his own pubic hair because he certainly wasn't going to let a nun do it.

At half-time, on Derek Dooley's fateful February day in 1953, the score was 0–0. In the dressing-room Sheffield Wednesday trainer-coach Alan Brown suggested playing through-balls more quickly, before the defenders moved up to catch Dooley offside.

In the fifty-ninth minute Wednesday inside forward Albert Quixall passed the ball through the middle of the pitch. Dooley galloped forward willingly. Preston goalkeeper George Thompson hesitated and then came out. Thompson reached the ball first and the two players collided. Dooley's right shin caught Thompson's flexed kneecap. The goalkeeper thought his knee was broken.

Seriously injured footballers react in various ways. Some scream. Some grip at the turf and grimace through the pain. Some clench their teeth or search for something to hold or bite on. Some, perhaps in shock, calmly summarise the story quietly and grimly when medical help arrives ('I think my leg's gone'). Some think only of the future ('Am I finished?'). All injured players want to put the clock back a few minutes.

Other players stand around. They may even talk to one another. They are glad it is not them who is lying injured. One or two may feel guilty, thinking that it was their pass or their challenge that caused the incident. Nearby spectators may faint at the sight of blood or a shattered bone.

Derek Dooley lifted his torso into a sitting position and waved urgently towards the trainers' bench. He knew immediately that his right leg was broken. He had fractured the fibula and tibia just above the right ankle.

Referee Arthur Ellis felt that Dooley had fouled the goalkeeper. He stopped the game, called for the trainer and allowed as much time as possible for Dooley to be made comfortable. The fractured limb was strapped to the player's other leg. Dooley was taken from the field on a stretcher and then to Preston Royal Infirmary.

Two days later, on the Monday, Derek Dooley cheerfully received visitors, but he would not have liked the *Lancashire Evening Post*'s account of Saturday's game. The reporter was critical of Sheffield Wednesday's defence ('vigour, heavy charges and the playing of the man felled ball-players of the calibre of Finney, Baxter and Wayman like corn at harvest time') and then he rounded on Dooley himself: 'This lumbering giant, of ponderous motion, and a stride almost half as long as a guardsman's pace-stick, has until next season to ruminate on the wisdom of refusing to give back before an advancing goalkeeper who has gained possession. Dooley could have avoided the hurt. There was little point in continuing his bull-like charge down the middle after Thompson had safely collected the ball and was preparing to clear. He had not even a half chance of scoring.'

Later that same Monday Dooley asked an Irish nurse to sign his plaster-cast. When she accidentally caught his toes she noticed that he showed no reaction and the toes were cold and blue. Was the cast too tight? A doctor was called and he found that the leg was seriously infected with gas gangrene.

The next day Derek Dooley was gravely ill. Anti-gangrene serum was used and Sheffield Wednesday sent a surgeon to Preston for a second opinion. Dooley's twenty-year-old wife, Sylvia, started a twenty-four-hour bedside vigil, and doctors whispered near to the player's bed. One told Dooley that the only way to save his life was to amputate the leg midway up his thigh.

'Well, if it's going to save me, do it now,' Dooley replied.

He went down to the operating theatre, doing his best to smile.

Sylvia Dooley didn't sleep for the rest of the week. By Thursday Dooley was out of danger. On Saturday he was able to follow Preston Reserves v Sheffield Wednesday Reserves on the hospital's new radio system.

'I would like to stay in football,' Dooley told a reporter. 'They can stick me up as a corner flag if they like.'

There was no denying his courage.

Injuries are a footballer's biggest frustration. Injuries are a nightmare beyond personal control. You can recover from bad form, you can solve a loss of confidence, but there is nothing you can do about injury. Disability brings anxiety, guilt, anger, uncertainty, embarrassment and sometimes depression. All you can do is accept a place on the sidelines, learn patience and develop your strength of character. But there is nothing like playing. If the team is doing well you want to be part of it. If the team is doing badly you think you could make the difference. But you can do nothing. You are injured.

Blackpool's Allan Brown had no chance of playing against Bolton

Wanderers in the 1953 FA Cup Final – his leg had been broken while scoring his side's semi-final winner – but Bolton's Eric Bell was in a more invidious position: a niggling injury had kept him out of the team.

According to historians Martin Johnes and Gavin Mellor, the story of the 1953 'Matthews Final' was beautifully constructed for and by the press. It was a tale of celebration and optimism, change and tradition. The new Queen was at Wembley to see the 38-year-old Maestro, Stanley Matthews, win his FA Cup-winners' medal after twice being a runner-up. The definitive moment came in the last minute of the match. With the score balanced at 3–3, Matthews beat one Bolton man on the inside, one on the outside, and cut the ball back for Bill Perry to score Blackpool's winning goal. The Wembley press box erupted. Pens, pencils, notebooks, writing papers and typewriters went everywhere.

Television coverage of the Final focused on the civic importance of the event, the presence of the Queen, the Matthews legend and how the event could appeal to a *general* audience and not just the fans of the two teams. The FA Cup Final had been televised since 1937, but now the number of television sets in England had reached a tipping point (20 per cent of British households). As the man in a newspaper cartoon said, after knocking on the neighbours' door, 'Can I watch the Final on your set, only I can't get near mine for all the neighbours and visitors?'

The 1953 FA Cup Final is conventionally known as 'The Matthews Final', but it could easily be called 'The Masseurs' Final'. It was really decided by injuries. Bolton Wanderers had only eight fit men when they were overrun in the last fifteen minutes. Eric Bell had returned to the team at left half but his injury recurred when he made a routine header after only seventeen minutes. Bell's thigh was strapped up, and he limped along on the left wing for the rest of the match. In the days before substitutes managers instructed injured players to stay on the pitch as 'nuisance value'. One of Bell's rare touches in the 1953 Final was the header that put Bolton 3–1 up early in the second half.

Soon afterwards Bolton left back Ralph Banks began to limp – he was off the pitch for three minutes at one stage – and Bolton centre forward Nat Lofthouse had to receive treatment three times. The fit Bolton men were working extra hard to compensate for the injured players, but Blackpool pulled the score back to 3–3. Two more Bolton players went down injured. Trainer Bert Sproston came on yet again.

'If they don't pay Bert Sproston double wages this week, he's certainly earned them,' said BBC television commentator Kenneth Wolstenholme.

In the last ten minutes Ralph Banks was seriously incapacitated by cramp and he was supposed to be marking Stanley Matthews, who had done very little up to that point. The absence of Bell had already created a gap in front of Banks. Then came the Matthews moment and Bill Perry's winning goal. 'The Masseurs' Final' was lost by injuries.

One day, playing at Anfield, Leon Leuty injured his ankle in front of a full house. The trainer ran on to the field and took off Leuty's boot.

'You shouldn't have done that,' a team-mate of Leuty's told the trainer. 'The ankle will swell up and you might not get the boot back on.'

Leuty gave a long sample of his infectious giggle. 'Don't worry,' he said. 'It's my other ankle that's injured.'

Here was the drawback. Some trainers had only minimal medical knowledge. They were usually appointed because they had been loyal servants as players. When Sunderland's Tommy Wright broke a leg he shouted, 'Don't let our trainer on,' but an opponent said, 'Ours is worse than yours.' One trainer ran on to the pitch with a sponge of cold water, but when he squeezed the sponge he found that he had forgotten to dip it in the bucket. Other times, on wintry days at Barrow or Buxton, the water would develop a layer of ice.

During the 1949–50 season Leuty kept his place in the Derby County team even though he was injured. Strained stomach muscles, they told him. One night before a match he couldn't sleep for pain so he left his hotel room for a midnight game of squash, just to keep moving. The next day he couldn't raise a gallop. He had a hernia operation in November 1949 and was out of the team for thirteen weeks.

After a £25,000 transfer Leuty played 185 League games in five seasons for Notts County, where he had once played as an amateur under Frank Womack. His last season, 1954–5, was the best. Notts County chased promotion to the First Division and they reached the FA Cup sixth round. 'Show me a better way to earn £15 a week,' Leuty told his team-mates. 'We're doing something that is enjoyable.'

Training was getting more interesting too. After Hungary's two convincing victories over England – 6–3 in November 1953 and 7–1 in May 1954 – it was clear that successful teamwork emanated from practising with the ball in small-sides games. Leuty's sixteen hours of training a week now included five-a-side games (defenders v forwards or England v Scotland). But Leon Leuty was taken ill during the 1955 close season. He recovered enough to join pre-season training, and he played in the first two games. But he was so weak that he had difficulty lifting his feet. He shuffled along like an old man. His hairline had receded into an M shape and the bones were showing in his face, but he kept going into work. One day the County trainer accused him of not trying. Leuty went home and cried.

At the start of September 1955 Leuty saw a specialist and was told to take a short holiday. He was treated at home by his wife. Then he went into hospital for observation. When Notts County won 2–0 at Nottingham Forest, Leuty sent his team-mates a telegram: 'THE WIN ON SATURDAY WAS BETTER THAN ALL THE MEDICINE IN THE WORLD.'

He was discharged after a month. He watched one Notts County match and visited the local racetrack. Then he travelled to Derby to watch a benefit match. He was far too ill to play.

'Have you seen Leon?' one player asked another. 'He looks like a ghost. It looks as if we'll be playing a game for his widow soon.'

Leuty went into hospital in the middle of December and had a blood transfusion. He told Notts County manager George Poyser that he was much improved. Poyser was relieved and asked him to do some scouting. But there was no time.

Leon Leuty died on Monday 19 December 1955. When the post-mortem was conducted the cause of death was found to be lymph sarcoma. At his funeral five Notts County players and manager Poyser acted as pall-bearers. You could have picked a great forward-line from the congregation: Stan Matthews and Sammy Crooks on the wings; Raich Carter and Peter Doherty inside; and either Jack Stamps or Tommy Lawton at centre forward. Leuty had played with them all. He left two young sons and his wife Wendy. The Notts County trainer apologised to Leuty's family. He had no idea that the player was so ill.

Football players have to accept the likelihood of injury as part of their job or hobby. You have to be brave to play. The sport has a natural affinity with hard physical labour in the coalmines, the armed forces and shipbuilding, where workers take risks and need the support of colleagues. In the post-war period football, injury and society were linked through the components of danger, youthfulness and masculinity. The professional game dealt with injuries in an amateurish, unsympathetic way.

Whether an injured player decides to play in the next match or not, there are consequences. When a professional player says, 'I'm not fit,' a sequence of events is set in train, power relationships within the club dictate decisions and attitudes towards the player change. If you decide to play, you are considered fit. Once you cross the white touchline you are perceived by supporters and the manager as ready to play (even if it is not your decision). Players who play when injured may harm their injuries, their psyches and their reputations, but there are times when it has to happen. Eric Bell played in an FA Cup Final and only he knew whether or not he was fit. Leon Leuty was sluggish in training but he was slowly dying. Derek Dooley had no decision to make. He would never play again. During his nine weeks in Preston Royal Infirmary he was visited by a group of Sheffield Wednesday players. He enjoyed the banter. But when they left he felt the emptiness of the room and confronted the loss of his career.

7

SHINE A LIGHT ON STANLEY

Patches of surface water shimmered under the Peel Park lights, footballers defied naturalism by sending their shadows in all directions and red flashes flickered across the dark terraces as Lancastrians inhaled on their cigarettes. Floodlit friendly matches had arrived in Accrington.

Soccer impresarios could now provide evening entertainment during the winter months. The atmosphere was described as electric, floodlights were considered to have a bright future and it became more common to depict a football ground as a theatre. Football directors, like stage directors, now needed charge-hand electricians. Years later, when asked about playing in floodlit matches in the fifties, Accrington Stanley's Joe Devlin recalled frosty nights when the sounds of spectators carried through the unusually clear black air and the players could hear every word, good and bad.

While cinema managers looked warily at their falling attendance figures, Accrington Stanley directors gloated when a ground-record 17,634 attended a floodlit friendly against Lancashire neighbours Blackburn Rovers on Monday 15 November 1954. Under lights the players seemed to play with a freedom that was lacking in grim Division Three (North) Saturday afternoon struggles. In one floodlit match, against the exotic-sounding East Fife, full back Jimmy Harrower dribbled through twenty yards of Peel Park mud and then scored with a powerful thirty-yard shot.

The advent of floodlights paved the way for more evening games, but reporters working for daily newspapers found themselves with tighter deadlines. Away-team supporters now had floodlight pylons to guide them to football grounds from a distance, and part-time professional players enjoyed an improvement in evening training facilities. Floodlit matches offered supporters an alternative to an evening's entertainment at a cinema, theatre or pub, but it meant more late-night travel, sometimes in poor weather. And children had another reason to stay up late. Mike Ferguson was an eleven-year-old boy when he travelled five miles by bus along the A679 from Burnley to Accrington, excited by the thought of a 7.30pm kick-off between Accrington Stanley and the likes of Tottenham Hotspur, Blackburn Rovers, Third Lanark, St Mirren or Alloa Athletic.

To understand the mindset of the Football Association in the 1950s, you have to imagine an old man in his seventies who doesn't want to upset anyone in his enormous extended family. He reckons that the easiest way to retain harmony is by not changing anything too quickly or too drastically. He waits until he is convinced that the change is inevitable and hopes for the best. He is an upstanding man, a little religious, scared of commerical organisations, and he often has a nap after lunch.

In August 1930 the FA had passed a resolution prohibiting member clubs from taking part in floodlit football, and that rule stayed in place for over twenty years. Experiments with floodlights had actually begun in the 1870s but top English clubs weren't persuaded until they sampled floodlights on foreign tours in the forties and fifties. In December 1950 the FA lifted their total ban by allowing friendly floodlit games but it took another four years for the FA to extend the experiment to FA Cup replays in the early rounds (if both clubs agreed) and rearranged League matches.

It was in August 1953 that Accrington Stanley shocked their neighbouring Lancashire clubs by spending £9,500 on floodlights. The installation – ten 500-watt lights on each of eight forty-foot pylons – was done by Alan E. Dent Ltd, an electrical contractor in nearby Burnley Road. All you had to do was phone Accrington 2732 and ask for a quote.

The test match came in January 1954 when Stanley Reserves played Nelson in the Lancashire Combination Cup. 'Sitting in the stand, the atmosphere seemed to be that of watching a match indoors,' wrote Jason in the *Accrington Observer & Times*. 'Every movement could be seen quite plainly and the 5,000 spectators obviously enjoyed the experience. There seems to be a future for the game at Accrington.'

A crowd of 4,794 attended, players of both teams were given commemorative ties, and the only hitch came when a fuse blew and all the lights on one pylon went out. Men on the terraces told spectators to raise their arms. 'Many hands make light work,' they claimed.

Jason's only criticism was that the goal-nets were not sprayed white. This was remedied before the Stanley floodlights were officially opened on

Monday 15 February 1954. 'Stanley Brilliance Matched the Lights' was the front-page headline in the *Accrington Observer & Times*. A crowd of 9,750 saw Stanley beat East Fife 4–1.

The attendance record, however, was reserved for the visit of Second Division Blackburn Rovers nine months later. 'The stands nearly blew away with the cheers, heard all over Accrington, when Stanley, swinging magnificently into action, were two goals up inside eight minutes,' wrote Jason. 'And two beauties they were.' The match finished 2–2.

In the mid-1950s it seemed like Accrington had a mill on every corner and a coalmine here and there. The Lancashire town was consumed with football. The 1954–5 season saw Accrington Stanley's best-ever Football League finish – second in Division Three (North) – and their average home League attendance (9,965) beat the previous highest by over 2,000. A crowd of 15,598 watched the match with York City on Easter Monday.

They say that success has many parents, and that was true at Accrington Stanley FC. Sam Pilkington, a local fent (cloth remnants) merchant, was considered to be 'Mr Accrington Stanley'. An ex-professional footballer, he had held a variety of key positions – secretary, director and now chairman – over a thirty-year period. Pilkington knew all about the hardships of the lower divisions and about Stanley's current £10,000 overdraft. He had experienced thirty years of creditors' writs and threats, bank negotiations, payment delays, wage reductions and the inevitability of outgoing transfers. He often recalled a time in the 1920s when the club refused good offers for two excellent young players, only for Freddie Kay to retire through injury at nineteen and Tommy Green to lose his form.

Third Division chairmen traded tales of escaping bankruptcy by a whisker, and Tom Booth's book on the history of Stanley had the ironic title *75 Years in the Red*. Insurance money on mysterious grandstand fires had saved a few clubs. One Third Division (South) chairman kept telling the trainer to leave the old dressing-room gas heater on overnight with the kit hanging over it. Freddie Westgarth, the secretary-manager of Hartlepools United (as the club was known until 1968), jokingly offered fellow managers an instruction kit on ways to thwart the efforts of the fire service, including pulling the pitch-roller over the hoses.

'I see you had a fire at your ground,' one club chairman told another.

'Keep your mouth shut – that's next Thursday.'

In 1954–5 the Accrington Stanley manager was Walter Galbraith, a

36-year-old Scot who was in his second season. Having arrived at Accrington when they were seeking re-election to the Football League, Galbraith set about improving the playing staff. He regularly returned to Scotland to sign promising lads, particularly from junior football. By 1955 Accrington Stanley had seventeen Scots among its twenty-five professional players, and in one match Galbraith fielded eleven of his compatriots. Some fans accused the manager of favouring Scots over Englishmen, and journalists became canny linguists when collecting quotes from players.

Some people thought the real Accrington Stanley star was Albert Lucas of the supporters' club. Lucas was a godsend. He was a great organiser – whist drives, domino drives, dances, concerts, quizzes, buses to away matches, season-ticket sales, and so on – but his most important contribution was the supporters' club lottery. Tickets were sold around the local factories. The skill was to pick the three home wins with the most goals. In 1954 the lottery proceeds were enough to pay the players' wage bill. Until, that is, a court case blew Accrington Stanley's finances wide open.

The 1934 Betting & Lotteries Act allowed *small* lotteries among a club's members. At one club, though, the police took the view that a club couldn't reasonably have 30,000 *members* as lottery participants if the average home attendance was only 2,000. Torquay United and Accrington Stanley were test cases. Albert Lucas and director Charlie Kilby received small fines after being found guilty of violating the Betting & Lotteries Act.

The months after the court case were bad ones for Accrington Stanley. Finances were badly affected by the withdrawal of lottery funding and, worse still, rivals Barnsley won eight consecutive games without conceding a goal. Stanley finished second in 1954–5, by four points, and only one team was promoted from Division Three (North) in those days. The directors were left with a lot of 'What ifs?'. What if Stanley had beaten champions Barnsley at home instead of losing to an own goal? What if that penalty-kick had been given at Darlington? And what if Stanley hadn't frittered away the lead at Tranmere Rovers in November? The last one really hurt. Tranmere's Abie Rosenthal cheekily came into the Accrington dressing-room after the match, bowed low to the downcast Stanley players and said, 'I am glad to meet so many wealthy men who could afford to throw away a £2 bonus.'

Charlie Kilby was another important man behind Accrington Stanley's rise. His forte was ground improvements. Kilby helped to raise the certified capacity of Peel Park from 15,000 to 24,500, with 9,200 spectators under cover. He oversaw the terracing of the steep bank at the Huncoat end of

Peel Park, a new red-shale running track and new roofing on the Manor Street side. An eight-foot wall was built at the back of the Burnley Road side because people had been sneaking in without paying, particularly during floodlit matches. Local comedians reasoned that the wall was to keep the fans inside.

Accrington Stanley was unquestionably a community club. The dozen directors were all local men. The one with the printing press printed the programmes and didn't always expect to get paid. Volunteers fixed the boiler, mended seats, unblocked drains and repaired broken panes of glass. Nellie Rishton and Ivy Sproul washed the kit, cleaned the dressing-rooms, ran a small canteen, hired out stand cushions on match days, painted the ground's woodwork and ironwork during the close season and looked after a bulldog mascot called Winston. Mrs Barton helped with heat treatment for the malingerers and casualties, Mrs Aspin looked after the young lads in the players' hostel in Avenue Parade and Nellie Smith sold tea and meat pies in the refreshment hut. The meat pies were truly pukka. Once, when a huge pie was generously placed in the away-team dressing-room, a visiting player took the blackened nail off his big toe and slipped it under the pie crust.

Of course, Stanley's success was mainly down to the players. Only a handful of Second World War veterans were in the dressing-room now, although most of the younger men had done their two-year National Service. Among the players with combat experience was Les Cocker, who had been part of the Reconnaissance Regiment of the 53rd Division when it went to France in 1944. Another was Archie Wright, who had also been part of the Normandy landings. Wright was married to a Belgian woman whom he had met in Ostend in 1946.

The only way to upstage a floodlit friendly was to host a *televised* floodlit friendly. Accrington Stanley's big occasion came in October 1955, when the annual Division Three (North) v Division Three (South) representative match was held at Sam Pilkington's new-look Peel Park. The goal areas were returfed and an alternative lighting system was put in place so that fans could leave the ground safely if the main lights failed. BBC cameras transmitted the second half as it happened. 'Maybe the players were a little TV conscious,' remarked the local reporter after the 3–3 draw.

One stay-at-home fan wrote to the local newspaper about his television-viewing experience: 'Those Stanley ground advertisers who had hoped for a bit of free "commercial" TV must have been disappointed, for their lettering was obscured by hordes of small boys who demonstrated that Accrington is not without its devotees of the "let's wave at Mum" brigade.'

Televised football was still of little significance in England. A *Soccer Star* straw poll suggested that fans would much rather be at the ground watching a match on a sunny day and might have second thoughts if it was pouring with rain. 'I do not think for one moment that people would much rather glue their eyes to a small screen watching the play of the ball only, and not always receiving a complete view of the game at once,' said the magazine's reporter.

The 1954–5 season was a watershed for floodlit football. Around the time that Accrington Stanley entertained Blackburn Rovers, Wolverhampton Wanderers were being hailed as the unofficial champions of Europe. Wearing fluorescent shirts, playing on a floodlit Molineux pitch that had been strategically watered and rolled, Wolves beat Spartak Moscow (USSR) and then Honved (Hungary). Many spectators walked home from the Honved match with only socks on their feet, having lost their boots in crowd surges.

By the end of the fifties the authorities were agreeing to floodlights for any match. The European Cup and the League Cup depended on floodlights. To factory managers' delight, afternoon midweek matches became a rarity after floodlights were installed. Floodlights also permitted consistent Saturday-afternoon kick-offs throughout the year. Previously during the winter months clubs had switched from 3pm to 2pm, 2.15pm or 2.30pm.

There were plenty of quirky early floodlight stories. At Kidderminster Harriers in 1952 Kettering Town players wore mascara on their cheeks to reduce the glare from the lights. At Manchester City in 1954 two players claimed to be blinded by a photographer's flashlight camera as the ball sailed into the net. At Stockport County in 1956 it was estimated that the new lights were the equivalent of lighting 500 houses. At Port Vale in 1958 a young player, Jim McLean, was dared to climb to the top of a floodlight pylon and the fire brigade had to bring him down.

At Accrington floodlit football generated mixed feelings. Once the initial euphoria had died down, attendances fell away, especially when it rained heavily. Referee Arthur Ellis abandoned the 1954 Monday match against Tottenham Hotspur after 'fifty-two minutes of muddy farce'. Sleet was falling, a gale was blowing, participants skated across the mud and players had to stop and look for the ball when it got buried. Only 6,286 turned up to watch that night. Stanley made a loss on the event and the groundsman had a few words to say about hosting two matches in three days. But the strongest criticism came when leading goalscorer George Stewart was injured in a friendly and had to miss an important League match.

'Are they worth it, even with the extra money they bring in?' moaned one fan. 'Injuries received in these games might well spoil the team for their more important League matches.'

The workers also threatened to revolt. Around the country, as new competitions and friendly matches proliferated, players wondered why they were playing so many games for the same basic wage. The ideal compromise, achieved at some clubs, was for the receipts from floodlit matches to go into a benefit fund for loyal players.

Undoubtedly, though, floodlights created an unforgettable atmosphere. Many football fans would look back on this era with great affection. Memories of those early floodlight days stayed as sharp and fresh as the extra oxygen in the night air. The lights created a dramatic and romantic scene, and the setting helped to focus attention on the pitch. This was like offering football supporters a candlelit dinner with their heroes.

8

ON THE ROAD

O N THE FIRST DAY OF the 1956–7 season Joe Thorpe drove a coachload of Barnsley footballers to Port Vale. Bus driver Thorpe was respected by the players for his safe driving, but that didn't stop the heckling.

'Get your boot down, Joe.'

'Drop her down a gear, Joe, or you'll be changing gears on the roundabout.'

'It's quicker down there.'

'Yes, fork off, Joe.'

Port Vale had been Thorpe's first-ever Barnsley Football Club driving assignment back in 1927. On the journey Thorpe stopped the coach outside a Buxton hotel so that the players could eat lunch. He stayed in the coach and took out his sandwiches, but the team captain approached him and said, 'The manager wants you to join us at lunch. When you travel with us, you're one of us.'

Joe Thorpe was 'one of us' for thirty-eight years. He drove Barnsley players and officials from 1927 to 1965, and all his matches were away from home. In his football driving career, covering first team and reserves, he visited 120 Football League grounds, all the Midland League grounds and lots of Southern League haunts. He travelled over 200,000 miles, always driving carefully and steadily, in case he had a nauseous player on board. He never owned a car of his own and he never achieved his career dream of driving an open-top bus with the Barnsley team carrying the FA Cup. Nor did Thorpe ever emulate an experience of his colleague Alma Bell, bus driver for the two lower Barnsley teams. In his mid-forties Bell played for Barnsley A team at Rawmarsh when a trialist failed to show up.

Thorpe always carried a set of tools and two bags of ashes in case the wheels got stuck. The only time he was late for a match was at Bury, on a terrible day, when a lorry blocked the road at Akinbrook, Blackstone Edge was closed, the Todmorden road was one-lane and the Gigg Lane pitch was miraculously playable. The only time he didn't bring the team home was when the brakes stuck after a match at Tranmere and he recommended that the team return by train. One of his proudest moments came when he heard long-serving secretary-manager Angus Seed say, 'Joe's never taken us on the wrong road.'

Joe Thorpe was a small man who was almost always seen in the uniform of the Yorkshire Traction bus company. He reminded the players of a bluff contemporary comedian called Arthur Haynes. Thorpe always liaised with the Barnsley officials about travel time and hotel arrangements, and he helped the trainer to pack the essentials (boots, shorts, shirts, socks, shin-pads, cotton wool, bandages, stitching equipment, towels, spare shorts, tie-ups, smelling salts, 'magic' sponge and so on). During matches he minded the players' valuables and the dressing-room key. Afterwards he took cups of tea to the players and helped to clean the boots. Given a spare moment he would collect autographs for one of his grandsons. The players usually had a whip-round for Thorpe, the club adding a little, and that paid for his children's shoes.

Joe Thorpe was a very helpful man. One time immediately after the war, when petrol rationing was in place, he drove the team to Birmingham. A Barnsley director asked him to go to a building contractor and pick up hundreds of kitchen taps while the match was in progress. Thorpe loaded the taps until the coach boot was overflowing, and the skip (the big wicker basket containing all the kit) had to travel back in the main body of the coach with a player sitting on top. After he had unloaded the taps in Barnsley the director said, 'Here you are, Joe, I told you I'd look after you,' and gave Thorpe sixpence (2½ p).

During the 'hungry thirties' a lot of Barnsley players came from very poor areas. Some had only one set of clothes. Others thought that Aston Villa was in Liverpool. One local lad had never been in a hotel before. When the waitress asked him what he would like for a sweet he replied, in all sincerity, 'A Nuttall's Mintoe.' Joe Thorpe acted as a chaperon for these lost young boys, especially those without fathers. But the local post-war youngsters were better prepared. The Barnsley Boys system was overseen by Harold Rushforth and Ted Davies, two forerunners of the specialist teacher-coach role. Rushforth and Davies laid down a high standard of dress, conduct and behaviour.

Joe Thorpe saw a lot of football-club dressing-rooms. Aston Villa had the biggest, with about eight separate slipper baths, just like those in private houses, but most clubs of this era provided a communal bath in which players could sit in water up to their shoulders. Newcastle United had an elaborate round one. At Workington both teams stripped in the same hut and used the same baths. At Hull City the bath was on a raised platform so that the water could drain away. At Rotherham visiting players had to be careful not to burn themselves on the boiler. The away changing-room at Chester was so small that the skip had to be left outside. The one at Crewe had a sloping ceiling and the smaller players were forced down one end. At Accrington a roller-blind was all that separated the home players from the away team, so players spoke more quietly than usual.

Joe Thorpe reckoned he could tell which young players would progress from Barnsley Reserves to the first team. He had little faith in those who would be saying 'What time are we due back?' and 'Can't you make it earlier, I've got a woman to see?' Thorpe knew that professional players had to be committed to travel schedules come what may. Travel was part of football.

During the process of travelling to and playing away games, local and professional footballers collect ideas about new surroundings and their inhabitants. They learn which places feel safe and which seem risky. Involvement in football provides an illustrated road map of a town, a region or a country. For a few at the top of their profession it is a window on the world.

Football taught people a selective geography of England. Football followers had heard of Walsall but not Cannock, Accrington rather than Darwen, Tottenham instead of Edmonton. People might have heard of Newcastle and Bristol anyway – they were both large cities – but football added to that awareness.

In the mid-fifties the players travelled much further than the fans. Connie Walden started watching Barnsley in 1920 when she was eleven. She got her first motorbike when she was seventeen and went as far as she could – Halifax, Bradford or Rochdale – to support her team. In the late 1940s, however, it wasn't always easy to go to away games as petrol rationing restricted travel. That restriction returned for five months during the 1956–7 season, with a limit of 200 miles a month during the Suez Crisis. Barnsley fans were limited to local derbies at Doncaster, Huddersfield, Rotherham and Sheffield.

On away trips professional footballers had to amuse themselves for long periods. The bad travellers sat at the front, kept their eyes straight ahead and avoided reading. Barnsley captain Norman Smith was a member of the Magic Circle so he practised his tricks. Other players organised sing-alongs, some chatted to each other, one or two read popular newspapers and a few napped. In all football clubs the banter made something out of nothing. The players ragged one another over women, clothes, haircuts and mannerisms.

The main time-passer was a game of cards. A few coach seats were replaced by tables, other seats were turned round and the lads played poker, brag, thirteen-card brag, solo, hearts or short pontoon. You could win or lose a week's wages on an away trip. Cards were sometimes banned until the return journey, and some managers would stop a game mid-flow if the mood was bad for team morale. When Norman Hallam played for Barnsley in the mid-1950s he hated bus journeys to away matches because he found that the culture of cards, swearing and smoking did not gel with his life as a Methodist minister. And David Wright, a grammar-school boy who won eighteen England Youth caps, was another exception. On away trips he quietly got on with his homework. He went to Cambridge University and never turned professional.

In the years to come this generation of Barnsley players retained memories of bed linen being stuffed in hotel washbasins full of water, team-mates being thrown in dressing-room baths and an impromptu rugby match staged in a hotel foyer. More than one player remembered towns by the nearest greyhound track. A trip to Plymouth resulted in a hot tip on a greyhound and it romped home at a good price. The players talked the owner into bringing the dog up to a Yorkshire track and they made another killing.

Gordon Duggins travelled more than other Barnsley players but he did so mostly on his own. He signed for the club as a part-timer because he didn't want to curtail a National Coal Board engineering apprenticeship that paid three pounds and fifteen shillings (£3.75) a week. His weekend football was merely to shrug off the working week, but those ninety minutes also determined what sort of week he would have.

Duggins stayed living in Staffordshire and trained on his own at nearby Gresley Rovers. If Barnsley had a match further south, he would join the team at the George Hotel in Lichfield. Otherwise he travelled seventy miles by train from Lichfield to Barnsley on Friday evenings, and stayed in the White Hart Hotel. Club rules banned him from drinking, but it was tempting as he had to walk through the bar to leave the pub. One time he had a half of shandy and was reported to the club manager.

If it was a home match, or a northern away match, Duggins would walk to the ground with half a dozen team-mates. In November 1956 he scored both goals in Barnsley's 2–1 victory at Bury. At the full-time whistle his first thought was about how he might get back to Lichfield. Coming off the pitch, he asked if anyone was going into Manchester.

'Yeah, me and me mate,' someone said.

He got a lift to Piccadilly station, bought a sports-special newspaper and was quite shocked to see his name in the headlines: 'Duggins Is Dynamite to Bury.' Then he got on the train for Lichfield.

At the end of 1956–7 Gordon Duggins decided to upgrade his bicycle to a 350cc BSA motorbike. Unfortunately, coming back from playing in a cricket match at Ashby de la Zouch, he had a crash and went through a car's windscreen. He spent two weeks in Burton General Hospital with head injuries and a badly broken nose. He bought a car for the next season and a friend came with him to teach him to drive.

Barnsley FC officials weren't in favour of cars for players. They were worried that it might make them lazy, and insurance companies considered footballers a bad risk for road accidents. One incident that deeply affected Barnsley people occurred at Easter 1960. Ex-Barnsley player Barry Barber was playing for Caernarfon Town at the time. He hired a big Ford Consul with a bench seat and picked up players along the journey to West Wales. Having hired the car for the whole weekend, he rang his mates and suggested a Sunday in Blackpool. There were four in the car when it hit a lamp-post early on the outward journey. Barber, twenty-three, died immediately.

Football sometimes finds unimaginable ways of replicating its past. In December 1960, nearly eight years after Derek Dooley's leg amputation, the Sheffield Wednesday players were travelling back from London when their coach hit a telegraph pole on the Great North Road in Huntingdonshire. Six people were injured, including nineteen-year-old twelfth man Doug McMillan, who had gone to the front to change the radio station. McMillan was trapped in the twisted metal. At the scene of the crash his right leg was amputated just below the knee.

A detailed study of the Barnsley players of the 1950s shows that the culture of professional footballers can be defined by a number of key factors: the inevitable travel; male camaraderie; a subculture that accepts banter, swearing and gambling; the threat of injury; the inevitable decline in physical power in a man's thirties; and the climactic focus on the match and its uncertain outcome. The players were able to continue their fantasy occupation, but there were positive and negative consequences of being in the public eye. There was also, of course, the ever-present possibility of enforced migration, perhaps to somewhere first visited on a Yorkshire Traction bus driven by Joe Thorpe.

In the 1950s Barnsley's professional footballers were, almost to a man, from working-class backgrounds. Almost half of them made a house move of more than ten miles during their careers, a far higher figure than that for the general population over the same period (6 per cent). About 24 per cent of these players had their Football League careers ended by a bad knee injury, and their median age of retirement from the game was twenty-eight. A further 10 per cent had careers ended by other serious injuries (mainly to the head). Although 10 per cent suffered a fractured leg, this was not considered to be as critical for a football career as a knee injury.

Professional players lived in an emotional world: the bitterness caused by rejection; the upheaval of an undesired transfer; the cruelty and kindness of supporters; the pain and frustration of injury; the antagonism towards some other players; the satisfaction of a job well done; the powerlessness of dealing with directors; and (occasionally) the joy of success. These footballers were generally more conservative than the general public. They were selected for the profession partly because they had a 'good attitude to the game'. They needed the requisite skills, but they needed other characteristics to succeed too – patience, restraint, clean living, self-discipline, pride in performance and dress, dedication, loyalty and ambition to reach the first team (but at an acceptable pace). Being a professional usually meant arranging an appropriate social life, marrying the right person, stabilising, never criticising the club, being sociable and yet tactful with the public and accepting authority.

In the late 1950s, all young men had to do their two years' National Service (unless they worked in the coalmines) but it was nothing like Joe Thorpe's period of nearly four years in France during the First World War. There was full employment now and people stayed put. The Suez scare passed and new Prime Minister Harold Macmillan was soon declaring that 'most of our people have never had it so good'.

Barnsley Football Club had some stability too – only two managers between 1946 and 1960, a long-serving secretary and trainer, a board of nine directors that was unchanged for six years and the same bus driver for thirty-eight years. In his Yorkshire Traction career Joe Thorpe earned thirty-two safe-driving medals. He once calculated that he had driven the equivalent of forty times round the world. Football was only a small part of his job but he was a friend to Barnsley players, a father-figure and, by the end, a surrogate grandfather. He was also a good role model for the players, particularly Eric Brook, who left Barnsley for Manchester City in March 1928 and played eighteen times for England. When Brook retired from football he became a bus driver in his home community around Mexborough. Brook became Joe Thorpe's colleague.

PART TWO

INTRODUCTION TO PART TWO

THE TOTAL NUMBER OF CLUBS in England rose from 17,973 (in 1948) to 25,217 (in 1964) and 30,862 (in 1967), partly owing to the legalisation of Sunday football. By the late 1960s the sport was played in 12,000 schools. A typical week during the season saw between 750,000 and a million boys, youths and men playing in football matches, and more than a million people watching. A major game shown on television could attract between seven and ten million viewers. Even more people connected to the sport through the football pools.

Football clearly remained a great source of entertainment and enthusiasm, but the late fifties and early sixties also brought growing concerns about the sport. The professional game was entering a new era of spectating. The composition of crowds was slowly changing, particularly in certain sections of the ground. Different generations began to take up separate positions inside stadiums. Patterns of support and expressions of partisanship were shifting. The rattles and rosettes of the forties and early fifties were being replaced by singing and chanting.

An oppositional youth culture, symbolised by pop music and clothes, made its impact inside and outside football. Some younger fans attacked football-special trains and attempted to storm the opposition's end of the ground. These early signs of serious hooliganism, much more Saturday-afternoon television coverage of sport, a general rise in income and the reduction of the working week helped to take some traditional supporters away from football (usually by means of a car). People increasingly migrated from urban streets of terraced houses not far from football stadiums to suburban semi-detached properties. Changes in the economic geography of Britain also benefited some thriving areas of the South at the expense of some traditional northern football strongholds.

For the professional game it was an era of industrial unrest, legal action and class conflict. The football authorities in England had to deal with illegal payments, match-fixing, worsening player discipline at all levels, the threat of a players' strike, court cases and financial concerns. Two conflicts were growing – European versus domestic football and club football versus the international game. International football dominated in July 1966 when England hosted the World Cup finals and won the trophy. England's great success brought national euphoria. It temporarily reversed the decline in League attendances and sparked new activity in the women's game, which had been largely dormant since 1921.

We begin and end this part with two immensely moving and important events involving Manchester United. The 1958 Munich air disaster and the club's 1968 European Cup success, against Benfica at Wembley, were the beginning and end of a ten-year story of tragedy, heroism and redemption that deeply affected the nation's people. Television captured and shaped that ten-year football journey, growing all the time in its stature. The transfer of the *Match of the Day* TV highlights programme from BBC2 to BBC1 in 1965, the launch of ITV's *The Big Match* and the transmission of the 1966 World Cup Final and European Cup Finals all helped to attract the nation's people to televised football.

9

'IF THIS IS DEATH . . .'

Part of football's egalitarianism is that power and size are not everything. Don Davies was only five foot three and eight stone, but he excelled as a fast, tricky, quick-thinking winger when playing as an amateur for Lancashire Wanderers, Northern Nomads and England. When Davies was twenty-two, in 1914, Stoke City approached him with a novel offer – they would pay his fees to study for a degree at Manchester University if he would play for them. Then came war and all deals were off.

Don Davies joined the Royal Flying Corps and became a bomber pilot, but he was shot down over Germany early in the First World War. He spent five years in a notoriously austere German prisoner-of-war camp at Holzminden. The brutal camp commandant gave the British prisoners little reason to smile, except for one time when he shouted at them, 'You fink I know no-fing but I know damn-all.'

At Holzminden Don Davies learned to speak fluent German, Spanish and French, and his language skills came in handy forty years later when following Manchester United in Europe. He also refined his appreciation of Wagner's music and read Goethe and Heine in German. But his weight slipped away, and so did the years from his promising sporting career.

After he had recovered from his wartime ordeal, Davies joined the engineering firm of Mather & Platt, based in Newton Heath, the birthplace of Manchester United. He worked there for thirty-eight years, as an assistant master in the firm's Day Continuation School (1919–35), as the school's headmaster (1935–50) and finally as the firm's education officer (1950–7). He taught the boys (and later a few girls) mathematics, English literature, physical training, science and drawing. During his summer holidays in the mid-1920s he played county cricket for Lancashire as an amateur.

Davies retired from playing sport at the age of thirty-eight. He was a committed teacher and scoutmaster, and used his spare time to write articles for the *Boy's Own Paper*. He also sent specimen football reports to the *Manchester Guardian*. He had followed football since he was very young, when he first sat on his father's shoulders to watch Bolton Wanderers at Burnden Park. He sensed his father reacting to the play with quick, convulsive movements and grunts. Each week his father vowed never to go again as long as he lived, 'yet each week saw him bolting his Saturday dinner and hurrying off as though his life depended on the struggle to get in'.

Halfway through the 1933–4 season the *Manchester Guardian*'s sports editor, Evelyn Montague, sent Don Davies to cover an exciting FA Cup third-round tie between Chesterfield and Aston Villa. Davies was assigned the byline 'An Old International' and spent the next twenty-four years as a *Manchester Guardian* sportswriter. He learned how to write for people who hadn't seen the game and people who had. He wrote in longhand on pages torn from an old exercise book, pinned them together and handed them in personally to the *Guardian* office.

'To say that the Cup favourites met their Waterloo would be both trite and trivial,' Davies once wrote about a major Cup upset. 'Say rather that they met their Marathon, their Arbela, their Hastings, their Bultowa, their Blenheim, their Saratoga, their anything and everything up to the limit of fifteen decisive battles of the world.'

In 1956 a new world opened up for Davies. His beat changed from England to Europe. The European Cup was seen as a means of healing war wounds and binding countries together to avoid future conflicts. In 1955 the League champions, Chelsea, had refused an invitation to play in the inaugural European Cup competition (on the advice of the Football League). The next League champions, Manchester United under Matt Busby, went against the League's wishes and tried their luck in Europe.

Busby was hailed as a pioneering genius. Davies attributed the manager's success to his personal qualities, first-hand knowledge of the top-level game, his ability to teach and handle men and a reasonable share of good fortune. Busby's assistant was Jimmy Murphy, a visionary recruiter of young players. Murphy could seduce the families of talented youngsters, and the capture of the brilliant Duncan Edwards was an astonishing coup. Dudley-born Edwards was a Wolves fan who lived only a few miles from the club's ground at a time when the team was one of the best in the country.

During the Second World War a group of local teachers had formed the Manchester United Junior Athletics Club to offer facilities for promising young footballers, and this structure helped develop young players for

Murphy and Busby. The Manchester United under-eighteen team won the first five FA Youth Cup competitions, starting in 1953. When these youngsters graduated en masse to the first team, they became known as the Busby Babes.

When the European adventure finally got under way for English clubs, in 1956–7, Don Davies had the chance to speak his foreign languages and sample the local culture in Dortmund, Brussels and Madrid before Manchester United lost their semi-final. In 1957–8 United beat Shamrock Rovers and Dukla Prague to reach the quarter-finals. Then, having beaten Red Star of Belgrade 2–1 in the first leg at Old Trafford, Busby's team faced a tricky return in Yugoslavia. Davies was initially unavailable for the Belgrade trip. The *Guardian*'s second football correspondent, John Arlott, was annoyed when Davies declared himself available and took his place on the plane.

The European Cup quarter-final second leg ended 3–3 after Manchester United had led 3–0 at one point, so United qualified for the semi-finals on a 5–4 aggregate score. Yugoslav journalists wrote about United's 'unsportsmanlike and often unscrupulous' tackling, but British journalists blamed the referee for being unduly harsh.

'The Blue Danube flows grey and cold through the city of Belgrade tonight,' wrote George Follows of the *Daily Herald*. 'And for all Manchester United care referee Karl Kainer of Vienna can jump in it – whistle and all.'

Despite the home team's elimination, relations were cordial during the post-match banquet at Belgrade's Majestic Hotel. When the lights were dimmed and the waiters entered with candles flaming on bowls of iced sweetmeats, the United players applauded and sang 'We'll Meet Again'.

'Why didn't you score just one more goal?' Don Davies told a Yugoslav journalist. 'Then we could have met a third time.'

The next day the Manchester United party flew from Belgrade to Munich's Reim Airport, where they refuelled for the journey to Manchester. At Munich Captain James Thain abandoned two attempts to take off on a runway covered with snow and slush. He taxied back to the terminal buildings to have the plane checked.

The passengers waited nervously in the airport lounge. After fifteen minutes they were called back on to the plane. It was approaching three o'clock in the afternoon. Just before the third attempt to take off, David Pegg moved to the back, saying, 'I don't like it here, it's not safe.'

With forty-three people aboard, including crew, the plane roared along the runway, past the point of no return. Ray Wood loosened his tie, took out his false teeth and leaned forward into an emergency position.

'Can you see whether that wheel has gone up yet, Dennis,' Frank Taylor of the *News Chronicle* asked Dennis Viollet of Manchester United.

'It's now or never,' said left back Roger Byrne, captain of Manchester United and England.

'I don't know what you're laughing at,' said Johnny Berry. 'We're all going to get killed here.'

'Well, if this is death, then I'm ready for it,' said Billy Whelan, the young Republic of Ireland international.

In Manchester that same Thursday Gertrude Davies happily went out and bought the ingredients for her husband Don's favourite meal – a casserole of lamb chops and mixed vegetables. She built a fire in the living-room and started to prepare the food.

At 4pm her telephone rang. It was her younger daughter, Deirdre.

'Mum,' Deirdre said. 'Pop hasn't gone to Belgrade, has he?'

Deirdre had heard a rumour.

Gertrude Davies rang the *Manchester Guardian*, the BBC Manchester studios and the city's Ringway Airport. She learned nothing. She paced up and down looking at the telephone. She rang Mather & Platt's offices and asked them to make urgent enquiries. As she talked the *Manchester Evening News* came through her letter-box. She scoured the paper and saw bad news in the stop-press: 'Manchester United Players in Plane Crash.'

The novelist H. E. Bates turned on his television at six o'clock. 'The normally urbane voice of the announcer seemed to turn into a sledge hammer,' he later wrote.

Eight young footballers died at Munich. Memories of them swelled up. As Jimmy Murphy wrote in his autobiography several years later, 'I can see them now.'

Eddie Colman was known as 'Snake Hips' because he had a deceptive body swerve. Before this trip his mother had made him a parcel of apples, oranges and tea. Don Davies's notebooks included personal details about the players. 'Colman: the premier danseur in a footballer's ballet. Humorous and chubby, shooting can be dangerous for two yards, sings ballads, sentimental, likes fish and chips.'

Tommy Taylor was a strong, stocky, ex-miner from Barnsley. ' "Babyface". Most lovable character, full of fun, imitates crooners.'

Mark Jones had grown up in Ardsley in south Yorkshire. His father had been a timekeeper at Wombwell Main Colliery. 'Life and soul of the party. Jones trains budgerigars, always ready for a talk.'

Liam (Billy) Whelan had great skill and was a wonderful improviser on the field, but he had an inferiority complex and was vulnerable to criticism. 'Quiet but with a ready smile.'

David Pegg was a skilful, tricky winger with a body swerve. 'Taylor's pal from Doncaster.'

Roger Byrne, captain of Manchester United and England, was studying physiotherapy for his next career. 'Well-educated, good home, amused twinkle, great confidence in own powers.'

Duncan Edwards died later in hospital after being in a coma. At twenty-one he already had everything as a footballer. He was strong, two-footed, skilful, and had a thirty-yard shot that could make a crossbar twang like a tuning-fork. Like his contemporary John Charles, he was a man of two first names and many positions. 'Good-natured, quiet speech, grand physique, modest bearing. How the air-hostesses hover over Duncan Edwards. Only equalled by the way Duncan Edwards hovers over air-hostesses.'

Geoff Bent had played only twelve League games in the United first team in nearly seven years. But high-class players could earn a good living as a regular reserve at their home-town club. Bent was in the plane as one of six reserves. He was a possible deputy for Roger Byrne, who had a bruised thigh. In the event Byrne was fit to play.

The Munich disaster changed the identity of Manchester United. It added an emotional charisma. A legend was created. United's European adventures coincided with the increasing prominence of television. Evening TV viewers grew to recognise these distinctive young men who were threatening to dominate English professional football and the new European game. There was enormous public sympathy for Manchester United Football Club. Complete strangers thought that they had lost part of their family in the tragedy. Funeral crowds lined the streets. A few southerners kept scrapbooks of Munich cuttings.

The pre-Munich Busby Babes had won two successive League Championships. The average age of the team in Belgrade was only twenty-three, and that was without young internationals like Whelan (twenty-two), Pegg (twenty-two) and Blanchflower (twenty-four), who were among the reserves. Woven into the Munich legend was wonder at what else the team might have achieved.

The Busby Babes also carried the hopes of the home football nations. Byrne (twenty-eight), Taylor (twenty-six) and Edwards (twenty-one) were already England regulars, and Pegg and Colman were candidates for the 1958 England World Cup party. Centre half Jackie Blanchflower was a certainty for the Northern Ireland squad for those Finals in Sweden. The what-might-have-been-but-for-Munich questions continued to the other side of the 1970 World Cup Finals. The continuing presence of Matt Busby and Bobby Charlton at Manchester United helped to cement the legend. Munich became deeply embedded in the day-to-day culture of the club, symbolised by the stadium clock outside Old Trafford, fixed at the time and date of the crash, and the memorial plaque.

After the Munich disaster almost every English person was aware of Manchester United FC, although this wasn't converted into a new wave of active supporters until the exciting United team of the late 1960s emerged. But United's European matches attracted City fans, and football followers elsewhere in the North-West used their newly acquired cars to see these special floodlit events.

In the immediate aftermath of the disaster the local community pulled together. Fans of both major Manchester teams felt the tragedy acutely. Manchester City had lost their legendary ex-goalkeeper Frank Swift and Matt Busby had once been a City player. Flags were at half-mast, factories held a minute's silence, City fans sympathised with United fans and the grief was shared. Here was *Manchester* united. But old divisions returned when the new normality settled, and not everyone was sympathetic. A few weeks after the disaster Burnley fans showed ill-feeling after seeing a catalogue of bad fouls by United's Greaves and Crowther, plus the sight of United goalkeeper Harry Gregg sitting astride Shackleton 'and hitting him with his fists', according to 'Sportsman' of the *Burnley Express and News*. After United's Pearson was sent off one Burnley fan said, 'It's a pity they didn't all die.' Another wrote to the local newspaper to say that he had 'never seen dirtier tactics than those displayed by United'.

Munich also created a trail of religious-type relics that eventually led to a memorabilia trade. The writer Gordon Burn, in *Best and Edwards*, says that the United items of real value are those connected in some way with Munich. These include ticket stubs for the match in Yugoslavia and the official programme for the first match after the disaster. Manchester United resumed their fixtures with a delayed FA Cup fifth-round tie against Sheffield Wednesday on Wednesday 19 February, thirteen days after the crash. The programme had blank spaces on the Manchester United side of the team sheet.

Three Manchester United club officials – Walter Crickmer (club secretary), Tom Curry (trainer) and Bert Whalley (coach) – died in the crash. The death-roll also included co-pilot Captain K. G. Rayment, a steward called W. T. Cable, travel agent B. P. Miklos and a United supporter called Willie Satinoff.

The story of the crash itself followed the prototype for disasters. There were heroic deeds – goalkeeper Harry Gregg was seen carrying a baby out of the wreckage – and narrow escapes. One Yugoslav journalist would have accompanied the United team to Manchester but he left his passport at home and missed the flight. Wilf McGuinness missed the trip because he was injured, and Colin Webster had flu.

The strangest regret, though, probably belonged to Arsenal's Dennis Evans. During Manchester United's amazing 5–4 win at Arsenal, on the Saturday before the crash, Evans was so incensed at seeing Duncan Edwards knock an Arsenal player over the cinder track that he set out to injure Edwards in response. But Evans pulled out from making the bad tackle at the last second. Later he wished he *had* injured the United player. It would have kept Edwards off the plane.

United assistant manager Jimmy Murphy learned about the disaster when he returned to Old Trafford from his duties as Wales manager in Cardiff. He took a bottle of whisky from a sideboard, retreated to his office and wept. Only seven of the seventeen travelling players were able to continue their football careers after the crash. Charlton, Viollet, Gregg and Foulkes played for United in the 1958 FA Cup Final team and continued their exceptional careers. But the two young wingers who played against Red Star Belgrade, eighteen-year-old Ken Morgans and 22-year-old Albert Scanlon, dropped into the lower divisions within four years, and 26-year-old Ray Wood moved to Second Division Huddersfield Town later in 1958. Jackie Blanchflower and Johnny Berry never played again. Berry was in a coma for two months. He had a fractured skull, a broken jaw, a shattered elbow joint and a broken pelvis.

The story of manager Matt Busby's heroic fight for life spread across the world. Busby twice received the last rites and confessed later that he had prayed for death. He had serious chest and lung damage and a smashed right foot, and it was only later that he was told about the extent of the disaster. The doctor in charge of the patients, Professor Maurer, complained about the aggressive and intrusive attitudes of the British press, especially when they were taking photographs of an unconscious Busby receiving an injection in an oxygen tent. Maurer said that the presence of the press interfered with the work of the doctors and nurses.

Matt Busby was fit enough to watch the FA Cup Final between Bolton Wanderers and Manchester United three months after the crash. Opponents Bolton Wanderers won 2–0 but felt justifiably aggrieved at playing in two FA Cup Finals (1953 and 1958) when the whole nation supported their opponents. As Bolton players passed through Manchester Piccadilly station on their return journey from London, they were pelted with clogs, tomatoes and bags of flour.

The Munich disaster story has always focused on the loss of young life and the growth of the Manchester United legend, but it was also a watershed for journalism. For the second time in his life, forty-four years apart, Don Davies was involved in a plane crash in Germany. This time he was killed.

Seven other reporters died in the crash. A number were Manchester United fans. Alf Clarke of the *Manchester Evening Chronicle*, a former United amateur player, had spent twenty-five years reporting on the club. 'There's only one team in this city,' Clarke once said, 'and you can't write enough about them.' George Follows of the *Daily Herald* wanted to see United win the European Cup. He had also marked his calendar with a date six years hence, in anticipation of his young son signing as a United professional at seventeen. Tom Jackson of the *Manchester Evening News* was 'more than a reporter – he was Manchester United's lifelong friend'.

The lost reporters were senior exponents of their craft. Archie Ledbrooke of the *Daily Mirror* was chairman of the Football Writers' Association. The *Daily Mail*'s Eric Thompson illustrated his own stories with cartoons. Frank Swift of the *News of the World* was, according to Don Davies, a 'goalkeeper, dressing-room chorister, and prince of travel companions'. Henry Rose of the *Daily Express* was a striking, mustachioed bachelor who smoked Havana cigars and wore a Stetson hat and a huge overcoat. He gave fans a voice in his 'Postbag' column and he was loved or hated for his opinions on the game. A devout Jew and proud Welshman, Rose told fellow reporters to 'never write anything of which you might later be ashamed'. He could attract more attention than the players.

After Munich, as always after disasters, the public was very dependent upon the media for news. But eight journalists had died and the only one to survive, Frank Taylor, was seriously injured. It was very difficult for the young replacement reporters to step into the shoes of these men, especially as some had to write obituaries on their colleagues. The replacements were the first of a new generation of reporters who would follow Henry Rose's lead by writing more about issues away from the match, such as who might sign for Aston Villa and which player was seen in which nightclub.

In the 1950s reporters were fans of the club and friendly with the staff. They went into the dressing-rooms and didn't always write about what they saw. They also approached stories in a more restrained manner. 'Secretly, Tom Jackson disliked the name "Red Devils" and the label "Busby Babes", for he loathed sensationalism,' wrote Jackson's obituarist. 'Football to him was sterner and more real. He never wrote a man off after a bad game or praised him extravagantly after a good one.'

After Munich the tabloid newspapers became much more aggressive in their coverage of the sport. More scandal-mongering and 'inside football' stories appeared, and the relationship between the press and football began to change. The FA, for example, complained to the Press Council about the 'quote system' and 'errors of fact, mis-truths and mis-statements' after the 1959 England tour to the Americas. The days of the sympathetic journalist were about to disappear.

10

ON THE PRODUCTION LINE

In 1949 Harry Thompson was a 34-year-old part-time professional footballer at Northampton Town. Looking forward to his next stage of life, he saw that Headington United were advertising for a player-coach. He didn't know where Headington was – he thought it was somewhere in Yorkshire – but he soon learned that it was a suburb of Oxford. Headington United appointed Harry Thompson and prepared for their first professional season.

On a wage budget of £120 per week Thompson put together a new team. He contacted friends he had made during his playing career with Wolves, Sunderland and York City, and signed a few players on their recommendations. Then he fell ill and was hospitalised with a touch of tuberculosis.

One of his visitors was Jim Howe, works manager at a local company called Pressed Steel. Howe told Thompson that he could fix him up with a job. He could also find work for a few of the Headington players. There were real prospects in the car industry at Cowley, three miles east of the centre of Oxford.

'If I can help you in any way, just let me know,' Howe told Thompson.

A selection committee picked the Headington team during the 1949–50 season. Then Harry Thompson was appointed player-manager with full responsibility. Over the next few years he was well supported. An electrician on the board of directors helped to set up some floodlights. Two builders set up a temporary stand for a big FA Cup match against First Division Bolton Wanderers. Professor Harold Thompson of Oxford University and Pegasus permitted amateur players to play for Headington United. And by 1954 the supporters' club had 20,000 members.

Thanks to people like Jim Howe, Harry Thompson could sign players on a part-time wage and find them a job at Morris Motors, Pressed Steel or Morris Radiators. The players could be better off than playing full-time football with a Football League club. Inside twenty years, between 1948 and 1968, Headington United rose from an amateur Spartan League club to a full-time professional club playing in Football League Division Two. It was an astonishing success story. Success happened because the club's directors appointed two sensible managers – Harry Thompson and Arthur Turner – who, in their respective ten-year stints, chose players well. Success happened because this was an era of stability and continuity which allowed a nucleus of eight Oxford United players to stay together for about ten years from the late 1950s. Success happened because ambitious directors were given good financial control by company secretary Edmund Gibbs. More than anything, though, success happened because Oxford was an expanding modern city with a thriving car industry. Simple statistics show the growth. The number of people working in the vehicle industry rose from 13,700 (in 1946) to 23,300 (in 1953) to a peak of 27,163 (in 1965). People migrated to Oxford. Some of them came from traditional football hotbeds. Some were professional footballers.

Harry Thompson turned up on Geoff Denial's Sheffield doorstep one day in September 1956. Denial was approaching twenty-five. He had been with Sheffield United for nearly five years and had played only ten first-team games. But he had served a pipe-fitting apprenticeship with the East Midlands Gas Board and that made him an ideal type for Headington United. Although Denial had switched to full-time football for the past two years, he now found that he had too much time on his hands.

'Come down and look at our ground at Headington,' Thompson suggested. He was mild-mannered, gentlemanly and very persuasive.

Geoff Denial took his wife down to Oxford and they talked it over. The player could easily have moved to a Second or Third Division club as a full-timer, but Harry Thompson was offering a better deal. Denial could return to part-time football, resume his trade and be comfortably off in the Oxford area. The only drawback was his call-up for National Service during the Suez Crisis.

Denial stayed at the club for eight years. He soon noticed that a lot of part-time Headington United players, particularly those without trades, worked at the Morris Motors factory. Theirs was a physically tough life but they earned good money. They worked full-time in the factory, trained two nights a week and played matches. After an evening match in Llanelli the team's factory workers got home at two in the morning and started work four hours later.

Halfway through the 1958–9 season Arthur Turner was on the verge of opening a business in his home town of Newcastle under Lyme. He had had enough of football management after being forced to resign at Birmingham City. Then journalist John Ross phoned to say that Headington United were looking for a manager. United chairman Ron Coppock talked Turner out of his retirement from football and gave him a better contract than the one he'd had at First Division Birmingham. Headington United's directors were very ambitious. They had ideas about getting into the Football League. But they were fortunate to scrape into the new Southern League Premier Division.

Turner knew that a stable team would reap benefits for the club as long as there was no conflict. He got rid of most of the existing staff and set about signing good young players. Turner looked to First Division clubs like Wolves, Birmingham City and Aston Villa, and he signed young men who had something to prove, family men with good character. He made sure that they knew that Oxford was well off for employment. It worked out well for Maurice Kyle (signed from Wolves) as he was a qualified electrician, and Tony Jones (from Birmingham City) did some lorry driving. Turner insisted that the players live in Oxford.

Southern League players of the 1950s tell stories of earning higher wages than in the Football League, low-rent housing, available jobs and backhanders disguised as removal expenses or travel costs. To hear them, there was more money in the Southern League than in parts of the Football League, but players were often left with a price on their heads if they wished to return to the League.

'Seventy-five per cent of Football League players didn't want the money [available in the Southern League],' said one experienced non-League player. 'They wanted the glory of playing in the Football League.'

At Headington United Arthur Turner wanted to organise the club along the lines of a full-time professional Football League club, and the directors matched his ambitions. Money was made available and there was great help from the supporters' club. Southern League success swiftly followed.

Arthur Turner retained Geoff Denial as his captain and built a team around him. Denial had developed his alternative career and was now in the heating and ventilation business. It was still in his interests to remain a part-time player while he continued his outside work in one of the many blossoming local businesses in an expanding economy.

The directors had a problem with the club's name. They had tried for years to switch from Headington United to Oxford United, but there was opposition from Oxford City and the Oxfordshire FA. On 4 May 1959 Headington United's Vic Couling wrote to FA secretary Sir Stanley Rous with a strong case for the name change. Couling argued that Headington had become a *city* team rather than a village (or suburb) team, and the new name would help the club's push to enter League football. Oxford City had now withdrawn their objections and, besides, Abbey United had been allowed to change *their* name to Cambridge United. In 1960 Headington United became Oxford United (after an interim year as Headington & Oxford United).

The next campaign was for Football League status. On 8 March 1961 Vic Couling wrote to League secretary Alan Hardaker on behalf of the Oxford United board. Couling outlined the club's healthy catchment area (150,000 people within fifteen miles), the lack of nearby competition (no League club within thirty miles), the club's administrative strengths and its financial circumstances. Oxford United owned their ground, had capital reserves of £52,000 and owned seven properties. There were eighteen full-time professional players, ten part-timers and five ground-staff boys. The wage bill was £400 per week, and gates varied from 4,500 to 17,000 according to the attraction. It was a convincing case. Oxford United were elected to the Football League in 1962.

Ronnie Atkinson had various nicknames. One was 'The Tank'. Another was 'The Oil King'. When he changed for a match he rolled over the top of his shorts so that they were high on his legs, exposing as much of his thick, muscular thighs as was decent. He looked more like a weightlifter than a footballer. Then he got out a bottle of olive oil and coated his legs until he glistened in floodlights.

'Is that in case the sun gets too strong?' other players asked him in December.

Atkinson used so much oil that he could have made a fortune from sponsoring it. Instead he worked as a representative for a hardware store and cleaned windows with his team-mate Bud Houghton.

Ronnie Atkinson signed for Headington United in July 1959, after three years at Aston Villa without a first-team game. He saw the move as a temporary one. He thought he would go to Headington, get some experience and make a big move from there. He stayed for over twelve years.

In his second year in Oxford Atkinson took over from Geoff Denial as club captain. Atkinson was only twenty-one, but Arthur Turner thought he had all the qualities for the job. Turner told Atkinson that one key rule of captaincy was to be bold enough to make sure others are doing their job even if you're not playing particularly well yourself. Throughout the 1960s, in more than a hundred dressing-rooms around the country, Atkinson would soak his body with oil and then try to punch anybody who was near him. He would tackle the wall to get himself aggressively wound up. He led his team out of the dressing-room like it was an explosion rather than a chore. He announced his presence to the crowd by whacking the ball up in the air. Here we are. We are Oxford United.

The Oxford United dressing-room became a stable place. The two full backs, Cyril Beavon (from Wolves) and local lad Pat Quartermain, went together like Morris and Cowley. There was Ronnie Atkinson and his brother Graham, Maurice Kyle, Tony Jones and, a little later, Colin Harrington and John Shuker. They all stayed at Oxford for more than ten years.

Arthur Turner particularly enjoyed watching Ronnie Atkinson lead out his team. It gave Turner the same kind of feeling as when his team went one–nil up.

'At Pressed Steel we talked about football all the time, especially on a Monday after the match,' said one former worker. 'Nearly everybody at Pressed Steel seemed to be a Headington supporter. We used to discuss the team, who they'd dropped and who they shouldn't have dropped, all that sort of thing. Pressed Steel was full of managers. Everybody knew more about it than the manager!'

The ambience of the factory floor suited this swift exchange of basic information. This helped the development of strike action, and it also worked to create a culture of football interest.

'Did you go on Saturday?'

'Of course!'

'What did you think?'

'They just need someone to knock in the goals.'

Working-class people were gradually becoming less tied to class and place. They were earning good money, growing more middle class in their lifestyles and getting more interested in consumption and style (cars, household appliances, DIY). In Oxford the economy was shifting from 'gown' to 'town'. Oxford had traditionally been a university city with university-related jobs and publishing-industry offshoots. Its town side had a greyhound track, factories, housing estates and Oxford United FC. Productivity in local factories and foundries rose after a good United win.

Arthur Turner organised a network of eight scouts around the country, arranged for good hotel meals on away trips, appointed a full-time secretary in the office (with assistance) and introduced some apprentice professional footballers to help the groundsman. Young players were recruited and developed. Here was another kind of production line.

Turner appointed Ken Fish as trainer-coach. Fish had been used to First Division clubs, so he wasn't impressed with Oxford United's ground. This is an education, he thought, when he spent the night on a camp-bed in the secretary's office. On his first day in charge he taped over the clock so the players couldn't see the time. He introduced novelty training techniques where he got players to compete with one another while doing bizarre things: 'Right arm in the air, touch your nose with your ring finger, keep running on the spot.'

Fish spoke with a South African accent and had an unorthodox approach to the job. He captivated the players and brought discipline, enjoyment and adventure to each day's training. The presence of Fish and Turner were signs that Oxford United could go much higher. Fish stayed for twenty-four years.

Town and gown stayed apart from each other, but some people occupied both camps. Ron Coppock, the long-standing Oxford United chairman, was managing director of Axtell & Perry, a firm of Oxford stonemasons who restored Oxford colleges. And during FA Cup runs press photographers would dress up Oxford United players in gowns and mortarboards in order to take a bizarre team picture.

Entry into the Football League brought a lot more travelling for Oxford United. Gone were the days when Headington United village players could jump on their push-bikes and pedal to Crescent Road to play Osberton Radiators. But there was still some semblance of village cohesion. A nucleus of eight lads had come together when they were young and talented and looking for opportunities. If they were on an away trip, they all went out as a group. They stuck together. Ronnie Atkinson thought that their togetherness showed through on the field.

A football club's fortunes can be mapped, albeit imprecisely, on to changes in the economic and cultural vibrancy of its local communities. The navy town of Portsmouth boomed around the war years, and its football team won successive League Championships in 1948–9 and 1949–50. In contrast Accrington was struck by a decline in the northern cloth trade in the late 1950s, Stanley fell into bankruptcy and their Football League place was filled by Oxford United. In football almost every success has an allied failure. Every victory brings a defeat.

England's sporting economic map was shifting. Some northern clubs – Accrington Stanley, Barrow, Bradford Park Avenue, Workington, Gateshead, Southport – were slowly being threatened, both economically and in a football sense, increasingly viewed as grim, unwanted trips by southern clubs. They would be replaced by the likes of Peterborough United, Oxford United, Cambridge United, Hereford United and Wimbledon, clubs from buoyant areas that were symbolic of economic change. Oxford was part of England's changing social geography. Oxford had regional prosperity and a nucleus of affluent workers, and Oxford United benefited accordingly. Their success signalled the South's post-war rise in the face of relative northern decline.

11

A BIT OF A FLUTTER

D URING THE 1950S ABOUT FOURTEEN million British people regularly connected with football through the ritual of completing and checking a pools coupon. They listened to the radio – or later television – at five o'clock on Saturdays, when the classified football results were broadcast with the resonance of an epic poem. Many a man sat in his armchair, noted the scores on a newspaper, looked at his coupon predictions and muttered, 'I suppose I'll have to go back to work on Monday.'

Pools coupons brought national fame to lesser-known football names. When it came to predicting results Aldershot held the same importance as Arsenal. Come Saturday tea-time households hushed as the music of 'Out of the Blue' introduced *Sports Report* and John Webster started to announce the final scores. Pools optimists tried to anticipate each result by the tone and tenor of the announcer's voice. Motorists cursed if their radios cut out when passing under a bridge.

The results service had the grandeur and familiarity of the shipping forecast. But, like a trip at sea, it could be dramatic. An episode of the television sitcom *Hancock's Half Hour* was set around a lonely man and his pools coupon, and the comedian Michael Bentine made a hit record in 1962 called 'Football Results'. Bentine began his rendition suitably slowly, but then completely lost his composure, screaming and crying out the scorelines. Finally he wiped away tears and returned to measured, neutral tones, accepting that it was yet another week without a pools win. As Michael Palin has put it, the announcer's word-perfect reading of the results was 'a quasi-religious experience' that left a 'trail of emotional havoc in his wake'.

Some people chose coupon numbers by the birthdays, anniversaries or door numbers of family and friends. Some did the same numbers each week and dare not stop for fear that the numbers would come up the following week. A few used a pin. Most football lovers studied the League tables and took recent form into account.

Newspaper experts offered offbeat advice ('It is a popular view that difference in the size of pitches accounts for a large percentage of home wins on the coupons'). Horace Batchelor of Bristol became a familiar voice on Radio Luxembourg as he repeatedly advertised his pools-winning system and gruffly announced his address ('That's Keynsham, spelt K-E-Y-N-S-H-A-M'). According to one big winner, pools companies wanted success to be seen as skill-related rather than 'picking numbers out of a water jug' as he had done.

About 39 per cent of the population did the pools, but nearly half of those aged twenty-one to forty-nine were involved. Working-class men were looking to escape their current life and the pools weren't seen as 'real gambling'. The game gave them a cheap thrill – a 'bit of a flutter' – and the chance of a fortune. What really hooked people, however, was the number of smaller wins. Most people heard about someone who was smiling because they had 'come up on the pools' and that maintained the dream. Twenty per cent of pools entrants were female, but they staked much less than the men. An estimated one in three *working* women did the pools in 1952, usually as part of a syndicate.

Most big-money pools winners were ordinary working-class people who stayed relatively close to their roots after their windfall. Their main ambitions were a house, a car and a holiday abroad. One business owner refused to put his winnings into his business because he wanted to retain his status as a self-made man.

Frank Wall was a 63-year-old baker when he won £275,235 on the pools on New Year's Day 1966. Before the win he worried about how he would continue to pay his council-house rent of £3 a week when he retired on a £4 weekly pension. Wall didn't want a car or holidays abroad, and his wife, a canteen cook, wasn't interested in jewellery or mink coats. She was happy with a night-out at bingo.

After the win Frank Wall opened his first-ever bank account. He bought a new home in Bournemouth for £8,800, gave his three children £20,000 each, put £1,000 in trust for each of his seven grandchildren and invested the rest. His wife continued to enjoy bingo and a £4 win left her feeling lucky.

Reporters craved rags-to-riches tales. A homeless man, winner of £23,000, remained homeless but lived in hotels rather than hostels. A convicted thief

(£26,000) was suddenly able to pay a £15 fine rather than serve a three-month sentence. Nellie McGrial (£205,235) was a widow raising two small children in Stockport on £6 a week. A 45-year-old writer of boys'-magazine stories found himself living an adventure himself when his coupon came up. A 30-year-old man (£105,507) gave up his job and spent his time playing football and going to the bowling alley (much like a professional footballer).

When Charlie Bragge (£112,904) was asked what he would do with the money, he said that his first purchase would be a dish of jellied eels. Betty Fox (£75,000) bought an Austin Princess car but was so anxious about driving it that she put little more than 4,000 miles a year on the car's clock. Raymond Smith (£28,649), a draughtsman and staunch Methodist from Bury, put his winnings into a trust fund and asked his trustees to distribute it all to charities. The win changed Smith in only one respect – he gave up doing the pools.

Most big winners had a period of major readjustment. Some were anxious about owning so much money and disoriented by having their ambitions changed. Some feared that their children might get kidnapped, and others were disturbed by the inevitable begging letters. Their close relationships usually changed in some way. Three-quarters of big winners in full employment gave up their job, but some of these started their own businesses later. They became much more likely to vote Conservative.

A few big winners suffered afterwards – one man had a nervous breakdown, another lost part of his winnings in a failed business and a third spent all his money betting on horses – but overall they were much less likely to feel bored or lonely than the general public. Years later almost all big winners were glad that they had won the money.

'I have enjoyed twenty-five years of holiday,' said one.

In September 1961 Keith Nicholson was a 23-year-old coalminer. He lived in a council house in Castleford, Yorkshire, and was married with three children under the age of four. He had been doing the football pools for two years. His routine was to spend three shillings and sixpence (17½p) a week on a Littlewoods coupon. Nicholson chose to perm any eight matches from his selected eleven (165 lines at a farthing a line), plus three separate lines of eight.

Late on the afternoon of Saturday 23 September 1961, Nicholson started shaving, ready for a night out with his wife Vivian. He could hear the football results announced on the television because the volume was turned up loud. As he heard draw after draw he became excited. According to his wife, Nicholson kept shaving, his hand shaking, and cut his face time and time again. He tore off most of the front page of the *Evening Post* to stem the bleeding.

Later Nicholson got hold of a Saturday-night sports paper and checked the results of his eleven selections very carefully. Sure enough, he had eight draws in the eleven. Unconcerned about the detail of the matches – what if Birmingham City goalkeeper John Schofield hadn't saved George Eastham's penalty-kick when Arsenal already led 1–0? – Nicholson immediately went to Castleford's main post office and sent a claim by telegram to Littlewoods.

Two days later a senior claims investigator visited the Nicholsons. All pools companies had strict security procedures. Winning coupons were checked for possible post-match tampering, and they were compared with the winner's previous coupons for consistency of handwriting and systems. The winner's background was investigated for fraud and the winner was asked a number of questions to confirm exactly how the coupon was collected and sent. Littlewoods had experience of all kinds of fraud; a Latvian man was fined £100 and ordered to pay fifty guineas in costs when he tried to gain £149,342 by false pretences.

Keith Nicholson passed all the checks. He was a legitimate, sole winner. He had sent off his coupon with an X to denote that he wanted no publicity, but now he changed his mind. Nicholson and his blonde wife – he called her Goldie – were whisked off to London to receive the cheque from Bruce Forsyth. A crowd of reporters were on the platform as their train from Leeds pulled in. One asked what the young couple would do with the money.

'I'm going to spend, spend, spend,' said Vivian Nicholson.

Keith Nicholson won £152,319. It was a staggering amount at a time when the average house cost £2,500. Financial experts from Littlewoods Winners Advisory Service talked to him about how to protect his fortune, and the company's liaison officer visited the Nicholsons' Kershaw Avenue house nineteen times. Advice was given on how to respond to begging letters and marriage proposals. Normally the publicity didn't matter too much as most big winners were soon left in peace. In the case of Keith and Vivian Nicholson, however, the publicity stayed with them. The general public was genuinely curious about how pools winners used their money.

Keith Nicholson gave up his coalmining job and Vivian gave up hers at a sweet factory. The Nicholsons splashed out money on cars – a reported eighteen in four years – and Vivian went shopping for clothes every day. Keith Nicholson started buying racehorses and took up shooting. There were stories in the press of household luxuries, daily trips to the hairdresser and parties till dawn.

In October 1965 Keith Nicholson was killed in a car crash when his new Jaguar left the A1 as he was returning from a visit to his racehorse trainer. He left £84,500, and that was reduced to £42,000 after payment of estate duty and other expenses. Vivian Nicholson had to fight to get her husband's pools win accepted as a joint marital asset. It wasn't long, though, before all the winnings had gone.

The Littlewoods Pools Company had been launched in the harsh economic climate of the 1920s and 1930s, largely due to the determination and imagination of Eccles-born John Moores, later chairman of Everton, and a ready supply of unemployed female labour on Merseyside. In the 1950s and 1960s Littlewoods held about half the market share for football pools; its customers had increased from 1.6 million in 1945 to six million in 1956. Turnover figures continued to rise dramatically – from £35.2 million in 1957 to £52 million in 1960. Thirty per cent of pools income went to the government in tax.

The Littlewoods operation grew more and more sophisticated. In 1951 the company took up the summer slack by including Australian soccer matches on coupons (two years after Sherman's had provided the lead). In 1957 coupon collectors were introduced, stockbrokers and bankers appointed as advisers to big winners and the £75,000 limit on the Treble Chance pool was removed. Then came optical scanning machines to check coupons (1961), magnetic tapes to replace stencilled customer addresses (1964), an IBM 360 computer system (1966) and optical character-reading machines to identify customers by a special code on the envelope (1967). By the end of the 1960s the number of staff needed to check seven million coupons a week had been reduced to 5,000, less than half that of a decade earlier.

In the 1962–3 season the pools companies faced a big problem – bad weather. Matches were often postponed and some clubs went two months without a League match. No football meant no pools. Some pools companies had to lay off staff. Then came an idea designed to circumvent the weather. A panel of experts (the pools panel) was introduced to predict results of postponed matches.

The first pools panels sat only when thirty or more matches were postponed. A panel was needed on Saturday 23 January 1963 and for the next three Saturdays. Chaired by a dignitary, such as Lord Brabazon, Sir Gerald Nabarro or Sir Douglas Bader, the panel was locked inside London's Connaught Rooms until the men had agreed all the imaginary results needed. Ex-referee Arthur Ellis joined four former footballers on the first panel. The ex-players were all internationals – George Young (Scotland), Tommy Lawton, Ted Drake and Tom Finney (all England).

The status of these men as *ex-players* showed that football was entering a new age. Tom Finney's retirement in 1960 was a particular watershed. Finney was the quintessential hero of the golden age of the forties and fifties. He was a one-club man with a local plumbing business. Finney turned down an offer to play in Italy in order to stay in Preston. His only appearance in a European club competition was as a guest for Distillery after he had retired.

The old football world, peopled by heroes such as Stanley Matthews and Finney, overlapped with the rising new world of celebrities such as George Best and Rodney Marsh. Modesty moved towards flamboyance, short, Brylcreemed hair grew into flowing locks, clean-shaven chins became bearded and the occasional drink in a pub and trip to a cinema gave way to nightclubs and boutiques. The old world was full of one-club men, the maximum wage and Anglocentrism. The new world would be one of unlimited wages, the League Cup, European competitions and a pools panel made up of players recruited from the old world.

The pools panel increased the number of gambling opportunities, as did national trends towards more slot machines and bingo. Betting on greyhound racing and horseracing continued apace. Also, in the 1960s, 'Spot the Ball' became more prominent in newspapers and on pools coupons. Regular competitions asked people to put an X where they thought the missing ball was in the photograph. Readers commented that it was easy to work out – you just kept putting in a pin in the paper and waited until you heard the hiss of escaping air.

In the two decades after the war, gambling on football matches became second nature in England. 'Until the coming of the football pools,' wrote the journalist Macdonald Hastings, 'the moral line was that any money won by chance never did anybody any good.'

'MR FOOTBALL'

O N SATURDAY I JUNE 1957 Barnsley FC chairman Joseph Richards left the bright London sunlight and walked into the Café Royal. At the age of sixty-nine Richards was the new president of the Football League. He would preside at the Annual General Meeting.

The first agenda item was a proposal to restructure the two regional Third Divisions into Division Three and Division Four. The lower-league clubs had fought against this idea, worried about increased transport costs, but their four votes (for forty-eight clubs) were insignificant because the top forty-four clubs had one vote each. So Exeter City and Hartlepools United would have to play each other in the inaugural Division Four season (1958–9).

The next item was the raising of the players' maximum wage. At a time when a postman's maximum weekly wage was nine pounds four shillings and sixpence (£9.23), a footballer's maximum was increased by £2 to £17 per week (£14 in the summer). Bonus payments went up to £4 (win) and £2 (draw), and benefit money was extended to £1,000 for ten years' service, although this was still at the discretion of the club. The Football League thought that the maximum wage was fundamental to healthy competition. If it were abolished, they argued, the good players would go to a few clubs, the money would go to a few players and the rest would starve.

'This is the first step towards a complete overhaul of the League's rules and regulations,' Richards told the gathering of forty-eight League members. He prepared for speeches with reams of papers, but he was never very fluent. 'Many of them are out of date. The revised rules can't be put in force for the coming season, but there will be a big change within twelve months.'

Richards would be League president for nine years. It was an eventful time.

Joe Richards was small in physical stature but cut an impressive figure puffing a Double Corona cigar in his chauffeur-driven Rolls. He bought his clothes from Austin Reed and cultivated a small moustache that increased his gravitas. His drink was whisky and milk.

Born in 1888, the year the Football League was founded, Joe Richards left school at eleven and worked underground at Barrow-Barnsley Main Colliery, where his father was manager. The young Joe also studied mining engineering at night school. Within a year, however, he broke a leg badly in an accident with a pit tub. The leg didn't set properly and thereafter needed a fresh bandage every morning. But it didn't stop Richards from climbing a tree at Crystal Palace to watch Barnsley play an FA Cup Final, or cycling fourteen miles to Sheffield to watch his team win the 1912 FA Cup Final replay.

After his accident Joe Richards started as an office boy and worked his way to the top. At the age of thirty-two he was colliery secretary and sales manager and a Barnsley FC director, and by 1945 he was managing director at Barrow-Barnsley Main Colliery. In the post-war era there were 116 collieries in Yorkshire.

Richards was an expert on the legal side of finance. He was a hard-working man, the first in the office, at 8am, and sometimes still studying paperwork at 2am. In 1948 he started his second spell as Barnsley FC chairman, and he joined the Football League management committee and the FA Council. Richards held numerous directorships, and his career reads like a social history of coalmining and football. He was also a freemason and a Conservative town councillor. In 1955 he became a selector for the England international team. Experienced club managers criticised the system.

'What right have you to be an England selector?' Derby County manager Harry Storer challenged Richards one night. 'Come on, tell me what your credentials are.'

'I've been watching football for fifty years,' Richards replied.

'We've got a corner flag at the Baseball Ground,' Storer continued. 'It's been there for fifty years and still knows bugger-all about the game.'

Joe Richards was typical of the Midlands and northern self-made men who had founded and developed the Football League. Within the professional game he became known as 'Mr Football'. In contrast to the public-school and upper-class amateurs who had traditionally run the Football Association for the benefit of the wider game and the national team, Richards promoted the interests of professional clubs. The amateur ethos, he thought, was relevant only for those who could afford it, not for working men. He thought that football should be run as a business, but that business values should not run football. He favoured the authoritarian fraternalism that had characterised his Methodist Football League predecessors back in the 1880s and 1890s – an authoritarianism for the poor.

Richards particularly disliked seeing good young Barnsley schoolboys 'kidnapped' or 'baby-snatched' by clubs from outside the area. He suspected that some deals were worth more than the regulatory £10 signing-on fee. There were tales of £300 changing hands, electrical appliances arriving in the family home, new cars on the street and jobs for the boy's relatives. More and more Barnsley youngsters rejected their local club for higher-level clubs. Richards much preferred signing a local lad first and selling him later, as he had with Tommy Taylor to Manchester United (for £29,999).

In the maximum-wage era professional clubs used subtle dodges to conceal under-the-counter payments. A chairman would claim to put some money on a horse 'on the player's behalf' and naturally it won. One manager regularly played snooker against his players for £2 a frame and he always lost. A director might buy a player's worthless mongrel for a tidy sum. Free cookers and refrigerators were conveniently slipped through the back doors of players' houses. Some players were given part-time jobs but they didn't have to show up, or money was given to the captain for clandestine distribution to the players. Cash was wrapped in brown paper and left in a safe place for a player to collect.

Some clubs paid out so many backhanders that they resorted to elaborate bookkeeping practices to hide the cash. They invented assistant groundsmen or scouts who made unusually long journeys. In 1957 Sunderland FC was caught moving money to and from outside companies. A joint Football League and Football Association inquiry fined the club £5,000, suspended two directors permanently, severely censured four other directors, suspended five players (for refusing to answer questions at the inquiry) and cut the benefits of ten players. All these punishments were later overturned; the inquiry had acted illegally by not allowing Sunderland's directors to have legal counsel present.

Perhaps it wasn't surprising that football was riddled with broken rules given England's thriving black-market economy in the post-war period. Joe Richards himself was scrupulously above board at his own club, but it still didn't prevent the odd incident. One Barnsley star found £5 notes in his jacket top pocket, donated by a mystery admirer, and the Barnsley manager once declined an approach from an opposing player who said that he could guarantee Barnsley a vital win if £200 was left in the visitors' boots.

One case that did come to Richards's attention, however, involved Angus Seed, Barnsley manager in the early 1950s. Seed went to the North-East and signed a player who insisted on a £100 backhander. Seed didn't like the idea but went along with it. Rather than involve Richards, he paid the money out of petty cash and set about slowly replacing it with his own money. The story came out years after the manager's death.

Early in his nine-year reign as Football League president, Joe Richards sealed the League's future with some typical hard bargaining. Together with another blunt Yorkshireman, new League secretary Alan Hardaker, he studied the 1956 Copyright Act and decided to make the pools companies pay for publishing the League's fixtures. Previously the Football League had been reluctant to take money from gambling organisations.

In *The Football League v Littlewoods* in 1959 the judge ruled in the League's favour. Copyright had been breached. The fixture list was judged a piece of literature as it required considerable compilational skills to juggle a range of tasks: preventing home-match clashes in the same region; avoiding long-distance journeys over holiday periods; arranging local derbies to suit local holidays; shifting home matches that clashed with significant local events; and making sure that clubs without floodlights would play midweek matches on shops' early-closing days. Four major pools companies signed a ten-year deal to grant the Football League 0.5 per cent of their gross stakes, with a minimum of £245,000 per season. The League chased down and struck deals with pools companies in ten other countries.

'This is the greatest day in football since the League was formed in 1888,' Joe Richards told reporters.

The pools-money episode confirmed Richards's understanding of the legal side of business and sealed his place as League president. But Barnsley people felt he was hobnobbing too much with the business crème and neglecting his own club. Richards, of course, was not being paid for either job.

Richards and Hardaker launched a new Cup competition, the League Cup, to add more purpose to floodlit matches – Richards bought the trophy with his own money – but the two men were on the defensive when the Players' and Trainers' Union began a campaign to overturn the limit on the maximum wage in football (raised to £20 a week in 1958). Although some professions had fixed pay scales, no other profession had anything similar to a maximum wage in circumstances where employers actually wanted to pay more. Some players had negotiated higher wages by going into non-League football. Others had emigrated to Colombia, Ireland or Italy.

'The players should be paid the maximum that clubs can afford to pay them,' argued Jimmy Hill, the union's chairman, a slim, bearded Fulham player. 'The players deserve the freedom to earn as much as they can negotiate with their employers. There should be no artificial ceiling.'

In a 1959 TV debate on whether footballers were treated like serfs, Richards was outwitted by Hill and Spurs captain Danny Blanchflower. Richards came over as curt and stubborn in interviews. League secretary Alan Hardaker could also appear unsympathetic in public. According to journalist Bryon Butler, Hardaker had 'an impish sense of humour, a crusty intolerance of fools, a prodigious memory, a respect for the past but also an ambitious eye for the future and an ungrudging willingness to devote just as many hours to a job as it needed'.

The players' union argued that the removal of the maximum wage would, by definition, do away with the prevalent under-the-counter payments. Jimmy Hill collected over 200 signatures from players saying they had received irregular payments. The union secretary, Cliff Lloyd, a quiet, self-effacing ex-player who was painstaking in his preparation, helped Hill to organise three major regional meetings. The one in Manchester proved a defining moment. In an atmosphere heavy with cigarette smoke a young Bury player called Alan Jackson argued for the status quo. Jackson said that a footballer's £20 a week was a very good wage for an open-air life when his father earned only £10 a week for eight-hour shifts down a Derbyshire coalmine.

'I know about tha father,' responded Tommy Banks, a tough Bolton Wanderers full back who, according to legend, would kick chunks out of a winger and then kick him across the pitch for his full-back partner Roy Hartle to do the same. 'Tell tha Dad I can do his job down the mines but he couldn't do my job, week in week out, which sometimes means marking Brother Matthews here.'

That brought the house down. Banks was standing next to the 46-year-old Stanley Matthews, who was the country's most senior and illustrious player. When Matthews showed his support for the union's action, Hill had the backing of almost all the players. In addition Hill and Lloyd had won the support of other trades unions and even a Conservative MP, Philip

Goodhart, who organised a special parliamentary debate and, astonishingly, called for a strike by footballers.

When a date was set for a strike – Saturday 21 January 1961 – the Football League capitulated and the maximum wage was abolished. Afterwards smaller clubs gradually found that they were reducing playing staffs, disbanding Reserve teams and curtailing youth policies. Transport costs were watched more carefully, and directors were unwilling to take calculated risks. But the game's financial problems were as much to do with falling attendances and rival leisure interests as they were with the maximum wage.

One of Cliff Lloyd's finest career moments came in June 1963 when he helped to change the contract system for players.

'I found convincing the evidence of Mr Lloyd, the secretary of the Professional Footballers' Association,' said Mr Justice Wilberforce, the judge in charge of *Eastham v Newcastle United Football Club and others*, 'a witness who seemed to be more in touch with the realities of professional football, and particularly the considerations affecting the supply and interests of players, than the other witnesses.'

In 1960 Newcastle United turned down three transfer requests from George Eastham – one Newcastle director said he'd rather see the player shovel coal than sign for Arsenal – so Eastham stopped playing and took a job as a salesman. In November 1960 Newcastle relented and sold Eastham to Arsenal for £47,500. Justice Wilberforce saw the idea of transfer fees as remarkable – 'unique both within and outside the field of sport' – but he concluded that the combination of the retention system and the transfer system was an unjustifiable restraint of trade.

'The retention system is, in my judgement, more of a restraint than is necessary to prevent richer clubs from buying all the best players,' Wilberforce said in his summing-up.

The club chairmen met at the Football League's new Lytham St Anne's headquarters to decide what to do about the Eastham case.

'Gentlemen,' said Joe Richards. 'This is probably one of the most – if not *the* most – important meetings held in connection with League affairs since the foundation.'

Burnley chairman Bob Lord suggested ignoring Wilberforce's judgement entirely, but Richards knew better. A new code of practice was drafted. Players were given the right to appeal to the League management committee and (if necessary) an independent tribunal, *with representation from the PFA*.

Benefit payments were left to the clubs and players. Players could not be transferred to a particular club for a lower fee, and option clauses were to be for no longer than the original contract.

It would take fifteen more years before the players became free to negotiate with new clubs at the end of their contracts, and thirty-two years before they could change clubs with no transfer fees involved when their contracts ended.

In January 1965 Joe Richards and Alan Hardaker saw professional football's image sink to a new low when ten players (or ex-players) were sent to prison for conspiracy to defraud. They had either fixed Football League matches or placed bets against their own team. Jimmy Gauld, who had played with five different clubs, was sentenced to four years' imprisonment with £5,000 costs. The judge called him the ringleader. The evidence showed that Gauld had made £3,275 from betting on matches and £7,420 for selling his story to the *Sunday People*. Alan Hardaker had interviewed Gauld in 1961 and passed on his worrying findings to Lancashire County Police, but the story was first revealed to the public by a team of *Sunday People* investigators led by Michael Gabbert. The newspaper called it 'the biggest sports scandal of the century'. Three Sheffield Wednesday players, including England regular Peter Swan, were sentenced to four months in prison. They were also banned from football *sine die* by the FA (although Swan returned to the Football League seven years later).

Joseph Richards was knighted in June 1966, three months before his reign as Football League president ended. One of his last acts as Barnsley chairman was to sell goalkeeper Alan Hill to Rotherham United for £12,000. Richards insisted on cash rather than instalments because his club needed the money. Fourth Division Barnsley were nearly bankrupt, close to what became known as 'doing an Accrington Stanley'.

In many ways Richards symbolised the Football League's values. He was a northern businessman who was ambitious, blunt and financially shrewd. He desperately wanted the League to thrive and he thought he knew what was best for it. He was a paternal authoritarian who was much more down to earth than any FA leader. But the League sometimes resisted change as much as the FA did. In 1963 Alan Hardaker put forward a 'Pattern for Football' which included 'four up and four down', five twenty-club divisions, a pre-season League Cup tournament played in regional leagues and various other changes. The League chairmen rejected the plan. Hardaker thought it was because clubs were too concerned with their own problems. They weren't interested in saving the game as a whole.

Sir Joseph Richards took ill a few hours before the 1968 FA Cup Final and died six days later. He was eighty. He had lived through the first eighty years of the Football League and had helped to shape its history.

13

SATURDAY AFTERNOON AND SUNDAY MORNING

P ETER SMITH WAS FIRST TAKEN to Reading Football Club when he was six years old. His father was a regular supporter who played in the band. Like almost every other boy, Peter Smith wanted to kick anything suitable in the street – a pebble, a fir cone, a cigarette packet or a ball.

Growing up in Reading in the 1930s and regularly watching the first team and Reserves, Smith soon realised that the club was important in local life. He felt he was born to support Reading FC. It was a natural tribal feeling; he simply *had* to follow the club's fortunes. In the days before supporters arrived in cars, he marched to and from the ground, shoulder to shoulder with other fans, part of the crowd. He identified with the club, grumbled about it and, occasionally, basked in its glory. What else could young men do in this town? Football was better than cinemas, billiard saloons, pubs and clubs.

On weekdays the Reading players were mysterious local heroes. They would come alive only when journalists wrote about their injuries, when a man in the barber's revealed third-hand gossip about a dressing-room feud or when a player was sighted on a bus or walking to the ground. Then the mystery would turn into companionship when the players appeared on the Elm Park pitch on a Saturday afternoon, sharing the same privations as the fans.

During the Second World War, when he was in West Africa, Peter Smith met a former Reading bus conductor. While other soldiers found the ex-clippie's stories boring, Smith enjoyed tales of how the bus crews would avoid the football crowd by hurrying to get past the Elm Park ground just before the final whistle. The two men shared an identity.

Peter Smith was just another football fan with attachments to his local community. Except, perhaps, for one thing – he was a vicar.

It shouldn't be that surprising to find the clergy among football fans. After all, the church had been connected to football from the start. About a third of top professional clubs owed their origins to church organisations, and Football League founder William McGregor was a committed Christian. Nevertheless, there were times when Reverend Peter Smith's work conflicted with his hobby.

On one occasion a couple booked their wedding well in advance. It was fixed for two o'clock on a Saturday in January, to be held at Reverend Smith's church, thirteen miles from where Reading played an attractive FA Cup tie at 3pm. The vicar asked the choir for 'no frills and fancies'. Afterwards he joined the happy couple and their family for photographs, and then slipped away to where his wife was sitting in the car. She drove into Reading, dropped him off outside the turnstiles and he dashed in to find his heroes already 2–1 down. Normally he disguised himself, so as not to inhibit nearby fans. This time he had forgotten to take off his dog-collar.

Reverend Peter Smith saw the links between football and religion. He said, light-heartedly, that churches and football clubs both tried to get as many as possible through the doors, but football fans paid when *entering* the ground whereas churchgoers paid when *leaving*. More seriously, they had lots of shared characteristics: attracting people who had a common devotion; serving as sites for emotional release and relieving distress; offering sacred ground for ashes to be interred; and providing locations for people to congregate and sing. Peter Smith thought that churches and football grounds all fulfilled essential parts of our human need – to identify with something bigger than ourselves, to feel a sense of our roots and to experience belonging.

There are differences too. Football is about winning and losing, and football clubs have as many connections with pubs as with churches. In local football some strict Methodists wouldn't even go into a pub to change. In football dressing-rooms swearing was de rigueur, although one notable exception was Port Vale trainer Lol Hammett ('If you get injured, it's your own fizzing fault, and the boss will stop your fizzing wages').

Overall, though, it is easier to argue a case for the *similarities* of religion and football. Football and religion both have symbolic neckwear and jewellery (scarves, crucifixes and so on) and both value ceremony and ritual. (Sometimes the symbols and ritual are the same – for example, black armbands and a minute's silence.) Both deal in faith and hope. Both offer support and security. Football stadiums and religious buildings can be hypnotic, mesmeric places where fanatics gather together, see magical moments and suspend their day-to-day life. A group of believers gather in an enclosed space with other devotees, search for perfection and look for guidance from superior beings. These fans know their Bible (or their team's history), enjoy the contemporary gossip about the new vicar (or new manager) and look forward to pleasurable celebrations, whether they be Harvest Festivals or laps of honour after the season's last match. Football managers are sometimes seen as miracle-workers . . . or devils.

Football isn't really a religion, of course, but it can operate in a similar way for individuals and groups. Football is a metaphor for religion.

Sunday is a sacred day. In the 1950s it was a day of rest for footballers as the FA had long outlawed Sunday play. The only exception had been a short period in the early 1940s, during the war, when workers were allowed some fun in the Sunday Works League. Otherwise the FA statutes included a threatening sentence: 'A person who takes part in Sunday football in the United Kingdom shall not be recognised by this association.'

Naturally that didn't stop people playing Sunday football, any more than Prohibition stopped Americans drinking. There would always be football bootleggers. One outraged cleric called them 'seventh day sinners'.

The FA was soon faced with a problem similar to the one they had with paid amateurs (shamateurs) – how could they police a rule that was so widely flouted? In 1955 the FA withdrew the draconian sentence threatening to ban players, but still refused to recognise, promote or organise the Sunday game. In the late 1950s Sunday football was still an illicit activity. Sunday friendly matches required clandestine operations. Council pitches were not officially available on Sundays, and the dressing-rooms were kept locked, so two teams might change by a hedge and grab one of the less conspicuous pitches for a ninety-minute run-out.

'If there's any trouble, there's enough of us,' the lads would say.

Finally, early in 1960, the FA accepted a committee recommendation that Sunday football should be permitted for registered players. The FA took over the running of the Sunday game, thus alienating the existing National Sunday Association (NSA). The NSA reckoned that they had 41,000 players in sixteen leagues and they didn't want affiliation to the county FAs.

The fifties and sixties were critical decades in the relationship between football and the Sabbath. As family life shifted from urban extended families to suburban nuclear ones, the Church lost some lobbying strength against Sunday activities. The family weekend was changing. People had more disposable income, women were becoming more influential in the family, men were drifting away from Saturday matches into other activities and too many weekend opportunities were now crammed into Saturdays. On Sundays shops were closed and professional sport was not allowed (until cricket started to offer admission by programme cost in the late 1960s). In 1968, however, ITV's *The Big Match* showed football highlights on Sunday afternoons. Football was slowly encroaching into the Sabbath. Football was challenging religion.

Football began to fulfil more of the inner values that had been the traditional preserve of religion. Examples included the Pentecostal-type singing at top matches. It took a while for the Church to realise that football could have a rival emotive and spiritual function. These football fans were *devotees*.

In professional football, however, there had always been a strange paradox. Between 1894 and 1957 professional clubs had played on Christmas Day – a few individual players and one club (Aston Villa) refused – but these same clubs were vehemently opposed to professional Sunday matches. They gave three reasons: (i) The FA argument, backed by the Lord's Day Observation Society, that Sunday was a religious day; (ii) English people preferred a quiet, restful day rather than following football teams; and (iii) public transport was poor on a Sunday. But a 1967 survey by National Opinion Polls found that 75 per cent of those interviewed were in favour of professional sport on Sundays, and the main opposition came from the over-fifty-fives. The first Sunday match between two sides with professional players came on 17 March 1963 when Desborough Town played Bletchley Town. Countries such as Italy had first-class Sunday football. Why not England?

Even after the FA took amateur Sunday football under its wing, there was a raw element to this form of the game. Sunday dressing-rooms could be pub snugs, sheds, old railway carriages, barns, houses or caravans without wheels. The pitches seemed worse on Sundays than Saturdays, probably because they had been used the previous day (sometimes twice). The playing kit was definitely worse: the socks and shorts were a mishmash from various teams, and some of the shirts were still in the possession of players who had been dropped or injured. Those who did turn out were often fractious, stiff from Saturday's match or hungover from a good night out. It took a while to crank up their muscles. At the end of the match there might be a couple of buckets of water for washing.

Sunday football was organised chaos. Its shambolic informality owed something to its illicit origins, but it also suited the attitudes of many of its participants. The Sunday game encouraged maverick players who didn't want to train, free spirits who didn't want to be part of a Saturday regimen, piss-artists who talked a good game, Fancy Dans who didn't want a manager bawling at them from the touchline, serious Saturday players who wanted to play for fun on Sundays and committed football fans whose Saturday was spent watching their team.

Welcome to the carnival. This was football for all.

Sundays often started with a search for players. In the early days of Sunday football people routinely had to go to houses and deal with tricky situations. A wife answers the door at 10am ('He hasn't come home yet'), or a mother sticks her head out of the window ('He doesn't tell me what he's doing').

One Leicester team had a star player who was out on parole. Every week it was a different story. One Sunday his wife answered the door and said, 'He's at the cop shop.' The next week she said, 'Fuck off.' Another time he had left his boots somewhere between 5pm Saturday and 10am Sunday, and it took half an hour of retracing steps to find them in a snooker hall. It was also a question of following the trail when a player picked up a girl on a Saturday night.

'Who did he go home with last night?'

'Where does she live?'

'Well, where does her *friend* live?'

At the ground (usually a public park) there was the need to put up goalposts, jammed upright in their bore holes with wooden wedges. Some posts leant backwards at an alarming angle that invited in-swinging corners. In the early days of Sunday football goalnets were not the norm. When they became more common, players would climb on to team-mates' shoulders and tie the netting to the crossbar with string or old tie-ups. It was do-it-yourself at a time when do-it-yourself was coming into vogue.

In the dressing-room all was not straightforward.

'Are you fit?'

'Aye, fit to drop.'

'Here, stick these shirts on, lads,' the manager says, producing a set that has been used the day before.

'This shirt stinks.'

'Fuck off. Just put it on.'

'I can't wear this.'

'Yeah, well, you go out and find another green shirt at this time on a Sunday morning.'

Players sniffed suspiciously at shirts and socks. A few players wore rugby shorts, betraying what they did on Saturdays. The matches didn't always start on time.

'Ball's soft.'

'Where's the pump?'

'It's in the van.'

'Where's the van?'

'Far side of the car park.'

'Who's got the keys to the van?'

Mostly, though, Sunday footballers just got on with it. Legitimate Sunday football blossomed. In some regions it became more prominent than the Saturday game. Sunday-morning matches prompted hangover bulletins in the dressing-rooms, strange pre-match tactical instructions from managers ('Call for Kev on your way and get him out of bed') and lengthy post-match discussions in the pub. Sunday-afternoon games were more dangerous if the players had met in the pub beforehand.

Proponents argued that the Sunday game was less manic and more matey. Few teams trained together in preparation for Sundays. It was more about pubs and enjoyment, much less serious than its Saturday counterpart. It wasn't unusual for Saturday's serious goalkeeper to 'play out' as a centre forward the next day, causing disputes among the Sunday-only players.

'Do we want these stars in our Sunday team?'

'They don't really give a toss.'

The Sunday players wanted to win but they also wanted to drink, mix and have a laugh. Jackson, for instance, was a Norfolk Sunday centre forward who liked his drink. One Saturday night he put himself under the alcohol hammer. The next morning, when his team got a corner, he held up his hand.

'Hold on,' he shouted. He walked behind the goal-line, vomited, walked back and waved for the corner-kick to be taken.

'That's right, Jackson,' his manager shouted. 'If you're sick again, I'm taking you off.'

Part of the Sunday ethic was playing with a group of lads who seemed committed but ill-prepared. The English syndrome called for a spirit of togetherness that could overcome the opposition's preparedness.

'This lot might have better facilities than us, a better pitch, better changing-rooms, clubhouse, kit,' says the manager in his Sunday team-talk, 'but we've got something they don't have – we're going to show these what we're made of.'

Some committed Sunday players would play for one team in the morning and another in the afternoon. They turned up for the afternoon's pre-match kick-in still bearing the morning mud and the smell of lunchtime beer. The stalwarts who ran Sunday leagues soon realised that Sunday morning was a better time of day for fixtures.

Young men bonded around drinks and pranks, curries and crisps, dancehalls and discos, cup games and drinking games, boys in Minis and girls in mini-skirts. At one club the lads compiled two sets of league tables: one was based on points accumulated by each team for matches won and drawn; the other was an individual competition with points awarded according to degree of success with women. The Sunday League season peaked with end-of-season dinners and exotic tours to Ostend, Barmouth or Skegness.

The Sunday subculture thrived on a series of zany anecdotes. The stimuli were a meeting with a particular opponent or former team-mate in a pub ('I'll tell you who I saw the other day'), referees ('This bastard booked me in injury-time when I told him I'd be late for Evensong'), events on the pitch ('And then the crossbar came down on his bonce and he let out that fuckin' hyena noise'), travel to and from the match ('What took you so long?') and Saturday-night action ('What did you get up to after we saw you in the Pheasant?'). Wherever Sunday players went, they found new mates through football.

What could vicars such as Peter Smith do to challenge this movement away from the Church?

14

FOOTBALL, YEAH, YEAH, YEAH

BILL SHANKLY: I THOUGHT THAT as a football manager I had a hard job, but I can tell you one thing: whereas I had to look after fifty-five thousand, you have to look after fifty-five million.

HAROLD WILSON: It's a very similar job, you know . . . When I formed the Cabinet for the first time, hardly anyone had ever sat in a Cabinet before. We'd been out of office for thirteen years. I used to say to myself, 'I take the penalties, I have to be the goalkeeper.' I went and took the corner-kicks, dashed down the wing.

Here were two key British figures talking together in the late 1960s. Bill Shankly's charisma seduced Liverpool FC fans of all ages in his fifteen years as manager, and Harold Wilson's Labour government made it fashionable to be young and working-class. Together they orchestrated a youth culture that blended music, clothes and football.

Harold Wilson was probably the first British Prime Minister to understand football's popularity. He had supported Huddersfield Town as a young man and, as MP for Huyton in Liverpool, he understood the impact of the game. In 1966 he commented that England had only ever won the World Cup under a Labour government. In 1970 he blamed his General Election defeat on West Germany's Gerd Müller, whose World Cup quarter-final goal had beaten England four days before the election.

'People say I get boring the way I use football analogies, even in the House of Commons, but it helps you understand it,' Wilson told Shankly when they met.

Bill Shankly was Liverpool manager from 1959 to 1974. A fantastic mythology grew up around the man. Like one of his heroes, Robbie Burns, Shankly was considered to be a poet, a philosopher and a prophet. He gave birth to an incredibly rich street literary culture around football in the city. His sayings became legendary in Liverpool:

'Our football was a form of socialism.'

'We beat them five–nil and they were lucky to get nil.'

'The best team drew.'

'He must be a good goalkeeper, he saved one of my shots last week.'

'There are two teams in Liverpool – Liverpool and Liverpool Reserves.'

'Some people talked about it [football] as if it were life and death itself, but it's much more serious than that.'

Shankly and Liverpool fans were compatible. Both sides of the equation were tough and cocky with plenty of swagger. Together they were a bit lippy, a touch crazy, and they made each other laugh. Merseyside led English popular culture in 1963 and 1964: Everton and Liverpool won successive Football League Championships, and for fifty-one of the sixty weeks between April 1963 and May 1964 there was a Merseybeat record at the top of the UK singles chart.

Bill Shankly's sayings spread like bushfires in a city that collected comic tales like museums collected artefacts. Shankly wasn't the first football manager to say these sorts of things but he was eminently quotable at a time when the media was reaching more people. Shankly had managed three outpost Division Three (North) clubs – Carlisle United, Grimsby Town and Workington Town – and that had brought him into contact with wise and wizened wordsmiths, such as Hartlepools United manager Freddie Westgarth.

Shankly's background was the Ayrshire coalmines, First Division football, the Scotland international team, the RAF during the Second World War and management in the lower divisions. He was an incredibly enthusiastic man, passionate about football in a way that bordered on the obsessive. Every day was 'A great day for fitba', even if there was six inches of snow and a howling gale. He also loved boxing and Chicago gangsters. His sheer intensity frightened some players.

Bill Shankly was a great motivator. He signed centre half Ron Yeats from Dundee United in 1961 and boosted the parochial Scotsman's ego ('Jesus Christ, son, you must be seven foot tall!'). On another occasion, in the dressing-room before a match, he told his players to take off their red shirts and have a shower because 'I'll throw these shirts out on the field and the shirts will beat Ipswich by themselves.'

But Shankly could also be harsh. He ignored players who were injured, seeing that as an opportunity for others, and he ruthlessly dismissed faint-hearted and clumsy players:

'He's got a heart as big as a caraway seed.'

'He'll only want to play if he can wear a numbered overcoat.'

'He couldn't trap a bag of concrete.'

Shankly was a Scottish socialist who believed in socialist football – keep the game simple, work hard for each other and share the load for the greater good. He was pleased that Liverpool wore red shirts and he thought that all players in the team should be paid the same wages. He didn't want prima donnas. He recruited tough, northern men who had either served apprenticeships or would have to serve one at Liverpool.

Ian St John signed as a part-time professional player for Motherwell in 1956 at the age of seventeen. He went into the first team soon afterwards. He was working in a steelworks at the time. He did his day job, trained two nights a week and played football on Saturdays. On Monday morning it was back to work to meet all the Motherwell fans. If he hadn't played well they were the first to tell him.

When he was twenty St John was selected by Scotland for a full international match against West Germany. He played at Hampden Park, Glasgow, on a Wednesday evening in May 1959 with 103,415 witnesses. The next morning he was back in the steelworks. It was a great leveller.

The following summer St John watched Real Madrid players train before the 1960 European Cup Final. The Motherwell lads couldn't stop talking about what they'd seen.

'Gento can run like the wind.'

'He could catch waste paper in a gale.'

'That Puskas could open cans with his left foot.'

'Di Stefano could play anywhere.'

Real Madrid crushed Eintracht Frankfurt 7–3 at Hampden Park with an exhibition of movement and skill. Ian St John started practising the tricks he had seen at Real Madrid training sessions. His skills at centre forward earned him a move to Liverpool in April 1961 – as a *full-time* footballer. Soon he would become a stylish young man of the sixties. In Liverpool he won medals, played in European competitions, bought sharp suits, met the Beatles and famously starred in an iconic piece of graffiti on a church sign in 1964:

'What shall we do when the Lord comes to Liverpool?'

'Move St John to inside left.'

*   *   *

Spectators felt both privileged and equal on the Spion Kop at Liverpool's Anfield Road ground. The Kop was as important to the city's heritage as the Liver Building, the two cathedrals and the Mersey ferry. Every young Liverpool supporter heard stories about the Kop, sensed the excitement surrounding the vast terrace and grew up wanting a small piece of it.

'It's somewhere where you can go and forget anything outside,' one Kopite said about the experience of watching a game in the sixties. 'You lose all your worries and for two hours that's all that matters. Everything outside is irrelevant. But what you do in that two hours lives with you for the rest of the week. You don't leave the Kop behind. That comes with you.'

The Kop held 28,000 people, all standing, jostling, pushing their way to a regular spec, organising themselves with a mixture of clever route planning, brute force and good manners. It was said that people with crutches could stand safely on the Kop.

On home Saturdays in the early 1960s fans of Bill Shankly's Liverpool woke up excited, adrenalin pumping, thinking only of the match. Some set off towards the ground at eleven o'clock, met their mates in a pub, drank a few pints of Higsons and walked on to Anfield. Others went straight to the ground from home or work. All discussed last week's game, previewed this week's game and prophesied about next week's game. At the ground they stood in fairly orderly queues and joked about whether the turnstile man had only one arm.

The Kop was a mostly male preserve. There were a few older women, but not many young women and girls. Some young boys paid to get into the Boys' Pen and then climbed over the railings into the adults' Kop. Occasionally small knots of opposition fans stood on the Kop, but that seemed to work out all right. People also made a helpful little circle if you wanted to pee, but some went home with wet clothes. The Kop crowd lurched back and forth; you could start a match standing next to your mate and end it thirty yards away. It was hard work. You built good thigh muscles from standing on your toes. Some complained of seasickness after an afternoon of crowd surges.

There were plenty of Kop characters. One man kept a running tally of Liverpool's corner-kicks for the season. A toothless old lady called Ma, dying of cancer, was regularly lifted by ambulancemen on to the running track so that she could watch the game from there. When a spectator died during a match, two Kopite gravediggers considerately scratched the final score on the deceased man's coffin.

The Kop was always a noisy place. People shouted and roared, and there was banter and bad language. In the early sixties, however, the noise changed. The Kop began to sing, and singing made the fans feel good.

Mention music, Merseyside and the sixties, and the automatic response is the Beatles. The Fab Four – George Harrison, John Lennon, Paul McCartney and Ringo Starr – achieved the first of eleven consecutive number-one UK hits with *From Me to You* on 2 May 1963. The Anfield Kop Choir covered a succession of Beatles songs soon after they appeared – from 'She Loves You' (1963) through to 'Hey Jude' (1968). But the Kop Choir had a whole array of local talent to mimic. There was also the Fourmost, the Merseybeats, the Searchers, the Swinging Blue Jeans, Rory Storm & the Hurricanes and Billy J. Kramer & the Dakotas. The Kop sang the whole of Liverpool's Cilla Black's 'Anyone Who Had a Heart' and adopted a new local anthem, 'You'll Never Walk Alone', a song from the musical *Carousel*, covered by Liverpool's Gerry & the Pacemakers.

Merseyside musicians owed a stylistic debt to Liverpool's history as an immigrant melting pot, a seaport looking west to Ireland and America's east coast. This brought a cosmopolitan air and a heady excitement that influenced the Beatles, whose early repertoire drew heavily on black rhythm-and-blues artists. In his book *Liverpool: Wondrous Place* Paul Du Noyer explains the city's music styles and notes how, despite these black musical influences and a vibrant black scene in Liverpool 8, Merseybeat was a cultural medium only for the *white* people of Liverpool. Music and football blended together on the Anfield Kop.

The Beatles themselves had little interest in football, but the Kop promoted their oeuvre to thousands and then, via television, to millions. Some spectators went to hear the Kop sing as much as watch the players play. The young people now differed from their parents – in their hairstyles, their clothes, their musical tastes and their English football experience.

Football had long had ritualised traditional chants (e.g. 'The Pompey Chimes') and club songs (e.g. West Ham United's 'I'm Forever Blowing Bubbles'). Mass conversations had taken place around a classic question-and-answer sequence ('Two-four-six-eight, who do we appreciate?') and the spelling of the team's name ('Give us a te – *te*'). At clubs such as Tottenham Hotspur and Spennymoor United, opponents' heads would sink as home fans set off on a spelling bee that lasted nearly a minute. It was less impressive at Bury.

At certain places, however, the singing and chanting suddenly became more spontaneous. Many Kopites fancied themselves as comedians. If local boys Ken Dodd and Jimmy Tarbuck could do it, 28,000 Scousers could surely come up with something. At an Anfield match in 1963 an opposing team's trainer ran on to the field, lifted a concussed player to his feet, then took his full weight as the player slumped forward, arms around the trainer's neck. The Kop, barely missing a beat, sang, 'He loves you, yeah, yeah, yeah.'

In the 1960s every Liverpool player had his own chant or song, and the terraces became a communal coach. Thousands of people now chanted or sang messages to the players:

'Attack, attack, attack, attack, attack . . .'

'No surrender, no surrender . . .'

In 1965, when Liverpool won the FA Cup for the first time, the Kop's number-one hit was an old playground song that could be used as commentary. Kopites would probably have been too embarrassed to have sung the original words ('Ee, aye, addio, the farmer wants a wife'), but it was fine to adapt it for Wembley ('Ee, aye, addio, we've scored a goal').

Some older people felt excluded from the new-style Kop. Anfield, like all English football venues, became naturally segregated inside the ground. If you were not young, if you didn't know the lyrics, you would have to find somewhere else in the stadium. The centre of the Kop was for the youth choir. Older fans moved to the periphery of the Kop or to other parts of the ground. In the early 1960s younger fans also began to travel further to away games, no longer accompanied by older fans.

'They shouldn't have stopped National Service,' one veteran fan said of the early 1960s. 'You had to cope. If you didn't, you got disciplined. You had to do what you were told. Once they stopped National Service, the yobbos started up.'

Two separate mythologies developed around the Kop. Metropolitan journalists, arriving like jobbing anthropologists, recorded the local tunes sung in communal, guttural accents and thought the Kopites were exotic, entertaining, fair and funny. This above-the-ground story proclaimed an engaging youth culture starring lovable scalliwags who were championing pop music and launching a carnival atmosphere. Their greatest festival event was when the Anfield Road end fans played the Kopites on the Anfield pitch. A European Cup match against Cologne had been postponed through snow but spectators were already in the ground. A fan found a small ball and hundreds piled on to the pitch to play. It must have been 250-a-side. Eventually a policeman took their ball away. That policeman was pelted with snowball after snowball. When he arrived home his wife thought he had fallen in the river.

But the real story of the Kop was a little more complex. The subterranean tale was of pickpockets who diligently worked the Kop, Reds fans who were handy with knives for visitors, and travelling Liverpudlians who gained admission by climbing over turnstiles, charging gates and throwing grappling hooks and rope ladders over stadium walls. The fans could occasionally be vicious towards other supporters or even home-team players. Goalkeeper Tommy Lawrence's nickname, 'The Flying Pig', showed both wit and cruelty. A succession of Liverpool schemers, such as Jack Balmer and Jimmy Melia, were unfairly lambasted. Opposing managers could be roughly abused.

Liverpool fans would say that the Kop was a safe place to stand because everyone looked after you, but it could also be a dangerous place. Sometimes people came straight to the match from pub or work and fainted through lack of food. Fans were carried out of the Kop during some major European-competition nights, either injured or gasping for air. Scrambled journeys out of the ground could be scary until fans learned the techniques, and the 1970 Liverpool–Everton derby was nearly a major disaster. The St John Ambulance dealt with crushing injuries – broken legs, fractured pelvises and broken ribs – and felt relieved that they could get the injured over the low wall at the front.

Identifiable youth ends spread across the country. Around 1966 and 1967 young skinhead fans began trying to 'take the ends' of rival fans and police responded by confiscating bovver boots. Supporters of big clubs began to arrive early at away grounds, sneak into the home end and await the locals. At big grounds, like Liverpool, that was not possible – no one could take the Kop – but elsewhere things were changing fast. At a Millwall match, in London, one fan threw a hand grenade on to the running track. 'Soccer Marches to War,' headlined one newspaper.

It was a sign of things to come.

Ian St John and the other top professionals found that their lives were changing too. Players became more professional. The maximum wage had disappeared and top-class players were now earning much more than the working man. Liverpool players routinely played in European competitions – from Sofia to Setúbal, from Dresden to Dundalk – and spent money on fashionable clothes. Elsewhere players such as Mike Summerbee (Manchester City) and George Best (Manchester United) started their own boutique business. Some of these younger players mixed with pop artists and went to discos. Here was the emergence of a new type of footballer: much more self-sufficient, more stylish, a little bit more brash, a regular at boutiques and nightclubs. The lives of most professional players, though, hadn't changed very much. But what had changed was the culture of the terraces. Music, youth culture and football fused in the 1960s in a way that was inventive and forceful. Bill Shankly and Harold Wilson both understood the vitality of working-class youths and made it work for them. They also realised that there was no way back to the pre-Beatle days of deference and austerity.

15

WEMBLEY 1966 AND AFTER

THE 1966 WORLD CUP FINAL was an apogee for the English game. It changed lives. It brought many English people closer to football and shifted their image of heroism. Gap-toothed Nobby Stiles, disliked by foreigners for kicking players, delighted England fans by dancing a jig on the Wembley pitch, socks around his ankles and the World Cup in his hand. Red-haired Alan Ball, only twenty-one years old, was worshipped for his youthful dynamism, offering fans a modern look that epitomised the new Britain. Bobby Charlton and Bobby Moore acquired stateliness to suit their elegant skills. Geoff Hurst scored a legendary hat-trick in the 4–2 win against West Germany.

Around the world about 400 million people watched the final match on television, and 1,392 journalists attended the World Cup finals. The three-week tournament was the first really global football event and the first major sporting event to be held in Britain during the television age. But it didn't totally unite the world. The South Americans felt let down by European referees: the brutal treatment of Brazil's Pelé by João Morais of Portugal; the sending-off of Argentina's Rattín against England when, according to the player, he kept repeating, '*Quiero a un interprete*' ('I want an interpreter'); and the sending-off of two Uruguay players against West Germany.

In England about thirty-three million people either watched the Final on television or listened to it on the radio. Some England fans couldn't bear it after West Germany's last-minute equaliser had taken the match into extra time; they walked the streets and listened to reaction from other people's houses. But England's eleven other squad members watched from the side of the pitch; Jimmy Armfield, the senior reserve, had brought them down from the stands to the bench with the score at 2–1, only to discover that celebrations were premature. Germany had equalised.

Extra time brought two iconic images for the national scrapbook. In the first period of extra time Geoff Hurst collected a cross from Alan Ball, swivelled and hit a right-foot shot which struck the crossbar and bounced down for a goal. At the end of the second period Bobby Moore's cool pass sent Hurst clear on the West Germany goal. 'There are people on the pitch,' said the BBC's Kenneth Wolstenholme, 'they think it's all over,' swiftly adding, when Hurst's shot made it 4–2, 'It is now.'

When the match ended Armfield and the reserves jumped up from the sidelines, all except the forlorn Jimmy Greaves, who had been omitted from the Final team despite considering himself recovered from a leg injury. Alf Ramsey, the England manager, was also amazingly restrained. On the pitch Bobby Charlton was openly crying because at last England had done something that people could cheer about. Jack Charlton, Bobby's brother, sank to his knees and held his face in his hands. Ray Wilson slapped his hands on the turf. In the stands Kay Stiles desperately wished that her husband Nobby would 'put his bloody teeth in'. Bobby Moore, the England captain, scaled the thirty-nine steps to the Royal Box, wiped his hands on any available material and received the Jules Rimet Trophy from Queen Elizabeth II.

After the match the England team partied until 4am at London's Royal Garden Hotel, but the players' wives were not invited to the official celebration. Hundreds of England fans danced a conga around Charing Cross Station, and Jack Charlton woke up next morning in a stranger's house in Leytonstone.

One incident forewarned Geoff Hurst that his life would change irrevocably. He was at home in Hornchurch when a large limousine arrived and cast an enormous shadow over the house. It was there to take him to a function for being England's top goalscorer in the tournament. Alan Ball was later grateful that his father kept his young feet on the ground.

England's win was a victory for a team plan. More English managers now wanted to emulate the England team's system of playing without wingers. More young players wanted to be midfield players like Ball, Stiles and Martin Peters. And more people watched professional matches. In 1966–7 Football League attendances increased for the first time since the late 1940s.

In the decades that followed, people treasured their 1966 World Cup stamps (designed by David Gentleman), cartoon images of World Cup Willie, a smiling lion in a Union Jack football shirt, and their sixty-eight-page souvenir programme, priced two shillings and sixpence (12½p). Film critic David Thomson dreamed for many years that he was coming on as a substitute to rescue England, dropping his false teeth into a startled Alf Ramsey's hand as he took to the pitch. Almost every day the team's stars faced a stranger coming up to them in a public place and saying, 'Aren't you Martin Peters?' or 'Aren't you Gordon Banks?' Players from England's World Cup-winning team toured the country and talked about the match. The most common question was 'Did Geoff Hurst's shot cross the line?'

The analysis of that one incident continued for ever. After Hurst's shot had hit the crossbar, the ball bounced on the ground and away from the goal. West Germany's Wolfgang Weber headed away for what he hoped was a corner-kick. England's nearest player, Roger Hunt, seemed convinced that it was a goal. The referee, Gottfried Dienst of Switzerland, talked to the Russian linesman, Tofik Bakhramov, who had witnessed the incident from the touchline, six yards from the goal-line, a far from perfect position. The linesman nodded to confirm the goal. More sophisticated later analysis suggested that the ball hadn't fully crossed the goal-line, but that didn't matter. The referee gave a goal, and the referee was the only person whose opinion counted.

Not every member of the 1966 England squad found his life enhanced by the victory. Jimmy Greaves, only twenty-six at the time and one of England's greatest-ever goalscorers, played only three more times for the national team and later attributed his decline and drinking problems to his omission from the team that day. Almost every 1966 contemporary could name Pickles, the dog that found the stolen World Cup trophy, but very few could recall the eleven squad members who didn't play in the Final. But all twenty-two squad members were given equal shares of the £22,000 team bonus for winning the World Cup; senior players overruled the FA's suggestion that the money be divided by the number of matches played by each player.

At school in Hampshire Sue Lopez played all the usual girl sports – netball, hockey, athletics and rounders – but what she enjoyed most was playing football. Like many girl footballers in the late 1950s, she learned her soccer skills informally, playing with and against boys. Her mother took her to watch their local village team, Marchwood, at the edge of the New Forest, and dressed her in the team's colours for a village cup final. Sue Lopez enjoyed the feeling of belonging to the team but hated Marchwood's horrible green.

When she was ten or eleven Sue's grandfather started taking her to watch

Football League matches at Southampton. She would jump into the back of one of the farmer's Land Rovers and set off for the Dell. She particularly liked watching two Saints forwards, John Sydenham and England international Terry Paine. If someone asked her what she wanted to be when she grew up, she said, right away, 'A footballer.' Everyone thought it was funny. Everyone except Sue Lopez.

When her mum took her to buy school shoes, Sue always wanted lace-ups rather than buckle shoes. Lace-ups looked more like football boots and allowed a better kick. When her mum remarried, Sue found an old pair of leather-soled football boots in a shed at their new house. The boots had no studs but it didn't stop her from wearing them. She ran around, thinking she was the bee's knees, wondering why she was slipping all over the place. She hadn't realised that boots needed studs. Years later, when she reflected on this experience, Sue wondered if it had helped to improve her balance for playing football.

Two other football-related incidents impacted strongly on Sue Lopez's childhood. After the 1958 Munich disaster her mother began supporting Manchester United from a distance. She compiled a 'Phoenix Rising' scrapbook with cuttings about the crash and its aftermath. A second big event was the high-profile wedding between Wolves and England captain Billy Wright and singer Joy Beverley, one of the famous Beverley Sisters singing trio. Hooked by the romance, Sue began supporting Wolves. Her favourite player was Peter Broadbent, another forward.

Then, on 30 July 1966, came the event that changed Sue's life. She watched the World Cup Final on television. I want to do this, she thought. I want to play this game.

The World Cup stimulated women's interest in football, but a great opportunity was missed. Had English grounds been more conducive to females, many more fans could have been cultivated. Instead the women's football revolution took another direction. More women started to play the game.

In August 1966, inspired by England's World Cup success, seven women's football clubs grew up almost overnight in the Southampton area. Most were office teams, like Flame United (from Southern Gas), Sunny Saints (from Sun Alliance Insurance) and Cunard (from the famous shipping company). One was a village club (North Baddesley).

Sue Lopez wrote to the local newspaper to ask for team contacts, and was granted a trial for Royex, the Royal Exchange Assurance team. Her career in women's football started in the new South Hants Ladies FA (Southampton & District) League. In her first match she played at right back but she wanted to be a forward. She spent the whole match charging up and down the wing and crossing the ball. She even scored a goal. It was the first time Sue Lopez had ever played organised football. Yet she was twenty-one years old and one of the most naturally gifted female players of her generation.

Like other forms of Sunday football, women's soccer lived an underground life in spartan conditions. Women's teams around Southampton used three football pitches on Southampton Common, all without goalnets. One pitch was next to a lake and the girls often waded in after the ball. There was a wooden changing hut, a toilet and an outside cold-water tap for cleaning boots and filling up the trainer's bucket. The referees and league organisers gave their time for free, and the girls' fathers usually did the work. But the Cunard manager was reported to the Hants FA because he was a registered player with Sholing FC and, since 1921, FA rules had banned affiliated clubs from having any association with the women's game. The long-term history of the women's game in England was one of condescension, paternalism and protectionism by the ruling authorities of the men's game.

The league's best players were brought together for a match between Southampton and Paulsgrove Ladies (Portsmouth) at Southampton Sports Centre. The Southampton players wore white shirts and black shorts because they wanted to be England. When their captain, Jill Long, led out her team that December day in 1966 she felt like she was emulating her own hero – World Cup-winning England captain Bobby Moore.

Nearly three years later, in November 1969, a group of people representing women's clubs met in London's Caxton Hall. The main proposal was to form 'The Ladies Football Association of Great Britain & Northern Ireland'.

'*Ladies* play golf,' said Olive Newsome of the Central Council for Physical Recreation (CCPR). '*Women* do football and athletics.'

The Women's Football Association (WFA) was thus formed, with forty-four member clubs. Like the men's FA, it became an *English* association. One of the many teething problems was negotiating with the men's FA. In January 1970, however, the 1921 resolution was rescinded. Well, not quite. The FA *recommended* that women's teams should be allowed to use

FA-affiliated grounds and registered referees, but not all local associations took up the suggestion immediately.

In November 1970 the WFA launched a new national knock-out competition (only ninety-nine years after the men's FA Cup had begun). Like the men's competition, Scottish teams were involved at the start. One, Stewarton & Thistle (Kilmarnock), was beaten 4–1 by Southampton in the first WFA (Mitre) Cup Final. Southampton scored thirty-four goals in the competition. Seven came from Sue Lopez.

Wendy Owen was born in Slough. At the time of England's World Cup win she was twelve. She watched the Final on television and shared the living-room euphoria at the full-time whistle. It was a defining moment. She spent hours juggling and kicking a ball in the back garden. With no female football role models, she imagined that she was Geoff Hurst or Martin Peters.

Wendy Owen's girls' grammar school didn't offer football, so she played with and against boys on the local green. When the boys started their own street youth team, she pestered her father into starting a Beaconsfield Youth Club girls' team. The team's star, Wendy Owen soon needed to play around better players. Thame Ladies, an Oxfordshire League team, offered her the chance. At the age of sixteen she took regular sixty-mile round trips between Slough and Thame, grateful to be playing in a higher standard.

In 1970 Thame Ladies had a taste of higher-level competition. They reached the final of the Butlin's Cup, a spin-off from Hughie Green's *Opportunity Knocks* television programme. In the national final, however, Thame were swamped 6–0 by Foden's Ladies (of Cheshire). *Opportunity Knocks* had reaped some publicity for the women's game but the real opportunity was missed – the chance of a structure that linked television and women's football. Instead the WFA fell out with the Butlin's organisers and the women's game continued in the excluded regions.

Thame Ladies joined a regional league, the Home Counties League, and raised money through player subscriptions, a weekly tote, a monthly disco and match-day collections. The young female players were looking for fun, friendship and new experiences. They stayed overnight at each other's houses before Sunday matches. In 1971–2 they won the Division Two championship, and they reached the semi-final of the Women's FA Cup, losing 4–3 to a Southampton Ladies team that included Sue Lopez, who was just back from a season playing football in Italy.

*   *   *

In the early 1960s a number of men's international players had left the English game to play for Italian clubs. Sue Lopez's chance came at the end of that decade.

Playing on Southampton Common provided a lot of enjoyment. The great Southampton and Wales striker Ron Davies often turned up to watch. He was a supporter of the women's game, offering kind words of advice and never refusing an autograph request. Sue Lopez had started out by watching great Southampton forwards at the Dell. Now one was watching her team.

After she played a match on tour in Italy in November 1969, two Italian women's clubs asked her to play for them. She took some time to organise her life and give up her secretarial job, and then signed for Roma. Four other British women went to Italy around that time. They included Rose Reilly, who had once been offered a trial with a Scottish League club. A scout had seen Reilly starring in an under-fourteen boys' match and had assumed that she was a boy.

Sue Lopez was careful to play for Roma as an amateur. She knew that if she played professionally she might be banned from the official English women's game. She stayed in Italy for a season (April to January), playing in front of crowds of several hundred. She was surprised at how much more the women's game was accepted and admired in Italy. One national sports paper, *Corriere dello Sport*, regularly devoted a whole page to women's football. And there was none of the condescension that went with the English game.

Although Sue Lopez returned home when there was talk of an England women's team being formed, she missed the first international match through injury. Later she wished she had stayed in Italy. She felt that the Italian game would have provided more respect and enjoyment, and she would have escaped the politics of English football.

Percy Ashley was manager of Manchester Corinthians. He had formed the ladies' club in 1949, because his football-mad daughter Doris needed a team to play for. Ashley was a good organiser who was very strict with the girls. He made sure they wore loose-fitting shirts and shorts rather than the men's tight-fitting kit, and he injected a little bit of fear into them. The girls had to be punctual, with clean boots, and they had to wear a dress or a skirt to and from matches. He dropped players if they didn't listen to him or if he thought they were getting big-headed. If anyone took the mickey out of the girls, however, Ashley was the first to protect them. If you play women's football, you don't want to be laughed at. You don't want men shouting,

'Show us your chest control, love,' 'Take her name, Ref . . . and her phone number,' 'Are you good at making passes, love?' or 'Don't forget to swap shirts at the final whistle.'

Before England's 1966 World Cup win there were too few women's teams for a full season's fixture list, so Percy Ashley arranged foreign tours. For the three-month South American trip in 1960, Manchester Corinthians started with three games in the Carácas area. The President of Venezuela turned up for the first match, the crowd was over 50,000, police patrolled with guns and the South American girls looked huge. The matches were well-organised, well-publicised and popular. Fans chased the coaches and the young women received telegrams afterwards.

The Corinthians also played in Portugal (1957–8), Madeira (1958), the Netherlands (1959), Ireland (1960), Italy (1962) and North Africa (1967). When they went to Berlin in 1957 Manchester City's German-born goalkeeper Bert Trautmann acted as interpreter. After returning from Tunisia one player was so tanned that her twin daughters didn't recognise her.

It was common to have male managers in the women's game. The women of that era conceded that the men probably knew more, and it was some time before women began to qualify as coaches. When the England women's team was formed in 1972 the FA asked one of their staff coaches, Eric Worthington, to take charge.

The England selection procedure was a reminder of early *men's* international trials (North v South or Possibles v Probables). The final trial for the women's team was held in September 1972. Sue Lopez was still recovering from injury, but Wendy Owen was selected for the England women's team's first-ever squad. She had just started her teacher-training course at Dartford College and needed permission for absence. That meant borrowing a skirt for an audience with the principal.

The sixteen-strong England women's squad met on the Thursday before the match against Scotland, trained at Wembley Stadium and travelled to Scotland by coach on the Friday. The average age was just under twenty-one. There weren't many experienced women players available.

The England players were mainly office girls, factory workers or schoolgirls. Wendy Owen's inexperience showed on the journey to Scotland when the older girls convinced her that she needed a passport to cross the Scottish border. Here was evidence of the joking that was rife in the men's game and, just like the men, the women formed a card school. At the local level, though, it was difficult to nurture a dressing-room culture if you had to arrive at matches already changed.

What was different, however, was the journalists' angle on the women's game. Local reporters generally concentrated on the sport, but national coverage was very prejudiced. In 1969 a shy northern female player was talked into posing for a *Daily Mirror* picture which showed her jumping to head the ball with her shorts down near her knees. When the England squad met for the first time, special tight shorts were provided for training, and the girls were embarrassed to be photographed. Wendy Owen was asked to pose in the dressing-room applying eye-shadow even though she had never used it before. When journalists discovered that England's Margaret 'Paddy' McGroarty had briefly joined a convent, she was dressed up in nun's clothing for more pictures. Elsewhere a *Daily Mirror* photographer managed to stage a photograph of twelve Orient Ladies players in a communal bath and the *Sun* was quick to publish a photo of an injured goalkeeper trading shirts with her nominated deputy.

Wendy Owen watched England's first women's international from the substitutes' bench. The match took place at Ravenscraig Stadium, Greenock, almost exactly a hundred years after the first Scotland–England men's international had been played. The English women's game was a century behind the men's.

The early history of the WFA was littered with tales of penny-pinching. There was never much money, very little sponsorship, and WFA funds stood at just over £76 in August 1970. International players received only one cap each, and that was painstakingly sewed together by Flo Bilton, who had borrowed a prototype England men's cap from Raich Carter, a near neighbour in Hull. Wendy Owen's fifteen England appearances were symbolically represented by one cap and fifteen plaques on a shield which was presented to her at the end of her career. Wendy retired from international football prematurely, at the age of twenty-three, with a chronic neck problem. Although she continued playing in club football, trying not to head the ball, she blossomed as a Higher Education teacher and football coach.

Home-and-away internationals against Sweden in the mid-1970s nearly bankrupted the WFA because they tried to match the Swedes' hospitality. The English women's game lagged well behind the Scandinavian model, and Britain had nothing like the USA's Title IX legislation, which in 1972 ensured equal access and equal funding for female sports in education.

Although Britain had the Sex Discrimination Act 1975, it exempted private clubs, where most sport was taking place.

In 1971 the Union of European Football Associations (UEFA) recommended that its members take control of the women's game in Europe. But it wasn't until May 1984 that the FA granted the WFA the equivalent of county FA affiliation, and another nine years passed before the FA acceded to UEFA's recommendation and took full control of the women's game. This was far later than in most other European countries.

The administration of the women's game showed similarities to that of the men's game. Those on the outside accused those on the inside of not making the necessary changes, while those on the inside accused those on the outside of not understanding how the system had to operate. Sue Lopez wanted to push harder for progress but found this difficult. The FA tended to settle for people who didn't want to change things too quickly.

In 2007, over forty years after England's World Cup success, an estimated 2,000 people attended Alan Ball's funeral at Winchester Cathedral. The momentous events of 1966 still resonated with England fans. The 1966 heroes had brought the country a rare world success in a sport where failure is the norm.

Sue Lopez had known Ball from his time at Southampton, where the men's club and women's club formed strong links and often celebrated their triumphs together. The crowd at Ball's funeral was so huge that Lopez was happy to stand outside the cathedral. She heard Nobby Stiles talk about how Ball was by far the best player on the pitch in the 1966 Final. Stiles recalled Ball's skills, his ferocious will to win and his incredible energy. It was very moving. But, unlike the male World Cup winners, Sue Lopez, a top-class England international player, stood largely unrecognised as the crowd drifted away.

16

CHESTER'S XI TAKES THE FIELD

O<small>N 23 JUNE 1966, JUST</small> before the World Cup Finals, an eleven-man team took the field – the field of football study.

The eleven men were briefed by Labour's Denis Howell, the minister responsible for sport at the Department of Education & Science. They were 'to enquire into the state of association football at all levels, including the organisation, management, finance and administration, and the means by which the game may be developed for the public good; and to make recommendations'.

'I'm very proud to be captain of this side,' said Norman Chester, the 58-year-old chairman of the Football Enquiry Committee (as it became known). 'There have been inquiries into railways and docks, but football, now there's something really fascinating.'

Norman Chester had been warden of Nuffield College, Oxford, for twelve years. A bluff, bespectacled, ruddy-faced Mancunian with grey hair and a dark moustache, he prepared for the first press conference by dressing in a dark suit with a white handkerchief in his top pocket, and a white dress shirt with cufflinks. Before talking to reporters he took out a fountain pen and wrote some personal notes on the page of an exercise book:

First watched M/c United in 1922 (long before Matt Busby).

Once said Oxford a wonderful university and a wonderful place to live but suffered from 2 disadvantages: (1) long way from the sea; (2) no first class soccer.

One is still true, but (2) has improved with Ox U now in 3rd Division – wd have got into second if they had had one consistent goalscorer.

But not an expert in how the game is run. Lots of ideas floating about. Our job is to study them.

I am interested in the game's finance – and social research.

Minister has chosen a very good team of eleven men.

Problem of finding a World Cup winning side on one hand . . . providing mass enjoyment for very large part of male adults on the other.

Norman Chester had helped transform Nuffield into a very wealthy college for its size. He was the author of a number of books on government and public administration. He had been a member of the War Cabinet secretariat and secretary of the Beveridge Committee.

Soon after being appointed to the Football Enquiry Committee he wrote, in an article about football for the *Spectator*: 'In this country probably a million play it every week in the season, and about twice as many watch. It is thus not surprising that the Prime Minister is known to favour the round not the long ball, and that he actively supports Huddersfield Town, narrowly beaten this year for promotion to the First Division.'

Chester argued that the major European club competitions were increasing British people's awareness of the continent. 'This and the car ferry are probably doing as much to make us European-conscious as all the activities of Mr Heath, Lord Gladwyn and their friends,' Chester told *Spectator* readers.

While England's elite players were winning the World Cup, Chester's XI began to analyse the game as a whole.

When Norman Chester worked for Manchester City Council's treasurer's department as a teenager, he enjoyed playing full back in what he called 'very minor football'. His experience of playing against the Gas B team in the Guild Cup at Manchester's Platt Fields was valuable enough. After all, the Football Enquiry Committee was briefed to study *all* levels of football, and only ninety-two of England's 30,862 football clubs were Football League members.

The amateur game had its own crises. Volunteers were working overtime to sustain county associations and local leagues. The number of local clubs had increased by 8,000 between 1961 and 1967, a rise of 34 per cent, thanks partly to Sunday football. The number of disciplinary cases had doubled during the same period, and the shortage of referees was chronic. Ernest Wilson of the West Riding County FA wrote to the Football Association complaining that volunteers were often out of pocket after fulfilling their duties: 'In my own case, as chairman of the Referees' Committee (twenty-six years) and as a retired person, on a fixed income, it is hardship and would not be accepted except for a desire to do the best one can for the game. It is fortunate that so many people are prepared to do this.'

Chester soon understood the range of tasks undertaken by these county FA people, and he also recognised how little publicity the grassroots game received. 'Most of the popular sports writers will highlight our main points about professional football and ignore much or all of the rest,' he told his committee. 'I doubt whether there is much we can do about this except give a good deal of thought to our relations with the press as publication draws near.'

Interest in professional football was declining in England in the face of alternative leisure activities. Workers had moved from a six-day week to a five-day week, and the weekend was more of a family affair. Aggregate League attendances had fallen from 41.3 million (in 1948–9) to 27.6 million (in 1964–5), and the lower divisions were the most affected. Now that the English had more money and time, some were rejecting football for more expensive pursuits, such as driving, photography, golf and even yachting.

Increasing home comforts, such as central heating, meant that fans of League clubs thought uncovered terraces more distasteful. In 1964 only 12 per cent of Football League accommodation was seated (compared with 80 per cent in Portugal's First Division), and Tottenham Hotspur's 28 per cent was top of the English range. Amateur players criticised changing facilities, while urban sprawl ate up available football pitches. Football was not keeping up with the Joneses.

Football League clubs faced major financial problems. Although First Division clubs were operating at an aggregate surplus (£1.7 million), there were aggregate deficits in Division Two (£140,000), Division Three (£260,000) and Division Four (£140,000). After the hullabaloo over the removal of the maximum wage there had been a shift towards higher wages in the top divisions. During the year ending 31 December 1966 the average annual earnings of players was £2,467 (Division One), £1,862 (Division Two), £1,446 (Division Three) and £1,130 (Division Four).

'Facts and figures, that's what we're after,' Chester told his committee. 'There are enough *opinions* around already.'

Chester's XI spent two years gathering information.

It was a visionary committee. Norman Chester belonged to a very traditional English institution, Oxford University, but he was avant-garde in his thinking. 'I imagine you may want to say something about amalgamation of grounds, the role of TV and such stratospheric ideas as large stadia catering for multi-sports activities,' he wrote to committee member Clifford Barclay.

Chester envisaged a future with pay television, more female spectators ('women provide a major and largely untapped source of support'), improved stadium facilities, amalgamation of same-city clubs, ground-sharing (like the Munich clubs), regional entertainment centres staging football and other events, clubs moving from one town to another (like American sports franchises), a more integrated relationship between the FA and the Football League, a League executive committee, a cadre of elite referees, supporters on club boards, and playing contracts of definite length with both parties free at the end of the contract (and transfer fees only when there was some part of the contract to serve). If England's Martin Peters was ten years ahead of his time as a player, Norman Chester was twenty, thirty, forty years ahead of his time as an analyst. He wanted the football authorities to embrace these possibilities. Better to take control of the future than let it run you down.

'It is a fine example of research and analysis,' Albert Barham wrote in the *Guardian*, when the report was published. 'The great question is one of getting the recommendations turned into legislation by the authorities.'

Indeed.

Maybe Chester had false hopes that the government would push the agenda. Instead the FA and, in particular, the Football League were innately conservative. As one wag put it, the Football League thought that Market Research was a non-League club in Lincolnshire.

'Between ourselves, I had Denis Follows [the FA secretary] for lunch last Thursday,' Chester told Clifford Barclay in 1969. 'It is a pity that relations between him and Hardaker [Football League secretary] are so bad, and it is also a pity that he is always so much on the defensive. Anyhow, he gave me the impression that the FA were in favour of most of our recommendations, but that the League were rather against them.'

FA chairman Harold Thompson would later claim that the FA acted immediately on Chester's recommendations. Chester was not so sure. 'Though the Football Association and the Football League catch the headlines and glamour,' he wrote in the final report, 'it is the county associations and the various League management committees which are responsible for the organisation and well-being for the mass of English football.'

In two years (1965 and 1966) the FA put £240,000 away to reserve and their total income was only £573,900. Some of this money clearly needed to go to county FAs. In a memo to his committee Chester wrote, 'I did not get the impression that they [the FA] were particularly good at finance and, indeed, I am told they have a very elderly and sick treasurer.' It wasn't until 1965 that the FA followed the Football League's lead and claimed copyright money from the pools companies for reproducing the FA Cup fixtures.

Chester recommended a compulsory retirement age of seventy for the eighty-four FA Council members (because the majority were older than that). 'We find it extraordinary that reaching the age of seventy-five should be regarded as a qualification for the main active offices in the Association,' Chester wrote, but there was no immediate change. Professional footballers continued to joke about FA councillors' ear-trumpets and Boer War injuries.

Very few grassroots clubs owned their own ground. Most rented from private landlords. A recommended figure of one pitch per 2,750 population offered Chester a benchmark. The statistics also showed that regions varied considerably from the professionally dominated to the largely amateur-oriented. In 1967 Norfolk had over 600 clubs and only one League club whereas Cumberland had two League clubs among its 183 clubs.

The thorny question of defining amateurism and professionalism was also on Chester's agenda. His committee recommended a new category of player, the 'semi-professional' or Form Z player. One member, Bill Slater, dissented. He thought the solution was graded open competitions that permitted teams of similar standard to meet regardless of status. Eventually, in 1976, the FA decided that all footballers should be called *players*. The FA Amateur Cup gave way to the FA Vase and FA Trophy, competitions that defined the *level* of football rather than the status of the players.

The Football League management committee thought that the Chester Report was factually correct but suffered from pre-conceived ideas and impractical recommendations. Theirs was an emotional response to Chester's scientific and considered proposals.

'All the officials that we saw from the football world were so full of themselves and so full of their own importance and so blasé about nothing being wrong, that one could have expected that the report would go on the shelf for some time,' a committee member told Chester some years later.

The Football League did appoint a director of referees – responsible for the training, selection and appointment of match officials – but it took longer for other recommendations to be noticed. It wasn't until 1973–4 that 'three up and three down' came to the top three divisions, but Chester had recommended 'four up and four down'. It wasn't until the early 1980s that the League accepted Chester's recommendation to permit managers or secretaries on boards and allow *paid* directors. In the early 1960s the average age of club directors was fifty-eight, with 38 per cent aged sixty or over.

Chester was aware of experiments with closed-circuit television. The 1965–6 Workington v Millwall match attracted more people to Millwall's big screen than to Workington's ground. He also promoted the idea of pay television as a way to solve the Football League's worries about television coverage reducing attendances.

'Pay TV can localise transmission,' said Chester. 'Thus if Manchester United were playing at Tottenham, transmission could be confined to the Manchester area. Moreover the owner of each set would have to pay a fee for viewing, probably of 7s 6d [37½p] or 10s [50p] and football would receive a substantial part of this. At the moment development of this system is limited by the number of people with pay sets and by the fact that the company is licensed to operate only in London and Sheffield.' Some of Chester's recommendations were totally ignored. There was no time given to the Chester XI's vision of a Football League with ninety-eight or 102 clubs and five divisions (including two regional divisions) as the clubs had already rejected Hardaker's similar proposal. The idea of an eighteen-club First Division was shelved, and it took nearly thirty years to reduce the top division to twenty.

'The League is only theoretically composed of ninety-two equal clubs,' Chester noted. 'In practice it has an established plutocracy, a middle class who normally just manage to keep their heads above water, and a large proletariat living in nearly permanent poverty.'

Chester showed the value of outside research. He collected evidence to disprove Hardaker's theory that transfer fees benefited the poorer clubs. In fact transfer fees were an added burden for smaller clubs. Whereas First Division clubs made an aggregate £318,565 *gain*, Third Division clubs made a £323,530 *loss* (between May 1964 and October 1966). A net figure of about £540,000 went *outside* the Football League – to Scottish League and Irish League clubs – and 40 per cent of English transfer fees were paid between clubs in the *same* division. Promising young players were enticed away by larger clubs, and the smaller clubs had to make do with what was left over when the larger clubs had finished their transfer dealing.

Chester told his committee that the story of Derek Dougan, a fiery Northern Ireland international and PFA committee member, was an example of football's poor labour relations. Dougan was called to the Leicester City manager's office at 11.50am on transfer deadline day (17 March 1967) and given ten minutes to decide about a transfer. Dougan thought it wrong that he didn't have the opportunity to consider arrangements about accommodation and schools. The outspoken player later adopted the Chester Report as his bible, mainly because Chester foresaw the complete freedom of transfer and even the possibility of the 1995 Bosman case, which allowed players free transfers at the end of contracts. But Chester's visionary ideas foundered partly on the conservatism of the ruling bodies and partly on the rising distraction of crowd-behaviour problems, an issue that was beyond his remit.

Manchester United, the club Norman Chester had supported since 1922, took off in the 1960s, thanks to its exciting players (Law, Best, Charlton), the growth of television, the lingering national sympathy for the club's loss and the continuing presence of Munich survivors (Charlton, Foulkes, Busby). In 1968 Manchester United beat Benfica 4–1 to win the European Cup at Wembley. As United manager Matt Busby and captain Bobby Charlton embraced afterwards, most football people's thoughts went back to Munich. The story was tragic, heroic, romantic, fabulous and full of glory. Here was some recovery and rehabilitation.

At 4.15pm on the day of the 1968 European Cup Final, Norman Chester received an honorary degree from Manchester University. At 5pm he was on his way to Manchester Airport. He arrived at London Airport at 6.40pm and reached Wembley with ten minutes to spare before the big match.

A few days later Chester wrote to thank Matt Busby for the tickets: 'Though you had me worried for the last fifteen minutes of full time, this only heightened the excitement of the first ten minutes of extra time. It was a wonderful occasion and it made one very proud to be a Manchester man and a Britisher.'

Typically, Chester also sent a cheque for £8 to cover the cost of the tickets.

PART THREE

INTRODUCTION TO PART THREE

'FOOTBALL MANAGERS HAVE COME TO rival the weather, the cost of living and the opposite sex as a topic for daily discussion,' wrote Stephen Wagg in *The Football World*. In this 1984 analysis managers of professional clubs had been transformed from sacrificial clerks (in the early twentieth century) to wily wheeler-dealers (in the 1930s) and then to miracle-working media personalities (in the late 1960s). In the late fifties some big clubs still employed figurehead managers who didn't select the team. Then, suddenly, managers became central figures in the drama.

This new era launched the early version of football's celebrity culture. Managers were now clearly responsible for player acquisition through a scouting network and team selection, and this suited everyone involved. Managers wanted full control, directors had a potential scapegoat for failure, fans knew who to worship or blame and the media had managerial hooks and headlines for stories. Managers even became part of the club name; it was 'Lawrie McMenemy's Southampton' after 1973 and 'Tommy Docherty's Preston' in 1981.

At the same time top-class players became more celebrated, more professional and more in control of their own careers. Players were no longer willing to put up with the conditions of the maximum-wage era. The journey to 'freedom of contract' was well under way, and a new deal was finally sealed in 1981. Professional clubs became more aware of the value of players as commodities, and this led to scientific examination of player injuries and stiffer pre-transfer medical examinations. Some players were shocked to find that major deals had fallen through on medical grounds.

Much of the new celebrity culture around the game was orchestrated through television. This era of TV football brought the launch of a panel of pundits, and Brian Clough and Jimmy Hill became household names. A study of 1974 World Cup broadcasts concluded that 'like language itself film and television operate as a system in which "messages" can only be understood in relation to a code'. The researchers argued that television programmers reconstructed the reality of football at almost every stage: the choice of match (to appeal to a mass audience); advance publicity conveying a particular story-line (e.g. via *Radio Times* and *TV Times*); the choice of images in the programme's opening sequence; the selection of issues in the preview of the match; the tone and substance of the commentary; camera placings and the framing of the action (including special shots of managers and the crowd); the selection of 'highlights'; the way the camera focused on particular players and managers to create star figures; the choice of slow-motion replays for special incidents; and the portrayal of an expert summariser as a superstar.

Not far behind the manager, as regards media attention, came the club chairman. Whereas chairmen had been mainly local figures in the late 1960s, in the early 1980s most football fans could name Ken Bates at Chelsea, Robert Maxwell at Oxford United and Jimmy Hill at Coventry City. These men were as newsworthy as managers, especially when it came to dealing with the exhausting hooliganism story. On top of the new expressions of support and partisanship, the actual behaviour of young male fans was becoming more unruly, more confrontational and more dangerous. Spectators increasingly attempted to manipulate the outcome of matches. There was an emerging consensus that supporter behaviour was growing out of control.

The English game faced a series of crisis points. Something had to be done, whether it was about spectator unrest, financial problems, player injuries or racist attitudes. Someone had to come up with scientific or otherwise sensible answers to the sport's problems. It was no use trying to muddle through with unprofessional, chaotic and amateurish attitudes.

While the professional game in England carried a sense of impending disaster, the amateur game continued relatively unscathed. A number of local clubs slowly followed the professionals by introducing floodlights, training pitches, youth teams and overseas tours. Fundraising became more critical, but the amateur game at the local level sustained its growth. The volunteer work continued.

17

THE BOSS AND HIS BOSSES

A GROUP OF FOUR PROFESSIONAL football-club managers were chatting after a match.

'If you're winning, the directors call it "our team",' said one. 'If you're losing, it's "your team".'

'One thing always amazes me,' said another. 'You try to sell a player because he's not good enough for your team and the directors say he's worth £20,000. You try to buy a player who you think will improve your team and they tell you to get him for £10,000.'

'I got a letter about my pension the other day. I thought, "Pension? In this game?" How do we get that far?'

They all nodded, deadpan.

'You know what the secret of good management is?'

'Good players?'

'Nah. It's keeping the five players who hate your guts away from the six who are not so sure. And keeping the five directors who want you out from the six who are on your side.'

'Harry Storer always said that the ideal board had only three directors – one dead, one dying and one in South America.'

More deadpan nods. Everyone had a strong image of Storer, a tough, sharp-tongued man who spent thirty-one years in management with Coventry City, Birmingham City and Derby County.

'They get on the board because they've got money or influence. A month later they think they've been elected because they know something about football.'

'I'll get you another drink,' the manager of the host club said.

'No, don't you go. Send your chairman.'

They had a good laugh about that.

*   *   *

Tim Ward more or less knew what was coming at the start of May 1967. He had been a football-club manager for fourteen years, at three different clubs, and he understood the precarious nature of the job. Now he was nearing the end of his five-year contract at Derby County and he hadn't achieved promotion to the First Division. The chairman, Sam Longson, stumbling over his words, told Ward that his contract wasn't being renewed. Ironically, Ward's wife had already heard the news from a friend who knew a director's wife.

The next day Ward received a two-word telegram from Bolton Wanderers manager Bill Riddings: 'THE BASTARDS.'

Ward collected his belongings from the Baseball Ground, returned the keys to his Vauxhall 101 car and thanked all the players. When he heard that chief scout Sammy Crooks and trainer Ralph Hann had also been sacked, Ward reacted more angrily than he had over his own situation. In his quiet voice he criticised the board of directors for being penny-pinching, controlling and failing to invest in the club. He told reporters that he couldn't use a tuppenny-halfpenny stamp without consulting the board.

This outburst was out of character for Ward. He was an unusually gentle man in the world of football. He didn't shout, he didn't swear and he had survived thirty years in professional football with a good reputation inside the game. He was a man of inner steel rather than outer bravado, and was almost Corinthian in his attitudes to the game.

'The trouble with Tim,' said chairman Sam Longson after the decision to sack him, 'is that he's too much of a gentleman.'

Sam Longson had a telephone call from Len Shackleton, a former England international player who was working as a journalist in the North-East.

'I'd like to recommend a lad from up here,' Shackleton said, 'but you won't have him in your applications.'

'OK, Len, who is it?'

'Brian Clough. He's at Hartlepools. He's a born leader of men.'

'Well, I'll think about it,' Longson said. A haulage contractor, he was gruff by nature.

'You'll have to think quick because West Brom are interested in him,' said Shackleton, stretching the truth.

'I'll see the directors tomorrow.'

Longson remembered Clough playing at the Baseball Ground, telling all the Sunderland players what to do. After speaking to Shackleton, Longson couldn't get the name out of his mind. *Brian Clough, Brian Clough, Brian Clough* . . .

He and three other directors travelled in his Rolls-Royce to meet Clough at Scotch Corner. Clough did all the talking.

'What do you think?' Longson asked his directors after the meeting.

'He talks too much.'

'He's big-headed. What did you think?'

'I like him,' Longson said. 'I like him a lot. He's just the opposite to Tim. Just the absolute opposite to him.'

Longson offered Clough £5,000 a year and was surprised to find that Clough had a partner called Peter Taylor. (Assistant managers were rare at this time.) More importantly, Longson, having recently sold his haulage business, agreed that £70,000 would be available to buy new players.

Tim Ward had five years' worth of stories about Derby County directors. He had a good relationship with his first Derby chairman, Fred Walters, but Walters was an outsider on the board. He wasn't one of the four Freemasons. Walters was ousted as chairman in 1964 and the new system gave each director a two-year stint in the chair.

Board meetings took place every Thursday at 7pm, with the manager excluded until team matters arose. Ward often waited in his office for over an hour before he was called. He got on with correspondence, but he was stopped from watching matches or seeing the part-timers, two of whom were regular first-team players. When he was called in to the meeting he had to assess the mood. Which directors couldn't look him in the eye? Who was red in the face, and why?

Ward told Fred Walters that the board meetings were too frequent and too awkward. Walters agreed but said that the other directors insisted on Ward being there. Ward assumed that this was because every month they wanted him to sign someone of their choosing.

On the directors' wish list was a lad from Sheffield Wednesday. Ward reluctantly telephoned a reporter friend.

'Don't go near him,' the reporter said. 'He can play, but don't have him at any price.'

Ward phoned Sheffield Wednesday manager Vic Buckingham.

'What do you want for this lad?' he asked.

'For you, Tim?' Buckingham replied. 'I'm not going to sell him to you.'

'I'm interested in him.'

'Look, Tim, we're mates, aren't we?'

'Yes.'

'And we want to stay mates?'

'Yes, of course.'

'So I'm not going to sell him to you. We wouldn't be mates afterwards.'

Ward got the message. But it took him a long time to convince his directors that the player was trouble.

Acting on the recommendation of his chief scout, Sammy Crooks, Ward chose two away matches to assess 21-year-old Kevin Hector of Bradford Park Avenue. The first match was on a beautiful day at Chester. Ward saw that Hector had pace and two good feet. Hector knew where the goal was, he was always close to the action and he wanted to play football in a simple and sensible way. In football parlance, Ward fancied the lad. He wanted to watch Hector every week. He wanted Hector in his team. He saw how he could fit in.

'Derby County couldn't afford him,' Bradford PA manager Walter Galbraith told Ward.

'Try me,' Ward said.

'We've been offered £30,000 for him.'

'Well, you've not frightened me off. You've probably frightened off my directors, but not me.'

The second time Ward watched Hector was on a dreadful day at Barnsley. Snow was blowing into the covered Centre Stand, the wind was bitterly cold and Ward smiled to himself because he couldn't imagine a better day for judging a player's character. Hector played well again.

Ward worked on the directors – and two chairmen – for six months. The directors were worried that Hector was only five foot eight, and, worse still, only a Fourth Division player.

'See if you can get him for ten thousand,' one director said.

Eventually, at a meeting with Bradford officials, Ward's latest chairman, Sam Longson, threatened to walk out on the whole Hector idea.

'Imagine, Mr Chairman,' Ward said. 'This could be a record fee for Derby County, a record fee for a Fourth Division player, and you're the chairman involved.'

Longson paused.

A fee of £34,000 was agreed and Derby County negotiated terms with the player. Hector signed and went on to become one of Derby County's all-time heroes, known to supporters as 'The King', even when he was surrounded by other great players.

'You're a lucky man,' Hartlepools United manager Brian Clough told Tim Ward a few days later. 'You've signed the best player in the Fourth Division.'

'Kevin Hector?'

'Kevin Hector.'

The two men were talking in the manager's office at the Baseball Ground. It was late on a Friday afternoon, the time of the week when most ordinary workers were euphoric. But Ward and Clough were on the cusp of yet another working weekend. Ward was glad of the company of the 31-year-old Clough, a man with enough energy and verve to learn his trade at a Division Four club. Ward believed that young managers should serve an apprenticeship at the lower levels. A knee injury had given Clough a premature opportunity – and the motivation – to develop his managerial skills. Both men had unfulfilled ambitions and a hunger to win trophies vicariously.

The two men knew each other already of course. Everybody in professional football knows everybody else, if only by repute. A couple of years earlier, when Clough was a coach at Sunderland, he once walked up to the Derby County dug-out and asked politely if he could watch the match with them. Clough had been away with Sunderland Juniors, and returned to find that there wasn't a seat in the home dug-out. Ward concentrated on the match, but he also had a chance to observe Clough at close quarters. In the years to come virtually everybody in the country had a personal perspective on Brian Clough, and Ward was no exception. It was just one of the many millions of relationships that football throws up.

The heart and soul of football lies in the relationships it generates. Football is not simply all about a ball; it is about the relationships that the ball provokes.

Player and player.

Spectator and player.

Brother and brother.

Father and son.

Spectator and rival spectator.

Player and manager.

Journalist and reader.

Player and God.

Us and them.

The list is endless.

The relationship between Brian Clough and Tim Ward fitted a number of categories. In the early days it was player and opposition manager, then coach and rival manager, then manager and manager . . . and then, in the summer of 1967, it became one of ancestor and successor. Clough took over from Ward as manager of Derby County, signalling a new era in English football, one in which managers featured much more prominently in the media coverage of the sport. Whereas Tim Ward's media involvement was limited to a weekly article for the *Derby Sports Special* – he received £3 an article and tried to avoid controversy – Brian Clough became a household name and professional controversialist.

Brian Clough arrived in the media spotlight in 1968, just when the spotlight was becoming a glare. Almost 90 per cent of homes had television, football highlights were televised on Saturday evenings and Sunday afternoons and preview programmes ran on Saturday lunchtimes. In the five years from 1968 to 1973 Derby County won the Second Division, the First Division, and reached a European Cup semi-final. The same five years saw the rise of *Match of the Day*, *The Big Match*, *Football Focus*, *On the Ball* and a network of local BBC and independent radio stations. Television stations launched panels of pundits for the 1970 World Cup Finals, and Brian Clough became a regular in the make-up room. He was one of a new breed of young, articulate, media-savvy managers who became bigger personalities than their players.

Clough was perfect for television because he was handsome and brash, frank and funny, controversial and opinionated. His perceptive insights, delivered in a distinctive strangulated north Yorkshire accent, gave him a powerful presence. He knew that television companies paid him for his opinions, and he thought that opinions were the earth's rotators. Clough's television career was initially supported by Sam Longson, who thought it good for the club. Longson later changed his mind.

Clough was a deep-thinking man of many personalities and mixtures. He was a tyrant who berated people and then gave them chocolates or flowers. He fined his own players for causing trouble on the field, but he didn't always stick to rules and regulations off it. He could be cruel but he could be very generous. He could turn up on time or off time. He was a fidgety man, fiddling with a squash ball or a cigarette lighter while talking in his office. He was iconoclastic, anti-establishment and unpredictable. Clough didn't mind arguments as long as it was his decision in the end.

In his early years at Derby County Brian Clough set about spending Sam Longson's money with great determination. He got Tranmere's nineteen-year-old Roy McFarland, a future England international, out of bed at 1am and convinced him to sign. He set off at dawn to sign legendary Scotland international David Mackay from Tottenham Hotspur. And he talked at length with Willie Carlin's wife when Sheffield United agreed to release the player after a twelve-month spell.

'Come and work for us,' Clough told one target. 'I'll give you the space, the opportunity, the grass and the oxygen to exploit your talents.'

Clough believed in class performers but he also knew that teams needed to be balanced. He signed the relatively timid Alan Hinton, tough-nut David Mackay and workhorses such as John McGovern and John O'Hare.

'We can't all be the same, you just mould a side together,' he once told a television interviewer. 'You know, you've got three guys behind you now. You're bloody hopeless at your job but they're making you look good. Only kidding.'

Early in their time at Derby Peter Taylor warned Clough that a manager shouldn't get too close to directors. But Longson and Clough initially got along like father and son. There was a chance it could go wrong, especially when Clough hired secretary Stuart Webb without telling Longson. Then Clough started making signings without the chairman's permission. Colin Todd came for £175,000 from Sunderland and Roger Davies for £14,000 from Worcester City.

'That's a lot for a non-League player,' one director said.

At Hartlepools United Clough and Taylor had helped a director to oust the chairman in a boardroom coup. At Derby in 1970 they colluded with Longson to jettison three directors – Ken Turner, Harry Payne and Bob Kirkland – and reinstate Longson as chairman. Rarely had a manager felt so much power.

Eventually – perhaps inevitably – Clough grew too big for Sam Longson's liking. The first two months of the 1972–3 season were exceptionally fractious, even by football standards. Clough and Taylor fell out when Taylor discovered that Clough had had a massive pay rise and he hadn't. Clough's drinking habits became a problem and the directors ordered the drinks cabinet to be emptied and locked. Clough wanted Longson out but the rest of the board refused to join the coup. Clough continued to talk to other clubs about managerial vacancies, and he became more outspoken in his television appearances and newspaper columns.

Longson was having difficulty when he visited other clubs.

'Who's running Derby County? Is it you, Sam or Cloughie?'

'He likes the sound of his own voice, doesn't he?'

Clough's major fault, to hear other managers, was telling other people how to do their jobs via the media.

'Brian Clough will be the next England coach,' a comedian said. 'They're going to take all his teeth out and replace them with seats.'

When Longson demanded to see Clough's press columns before they were published, Clough was outraged. Clough then accepted an additional ITV job, appeared on chat shows and was the subject of a Mike Yarwood impression. Longson argued that it was all interfering with Clough's Derby County duties. Taylor and Clough offered their resignations and, to their surprise, they were accepted.

It was really a matter of power. Clough thought Clough should dictate. Longson knew Longson was in charge.

In the first few years after Tim Ward's departure from Derby County, people would often sidle up to him in football-club tea-rooms and boardrooms and, while feeding themselves with a pork pie or cake, they would feed Ward with rumours and stories about Brian Clough.

'They say he took Peter Taylor to Hartlepool because Taylor had owed him money from their Middlesbrough days, and Clough was then able to stop the money from Taylor's wages.'

'Uncle Sam's looking after Cloughie so well that he doesn't have to touch his own wages.'

'He had a fight with Jimmy Scoular. Cloughie was standing at the top of the passage telling Cardiff players that they shouldn't play for such a shower. They had to drag Scoular off him.'

People must have thought that these were stories that Tim Ward wanted to hear, but Ward was wise enough to understand that all arrogant, young, successful managers attracted scurrilous tales. When people told Ward that Clough's Derby had lost a match, they seemed to expect him to cheer. Ward might have felt hostile to Sam Longson and two or three of the other Derby directors, but he didn't feel hostile to Brian Clough. He also knew that the football world was changing. Of course, Ward would have loved to have had the transfer money to achieve what Clough did at Derby County, but he also recognised that Cloughie was an exceptional manager who had done a wonderful job. While Derby County fans debated about which of Clough's signings was his biggest success, Ward thought that Clough's most amazing achievement was getting rid of three Derby County directors.

18

THE REFEREE SAID, 'PLAY ON'

Hunter . . . pass intercepted, but Suggett is offside. The referee is waving him on. Brown is going through . . . taking on Sprake . . . and the goal . . . by Astle . . . and Leeds will go mad and they've every right to go mad because everybody stopped with the linesman's flag.

ACCORDING TO STEPHEN POTTER IN *The Theory and Practice of Gamesmanship*, the art of gamesmanship is to use dubious, but technically legal, tactics to win a game. Gamesmanship is usually against the spirit of the game but not against the laws.

'We would have used the word "professionalism", not "gamesmanship",' said Jack Charlton, who played for Leeds United for twenty-one years (1952–73). 'There's so much professionalism in the game of football now, and the more they try to stop it the more coaches will invent ways round it. We were probably the first professional outfit, and we used the rules within the laws of the game to our advantage.'

'They time-wasted, they pulled your shirt,' said George Best (Manchester United) about Leeds. 'If it was a corner they pulled your hair, but the most exasperating thing was that they could actually play as well.'

'I think it was probably openly encouraged at Leeds that you get the ball into the corner to waste time,' said John Giles (Leeds United and Eire). 'You knock it up into the corners and get tight on the opposition rather than keep possession of the ball. It's not attractive and it is certainly frustrating for fans and opposition players alike.'

Leeds United manager Don Revie was an ambitious man with a sophisticated football mind. He paid great attention to detail. Revie changed the club's colours to all-white, not only to emulate Real Madrid but also because it was easier to spot team-mates on a grey day. The team's array of superstitions included Revie's lucky mohair suit and Norman Hunter's ritual of picking up a football and throwing it to the captain as they left the dressing-room. With the help of his scouts, and assistant Syd Owen, Revie compiled dossiers on opponents. United players were briefed on the obvious ('Keep Jimmy Greaves away from his left foot') and the not-so-obvious ('This is how our opposition will be taking free-kicks . . .').

'You weren't there to enjoy the game, enjoy yourself,' Jack Charlton once mused. 'You were there to get results and to win games and to work hard at every game and to produce what you had to produce.'

'I was told that Leeds United had a list of referees in the manager's office,' said one ex-referee. 'Each of the eighty-one referees was listed and then opposite their names were free-kicks, penalties and all that sort of thing. "Give a penalty for anything." "Don't show any dissent." ' Some referees even claimed that Leeds United players deliberately used the referee as a shield in passing movements.

Top-class referees were generally thick-skinned, confident and capable of handling abuse. They had heard all the usual insults. But they were presented with a new challenge by the gamesmanship (or professionalism) at Leeds United (and other clubs) in the late sixties and early seventies. Referees also became increasingly in the television spotlight.

On Saturday 17 April 1971 Leeds United played West Bromwich Albion in a First Division match. An incident in the sixty-ninth minute symbolised the coming of a new montage for professional football – gamesmanship (or professionalism), challenges to the referee's authority, spectators behaving badly and trial by television.

The First Division Championship was at stake. On the morning of the West Brom match Leeds United topped the table by two points (one win), but second-placed Arsenal had two games in hand. Leeds United had only four League matches to play (including the one with West Brom).

On the surface it looked an odds-on home win. Leeds had lost only seven home matches in five years, whereas West Brom had not won away in sixteen months. That same year, it was said, a Japanese soldier returned to civilisation after living in the jungle for over twenty-five years, and Midland wags guessed the man's first words: 'Is Churchill still alive? Is Roosevelt still alive? Have West Brom won an away game yet?'

But at Elland Road West Brom's Tony Brown scored a fifteenth-minute goal and Leeds United trailed 1–0 at half-time. West Brom's central defenders, John Wile and John Kaye, used the offside trap to smother the Leeds United strikers. Football thrives on discussion and disagreement, and what would men have to talk about in the pub if it wasn't for offside?

On the pitch footballers with short fuses and threatening body language take part in something which is very combative, very competitive, and yet, for most of the time, the system works amazingly well. It works because the International Football Association Board (IFAB) has developed an acceptable set of laws. It works because of the symbolic authority of the referee. It works so well that football has the most pervasive international legal system on the planet. Football has reached places that would make Esperanto speakers envious. FIFA has recruited more member countries than the United Nations. It has been an incredible success. Football's legal system has something to teach us all. People can learn to live together through football.

In most other contexts players would have little respect for the sort of people who become referees. On the field, however, players succumb. It is an incredibly powerful message about what football can do. At the lower level referees work alone, stand completely outside the event and are often regarded as the enemy. Yet the system still functions.

Judging offside has always been difficult. Linesmen have to stay level with the second-last defender, note the position of the forwards and assess the picture at the exact moment the attacking team played the ball. Linesmen are like old-time horseracing judges, deciding a photo-finish without a camera – except that the finishing-line keeps moving and a ball is somewhere else on the pitch. Researchers into eye movement have argued that a linesman cannot assess the relative position of several key players and the ball *at the same time*.

One confusing aspect of the offside law is the caveat that players can be offside only if they are interfering with play and/or seeking to gain an advantage. An early Football Association decision (19 December 1910) made it clear that referees shouldn't award a free-kick simply for seeing a player in an offside position. In the 1920s it was stated that players had a duty to keep clear of the play if they were in an offside position. In the 1960s most referees took a safe stance on offside, assuming that anyone on the field was automatically interfering with play.

At Elland Road, in the sixty-ninth minute of the Leeds United v West Brom match, Norman Hunter (Leeds) lost the ball ten yards inside the West Brom half. Hunter's pass was intercepted by Tony Brown (West Brom), who kicked the ball into open space on the West Brom right.

Brown's team-mate Colin Suggett was apparently in an offside position in the centre of the field. The Leeds United defenders stopped. But Suggett, after taking two or three strides towards the ball, then turned his back on the play, and Brown, after briefly hesitating, set off on his own. The linesman, Bill Troupe, saw Suggett in an offside position and dutifully raised his flag.

'All the way along he had used his linesman for offside,' Norman Hunter said years later. 'Tony Brown won the ball from me, and there was a lad called Colin Suggett who was way offside. He must have been nearly ten yards offside. And Tony Brown carried on and then he turned round and the referee said, "Play on," and he went on.'

The referee, Ray Tinkler, had raised his whistle towards his mouth, anticipating Brown passing to Suggett. Then he saw Brown take the ball through himself. In that moment Tinkler judged Suggett's intentions to be innocent. Suggett was a long way from the ball and not seeking to gain an advantage. The referee lowered his whistle and waved play on. Referees carry whistles in their hand rather than in their mouths to give themselves extra thinking time.

Tinkler had every right to make such a decision. In football the referee always has the final say on matters of opinion and fact. The only time a result can be changed is if it can be proven that the referee has got a law wrong when making a decision. Linesmen are there only to advise and assist.

Tony Brown ran forty yards with the ball, and then played it across goal for Jeff Astle to score.

'If you look at the tape again, Tony Brown knocked it forward and Astle's offside,' said Norman Hunter. 'He [the referee] had used his linesmen over and over again, and before that there had been an incident where we had scored. Mick Jones got up and scored a great header, and then the linesman's flag was up for some incident and we couldn't see why. It all seemed to build up and build up, and the referee went to the linesman and gave the goal, and there was absolute pandemonium.'

The linesman was now out of position, but referee Tinkler judged that Astle ran from a position behind Brown (and Tinkler was probably correct). As soon as he awarded the goal, Tinkler explained later, he knew there would be some kind of trouble because Leeds United were involved. And BBC TV commentator Barry Davies was sympathetic to Leeds:

Leeds have every justification for going mad, although one must add that they played to the linesman and not to the whistle. But you can understand the feelings of these Leeds players . . . Don Revie on the pitch . . . the linesman going over to talk to the referee . . . Don Revie, a sickened man . . . look at him, looking up to the heavens in disgust.

After Jeff Astle's goal for West Brom, most of the Leeds United players, including the goalkeeper, surrounded the referee. (Had a 1968 Chester Report recommendation been adopted, only the two captains would have been permitted to speak with the referee.) Some players protected the referee, but the linesman over the other side of the ground, Colin Cartlich, sank to his knees after being hit on the head by a can.

About twenty spectators, young and middle-aged, ran on to the field and swirled around angrily until police took charge. Others sat in the West Brom goal area. Beer cans, toilet rolls and sandwiches were thrown from the Kop, and cushions and coins tossed from the stand. It was some time before order was restored. West Brom went on to win 2–1, and Arsenal ended the season as champions.

After the match hundreds of Leeds United supporters went on a rampage in the city, and a small crowd gathered near the club entrance.

'Don't spare the Ref when he comes out,' shouted one man.

Ten months before this drama a group of twenty-four delegates had gathered for a four-day weekend at the Caledonian Hotel in Inverness. They attended a sumptuous Saturday-night dinner – 'dark lounge suits will be used' – and chose from a menu which included haggis and neeps, rainbow-trout meunière, tournedos Caledonian, roast Moray duckling and Scotch cheese.

The 1970 IFAB Annual General Meeting started at 10am on the Saturday morning. A working party had already studied possible changes to the wording of the world's football laws. Also on the agenda was a new system for deciding drawn Cup ties – kicks from the penalty mark.

The IFAB had ten voting members – two from each of the four British Associations and two from FIFA – and it needed agreement from four-fifths to instigate a change. The lawmakers weighed up evidence from around the world, resisting radical changes because the game was already so successful. At the same time they knew they had to tinker with a few parts to eliminate abuse of the system and maximise the enjoyment of football.

One particularly significant item was recorded in the 1970 IFAB minutes: 'The Board deprecated the emphasis placed in television recordings and television comment which challenged the authority of the referee. It was agreed to request the television authorities to refrain from any slow-motion play-back which reflected, or might reflect, adversely, on any decision of the referee.'

But IFAB had as much control over television-company policy as an Inverness shepherd over a border collie in Shepherd's Bush. In 1961 a disputed goal meant a *local* dispute; in 1971 a televised disputed goal meant a *national* dispute.

An estimated 10.85 million people watched *Match of the Day* on 17 April 1971. Television images of the Leeds United–West Brom incident show Don Revie gently putting his arm around linesman Bill Troupe and urging him to speak to the referee. The tall Ray Tinkler bends to listen to Troupe, while players strain to hear. Revie departs from the pitch shaking his head, later saying, 'Tinkler ruined nine months of hard work.' And West Brom manager Alan Ashman was annoyed that the *Match of the Day* coverage detracted from West Brom's fine performance and well-deserved win.

On the Sunday after the match Ray Tinkler's wife fielded supportive phone calls from 8.30am to 10.30pm. The abuse came later. While Tinkler tried to get on with his day job as a company secretary, he was condemned by the *Evening Post* in Leeds ('The Goal That Never Should Have Been') and had to deal with a bomb threat, abusive phone calls and poison-pen letters. He described the letters as 'postmarked Leeds, not very well written and all anonymous'. Police protection was needed.

One good thing about the television coverage was that Tinkler was able to watch the incidents himself and feel relieved that his decisions were correct. Other referees might (or might not) have viewed the incident differently, but there should have been no challenging of Tinkler's decision. Leeds United fans were unwilling to blame Norman Hunter for his *two* intercepted passes within a few seconds. Most would have agreed with Mrs P Kirkham of Strickland Avenue, who wrote to the local newspaper to say 'they always seem to have to play eleven men, a referee and a linesman'.

Don Revie called for full-time referees and said he could understand why the crowd cut loose. His chairman, Alderman Percy Woodward, was even more inflammatory. 'They were men of maturity who acted as they did because they were incensed by the decision of one man,' Woodward said of the pitch invaders. 'There was every justification for it.' Leeds United were eventually fined £750 by a joint Football League and FA inquiry, and Elland Road was closed for the first four home matches of the following season.

Inside a professional football club the manager is clearly the manager. He runs the playing side of the club and is called Boss or Gaffer as a measure of respect. He generally has the final say on team selection and player recruitment. At Leeds United in April 1971 Don Revie had just completed ten years in charge. Revie dictated his players' lives. He banned long hair, beards, moustaches and jeans. He demanded ties and grey suits on match days. He sent little presents to the players' wives.

Revie had a lot of control but, like all football managers, he had to concede authority for the most important period of the week – from when the referee steps on to the pitch before a match to when the referee leaves at the end. Giving up control isn't always an easy thing for a Boss to do. Sometimes he will walk into a post-match press conference and behave like a referee's assessor – 'The referee got it wrong' – as if to reassert his own authority. Yet most managers have very little refereeing experience themselves.

In April 1971 Leeds United lost a key match they thought they should have won. But their general approach to football left them with little sympathy. More importantly, they discovered that their persuasive brand of professionalism could not influence the decision of a strong-willed referee who knew what he saw and stuck by his decision. The moral of the story should have been simple: play to the whistle and abide by the referee's decision. But the matter was complicated by two new core features of modern football – gamesmanship and television.

19

'MUM, THEY HAVEN'T GOT TAILS'

THE FIRST-EVER HIGHFIELD RANGERS MATCH was at Peckleton, a small village eight miles west of Leicester. The Highfield Rangers' under-eighteen players and supporters arrived in a hired double-decker bus, and it was like they had come from another planet. Curtains twitched and local people laughed. It must have been very strange for all those white people to see a group of black lads turn up for a game of football in England in 1970. Maybe they were laughing at the rickety bus or, more likely, at the whole idea of black people playing football. They soon stopped laughing. Highfield Rangers won that game easily.

That first match set a pattern. Everywhere they played, especially in the country villages, Rangers could sense the locals talking about them. On the pitch they called for the ball from Kenrick, Solomon and Delroy rather than, say, Kev, Steve and Dave.

The Rangers players had their patience stretched by on-the-pitch insults and touchline taunts:

'Get these black bastards.'

'They're no better than animals.'

'Mum, they haven't got tails like you said they would have.'

The Highfield Rangers' discipline was poor in those early days. They were young bucks. There were fines for late starts or for playing with ten men. When the insults came flying their way, when they were constantly called 'Nigger', 'Coon', 'Wog' and 'Golly off the jam jar', when the monkey noises were chorused from the sidelines, the Rangers players sometimes felt the need to respond. They had set about proving themselves as footballers and now they had to prove themselves as men.

One day, early in the club's history, Rangers played a Cup tie in a Leicestershire village. This was probably the villagers' first face-to-face meeting with African-Caribbeans. The two teams changed in different sheds.

When Highfield Rangers came out, a little late, they were laughed at. Their kit was not ironed and looked a mess, and, of course, they were abused about their colour.

On the field that day the tension built up until a fight broke out between two opponents. Both players were sent off. But it didn't stop there. The Rangers player followed his opponent into the home-team shed and soon there was a rumpus with lots of hollering and the shed moving from side to side. The game stopped and everyone rushed over. The fight was broken up – just before the shed was – and, after a few minutes of discussion, the match continued.

In the 1960s a wave of young children came to Leicester from the Caribbean. Usually their fathers arrived first, found jobs and sent for the rest of the family. In some cases the children were left in the West Indies with grandparents, who later waved the kids on to planes or saw them off on nineteen-day boat trips, telling them that the streets of the Mother Country were paved with gold. In Britain life would be better, happier and richer.

The Caribbean children came from different West Indian islands. They had been mostly raised in rural communities where coconuts grew and sheep roamed. In the West Indies they had dirt tracks. The children could go around barefoot and enjoy swimming in the sun or playing on the beach. They could fish or kill birds with a catapult. The only threat to the relaxed lifestyle was an occasional hurricane or whirlwind. But Leicester's Highfields housing estate was very different. The West Indian families clustered together in flats in converted large houses. Later shale-coloured tower blocks were erected to accommodate them.

In the West Indies almost everybody was black. In England almost everybody was white. The language was the same but the language was different; West Indian patois was not the same as BBC English. One child was warned that when men started beating you up in England it was a problem because there was no loose stones on the English roads and therefore nothing to hit back with.

Arriving in Britain was certainly a shock. In Leicester the young Caribbean children learned about snow and ice, and they experienced chilblains and freezing ears. Instead of being barefoot they needed fur boots. Early-morning wake-up calls came from an alarm clock rather than a crowing cock, and life was much less easy-going. There were more rules in the United Kingdom. You couldn't fire a catapult at birds and you had to go to school. The streets were paved with concrete rather than gold and the new M1 motorway carried traffic past Leicester.

In the West Indies sport meant *cricket* – these children worshipped Garfield Sobers and Wesley Hall – but a Leicester winter called for football and rugby. Slowly these Caribbean boys began to study black international footballers such as Eusebio and Pelé. When the *Match of the Day* highlights programme was switched from BBC2 to BBC1 in 1965 the black kids of Highfields were inspired by two professional players called Best. Manchester United's working-class Irish Protestant George Best was an icon because of his Brazilian-style dribbling, trickery and arrogance, and West Ham United's Clyde Best was a role model because he had been born in Bermuda and brought up in London. Clyde Best proved that it was possible to come from the Caribbean and become a professional footballer.

The young West Indian immigrants played for their school team in Leicester and joined a youth club. A report by a white youth worker captured the mood of the young Caribbean lads in 1969: 'The older five contained a number of brilliant footballers but their biggest enemies were themselves. They were players of extremes; when on top they were devastating, but if they got off to a bad start they would go completely to pieces. A marked shortness of temper characterised this team and the leader with them needed to be one move ahead all the time to foresee what might happen next. As with the basketball team, these lads needed plenty of encouragement, especially when things were going wrong.'

In Leicester there were already ethnic-minority adult teams. A Saturday team, Sapna Old Boys, consisting mainly of Asian Sikhs, trained twice a week and played in Spinney Hill Park. A Sunday team called Caribbean were becoming established. Then, one day, around the time of the 1970 World Cup Finals, the Highfields boys sensed the scale of their football interest and said, 'Let's make our own football team. Let's play on a more organised basis rather than kicking around with ourselves.'

This rallying call is as old as organised football. It may come from a bunch of pub regulars, workmates, churchgoers, school-leavers, cricketers, villagers, youth-club members or rebels from another football club. Some clubs are short-lived, many achieve local stability and a few achieve national notoriety. Even the big clubs started in such a manner. Newton Heath (later Manchester United) was once a district club. Thames Ironworks (later West Ham United) was a works club set up by a patrician East End industrialist.

Every new club needs a name. The Caribbean boys assessed several alternatives – Raven, Highfield United, Biafran Underdogs – before choosing Highfield Rangers. They all lived in Highfields and they wanted to represent the area. They began with an under-eighteen team in the Leicestershire & Rutland Under-Eighteen Youth Competition.

The young lads learned that people were needed to handle bank accounts, match fees and balance sheets (a treasurer), fixtures and transport (a secretary) and the playing side (a manager). The secretary also had to learn the regulations for local leagues and the Leicestershire FA – colour clashes, player eligibility, pitch regulations, goalnets, substitutes, team information sheets, postponements, payment of referees, protests, appeals, Cup ties and even the maintenance of trophies.

There are books on how to form your own club. What the books don't tell you is how your club survives when almost all your players are black and theirs are all white. You form a club to feel safe in the local community and to provide community spirit, then you find that every match leaves you feeling unsafe. Nevertheless, the tasks of running a club enabled the committee members to develop useful skills and establish some control over their lives.

The founders of Highfield Rangers wanted to build something they could call their own in order to deal with the key problem they were facing – racial prejudice. In the act of building their community, however, they had to face up to the very thing they were trying to protect themselves from. They had to travel to hostile villages. They had to recognise that football could be ugly at times.

The Highfield Rangers team usually had a couple of white players and a couple of Asian origin. One white Rangers player, Malcolm, played for years and for a long time never really noticed being the only white player in the team (because he had grown up with the other lads and gone to school with them). Then he found himself thinking about it a lot, especially when opponents abused him ('What are you doing playing for these black bastards?'). Malcolm stayed loyal to his team-mates, who told him that he was now getting some idea of how they were feeling.

Rangers players were also suspicious of referees. They thought that white referees were biased in their decisions, and even in their choice of where to change and in their handshakes. There were no black referees. Combating racism wasn't high on a white referee's agenda in the 1970s.

*   *   *

Highfield Rangers players believed in a particular style of football. The game should be played at a fast pace, and players should be given the opportunity to express themselves. The lads were allowed their little tricks and flicks on the ball, and were encouraged to dribble past opponents. It was positive football and team-mates expected the unexpected. It was the football equivalent of calypso-style cricket, where players were encouraged to go for their shots.

When the original cohort of players became too old for youth football, Rangers became a club for adult players and joined the Leicester Mutual League (in 1972). Starting in Division Eight, they won promotion after promotion, until they reached the League's Premier Division in 1978. Later, when three applications to the elite Leicestershire Senior League were rejected, Rangers players and officials claimed that it was because they were good and black, and because other teams felt threatened by such an unusual and successful club. The official explanation was that their facilities and poor disciplinary record counted against them. But it took twenty years for the Leicestershire Senior League to relent.

Highfield Rangers worked on improving their discipline without losing their distinctive style. They gradually internalised the idea that beating teams at football was the best retort to racism. They learned to unclench their fists and hold their tongues, and they hoped that people might dismantle their racist attitudes if Rangers were seen to be winning. There were even places where the Rangers players were applauded off the field.

For years Rangers looked around for a ground of their own. Their opportunity, perversely, came after the 1981 riots. Lord Scarman's report on the Brixton riots called for local authorities and central government to provide resources and support for inner-city areas. Scarman singled out the need to take positive action to overcome the disadvantages suffered by black people. The idea was that rioting could be quelled by offering sports facilities.

There was no green space in Highfields, but Rangers' application to develop a site in nearby Rushey Mead was accepted. A grant came from the local authority, and work began on levelling the old rubbish tip and picking stones off the ground. A year was spent waiting for the land to settle. The Rangers players and the club's supporters were thrilled, though others warned that this was just another form of racism – pigeon-holing black people as 'good for sport but little else'. The new clubhouse became a social club, hosting social events and other games, and a women's team and an under-twelve boys' team were later formed.

*   *   *

The second generation of African-Caribbeans in Leicester perhaps took more for granted than did their parents (but that is said in most amateur clubs). This new generation were born and bred in Britain, and they were brought up with more of an English-style game. When the distinction between amateurs and professionals was ditched, cash payments became more commonplace in local leagues. The best players in the Highfields catchment area now went off to local senior league clubs for £40 or £50 a match. The older generation called them a bunch of mercenaries.

The progress of black players into top-class professional football was slower than their talent deserved. The Highfield Rangers lads suspected that the culture wasn't ready for them at high-level clubs, and it wasn't until the late 1980s that an ex-Rangers player, Dion Dublin, got a sustained chance at the professional game.

In the sixties and seventies the prevailing feeling among Football League managers was that black players couldn't handle the cold or the tough atmosphere of football. Black players were labelled 'chicken' and 'coward' and tactical talks from white managers suggested 'Kick this coloured lad early on'. In his book *Colouring Over the White Line* Phil Vasili shows that this is a complicated tale, stretching back to black professionals such as Arthur Wharton and Walter Tull before the First World War. Those who did make it through had to accept matey jokes about their colour.

'At least your bruises don't show.'

'You've got an unfair advantage in the dark.'

'Next tackle, I'll squeeze you like a blackhead.'

Charlie Williams, a tough black defender, played for Doncaster Rovers throughout the 1950s and later forged a career as a stand-up comedian. His stories were about terraced houses, outside toilets, coalmining and sport. His jokes often played to people's racial prejudices by highlighting his own origins ('I've been left in the oven too long'). Williams decided to deal with racial prejudice by making people laugh rather than by fighting.

The Caribbean lads of Highfield Rangers, raised in warm rural areas, clearly adapted to the colder urban setting of an English football season. They proved wrong the notion that black players couldn't handle an English winter or the physicality of football. And the influx of more and more black professional footballers has reinforced that point. But this raises other questions about the English climate. Was there something about the weather that enabled football to develop at the expense of cricket, rugby or hockey?

Does the national style of play depend on climate, which itself shapes the characteristics of local people?

'I can't see myself leaving Rangers, I'll always be a member,' said one Highfield Rangers veteran, when interviewed in the early 1990s. 'As long as I am around and have got any sense, Highfield Rangers will remain, it will never change. I can go into Highfields and feel at home.'

20

'NEVER IN MY LIFE . . .'

We have an absolute explosion up here. Thousands of them have invaded the field. They've rushed from one end to the other. From the Newcastle end to where the Nottingham Forest spectators are. The game has stopped altogether. The players are off the field. The referee has taken the players off the field. There's only one reason for them doing this – it's to stop this wonderful Cup tie. Some are fighting with the police. We've had a stand-up battle in the middle of the field with one man on top of a policeman, and now the policemen are yanking them off, several at a time. They are just yanking them off. They're frog-marching them off. Never in my life have I seen a situation, or a scene, on any English football ground, quite like this.

B EFORE THE SIXTH-ROUND FA CUP tie between Newcastle United and Nottingham Forest, John Lawson of the *Nottingham Evening Post* wrote that Newcastle United had experienced 'a recent Cup history as black as the stripe in their shirts'. The past sixteen seasons had brought Newcastle nine third-round exits and six fourth-round defeats. There had been defeats by Third Division Peterborough United, non-League Bedford Town, Second Division Carlisle United, Third Division (North) Scunthorpe United and non-League Hereford United.

Newcastle's failure was aggravated by Second Division Sunderland's 1973 FA Cup Final victory over hot favourites Leeds United. Despite unemployment running at 7.5 per cent, that FA Cup success had boosted Sunderland to the envy of the Geordies. At Wearmouth Colliery, in the heart of the Sunderland FC catchment area, production rose by 30 per cent in the spring of 1973, and record levels of output were reported in the Sunderland shipyards and light-engineering factories.

Newcastle United fans, by comparison, were in the FA Cup doldrums. In 1974 they feared a Hereford repeat after home draws to non-League

Hendon (in the third round) and Fourth Division Scunthorpe United (in the fourth round). But Newcastle won the replays comfortably and beat West Brom away in the fifth. All seemed to be back on track, until they fell 3–1 behind to Second Division Nottingham Forest at St James' Park on Saturday 9 March 1974. That was when the distinctive voice of BBC radio correspondent Bill Bothwell was heard across the country and the game's ruling authorities simply had to consider their response.

We have an absolute explosion up here . . .

Jim Barron came from Tantobie, a village about eight miles from Newcastle upon Tyne. He grew up supporting Newcastle United and learned that football was life or death on Tyneside. When United won the 1955 FA Cup Final Barron was an eleven-year-old boy who worshipped 'Wor' Jackie Milburn. En route to that Final Newcastle beat Nottingham Forest after three matches. In the second replay Jack Milburn tore stomach muscles, an injury that thereafter dogged his career.

As a promising teenage goalkeeper Jim Barron went for trials at St James' Park, but he opted to move from the Newcastle area. He signed for Wolves, then transferred to Chelsea, where he got stuck in the Reserves behind England goalkeeper Peter Bonetti. Barron was nearly twenty-seven when Nottingham Forest signed him for £35,000 from Oxford United.

Jim Barron was superstitious. On a winning streak he would dress for match days in the same suit, same shirt, same tie and same underpants. In the goal-mouth before a game he would ritually touch the floor, touch the crossbar and kick both posts. For years he scored a line through the grass from the middle of the six-yard line to the goal-line – until referees started cautioning goalkeepers for marking the pitch. Lately, however, Barron's Saturday routine had occasionally become a Sunday routine. (The coalminers' ban on overtime had led to energy shortages, forcing the football authorities to stop floodlight matches and switch some matches to Sundays.)

Barron still had friends and relatives who were Newcastle United season-ticket holders. For the Cup tie at Newcastle he made sure that his mother was there because she was Nottingham Forest's lucky mascot. Having watched Forest six times that season, she had yet to see them lose. Barron's Forest team-mates felt reassured at her presence, just as they were boosted by Duncan McKenzie's 'lucky haircut' on the Friday before the match.

*   *   *

The all-ticket St James' Park crowd of 54,500 included 13,000 Nottingham Forest fans. The basic entrance fee was 50p. The match was thrilling. The atmosphere was electric.

The captains tossed up. Newcastle fans sang 'Blaydon Races' and Forest fans sang 'Robin Hood'. Inside the first two minutes Ian Bowyer collected a through-pass from Martin O'Neill and scored for Forest. Fighting had already started behind the Gallowgate goal and police went to sort it out.

Newcastle fans chanted 'Ha'way the lads'. Police had words with fans as Forest's George Lyall tried to take a corner-kick. The fighting continued and fans of both clubs were ejected. David Craig equalised for Newcastle after twenty-six minutes, but Liam O'Kane put Forest ahead again just before half-time.

Then, in the fifty-fifth minute, a crucial incident occurred. Referee Gordon Kew awarded Forest a penalty-kick. Craig was adjudged to have held the troublesome McKenzie. The Newcastle United fans in the Leazes End were angry.

'Craig was off-balance and falling.'

'McKenzie's made the most of it.'

Frustrated home fans pushed forward and began to crush younger fans at the front. The Leazes End was clearly too full. Some youths went pitch-side to escape the pressure. The police contained the spill-over.

Then, before the penalty-kick was taken, the combustible Newcastle United centre half Pat Howard was sent off. Lyall scored from the penalty and Forest led ten-man Newcastle 3–1. A few Forest fans celebrated on the pitch in front of the Gallowgate End.

Play continued but the ground was now seething. Two goals down with ten men seemed like a hopeless position for the home team. Three minutes after the penalty Forest were awarded a free-kick ten yards outside the Newcastle penalty area. It was the signal for a balding 45-year-old self-employed builder called Leonard Conroy to make his way through the packed crowd to the front of the terrace.

'Come on,' he shouted to no one in particular. 'Let's stop the game.'

'We want a riot,' others responded.

'We're going on the pitch.'

Conroy was no typical football hooligan. A father of five schoolchildren, he was watching his first match for twenty-five years. But he had been drinking heavily. Now he moved on to the pitch, leading the cavalry charge, and it looked like he wanted to take on the police force single-handedly. He hit one policeman in the face and kicked another in the back. Between 300 and 500 spectators followed him. Most were teenagers.

As the referee took the players off, Forest defender Dave Serella was attacked by twin brothers. One jumped at him with both feet and knocked him over. The other tried to kick him. When a linesman stepped in to protect Serella, he was knocked down too. Forest's Martin O'Neill was also struck.

The game has stopped altogether . . .

Jim Barron was the last player to leave the field. He was later accused of making a V-sign to the crowd after the third Forest goal. He explained that he had been showing the score (three fingers on one hand and one on the other). Also, he said, he couldn't have caused the trouble because the pitch invaders ran past him. He was able to leave the field safely.

There were seventy police officers inside the ground, seventy outside and a few police dogs and police horses. They dealt with the trouble quickly. Forty fans were ejected that day (including a few Forest fans) and thirty-nine spectators were later charged with violent conduct (including fourteen from Forest). Twenty-three people required hospital treatment (two with fractured skulls) and 103 received first-aid treatment at the ground, including some youngsters who had been crushed against barriers. Leonard Conroy was arrested and later sentenced to six months in prison.

During the eight-minute delay before the match continued referee Gordon Kew surveyed the pitch scene wearing a detective's raincoat over his refereeing kit. It was a traumatic experience for him but he had no thought of abandoning the game, no desire to let the hooligans win. His main worry was for the safety of the players, and how long the delay would be. Dave Serella received some treatment in the dressing-room and Jim Barron began working through his superstitions again.

In the Newcastle United dressing-room one player was Barron's mirror image. While Barron had grown up eight miles from Newcastle and had once been on trial at Newcastle United, striker John Tudor hailed from Ilkeston, eight miles from Nottingham, and was on Forest's books as a fifteen-year-old. Three of Tudor's Forest-supporting relatives were at the match.

It was Tudor who now cajoled the Newcastle players.

'We can still win this game,' he told them, when he saw team-mates with their heads down, 'even with ten men.'

Tudor honestly believed that Newcastle had a chance. After all, Forest had a young team, their rhythm would be disturbed and St James' Park was feverish.

The referee has taken the players off the field . . .

The last thirty-five minutes of this turbulent Cup tie belonged to a different game. Newcastle's ten men gave it everything, the raucous crowd sensed a possible transformation and the Forest lads lost momentum and cohesion.

The referee awarded Newcastle a penalty for an alleged push by goalkeeper Jim Barron on Malcolm Macdonald. Barron was furious, but Terry McDermott scored.

Newcastle United 2 Nottingham Forest 3.

John Tudor equalised with a flying header.

Newcastle United 3 Nottingham Forest 3.

Bedlam.

Bobby Moncur scored Newcastle's winning goal, but Forest manager Allan Brown later claimed that the referee favoured Newcastle after the hold-up.

Newcastle United 4 Nottingham Forest 3.

The final result.

Well, not quite.

The FA Cup still offered a special kind of entertainment. Each tie was decided by chance, so the FA Cup created unfamiliar fixtures. In the 1973–4 season the draw produced Formby v Oldham Athletic, Bideford v Bristol Rovers and Grantham v Middlesbrough. Ties like these brought excitement and novelty for small clubs, whose officials had to organise ticket sales, extra police and sometimes a different venue. Clubs tried to identify – and give first choice of tickets to – diehard supporters by asking them to save vouchers from match programmes.

Above all, FA Cup ties offered fans of smaller clubs the chance to see major stars and visit new places. In January 1974 Oxford United supporters watched Denis Law, Mike Summerbee and Rodney Marsh share five Manchester City goals, and fans of Willington FC set off from the North-East for a replay at Blackburn Rovers, a top club with a great Cup tradition.

Reporters commonly described the FA Cup as magical, romantic and special. They kept clichés about 'giantkilling' and 'major upset' at the ready. During the 1970s Wrexham FC played thirty-eight FA Cup matches, and only eight were against teams from the same division. Only the FA Cup could take Wrexham fans on adventures to Southampton, Goole, Blyth,

Tottenham, Sunderland and Newcastle. Of course, it helped that Wrexham got wins or draws at all those places.

There was one other important difference about the FA Cup. It was organised and managed by the FA rather than by the Football League, a point that would prove significant when it came to the Newcastle–Forest tie.

'The sympathy to be extended to Nottingham Forest is now of no avail,' wrote Geoffrey Green in Monday's edition of *The Times*. 'They were hounded out of the Cup by the criminal behaviour of an undisciplined horde who think that they own football. Unfortunately they can certainly influence it. The real punishment for the Tyneside hooligans would have been for the match to be abandoned and awarded to Nottingham Forest.'

Forest appealed to the FA and their secretary, Ken Smales, personally delivered a written submission to London. Forest chairman Jim Willmer said, 'If this result is allowed to stand, it will be the biggest mockery football in this country has ever known.'

The *Nottingham Evening Post*'s leading letter that evening was from a Newcastle United fan, Jean Yates, who said that 'the vast majority of Geordie fans were as appalled by this behaviour as were the supporters from Nottingham'. The *Newcastle Evening Chronicle* also led with a fan of the other side. S. A. W. Simpson, a Forest fan for forty years, expressed his 'utter disgust at the scenes of bad sportsmanship displayed by the crowd'.

In Newcastle two letter-writers focused solely on the great fight-back. Another praised the police for dealing with the problem 'quickly and professionally', and M. Conroy of Ashington suggested that Newcastle should concede the tie to Forest as a gesture of sportsmanship. Nobody blamed Pat Howard for getting sent off, but two Geordies were quick to chastise Jim Barron – one for his alleged V-sign, the other for giving away a silly penalty.

The most severe criticism, however, was directed at the BBC's Bill Bothwell. M. Rose of Newcastle pointed out that the commentator's description of the pitch being invaded by 'thousands of hooligans' was 'the grossest exaggeration'.

Thousands of them have invaded the field . . .

At a four-man FA Cup committee meeting held on the following Thursday, the 4–3 match was declared 'null and void'. It would have to be played again at a neutral venue. Also, Newcastle United were banned from playing any 1975 FA Cup matches at home.

Edward Grayson, a barrister who specialised in sports law, felt that the FA and the clubs had missed a great opportunity.

'That really was the green light to hooliganism,' Grayson said twenty years after the incident at St James' Park, 'because the FA failed to grasp the nettle and do their job and their duty to the game which they inherited from the great pioneers in the past.'

'My reaction is one of disgust, but not surprise,' said Newcastle United striker Malcolm Macdonald. 'I half expected a ridiculous solution and they have certainly come up with one.' Macdonald was charged with bringing the game into disrepute.

Ian Jones, a Nottingham Forest fan, reflected on the incident years later: 'I was at the Newcastle v Forest FA Cup tie in 1974, and for the only time in my life I was frightened at a football match. The FA's answer to this? Nothing.'

A compromise solution was to be expected. Three members of the four-man committee were directors of League clubs. They mixed in boardrooms with directors from other clubs and wanted to keep the harmony. One of this particular committee, Sam Bolton, had been on trial with his club, Leeds United, after the 1971 offside incident. Now it was the turn of Lord Westwood (Newcastle United), another FA Council member, to defend his club. Newcastle United had already been in trouble for a series of pitch invasions, including a serious one during the Manchester United match in November 1973. The FA failed to get a grip on this latest incident because there was no independent judgement, no clearly defined rules and no designated punishment laid out in advance.

Denis Howell, the minister responsible for sport, set up a working party to consider football hooliganism. Between August 1970, when spectators invaded Plymouth Argyle's pitch after the match, and October 1976, when drunken Glasgow Rangers fans caused the abandonment of a friendly at Aston Villa, the FA dealt with 129 spectator incidents. These included pitch invasions (38 per cent), the throwing of objects such as beer bottles, whisky bottles, billiard balls, cushions, coins, stones, darts, cans, a six-foot length of steel, a lump of coal, a cup, a roof tile, a thermos flask and a smoke bomb (33 per cent), match officials being threatened or attacked (15 per cent) and match officials or players being hit by missiles (11 per cent).

The FA's overall punishment record was incredibly light-handed. In sixty-two of the 129 cases the FA took no action because the club had taken 'all reasonable precautions'. In most other cases clubs were asked to post warning notices in the official programme and around the ground. Only seven cases warranted further punishment. Five were fines between £50 and £200 and the other two were the ground closures (and fines) at Leeds United and Manchester United.

'What a load of yellow-bellied people you have become,' H. Johnson of Ware wrote to the FA, before suggesting that offending clubs should be suspended from all matches for a month (with loss of points). 'Where you get roughnecks like McKay [sic], Docherty and the present England manager [Don Revie] having charge of teams, it certainly is to do with the clubs.'

'Fencing them in at the grounds wont [sic] help people outside the grounds,' wrote Mrs Z. Price of Withington, Manchester. 'These BARBARIC SAVAGES commit most of their destruction after they have left the match. When United lost to Ipswich at the end of last season, some of the United thugs went round with broom handles sawn in half, and nails knocked in the end, bashing up innocent animals. My cat was a victim, and my sister's poor thing had her head nearly bashed off. A dog near here had a knife plunged in its side. And had to be destroyed. Yet United wont [sic] listen, they never even acknowledge your letters.'

Other ideas from members of the public included taking teams off the field for at least ten minutes, introducing identity cards, getting culprits to pay their fines in instalments at 3.30pm on Saturdays, stopping all the 'progressive teaching' in schools and flogging the hooligans.

There was more drama left in the Newcastle United v Nottingham Forest Cup saga. When the rescheduled match ended 0–0 at Goodison Park, extra time was played, as if it were a replay after all. A third meeting proved necessary and the FA had to make another decision about the venue. They opted for a neutral ground again. This time Newcastle won 1–0 at Goodison.

Not one of the three matches was staged in Nottingham. The FA committee felt that the atmosphere at the City Ground would be too intimidating and that there might be reprisals if Forest fell behind. It was no comfort to Forest fans.

In fact Newcastle United did very well out of the pitch invasion. They came back to win a match that was all but lost, and gained television income and gate receipts from four more FA Cup matches – two against Forest on a neutral ground, a semi-final against Burnley and a lucrative Wembley Final which they lost 3–0 to Liverpool.

The FA's leniency in the Newcastle case inadvertently made father-of-five pitch-invader Leonard Conroy an unlikely figure in the escalation of terrace belligerence in the late 1970s.

Never in my life have I seen a situation, or a scene, on any English football ground, quite like this . . .

DON'T CALL US, WE'LL CALL YOU

T HE GREY-HAIRED MAN HAS THE walk of a former footballer. He is pigeon-toed, well-balanced and seems sprightly for a man of his age. His aura conveys gravitas and experience. Other spectators think there is something familiar about him.

He makes his way to a seat in the grandstand or, if he is lucky, towards a seat in the directors' box. Occasionally he stands on the touchline. Today he sits near the halfway-line, where he can study the whole of the ground.

He leans forward slightly in his seat, his hands clasped between his knees, concentrating on the play. He assesses everything quietly. He has seen it all before; or it feels that way to him. He sits among strangers and the match result does not particularly interest him. He may not stay to watch the whole match. When controversy breaks out around him, while fans curse and shout, the grey-haired man sits quietly and smiles to himself.

He is a scout.

He is involved.

He worked for Nottingham Forest in the early 1970s, after Forest assistant manager Bill Anderson phoned him out of the blue and offered decent expenses. He soon discovered that Anderson, strangely for a football man, had a poor sense of geography.

Scouting involved travel, and travel involved danger. Floodlit fixtures added to the problem and there were instances of scouts being killed or maimed late at night on icy roads. This Forest scout worked as a sales representative and lived near the A38 in Staffordshire. He was well situated for a lot of football grounds and, in five years of scouting, Bill Anderson sent him to most of them, particularly Walsall, Chesterfield and Sheffield. The scout never turned a match down, even if it meant a long trip, but he learned to confirm the game before setting off. On two occasions he arrived to find that Anderson had read the fixtures incorrectly.

Football scouts could be unlucky. Our man went to watch Bruce Bannister (Bradford City) and Michael Elwiss (Doncaster Rovers) only to find that they weren't playing that day. He travelled to Hull to see Chris Garland (Bristol City) and arrived a few minutes late, just as they were carrying the unfortunate player off on a stretcher with concussion and a broken nose. In his report he said, 'I can't comment on his play but he bleeds well.' Garland later moved to Chelsea for £100,000.

One Saturday he was six miles south of Preston when he heard on the radio that Preston North End's match was one of only two postponements in the country. A match at Mansfield was called off just as he arrived at the ground, and it took him three hours to drive the thirty-six miles home in the snow. Kettering was always a frustrating ground to reach; he could see the floodlights but the one-way system always seemed to divert him into the railway station. On another Saturday, during the coalminers' overtime ban in December 1974, a reserve match at West Bromwich started at 2pm so he missed the first half.

When watching a match he assessed the standard of the play, the pace of the game and its skill level. His first question was, 'What would happen if we took a player out of this match and put him in another team in another league?' Then he looked at the individual. Does he have good balance? Does he have pace and speed off the mark? Does he have determination and courage? Does he have the necessary ball skills? Is he capable of 'reading the game' by predicting the course of the ball and other players.

Skill is making the difficult look easy in the shortest time to the greatest effect with the minimum amount of effort. It must be transferable from one situation to another, in particular to situations of greater importance. It must also be sustainable – from match to match, week to week, month to month. Scouts studied a player's injury and illness history. Assessing the player's character involved chatting to trusted people about the player's reputation and habits, watching his interaction with other players on the field and studying his body language. It could involve a bit of snooping and questions about his family. Let's stand on the terrace and hear what spectators say about him. What does his previous manager think? What's he like with the other players in the dressing-room? Above all, does he desperately want to win? It was even worthwhile standing next to a fancied player and judging his true height and weight. Sometimes statistics were designed to deceive.

When submitting reports our anonymous scout worked on the principle that the manager and chief scout were busy men. He kept his reports brief. Some scouts used a teacher's marking system. Harry Storer, scouting for Everton, once wrote 'COWARD' across a report form.

On the one hand football's recruitment system was full of subjectivity and personal judgement. On the other hand it was very sophisticated. Where else in the world of employment would a recruiter travel to a competitor's workplace, watch the candidate work and listen to what others say? Football clubs looked for direct evidence of a player's ability to do the job. The candidate was watched in action. Football's recruitment system didn't depend on notoriously unreliable interviews. Even when recruitment eventually involved agents, academies and work permits, there was still a place for the dogged scout, putting in the miles, searching for gems.

In lower-league football the recruitment of players was more haphazard. The rewards were smaller, the mistakes less costly. Recruitment was often made through an informal contact. The incentives could be a little money, a good atmosphere, a better standard of play or the chance to win a trophy. The higher levels of local football were full of very talented players whose progress had been stopped by discipline flaws – a weakness for drink or women, a liking for their beds rather than hard work, or an overdeveloped sense of self-preservation.

Some scouts spent all their time watching young players in local football. They bought maps of their local area and marked the playing fields. They collected handbooks of local leagues and made contacts with club officials and teachers. They read reports of local matches. They watched players of eleven and older, usually viewing them at least twice, and they approached promising boys through their teachers, headmasters and parents. If a scout lived near the club ground he became a general factotum – picking up parcels, organising trials, acting as a taxi driver and carrying the sponge at lower-team matches.

Our Forest scout met a lot of ex-players who were also scouting, and they enjoyed each other's company. Sitting next to Joe Mercer at Crewe one day, listening to Mercer's comments on Crewe's Stan Bowles ('If only he could go past bookmakers like he goes past opponents'), they all agreed that a tall, raw Gillingham wing half was overrated. Just before the end of the match the player was completely outpaced by the Crewe winger.

'Christ,' said Mercer, 'He can't run either.'

Another time at Crewe a group of scouts talked for so long after a Saturday-afternoon match that they had to lock up the ground themselves and push the keys through the groundsman's letter-box.

'I could have had Bryan Robson for free, y'know.'

'You're the sixth one I've heard say that.'

'I'll probably see you next Saturday as well.'

'Yeah, we can't go on meeting like this.'

'I think you must be scouting me.'

One day Bill Anderson sent his Midlands man to Redditch to assess a young prospect. In the town centre the scout got caught up in the one-way system while looking for the ground. He stopped his car and asked in a shop for directions.

'I'm going to write this down,' the shopkeeper said. 'If you miss one turn, you'll have to go round again.'

The scout found the ground but it was deserted. The pitch looked immaculate, but there was no game. While exploring the Redditch one-way system again he took a wrong turn and suddenly saw a football match in a local park. Outside was a visitors' bus marked 'CAMBRIDGE CITY'.

'Yes, we're playing here now,' he was told on the gate. 'The ground's not ready for another three weeks.'

As he walked in, halfway through the first half, he saw raffle tickets on sale. He bought a ticket and won a big basket of vegetables and a chicken.

That Redditch trip was a metaphor for the whole scouting business. Scouts went all around the houses, looking for something elusive, and occasionally won an excellent prize. They watched players develop, reviewed their previous judgement and occasionally, during a match, gazed in the direction of their own youth.

22

JIMMY HILL WILL FIX IT

I T WAS THE FIRST TIME the retired hosiery mechanic had ever been afraid at a football match. The approach to his normal entrance was chock-a-block with visiting fans. It would take some nerve for a man of seventy-four to go through them and into the ground.

As a schoolboy he had regularly walked the five miles from Bedworth to watch Coventry City. He had been a lifelong City fan. He had lived through two World Wars and had seen City grow from a run-of-the-mill Third Division (South) outfit to an established First Division club.

In September 1981 this aged City fan knew that Jimmy Hill had been a very popular Coventry City manager in the 1960s, but he also knew that Hill was unpopular now that he was chairman and managing director of the club. Take this idea of replacing all the Highfield Road terraces with seats, and look at how news of the all-seater plan had been announced. Hill and his directors had alienated the fans. Many supporters had met their mates on the Spion Kop year after year after year. But not any more. Their favourite spot and their favourite friends had gone. Standing on the terraces you could talk to ten other men; sitting down you had to limit the conversation to the two next to you.

It's not a football club any more, he thought, it's a business. He'd heard more and more City fans say that recently. Look at the £1.5 million Sky Blue Connexion leisure centre that had been built by the club at Ryton. That was just a business venture, nothing to do with football, and yet it was built with money from the £1 million sale of striker Ian Wallace to Nottingham Forest. Very few Coventry fans went to the Connexion. Some called it 'The Ian Wallace Connexion'. Look, too, at the £595,000 the club had lost by investing in Washington Diplomats, an *American* soccer franchise. No Coventry fan would ever watch the Washington Diplomats. And now £350,000 had been spent on converting Highfield Road to an all-seater stadium. Think of all that money Coventry City could have spent on players.

The retired hosiery mechanic didn't like this new-look stadium. Part of the Sky Blue Stand had been allocated to away-team supporters, so the two sets of fans now mixed in the stands, in the toilets and outside the ground. There was no formal segregation. Would violent rivalries between English football fans magically disappear by forcing them into seats?

It took some nerve to go through the turnstile when surrounded by visiting Leeds United fans. Inside the ground he was even more frightened. Young fans stood on seats, broke them and threw the pieces at the police. Three officers were injured, and one required fifteen stitches to a facial cut.

One hundred seats, a toilet and a bar were seriously damaged. So much for theories about all-seater stadiums deterring troublemakers, the 74-year-old thought. And selling beer at a football ground is a bad idea. In his opinion it all worsened behaviour. OK, the view was better from seats, but that wasn't much good if you were watching hooliganism.

It was 12 September 1981. This was the second-ever match at an all-seater football stadium in England. The only good thing, for the retired hosiery mechanic, was the result. Coventry City beat Leeds United 4–0.

Six months earlier, towards the end of the 1980–1 season, Coventry City chairman Jimmy Hill talked with his board of directors about the problems within football. Hill could sense ailing finances ahead. The large crowds of the late 1960s had gone. The Football League's season aggregate attendance was below twenty million for the first time since the First World War.

People had looked at all sorts of methods for taming crowds. Coventry City had even considered a 'thumbs down to hooliganism' idea whereby all spectators would be fingerprinted so that anybody evicted from the stadium could be banned for life. But Jimmy Hill thought he had a much better plan.

'It's harder to be a hooligan when you're sitting down,' said Hill. 'Let's create an all-seater stadium.'

Some people in football saw it as another one of 'Jimmy's gimmicks'.

Jimmy Hill first came to Coventry City as manager in November 1961, shortly after a shocking 2–1 home FA Cup defeat to non-League King's Lynn. City were a Third Division club then, but Hill brought them two championships in four seasons. Home gates averaged 26,000 in 1963–4 and shortly afterwards Coventry City paid Crystal Palace a world record fee for a goalkeeper (Bill Glazier).

When local journalist Derek Henderson referred to Coventry City as the 'Sky Blues', reflecting the colour of their kit, Jimmy Hill sensed a marketing opportunity. The Sky Blue name was applied to everything associated with the club, including the official programme (*Sky Blue Magazine*) and innovative match-day trains (Sky Blue Away Day Specials).

After steering Coventry City into Division One in 1967, Jimmy Hill resigned suddenly and became Head of Sport at ITV's London Weekend Television. There he helped to create *The Big Match*, and he appeared frequently in ITV's Saturday-lunchtime programme *On the Ball*. Hill stayed five years with ITV and then set up his own football consultancy group (Jimmy Hill Ltd). He also joined the BBC *Match of the Day* team as a presenter and analyst. Hill's move from ITV to BBC was as newsworthy as Denis Law's move from Manchester United to Manchester City.

Jimmy Hill became the voice (and bearded face) of *Match of the Day* for over 600 programmes (from 1973 to 1999), during an era when television increasingly set the agenda for sport. In June 1974 he dressed as a referee for a *Radio Times* World Cup cover, his arm around Scotland captain Billy Bremner. In November 1978, when ITV broke the cosy BBC–ITV cartel (the 'Snatch of the Day'), Hill led a campaign to overturn the contract and the Office of Fair Trading eventually quashed the ITV deal as being too monopolistic. (The Football League brought legal action against Hill for remarks he made during the negotiations but the matter was settled out of court with a confidentiality clause.)

Hill wanted football to change, whereas Football League secretary Alan Hardaker was initially against the adoption of shirt-advertising ('Those who go to soccer want to see a game of football, not to be reminded every time they look at a player that they must go home and tell the wife to change her soap powder') and the exodus of players to the United States ('The League are concerned about the growing intervention of agents acting on players' behalf'). One of Hill's companies, World Sports Academy, invested profit from a Saudi Arabia contract in a money-losing American club called Detroit Express. On 27 February 1981 the Detroit franchise was moved to Washington DC, where the club became the Washington Diplomats. Coventry City joined the investors in US soccer.

English club players enjoyed good summer contracts in the USA until the League outlawed transatlantic loan deals in 1979. But English soccer was unquestionably becoming more worldly. Don Revie controversially left his job as England manager to work in the United Emirates. Tottenham Hotspur spent £700,000 on two players from Argentina's World Cup-winning team, Ossie Ardiles and Ricky Villa, and Ipswich Town signed Dutchman Arnold Muhren. Britain had joined the Common Market and each English football club was allowed two foreign players.

Hill was greeted with mixed feelings inside the world of football. He was too flash and gimmicky for some and he made enemies through his trenchant *Match of the Day* inquests. Managers moaned when Hill criticised one of their players to the nation (even if it was justified). As a qualified referee, however, Hill was concerned about the trend towards more cautions, more sendings-off and more suspensions (via the new totting-up system).

The late 1970s were an insecure time for directors of professional football clubs. Top-level transfer fees rose very sharply from £350,000 (for Joe Jordan in January 1978) to £1 million (for Trevor Francis in February 1979) and £1,469,000 (for Andy Gray in September 1979). The players' new freedom of contract would surely affect the game, and the older generation had to accept modern fashions such as long hair, flared trousers, scraggly beards and graffiti on stadium walls:

'United rule OK.'

'Chelsea are magic.'

'Watch them disappear from Division One.'

Most of all, the rulers of English soccer were concerned about what FA chairman Sir Harold Thompson called 'moronic louts and saboteurs'. Manchester United were thrown out of the European Cup Winners' Cup (but later reinstated) after crowd trouble in France, England fans caused mayhem in Luxembourg and Denmark, and Leeds United and Millwall had their grounds closed in punishment for disorder.

Jimmy Hill had his own ideas about dealing with spectators. He was an astute operator in a sport which had few of them. Maybe it was his year on the Stock Exchange that had given him confidence. Or his time as an army drill sergeant, standing in front of men and talking to them. Or perhaps it was listening to the man on the microphone at Wimbledon speedway, learning how to captivate people with clever words.

When Hill returned to Coventry City as managing director in 1975, the club was heavily in debt. Attendances then fell by 20 per cent between 1976 and 1981, part of the general trend. The authorities had tried to counter defensive football by promoting and relegating more teams and allocating three points for a win, but the truth was that football was becoming an inferior product. Poor facilities, spectator disorder and boring play all tainted the sport. Successful national teams usually stimulated spectator interest, but the England team had performed poorly in the 1970s. After her election in 1979 Prime Minister Margaret Thatcher had curbed inflation at the expense of an economic recession and massive unemployment. Many people couldn't afford to attend matches.

A *Daily Mail* survey found that fans' main reasons for staying away from matches were 'Not interested/don't enjoy it' (29 per cent) and 'No time' (29 per cent). Hooliganism was third (18 per cent) and 'Ill health/age' was fourth (10 per cent). Hooliganism was a big problem in the English game at this time – but other things were wrong too.

In his 1969 report into crowd behaviour at matches, John Lang commented that increased seating facilities could aid detection and apprehension of offenders, although it was obviously at a cost of investing in seats. An FA inquiry into the death of a fan at a 1974 Blackpool match called for 'seating all round the ground so that people can go to a match in safety'. In Scotland in the summer of 1978 Aberdeen FC made Pittodrie Park an all-seater at a cost of £1.5 million. Aberdeen took care to add toilets and washrooms of hotel standard, and the design included bright colours and plenty of room for people to circulate. The stadium capacity fell from 45,000 to 25,000, but fans were pacified. Aberdeen entered one of their most successful eras, inspired by an ambitious young manager – Alex Ferguson.

Unlike canny Aberdeen, however, Coventry City simply plonked seats on open terraces and aimed to play home matches with as few away fans present as possible. What mattered to Coventry City officials was *overall gate receipts* rather than the number of fans attending. If fewer away fans paid more for tickets that would mean higher profits and reduced crowd trouble.

In 1981 many Coventry City fans took umbrage when Jimmy Hill implied that City needed to attract a new type of supporter. Letters poured into the *Coventry Evening Telegraph* offices:

'How do thousands of loyal and sensible supporters from the terraces feel when they hear that seats will attract "the better class of supporters"?'

'There are thousands of us who prefer to stand but obviously we don't count.'

'Insulting and derisive, based on an unproven theory about hooliganism.'

Protest banners appeared, but Coventry City went ahead. Then came another storm. All Coventry City's home matches would now be all-ticket affairs.

The Football League had always set a minimum admission price, never a maximum. Now, for 1981–2, Coventry City fans could buy tickets (minimum price £2) in advance of the match, either from the official ticket office or from official ticket agencies (such as travel agents), or they could buy tickets on the day of the match (at £5 or £6). The advanced prices for away fans were the same as match-day prices for home fans. The club made it clear that they would be happy if away fans were frozen out altogether by these new pricing arrangements.

The all-seater stadium housed 19,329 people for its first match – against Manchester United. This was fewer than for the match against the same opponents less than five months earlier (20,201). This time, though, the gate receipts were £39,506 rather than £25,068.

Some supporters were suspicious of Jimmy Hill's motives. One letter-writer saw the club as 'a useful hobby for Jimmy Hill Enterprises and his socially divisive schemes'. Other fans pointed out that Hill rarely attended home matches because of his duties on the BBC's *Match of the Day*. They thought the club was just a vehicle for Hill to experiment with schemes that he had talked about on television.

Not surprisingly Coventry City's pricing policies were unpopular with the fans and officials of visiting clubs. Away-fan numbers were reduced by more than half, but *receipts* from away fans went up by around 50 per cent. The only serious hooliganism came at the Leeds United match and during an FA Cup match with Oxford United.

The Sky Blues also lost home fans. The aggregate season's attendance was down by 22 per cent on the previous season, but receipts were 15 per cent up. More importantly Coventry City's lower break-even attendance figure was the envy of almost all the First Division clubs and many Second Division clubs. There were talks of boycotts, especially among away fans, and the *Liverpool Echo* referred to Liverpool fans 'paying through the nose' at Highfield Road. The big danger was that football fans might lose the habit of attending matches.

The 74-year-old retired hosiery engineer had been a supporter too long to boycott Coventry City. Instead he moved from the Sky Blue Stand to the Main Stand. 'You enjoy the game better in the Main Stand than you do amongst that rabble,' he said. From his new seat in the Main Stand he could look directly across the ground at the Sky Blue Stand and gaze at where he used to sit. Two years later his old section in the Sky Blue Stand was almost always completely empty. He'd moved from his old seat and then nobody used it.

Coventry's population declined by 8 per cent between 1971 and 1983, average earnings fell well below the national average and its 17 per cent unemployment in 1983 was double the national figure. The boomtown of the 1960s was now, according to the number-one hit by the Specials, a 'ghost town'. Coventry City's break-even figure depended on at least 11,500 loyal fans being willing to pay the increased prices, but attendances dropped to just over 8,000 early in the 1982–3 season. Jimmy Hill argued that at least the club was finally winning the battle against hooliganism, but a home match against Aston Villa saw forty-three fans arrested, including sixteen inside the ground. After difficulty explaining some of their special ticket offers, the club eventually relented and relaxed the '£5 on the day' scheme for home fans.

In November 1982 a survey of supporters showed that Coventry City fans were 88 per cent male and 12 per cent female and they lived more locally than supporters of other top clubs. Some 90 per cent lived in Warwickshire and 65 per cent in Coventry itself. They travelled to the ground by car (68.5 per cent), bus (15.2 per cent) or on foot (11.4 per cent). Fifteen per cent had been watching for over thirty years. Here was evidence of habit.

There was some small indication that the fan base was moving up-market. Fifty per cent were non-manual workers, much higher than the composition at, say, Tottenham Hotspur (30 per cent).

'I've only just started to watch Coventry City this season,' said a 21-year-old installation engineer from Northampton. 'Three of us have bought season tickets. I've been impressed by the ground and I enjoy every game in comfort.'

Was this Jimmy Hill's 'better class of supporter'?

'For the comfort of seeing the game without having to peer through barrier fencing, for the comfort in enabling one to approach the ground without interference from hooligans and drunks, Jimmy Hill earns my eternal gratitude,' said a 67-year-old retired Rolls-Royce inspector.

When responding to a question about the perceived advantages and disadvantages of the all-seater stadium, however, it was clear that the disadvantages were uppermost in fans' minds. The negative aspects scored highly – loss of atmosphere (79.3 per cent), the inconvenience of all-ticket matches (60.5 per cent), and expense (55.8 per cent). The positive aspects were not as striking – less hooliganism (46.9 per cent), more attractive to a family audience (38.1 per cent), safer (37.2 per cent) and more comfortable (34.6 per cent).

Some people indicated that they actually felt *less safe* inside and outside the all-seater stadium.

'The atmosphere on the Sky Blue Terrace has degenerated into hate and fear, and pockets of opposition fans may be observed in verbal and physical conflict with Coventry supporters on the other terraces as well,' wrote a 21-year-old trainee surveyor. 'The chairman [Jimmy Hill] would observe the realities of the situation if he actually attended some games, preferably from the Sky Blue Stand.'

An eleven-year-old boy had some advice for the chairman: 'I think they should buy more players. You don't supply hot-water bottles so when a goal comes we are too froze to clap, we are like monuments. Mind the moth when you get your wallet out, Jim.'

Almost a quarter of the respondents called for the club to convert at least one section of the ground back to terracing. 'Stand in the rain and not get wet,' said one fan. 'Sit in the rain and you'll get soaked.' Some fans under cover actually had their enjoyment spoiled by seeing uncovered fans getting so wet.

'For many years up to a dozen of us attended matches,' wrote one fan, 'we always stood in the same place and so a last-minute decision to attend could be made and we could meet up at the same spot. The introduction of seats has meant this is no longer possible and the all-ticket games have meant that last-minute decisions cannot be made. From the dozen, only three of us are regulars (season ticket), the other nine hardly ever attend. Furthermore, now the habit has been broken, I see little prospect of getting them back.'

Perhaps the most telling comments came from an advertising executive who felt that the club's image was losing Coventry City valuable support.

'I think that the club has alienated groups of supporters, probably by class,' he wrote on his questionnaire. 'The introduction of nice facilities, restaurants, company boxes, presidents' club etc does *absolutely nothing* to attract the average working-class supporter, and he is the one who should matter most, if the average attendance is to be maintained at all.'

Coventry City's debt of £565,000 compared favourably with the debts of local rivals at Leicester City (£1.25 million), Birmingham City (£1.5

million) and Nottingham Forest (£2 million), but the playing staff had been reduced from thirty to nineteen, and there was now a £200,000 Sky Blue overdraft. Debts increased to £700,000 by January 1983, and the following month City striker Gary Thompson was sold to West Brom for £225,000 because of growing financial pressures.

Despite all this, the team did well. City were fifth in Division One when fewer than 10,000 fans watched a 0–0 league draw with Swansea City on 22 January 1983. But then a slump set in, and the Sky Blues eventually escaped relegation by only one point. Jimmy Hill was asked to resign as chairman, and manager Dave Sexton was sacked. The following season a small section of the Coventry City Kop was converted back to terracing for home supporters.

In the 1960s Jimmy Hill had brought City fans and the club closer together. In the 1980s they grew further apart. But the Coventry City scheme was about giving English football a new direction in terms of stadium facilities and spectator profiles.

Undoubtedly Hill's pioneering all-seater idea would have worked better had the Highfield Road stadium been adequately prepared for seats and all parts covered. But Jimmy Hill's self-belief and spirit of adventure meant there was no time (or money) to waste on such niceties. Hill's flirtation with the all-seater stadium was seen by many as 'just another gimmick' but Coventry City's prototype was soon to attract more interest. Professional football had come a long way from the 1950s, when less than 1 per cent of the crowd at Peel Park in Accrington were able to sit down. There was something in Hill's idea that would eventually help to save professional football.

23

IF YOU THINK YOU'RE HARD ENOUGH

'I T'S BEEN GOING ON FOR years really,' said a West Ham fan. He was sitting in the Britannia pub in East London, talking about the timeless rivalry between West Ham United and Millwall followers. 'They're the nearest thing to us sport-wise, you know. There's less of them than us, but obviously, over the years, they've got a reputation. We've had a reputation, you know, and we've always classed ourselves as pretty much top firm who travel away. And so do Millwall. They reckon they're better than us, and we obviously think we're better than them.'

'They say they're East Londoners and cockneys, but they're South Londoners,' said one of the other West Ham fans in the group. 'We're the proper cockneys, not them. And they say they come from Docklands but they don't come from Docklands.'

'They've only ever played in Second and Third Division grounds, they've never been in the First Division yet,' said a third West Ham fan. 'We've done it in the First Division. We've been everywhere in the First Division. We've been in the Second and come back up again, and we've been everywhere. What they've done is make their names for smashing things up.'

These young men were talking about intense competition and deep territorial antipathy. Football hooliganism picked up pace in England in the 1960s, 1970s and 1980s, and here was one of its key facets: *Violence at football matches was the acting out of rivalry between groups of young men in different working-class communities.*

In the late 1970s one Leicester council estate was known as Dodge City. It was so called because it was reputed to be as tough as Kansas's notorious nineteenth-century Dodge City. Also, some of its residents were known to *dodge* milkmen, rentmen and police officers. In the late 1960s British Debt

Services ranked Leicester's Dodge City as the joint biggest debtors in Britain. Some young lads had 'Dodge' tattoos. There was local pride.

Most Dodge families had a classic lower-working-class set-up. The mother was in charge of the home; the father was out, either on the scrounge or in the pub. Young men exerted proprietorial rights over their women. Fights broke out if someone was 'shagging someone else's missus' or if a boy from outside the area even looked at a Dodge girl.

It was a rough world where boys were taught not to be sissies, and sometimes that meant fighting. This led to the routine formation of male street gangs in which every member knew his place. The gang's hierarchy could be changed, of course, through special 'gameness' (aggressive behaviour that worked out to an upstart's advantage).

Football was an interest – school was not – but most Dodge football conversations were not about players, managers or matches. They were about rival ends, fights and the police response. Their Saturdays were a full day's entertainment. Their match was about far more than kicking a ball about. It was about action: clearing the home end of rival fans by threat or by force; shouting, singing, chanting, gesticulating, spitting and throwing missiles at opposing spectators, opposing players and the police; settling local disputes; boozing and 'having a laugh'; and monitoring, goading and obstructing stewards and police. It was about hanging around toilets and refreshment stalls in order to plan post-match tactics and assess thieving opportunities. It was about defending the reputation of Leicester and the Dodge City estate.

Hooligan apprenticeships began at twelve, thirteen or fourteen, when the young Dodge lads began going to matches with their elders. They learned that if one Dodge male went to a match they all went. In their football context they earned local and national respect for being known as good battlers. Respect was shown to them locally through a number of small gestures: the way other Leicester males stepped aside and strove to be on nodding terms with the key Dodge boys; the caution shown around Dodge boys by other estate crews; and the fearful stiffening of bar staff and clientele when Dodge boys walked into their usual pubs. Here was another key feature: *Hooliganism was a display of traditional working-class masculine characteristics.*

They called him 'Animal'. He originated from an East Anglian village. When he went to London he fell in love with West Ham United. He started travelling to away matches. Then, during a match at Wolves, a policeman pulled his hair.

'So I started fighting the Old Bill,' Animal said later. 'And I got arrested, like, and I got three months DC [detention centre].'

That was the first of Animal's numerous arrests. Most were for fighting at football; one was for biting a police horse.

'The reason we have to fight at football is because you've got other people, like Mancs [Manchester United and Manchester City] or Scousers [Liverpool or Everton] or Yids [Spurs] trying to take us,' explained Animal. 'They always want to fight us, because they think they can take your name and denounce you. So they can go running round, like, saying "the dumb West Ham". But they haven't, they never will. In a way you are fighting for East London, I suppose.'

When Animal travelled north for a West Ham match at Manchester United he knew something would happen. Thousands of Hammers fans made the trip. Arriving in Manchester, Animal and his InterCity Firm (ICF) mates found three or four hundred Manchester United fans waiting.

'You go through here to get the coach,' the police told the West Ham fans. The plan was to escort the visitors safely to the ground. Instead the Hammers fans broke off and ran through the lines of police. Some went round the front of the rail station; others round the side. The smaller group of West Ham fans were coming down the slope from Manchester Piccadilly station when the Manchester United fans ran at them.

'Stand,' shouted someone from West Ham. 'Just stand and 'ave it.'

They stood and fights broke out. But other West Ham groups suddenly came from behind the Manchester lads.

'We just caned them,' Animal said later. 'That was it. We just mollied 'em. That was really good.'

This was a classic example of a confrontation between rival groups of English hooligan fans: *Hooliganism was about defending your territory against the enemy and trying to take the enemy's territory.*

'British Rail used to lay special trains on,' said a West Ham fan in the Britannia pub. 'These trains were like a carriage and, you know, you sit there and you behave yourself. Loads of Old Bill on it.'

'Like cattle trucks, weren't it?' said his mate.

'Like cattle trucks, you know what I mean? Like old mail trains, you know what I mean? You sit on that and you behave yourself, and you'd ship from one station to the other, and you're led out there on to the ground. So, like, people started going by [British Rail] InterCity, like InterCity Firm. ICF.

Loads of people started doing it because they was fed up of getting pushed around by the Old Bill.'

'Then the ICF vans started. You'd hire a van for the weekend. You'd go up by van and cars. People got out of that stage of going by train.'

'West Ham's got everything.'

'It's like the whole spectrum of the thing, like being mobile to go to the game.'

'It's tribal, innit? Football is just tribal. One tribe on to another tribe. Who can go and do the next tribe. Boils down to human nature, ain't it? Any male of any species will fight another male for his territory. Like our away games. For instance, we went to Sunderland one year, right?'

'Two vans.'

'Yeah, vans. We went on a Friday night 'cos football was the whole weekend, like. You lived for your football on a Saturday.'

'We're going back now.'

'Yeah, and we was in a pub. We stopped off at a diner on the way home from Sunderland, didn't we, for a drink, right?'

'We was in a square. There was like thirty West Ham supporters and we found a pub and we only wanted a drink and a laugh. What we didn't know was that there was, like, five or six coaches of Newcastle in town. They've heard cockneys in the pub and they've come looking for us, right. The windows have come through and everything like that.'

'Some old woman got it, didn't she?'

'Yeah. But we was only interested in having a drink and a laugh, weren't we? A weekend break. Next thing we know, like, the windows come through the pub.'

'We got out. When we got out the pub, we chased them round the town.'

That incident occurred in September 1978, when West Ham played at Sunderland (a 600-mile round trip) and Newcastle United played at Nottingham Forest on the same day. In that era local residents boarded up their windows in what newspapers called 'Streets of Fear'. The British tabloid press had begun to identify hooligan firms publicly, and Manchester United had erected six-foot steel fences around the pitch to keep 'the savages' at bay. Private transport was expanding, the motorway network had reduced journey times and hooligans were more willing to spend money on travel. *Hooliganism became a major problem when it became easier and more desirable for away fans to travel to matches and confront rival fans in larger numbers.*

A battle broke out on Middlewich Station after the Cheshire Cup Final between Nantwich and Crewe. Fans of the two teams gathered on opposite platforms as they waited for their respective trains. They shouted at one another across the tracks. Then one fan picked out a specific rival and challenged him to a fight. The offer was accepted.

The two men jumped down to the railway line and began to slug it out. Railway officials followed them on to the tracks and tried to break up the fight.

Then a large number of Nantwich fans charged across the line and stormed the Crewe fans on the other platform. Neutral passengers scampered out of the way. It was a fierce battle with a number of casualties. Then the police arrived.

The year was 1889. *Eighteen* eighty-nine.

Hooliganism has been happening since football began (although there is no doubt that it increased from the mid-1960s). Unrest could be triggered by controversial events on the field but other pre-conditions towards hooliganism had to be in place.

When Animal came out of the detention centre after his first three-month sentence, his foster parents deserted him. He turned to football. The West Ham boys became his family. He enjoyed talking to them. He enjoyed fighting alongside them. He liked the way that West Ham boys stuck together.

The pressure built up during the week. It built up if you were out of work; it built up if you were employed in a crap job. At work some people called Animal names and that got to him because he wanted their respect. He had problems at home. It all built up until he wanted to explode. On Saturdays he did explode, and it became like a drug. He was addicted to football and fighting.

'I think I fight, like, so I can make a name for meself and that, you know,' he said. 'Hope people respect me for what I did, like. It's the only reason I can think of.'

Animal never cared how many opposing fans were up for a fight, or how many police were around. He just piled in. He took some beatings and he kept getting nicked by the police. When he was eventually banned from football grounds he would go along anyway. He didn't go through the turnstiles. He stayed outside the ground and went in the pub until three o'clock. Then he came out and hung around the ground until after the match. He'd see what happened then. West Ham was all he had. He'd lost his parents.

There were major structural changes in English society in the 1970s and 1980s. There was a breakdown in the extended family, a rise in divorce and separation rates, more absentee fathers and children in care, and increasingly fewer work opportunities for young people.

'Say we meet up with a bunch of Northerners, like Liverpool. Four or five hundred of their mob'll come round the corner. We're probably fifty- or sixty-handed, like, always outnumbered. Half the time it's just jumping up and down, a bit of fun, a little bit of noise, you know. We show a bit more arsehole than them. We'll go towards them, and half the time, you watch, there ain't even a punch thrown. We'll run at them, and that mob will be running, and the police will move in. They'll grab you. "Using threatening behaviour", whatever. They'll take ten or twenty people out, take them away, charge them, let them out after the game, whatever. But half the rows are not rows. People ain't getting hit.'

We are back with the West Ham fans in the Britannia.

'It's in the *Sun* that Fred Bloggs got a golf ball in his eye with nails hanging out of it, and all the geezer's got is a black eye, know what I mean, because a golf ball hits him.'

'What about in the *News of the World* when they have different things? They talk about the ICF and everything, like, and they've hung things on people who go to football and they've never said these things. They've got hold of things and pictures and things . . .'

'. . . and twisted them . . .'

'And twisted them and made their own thing up, you know what I mean?'

'This geezer's never been there.'

'The media make it their big paper sellers so they put it all over the front of the paper: "So and So Gets Beaten Up at Football Ground." It's like if someone gets killed in Northern Ireland. They're not really bothered who got killed or why they got killed, it's, like, it'll sell papers. So a soldier blown to bits in Northern Ireland is all over the front page. Or someone got twenty-odd stitches up the back from a Stanley knife at Liverpool v Man United, so it's on the front page. You know, there's worse things happen than that, just in day-to-day life.'

Hooliganism has more shows of ritualised aggression ('aggro') than actual violence. The tabloid press is competition-generated and commercially oriented, so actual incidents of grotesque violence are more newsworthy than stand-offs.

*   *   *

The hooligan lads were interested in their own reputations and their sense of manliness. It was generally considered cowardly and unmanly to attack innocent people who were not interested in fighting. The hooligans sought to match themselves against similar groups. The only times older bystanders were dragged in was when it 'went off' spontaneously outside grounds, causing chaos, or when seats or missiles were thrown randomly into groups of opposing supporters. But 'top boys' could actually lose status inside their firm by doing such cowardly things.

Hooligans spent time searching for lads whom they considered to be like themselves. They wanted to find rivals who were credible and worth opposing. They wanted to be in situations where they felt a real buzz (a mixture of anticipation and fear) and where they could increase their masculine status and improve their self-esteem.

Hooligans also studied the actions of the police. While the clubs and the police instigated more sophisticated techniques, and short-term measures – segregation, escorts, cameras, fencing, all-ticket fixtures – the hooligans found ways to outwit the police. Many hooligan procedures were informal and haphazard – plans were discussed by organisers in pubs during the week – but the hooligans had an internal structure and a viable communication network.

'The police are two steps behind us,' said one West Ham fan in the Britannia.

Spontaneous events certainly happened at football. People had too much to drink, sometimes got into arguments and lost control. Individuals could go wild at matches. But the whole scene was far from amorphous. *Hooliganism was not random violence or mindless violence. It was often organised and there were reasons for it.*

'The British race are violent people,' said another West Ham fan in the Britannia. 'We've always been outnumbered by whoever we've fought, whether we've fought in India, the Germans, whatever.'

'Yeah, so when you boil down to it, the British people are violent people, through all courses of history. The young generation now, there's never been any kind of a fire, so how do you let your aggression out?'

'There's thousands of outlets. You can run down the road and you can bash people or you can have a fight . . .'

'Four million on the dole.'

'Four million on the dole. How do you let it out? You're pulling your hair out.'

The British media suggested that football hooliganism was irrational violence. Hooligans were called names that implied irrational behaviour – animals, yobs, thugs, morons, scum and, well, hooligans. This helped the authorities to disown *society's* responsibility for what was happening at football matches. To the media and the authorities football hooligans were *football* hooligans. In fact they were 'fighting gangs'.

'If I fight, it don't have to do with the football match,' said one West Ham fan in the Britannia. 'I'll fight anywhere.'

The authorities saw it as *football* hooliganism. They saw it as a *football* problem, something that could be contained within *football*, something that had no links outside of *football*, something that was rooted in the football context.

The roots of football violence lay outside of football, deep in English society. Spectator disorder arose from a combination of causes.

24

DODGY KNEES, GROIN STRAINS
AND METATARSALS

'Before the match is the occasion for chatting,' Dr Stuart Carne told his audience in the Hyde Park Hotel ballroom in London. 'This is the occasion when most frequently in the week I am consulted, not about the player's problems but the problems with his wife and children.

'His mind is on almost any subject at that particular moment, and my job is to keep his mind off some of the immediate stresses. It is the job of the expert, the physiotherapist, to do the rubbing-down and to prepare the players.

'I am there after the game, and I am very careful if it has been a difficult game to have at least one cup of tea before I go down, because the manager wants his privacy,' Dr Carne continued. 'I do not go in until at least four of the players are in the bath. If we win 6–0 against a First Division team I am there in the dressing-room waiting for them to come in because there is no talk from the manager and I am waiting for the champagne bottle to be opened, and I would like my share of it.'

Dr Carne was talking to fifty football men at a ground-breaking conference on Football Injuries. He was the honorary medical officer at Queen's Park Rangers. The date was Wednesday 17 February 1982. Science was coming to football.

The conference was sponsored by the Football Trust, whose chairman was Sir Norman Chester (knighted in 1974 for services to public and academic life). Chester was now three years into his retirement. He worked from a study in his home in Woodstock Road, Oxford. His wife had died, he had no children, but he kept himself busy by writing books, reading detective stories, walking in Exmoor and the Pennines, enjoying ornithology and studying football.

Chester had unfinished business with the sport. He was aware of the rising problems but he didn't believe that the game was in crisis. England had nearly 40,000 registered clubs (29 per cent up on 1968), and that wasn't the sign of a game in decline. In his remaining years Chester hoped to see British football flourish like never before. He strongly believed that the football authorities needed more scientific data about the game. He wanted basic statistics – about crowds, finances, spectator behaviour and player injuries – so that decisions could be grounded in reliable research. He dreamed of an annual digest of football statistics.

In his 1968 report for the Football Enquiry Chester had asked for a small levy to be taken from pools companies for a Football Levy Board. That idea was quashed when the Chancellor of the Exchequer raised the football pools tax from 25 per cent to 40 per cent (and later to 42.5 per cent). Then came the Ibrox Park disaster at the end of a Rangers–Celtic match on 2 January 1971. Sixty-six people were crushed to death and more than 140 injured. The resulting Wheatley Report highlighted the need for ground improvements and led to the Safety of Sports Grounds Act 1975. Discussions with the Pools Promoters' Association led to the formation of the Football Grounds Improvement Trust (FGIT), funded from money made from spot-the-ball competitions. In 1980 the Football Trust was formed and given a wider remit. Of the Trust's funds (£4.75 million a year by 1982), 60 per cent went to the FGIT and the rest was spent on a number of projects relating to the sport, including research into hooliganism and football injuries.

The first speaker at the 1982 Football Injuries conference was Nigel Harris, specialist adviser to the Football League's insurance scheme and a consultant orthopaedic surgeon to Arsenal FC. Harris identified the main types of career-ending injuries – knee joint (61 per cent), ankle joint (8 per cent), lower back (6 per cent) and symphysis pubis, i.e. ligament damage in the pubic area (6 per cent).

'There is no doubt whatever that the vast majority of injuries are to the soft tissues, of various sorts, and not necessarily particularly serious,' Harris said. 'In my experience many of them are simply due to over-use. Some of these relatively minor injuries become disabling because of inappropriate treatment, for example, the giving of injections and immediate mobilisation – a controversial subject in the medical world. It is my view that total and complete rest from physical activity is still by far the best and quickest method of treatment in the long run. Very often there are no short cuts to that and it is a very difficult message to get across in many clubs.'

Harris believed that seriously injured players were poorly served by the system. There were delays in appointments with doctors and specialists. There were some misdiagnoses, as well as instances of poor rehabilitation after injury, both at the hospital and at the club. Sometimes communication was poor between the major parties – player, club doctor, specialist, physiotherapist and manager.

'We need much more detailed information,' Harris said. 'Clubs should have a duty to maintain accurate records of all injuries which necessitated the player being away from his playing and training for more than a matter of days. A standard accident form should be completed and should contain such information as the mechanism of injury and whether an injury was related to foul play.'

Sir Norman Chester nodded. So did Gordon Taylor, secretary of the Professional Footballers' Association (PFA). Taylor had long believed in centralised data on football injuries. After all, horseracing had a national register for injuries to jockeys.

Watford assistant manager Bertie Mee now spoke about the pioneering statistics he had collected on Arsenal players during his six-year spell as club physiotherapist in the early 1960s. The club had reduced knee-injury recovery time from 36.9 days to 17.1 days, and ankle-injury recovery from 39.2 days to 18.1.

'What disturbs me greatly is the over-use injuries that are occurring at school level, at fourteen and fifteen years of age,' said Mee, who had been forced to retire early from his own playing career. 'The increase in Osgood-Schlatter's disease [a persistent pain just below the kneecap], [and] the increase in soft tissue injuries is very disturbing. I like to think that with our apprentice players our education over the years certainly helps to prevent some of the injuries that used to occur. We used to have a lot of stress injuries of the metatarsals as a result of old-fashioned managers pounding their players round the track. I like to think that we have progressed beyond that.'

Mee was compelling when it came to the crucial role of club managers. He had managed Arsenal for ten years, taking them to the League and FA Cup double in 1970–1. As a manager he had expected injured players to work harder than the so-called fit ones.

'The manager – and I say this with great feeling and commitment – usually produces discord in the treatment room,' Mee told the conference delegates. 'He tends to make emotional judgements when a player's fitness to play is discussed. The fitness to play of an injured player should be subject to discussion between the doctor, the manager, the physiotherapist and indeed the player.

'A manager is not in a position to make this decision on his own but may well make the final decision when his advisers have provided him with the various clinical and other factors involved. Calculated risks are taken, but the consequences should be known to all concerned. The doctor cannot overlook his medical ethics. Indeed, everyone should be made aware of the long-term effect of certain chronic injuries. I have seen some pretty shattering injuries twenty or thirty years after, in people in their fifties.'

'We are finding that a lot of these players date their onset of the problem to pre-season training,' said David Muckle, a surgeon and football-club adviser in the North-East, during the general discussion. 'When I went through my statistics – and this has been found in France and Yugoslavia – 40 per cent of the problems later on in the season are referable to the pre-season training sessions. Injudicious use of weights, training on gymnasia floors, cross-country runs and certain types of running that are prevalent in the North-East, on the concrete road, down to the beaches and back again, tend to be the precipitating factors. Often it is described as a disc syndrome until the stress syndrome becomes manifest, which may be one, two or even three years later.'

Muckle was the author of *Get Fit for Soccer*, an early scientific study of what footballers actually did on the pitch and how diet, training, pre-match routines, injury rehabilitation and acclimatisation could help. Muckle recognised that England lagged behind other countries when it came to scientific preparation.

'Bertie Mee talked about the fourteen-year-olds and fifteen-year-olds who are being encouraged to play too much football,' said Dr Vernon Edwards. 'I had in my consulting rooms recently, as a general practitioner, a boy of eleven whose mother brought him to me with a problem of the knee. He was a lovely kid and very keen on football. I asked him how many games he played a week and he told me it was usually nine. This was about April. Nine competitive matches a week! How can it be done? He played for the Cubs. He played for his school. He played for his form. He had a club. Nine competitive matches a week! Was there any wonder that he was developing some tremendous problems with his knee?'

*   *   *

The Football Trust had already collected some basic statistics on treatment practices. In December 1981 a questionnaire was sent out to ninety-two Football League clubs. Seventy-three replied.

All except one of the respondents had a club doctor attending home matches, and five clubs had a surgeon or general practitioner on their board of directors. In a few cases the doctor attended only first-team matches. In at least thirteen cases, however, the club doctor had no specialist training in sports injuries. PFA secretary Gordon Taylor had already approached the authorities to ask them to compel each club to have a doctor present at home matches. Taylor also wanted more accessible lists of specialists.

The questionnaire showed that seventeen professional clubs did not employ a full-time physiotherapist. Only sixteen League-club physiotherapists were members of the Chartered Society of Physiotherapists and only eight were members of the Society of Remedial Gymnasts.

Answering a question on injured players' referrals to specialists, almost all clubs referred to speedy attention, using words such as 'immediately', 'almost immediately', 'no waiting' or 'within twenty-four hours'. A few clubs mentioned 'two or three days' or 'within seven days' but astonishingly one lowly Fourth Division club replied 'does not normally take longer than two or three weeks'.

After a good lunch Dr Vernon Edwards and Dr Stuart Carne spoke about the club doctor's role. Edwards reckoned that being an honorary club doctor took up about three hours of his working week on top of attending matches. Should the job be paid?

'The subject of transfers was raised over lunch,' said Dr Edwards. 'This is a very vexed problem indeed. To whom is the club doctor to be loyal? To the boy who wants to move, even though the doctor perhaps knows that he has got some problems with certain joints? There are many ethical problems here that are very difficult for our profession; very difficult indeed. Surely the onus must be on a full proper medical examination of the club who is buying the player? If that club does not have a club doctor who is skilled enough in looking for the right things, then they ought to have one.'

'In the past many football clubs have relied on the old boy network,' said Dr Carne. 'The orthopaedic surgeon has had a side door in the hospital which is open, to which players can be taken relatively quickly. Criticisms have been made. Why should a professional footballer be given priority over a factory worker who has an identical injury? I must confess it is very difficult to argue why a professional footballer should be given priority.'

'There are still people running on with the sponge who haven't got a St John's First Aid Certificate to their name,' said Dr Edwards. 'And that is the truth. There are! And I see people nodding because they know it is the truth. Who would want somebody without a first-aid certificate to come and look after him if he had had a head injury on the playing field? I am jolly sure I would not!'

'When I first joined the club I was informed that I was expected to attend the first-team games and reserve-team games,' said Dr Michael Hutson, honorary medical officer at Nottingham Forest, when a discussion started up. 'I subsequently asked myself why I should not attend A team games, practice games or training. The sixteen-year-old playing for the A team is just as likely to be injured.'

The discussion on substitutes raised a number of points. Since their introduction in England in 1965 substitutions had helped to prevent injured players from aggravating injuries, and they allowed players returning from injury to be tried out for forty-five minutes. But didn't they also encourage a manager to use an injured player for *part* of the game?

'I want to finish by putting in front of the younger members of the audience a dream that I have had for many, many years,' said Bertie Mee at the end of the conference. 'Sooner or later Wembley will fall down, and then the Football Association will – I hope – develop its own national stadium. I should like to think in that national stadium we shall establish our own rehabilitation centre whereby we can channel from clubs the more serious injuries, such as fractured tibs and fibs, and so on and so forth, where they can be all treated together in a dynamic environment, and then back to their clubs when they reach the stage of functional assessment. There we could run all our treatment-of-injury courses, our coaching courses, if need be a physiological research unit. We could correlate all our statistics that we have been talking about, and so on.'

Sir Norman Chester promised that the Football Trust would collect standardised statistics on player injuries. When this was followed up, figures for the last six months of the 1983–4 season showed 878 player injuries. The most common cause of injury was 'no contact' (51 per cent of training injuries and 30.7 per cent of match injuries). The most common injury sites were the lower leg or foot (34.2 per cent) and upper leg or thigh (27.6 per cent), and the most common nature of the injury was a twist, pull, sprain, tear or rupture (62.6 per cent). Some 26 per cent of injuries occurred during training.

Here was one small step towards a more rigorous scientific analysis of the sport. As Chester knew by now, football was a very fast game on the pitch, but elsewhere its authorities moved . . . oh . . . so . . . very . . . suh . . . low . . . ly.

PART FOUR

INTRODUCTION TO PART FOUR

THE PERIOD FROM 1981 TO 1989 was a catastrophic one for Britain. The nation suffered a litany of fatal disasters in public settings, and some of them happened at football grounds. There were the inner-city riots in London, Bristol and Liverpool (early 1980s), the Manchester Airport crash (August 1985), the sinking of the *Herald of Free Enterprise* in Zeebrugge Harbour (March 1987), the fire at King's Cross Underground Station (November 1987), the Piper Alpha oil-rig fire (July 1988), the Clapham Junction rail crash (December 1988), the Kegworth air disaster (January 1989) and the sinking of the *Marchioness* on the River Thames (August 1989). Professional football had disasters at Birmingham, Bradford, Brussels and Sheffield.

Under neo-liberal governments that stressed private enterprise and profit over public good, the nation lacked adequate and well-maintained provision in public space, leisure and transport. This was an era of public inquiries rather than public safety. Analysis of these disasters revealed poor communications, poor situational awareness, a lack of leadership, poor decision-making, inadequately trained staff and dilapidated public facilities.

Memories of the 1946 Bolton tragedy had virtually disappeared. The sporting disasters of the 1980s were a terrible, logical end to what had been building up for over twenty years. Spectators were badly managed by relatively uncaring club officials in poorly appointed stadiums. Facilities, spectator behaviour and the policing of football crowds had all worsened.

Also, in the 1980s football became more international. The England national team had fallen away after the 1970 World Cup Finals, but English club teams dominated in European competitions. If one cause of rising hooliganism was the ease of travel within England, then the problem was aggravated by the ease of travelling abroad. English fans became successful at continental travel and disorder, and the almost inevitable climax came in Belgium in 1985. After the Heysel Stadium disaster English clubs were banned from European competitions.

During the 1980s some figures in the British government seriously questioned whether the professional game was worth saving. At one point the *Sunday Times* dismissed football as 'a slum sport played in slum stadiums increasingly watched by slum people', and Football League aggregate attendances fell to an all-time low of 16.4 million in the 1985–6 season.

There was still some hope. People inside the game, drawn from different political philosophies, began to experiment with possible solutions to crowd problems, and orderly spectators began to activate themselves, saying, 'We're not the perpetrators here, we're also the victims.' For professional football to survive, either the troublemakers had to be forcibly excluded (according to one school of thought) or the clubs had to become more democratic and more open (according to another view). Certainly the quality of policing and crowd management had to improve.

Meanwhile relatively little had changed in the amateur game. Local football could be rough and tough, but there were no major non-League catastrophes to match those in the professional game. Amateur football remained an important source of local stability, community and continuity. Away from the headlines hundreds of thousands of people played football every week with little thought of the uncertainties facing the professional game. Facilities could be poor, but teams from rival neighbourhoods generally finished the ninety minutes without anything terrible happening. As Sir Norman Chester had pointed out, there was still hope for football while so many played the game.

25

THE CLUB V COUNTRY SHOW

THE SETTING IS A FICTIONAL radio station in West London in June 1982. The producer holds up an 'Applause' sign.

PRESENTER: Welcome and thank you for joining us for this evening's great football debate. Some of the game's biggest names are here tonight to discuss a topical football issue – club versus country. Why has the England national team performed so poorly, and yet English club teams have won six successive European Cup Finals? England *failed* to qualify for four successive major Championships between 1972 and 1978, and their appearance at the 1980 European Championship Finals wasn't too successful. But Liverpool, Nottingham Forest and Aston Villa have won the European Cup every year between 1977 and 1982. Why does it all go so well for the clubs and so wrong for the national team?

We have with us tonight eight men who know football inside out. Each will put forward his own explanation. Before we went on air tonight we had our own little FA Cup draw to decide the order for our speakers. And the first out of the hat was a journalist. Step this way, please.

JOURNALIST: Thanks. I think the main difficulty for the England national team manager is that it is so hard to create anything that matches the English club spirit. Don Revie took over as England manager in July 1974. He won trophies at Leeds United because he worked with his players *on a daily basis*. He made sure they prepared well and lived right. Revie and his staff rectified any problems as soon as possible. He was very personally involved with the players. He took players away on Friday nights to play carpet bowls and bingo, and he provided dossiers on opponents. Togetherness was the key.

'You can't turn it on like a tap,' Revie told his players. But on international duty you *do* have to turn it on like a tap. Some England players report for duty on the Saturday night. Others are injured and turn up later; some need rest. Revie couldn't have a post-mortem two or three days after the match like he did at club level. He found it impossible to create the same family-like intensity with England. When he got the England players together he realised just how professional the Leeds team was. His management skills disappeared in the international context.

The Leeds players enjoyed the indoor bowls and bingo, but some senior England players didn't take part. They thought Revie was treating players as if they were children. International teams don't bond in that way. At clubs players bond every Saturday, especially if they drink together after the match. With England it's very different.

PRESENTER: Thank you. Now our next speaker is a famous Scotland international who plays for an English club. I think he might be talking about the Scots tonight.

SCOTLAND PLAYER: Aye. The reason why English club sides do better is obvious. Club managers can choose the Scots, the Irish and the Welsh. The England manager cannae choose them. The United Kingdom is allowed four separate national teams, yet it's the combination of British national identities that brings out the best at club level.

Take John Robertson at Nottingham Forest. He is a Scottish match-winner. He crafted the 1979 European Cup Final-winning goal and then scored the winner himself the following year. Liverpool have three key Scots – Souness, Dalglish and Alan Hansen. Aston Villa have Ken McNaught, Allan Evans and Des Bremner. When Leeds United got to the 1975 European Cup Final they had Billy Bremner, Lorimer and Eddie Gray, and they would have won the trophy that year but for the referee. Scottish football has been particularly strong in the last ten years. Scotland have now qualified for the 1974, 1978 and 1982 World Cup Finals.

PRESENTER: Do you think a united British team could do better at international level?

SCOTLAND PLAYER: Aye. But we wouldnae want to lose our Scottish identity. International football is the one way we Scots can still show the world that we exist as a nation. Don't forget, Scotland have done better than England in the last two World Cups.

PRESENTER: Thank you. And now the views of a well-known English club manager. Does he think the FA picks the right man for the England job?

CLUB MANAGER: Nah, they keep choosing the wrong one. They think they need someone who can fit in with their coaching structure, but they really need someone different. The FA coaching system has become too predictable, thanks to the system of schoolteachers as coaches and Allen Wade's classic book on coaching. It's like two hypnotists reading the same book on hypnotism. Whoever's read the most chapters has the other one in his control.

Most top managers are non-conformists. Brian Clough, Bob Paisley, Don Revie and Ron Saunders are as different as chalk, cheese, chutney and chopsticks. There is no formula for management. You have to do it your own way. When I started out in management I rang Sir Matt Busby and Don Revie and said, 'Can I come and see you?' I had an hour with Don and an hour with Matt. What they told me was like talking to two complete strangers. They had opposite views. I had to listen to them and then go my own way.

English clubs have won the European trophies with managers who went their own way, but the FA wants dignity rather than controversy. It would rather have diplomacy than success. The FA had a great chance of changing tack in 1977 but they appointed Ron Greenwood rather than Cloughie. Ron Greenwood had an excellent club pedigree and coaching expertise, but he wasn't the people's choice. When Cloughie went for his interview he told them the truth. He told them that he was the best man for the job, but they were worried that he might take over the entire FA, which he would have done.

PRESENTER: Strong views there from another non-conformist. Now our next speaker is a fan. He's a Liverpool fan. But he seems lukewarm on England.

LIVERPOOL FAN: Yeah, that's right. I just want to say that the fans have become more committed to their clubs. No one round Liverpool cares much about England any more. Our European adventures have turned people into *club* fans rather than England fans. These fans have very strong club identities. In the last six years Liverpool fans have been able to travel to sixteen European Cup matches away from home. These fans don't *need* the England team any more.

Being an active young Liverpool fan is the full-time equivalent of having a job. While Yosser Hughes was saying, 'Gissa job' in *The Boys from the Blackstuff* on the telly, most Liverpool fans were asking, 'How we gonna get to the game in Tbilisi?'

These are resourceful, risk-taking, working-class fellas who watch Liverpool wherever they play. They won't be denied adventures just because they live in a so-called depressed northern-English city. They hitch-hike hundreds of miles, bribe coach drivers to take them on board, stow away on trains, live off the land and bivouac anywhere. They bunk into matches, raid shops and leg it from shopkeepers and coppers. Following the Reds in Europe is like having exciting football gap years. We bring back treasures from our expeditions – new trainers, shirts, scarves, hats – and we don't always pay for them. These sorts of fans don't have any faith in *national* politics or the *national* team. Their main identity these days is with their city and their region – and with football.

PRESENTER: Yes, thank . . .

LIVERPOOL FAN: Look, lots of club fans are cagey about watching the national team. England fans are treated with contempt. The England team promotes a southern-based culture for hooligans. Anyway, talk to fans of Leeds, Liverpool, Man United, Forest and Villa, and they will tell you that their club team could beat the England team. And where are the great England matches anyway? Nothing much to talk about since 1970. Nothing to match the great Liverpool FC party in Rome on 25 May 1977, when 26,000 went to see Liverpool win the European Cup. Everyone had a brilliant story to tell about Rome. That Colosseum'll be sound when it's finished.

PRESENTER: Thank you very much for coming along tonight and for being so forthright. I won't ask you how you got to London . . . Our next speaker works for the FA. Has playing for England become devalued today?

FA REPRESENTATIVE: I'm afraid that's true. It's all about money now. Playing for England used to be based on a particular set of values – national pride, responsibility, duty and so on. But money has become more important to the clubs in the last few years. As the smaller clubs struggle to make ends meet, the top clubs have chances of earning substantial sums in Europe. One long-standing area of conflict between clubs and national teams is a player's unavailability due to injury. Top clubs can't afford to have a star player missing from a European club match these days. So players get withdrawn from England squads with minor injuries.

There are many things that are totally beyond the control of the England manager or the national-team coaches. Players are recruited by *clubs*, paid by *clubs*, developed through *clubs* and motivated – or demotivated – by *clubs*. It's the clubs who find young players and teach them how to fit in. The top clubs want more European fixtures, and international matches are simply an unwelcome intrusion. The clubs are surrogate parents, and the international team is an occasional visitor. The clubs have all the control and the England team suffers.

PRESENTER: Thank you. Now we turn to a current international player. What does he think is going wrong with England?

INTERNATIONAL PLAYER: The real problem is that the English First Division clubs play twenty-two different systems. As the tactical stuff gets more and more complicated, it gets more difficult to make things work in the England set-up. The England manager has a lot to sort out. Where will we hold the defensive line? Three at the back, a flat back four or a sweeper system? Who will take the key set-pieces? Long ball or short passes? In the air or on the deck? Orthodox wingers or workhorses?

We have to switch quickly from familiar team-mates and our action-packed playing style to something much slower and considered, all while under intense scrutiny. Club teams work as a unit whereas international teams are fragmented.

When Ron Greenwood started out as England manager he arranged a meeting with Liverpool's England players and suddenly realised how many England players Liverpool had. They were the dominant club. Greenwood decided to pick more of their players so that the tactics would gel more easily. The next season he chose seven of Liverpool's 1977 European Cup-winning team for a match against Switzerland. OK, the 0–0 draw wasn't a great result, but I could see what Ron was getting at. He knew what the problem was.

PRESENTER: Thank you. And now the views of another legendary England international player. What has changed since his days as an England player?

FORMER ENGLAND INTERNATIONAL STAR: Talk to people of my era and they don't talk about the decline of the England national team; they talk about the improvement in other nations. Look at Holland. Just after the war an England team scored eight against Holland. Then an Englishman, Vic Buckingham, coached Ajax to the Dutch Championship, and Rinus Michels took Holland to two successive World Cup Finals in the 1970s. Here was organisation matched with physical conditioning and great technical ability. Some of the Dutch players were pencil-thin but as hard as teak. Continentals were no longer intimidated by the England bulldog spirit.

Another thing: the other home countries are now competing for some of England's players. Parents and grandparents can now be taken into account. Liverpool's Mark Lawrenson plays for Ireland. He's an Englishman with Irish heritage, snapped up by the Republic of Ireland when he was a nineteen-year-old Third Division player at Preston North End, as thin as a British Rail sandwich. Lawrenson has played in two European Cup Finals, and he would surely have been a key player for England.

In the last few years Denmark, USSR and Spain have all recorded their first wins at Wembley. England used to win easily against Norway, but then came that match in Oslo when England lost 2–1. There are no easy matches these days.

PRESENTER: We have a little reminder of that 2–1 defeat in September 1981 for you here – Bjorge Lillelien's famous words of commentary: 'Lord Nelson, Lord Beaverbrook, Winston Churchill, Sir Anthony Eden, Clement Attlee, Henry Cooper, Lady Diana . . . Maggie Thatcher . . . Your boys took one hell of a beating.' And now we come to our final speaker, a top football coach who has worked with some great managers. Is there too much pressure playing for England today?

TOP COACH: I think it's hard to relax England players like you can relax them at club level. There's too much at stake. And players do need to relax before a match. That's why managers get comedians in the dressing-room or get them to play bingo. You get the best out of yourself when you've prepared well beforehand and you're relaxed on the day, and that applies to sex, driving a car and doing your daily job. If you're relaxed and have a bit of talent, it will ooze out of you.

Unrealistic media expectations make it harder for England managers to create a relaxed environment these days. Some press men plant doubts, create tension and hound the players and the manager. Because of time constraints, England managers cannot influence their players enormously, but those managers are still portrayed as the cause of everything.

There's one other point I want to make. I see some kids who would make great footballers. They are intelligent, good decision-makers, athletic, good learners, but they don't play football at school. They are middle-class kids who play rugby union. England has always suffered from this class divide in winter sport. Other countries don't have that problem to the same extent.

PRESENTER: Thank you. We've just got time to take a couple of views from our studio audience. Yes, sir, you at the front.

STUDIO GUEST 1: Perhaps the real question is not why the English clubs are so strong at this time but why the Italian and Spanish clubs are so weak.

PRESENTER: And the other gentleman, at the side. Do you have a quick point to make?

STUDIO GUEST 2: Yes. Maybe there's not much difference between the fortunes of the national team and the club teams. Maybe it's all down to luck. Most European Cup Finals were won 1–0 and could have gone either way. Some of the England national team's so-called failures could easily have gone the other way. England played Poland off the park at Wembley in 1973 but could only draw 1–1 in a fluke result. What if Trevor Francis had not been injured in the 1980 European Championships? Keegan and Brooking are injured now. It's just luck.

PRESENTER: Thank you. And thank you to all our guests. Congratulations, too, to Aston Villa for bringing the European Cup back to England once again. Our great football debate this evening has been Club v Country. Tune in at the same time next week, when we will be asking why so many England fans behave so badly abroad.

26

TASK FORCE

'WITH FOOTBALL, RIGHT, IT'S LIKE countries fighting over territory, you know what I mean,' said a man in an East London pub in the early 1980s.

'Or religion,' another fan responded.

'Yeah. Or religion. Whatever. Like the Communists are fighting these because they're not Communists, and they're Communists, like, and they're at war because of them two things. They're at war over politics, right? Well, it ain't a war with us. You wanna be the tops in life, whatever it is, and our thing's been football. We've been involved in violence and it's there. It's never gonna go. There's always gonna be that rivalry. There's always rivalry in life. There's you, and then there's us.'

'We never said to the government, "Why'd you sink the *Belgrano*?" I mean, they went and murdered all them geezers on the ship. We didn't slag them off for doing that. And they wanna electrocute fences now [at football grounds], so people can't touch the fences, know what I mean?'

'It's still wrong, though.'

'There's always been football violence.'

'English supporters are the worst.'

'As soon as an English supporter goes abroad he is the worst thing ever to set foot in that country.'

'The police was just trying to batter us silly because we was British supporters out there supporting our team, and they do not like it. They don't like yer. The British are a hated race.'

'No one actually clumped anyone, out of all the people who went out there. But when we come home, in the papers we was scum, thugs, everything was . . .'

'The British race are violent people.'

In the South Atlantic on 2 April 1982, Argentina invaded the Falkland

Islands and claimed Britain's overseas territory as its own. Britain's Prime Minister, Margaret Thatcher, desperate for a lift in the polls, sent a Task Force across the world. British troops heroically recaptured the Falkland Islands with the loss of 255 British troops. An Argentinian ship, the *General Belgrano*, was sunk with the loss of 323 lives.

Now come with us on another crusade abroad. It is the summer of 1982. England has qualified for the World Cup Finals. Argentina holds the World Cup after beating the Netherlands in the 1978 Final, but England manager Ron Greenwood is taking a team to Spain to reclaim what England had won in 1966. Kevin Keegan and Trevor Brooking have been injured but they are in the squad of potential heroes. Lots of England supporters are volunteering to help. The Task Force sets off for Spain.

The travelling fans 'will be as good representatives of this country as our armed forces have been in the South Atlantic', says Margaret Thatcher in the House of Commons.

As soon as England qualified for the 1982 World Cup Finals the authorities feared outbreaks of England fan violence to rival those in Luxembourg (1977), Turin (1980), Basle (1981) and Oslo (1981). One Conservative MP, John Butcher, spoke about how massive precautions were needed to stop large international television audiences experiencing 'scenes of the degrading and humiliating behaviour exhibited by a certain element of British supporters whenever they visit the continent'. The new FA chairman, Bert Millichip, spoke of his ten-point plan to combat hooliganism at home and abroad. His suggestions included a return of corporal punishment in schools, the prevention of travel for offensively dressed fans and the return of the Riot Act.

England's first group matches were in Bilbao in northern Spain. At the time, Bilbao was known in England as the Middlesbrough of Spain. One theory was that the England fans had been put there because there was nothing valuable to destroy. The social and political chemistry in northern Spain was very different from the rest of the country. The Basques had little time for the Spanish government or their national football team, so England fans felt some affinity with the locals. The Spanish government was pro-Argentina, so England's natural enemy was Spain. But the Basques were anti-Spain, so England fans were pro-Basque. Your enemy's enemy is your friend. Some England fans even carried the Ikurriña, the Basque flag.

In northern Spain during the first group matches there was very little serious disorder. Deep down, however, the England followers were menacing.

Some arrived in Spain with hardly any money, others avoided paying bills in bars and restaurants and lots connived to get free train rides. Large groups of England fans shared double rooms in hostels or hotels. Fans scrounged tickets or snuck in. Wearing only Union Jacks, patriotic tattoos visible, skin often severely sunburnt, they stole food and taunted locals until dawn (and later) with chants of 'England, England, England' and 'We're on the March with Greenwood's Army.'

Some England fans came to Spain with a National Front agenda. These included squaddies based abroad. At impromptu street meetings they discussed getting black Britons out of the country and not supporting the black players in the England team. Black England players had been jeered by their own fans in the recent past.

The England fans in Bilbao were predominantly young, drawn mainly from the home ends of First Division grounds (except that there were none of the fourteen- or fifteen-year-olds who usually hung around the hard lads at matches in England). The fans looked forward to trouble. One was a bald skinhead from Peterborough. He was probably in his early twenties and spoke in monosyllables of his support for the British Movement, an ultra-right-wing spin-off from the National Front. His allegiance to West Ham was tattooed across both arms and a Viking ship sailed silently across his bare chest. He wore braces, jeans, black Doc Marten boots and a black Basque beret. He came without tickets.

Another Bilbao visitor was 'Kellerway', a railway ticket collector from Battersea, London. In his late thirties, he was one of Chelsea's long-standing chant leaders and fighters. He had quite a following. Throughout the match against Czechoslovakia he conducted supporters' chants. After the match he toured coaches from Mundiespana (the official World Cup organisers), making a collection for a fictitious female fan who had allegedly been robbed by local thugs. He kept the money.

Between matches England fans went to the seaside for a few days' rest and recuperation. Sportsworld, the tour operator with sole rights to World Cup tickets, had organised a campsite for 600 English customers on a hill west of San Sebastián bay. Almost all the campers were males under twenty-five.

One night half a dozen lads walked along San Sebastián's sea front. They looked English but none wore English colours. It was 11.15 at night, after a few drinks, but it was just a normal night-out. It wasn't even a match day. These lads were not mainstream hooligans looking for trouble.

Then a police van screeched to a halt alongside them. Police poured out, speaking Spanish, grabbed the fans, handcuffed them and threw them into the van. The England fans were scared and edgy.

'Why are you arresting us?' one started to ask. He got as far as 'Why' when a policeman silenced him with a truncheon blow across the shoulder.

They've made a mistake, thought the England fans, but it will be cleared up when we get to the police station. Some English official will come along and sort it out, we'll be released and it will be a good story to tell.

In the police station they were taken down a corridor and into a room with other England fans. Another small group of fans arrived.

Ah, these must be the real bad guys, the larger group thought. We'll get released now and these hooligans will get done.

By now there were twenty-odd England fans of various shapes and sizes. They were told, in Spanish, to line up facing the wall. The police showed them exactly how to stand – by hitting them on the inside of their legs with truncheons. Some fans decided to speak out and the police whacked them. The police talked to one another in Spanish, saying something about Las Malvinas (the Falkland Islands). One fan in the line started humming and singing 'Rule Britannia', a typically defiant England fan's action, as if to say, 'You can't do anything to us, we're English.' He was beaten up.

The fans stayed like that for more than two hours. Then they heard a voice speaking in broken English. A nervous Spanish courier had arrived from Mundiespana. She spoke with the Policia Nacional and then addressed the fans in English: 'There has been some damage in San Sebastián tonight which you are supposed to have committed. The police are going to put you in jail and you will come up before the judge tomorrow. Like last time, you will have to pay for the damage.'

'Last time' was an incident the previous week when the police had held ten England fans in custody after some damage to property.

About ten minutes later the courier returned with a different message: 'Listen, you have been very lucky. You are going to be released. But, please, you must be polite to everyone here. Say, "Thank you" and "Goodnight" to everybody, and the Inspector says that you must be nice here and no more fighting now. You must not cause any more damage. Please, don't say anything as we leave. Just walk out with me. I will be responsible for you.'

The fans apologised, but everyone was really angry.

We haven't done anything, they raged.

The Spanish police were sending a message. It was like saying, 'Tell the other England fans that if they misbehave in this town the police won't care who they get.' Spain wasn't long out of General Franco's control. Few people in Spain trusted the police.

But there had indeed been trouble in the town. England fans had taken a donkey into a high-class discothèque, causing a fight and a lot of damage. There had been disturbances at nearby coastal resorts in Spain (Santander and Zarauz) and in France (Biarritz and St Jean de Luz).

The rumour mill took the San Sebastián incident and turned it into something unrecognisable.

'Loads of English guys were beaten up.'

'One was stabbed.'

'The police are bastards.'

'There's all this Las Malvinas stuff going about.'

'There's no justice.'

'These fuckin' barbarians don't have the British sense of fairness and justice.'

'For fuck's sake, we *invented* fairness.'

'We've got to stick together and look after each other because these guys will abuse you.'

'Bad things will make us stronger,' the fans told one another. It was exactly the sort of thing that England players would say. The England players had their own 'backs against the wall' attitude. In Bilbao, where England won all three matches, they had built up hope of World Cup success.

Next stop was Madrid, where Spain was definitely the enemy.

In the second group stage England would play West Germany and Spain. England fans went on manoeuvres to Madrid.

The great patriotic adventure continued.

Show you are English.

Wear England shirts.

Wear the uniform.

Don't be ashamed of being English, even if it is dangerous.

Neutrals sensed that England provided both the best and worst fans for World Cups. The best were the older football nuts who travelled around in twos and fours, buying tickets for low-interest matches, such as Yugoslavia against Honduras. The worst were the trouble-seeking young, white, male hooligans.

Derby County's Leon Leuty (left) and Jack Nicholas (with FA Cup), 1946

Young children passed overhead to safety at Chelsea's Stamford Bridge, 1947

FA Cup Finals were national celebrations:
Aston Villa fans at Wembley, 1957

Spectators at Millwall supporting 'the Lions', 1957

An enthusiastic fan shows her allegiance to Banstead Athletic,
a Surrey League team near Epsom, 1955

Aerial view of 111 football pitches, Hackney Marshes, London, 1962

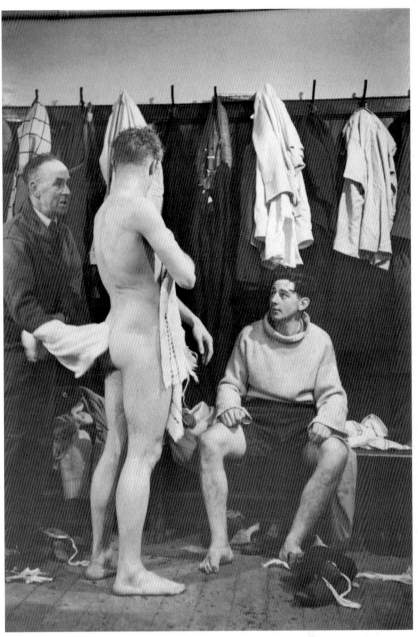

The inner chamber: Manchester City's dressing-room, 1951

Orderly, respectable fans watching Wolverhampton Wanderers, 1949

A Sheffield & Hallamshire county FA fixture at Worksop, 1950s

An early floodlit match intrigues Arsenal fans at Highbury's Clock End, 1951

FA Cup winners Nottingham Forest at Canning Circus, Nottingham, 1959

Players' union chairman Jimmy Hill (left), Minister of Labour John Hare (centre) and Football League president Joseph Richards (right foreground) after resolving the players' dispute, 1961

Tom Finney (left), Preston plumber and England footballer, meets George Best (right), a celebrity player of the next generation, 1969

England women's international Sue Lopez playing in Italy, 1971

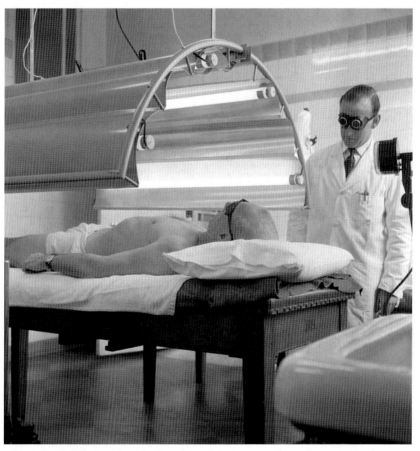

Arsenal physiotherapist Bertie Mee applies science to his profession, 1961

Derby County manager and media pundit Brian Clough (right)
with his son Nigel, 1968

The singing sixties: Wolverhampton Wanderers' fans in a Kop choir

A boot up the backside wouldn't always be enough, Blackpool, 1970

African-Caribbean pioneers Highfield Rangers in the Leicestershire Youth League, 1971–2

Two members of England's 'Task Force' camp in Spain during the 1982 World Cup Finals

The Bradford City fire, 11 May 1985

The dressing-room: A place for banter, speeches and fears, Stevenage Borough, 1998

In Madrid England fans got on surprisingly well with West Germany fans. There were even times when they joined forces to fight the Spaniards. The first hint of serious disorder came three hours before the England–West Germany match. Spanish nationalists paraded in front of the English. The locals, mainly from the right-wing Fuerza Nueva (New Force), chanted slogans about Las Malvinas and Gibraltar, and the English responded with, 'Malvinas, Malvinas, Inglaterra.'

Officers of the Policia Nacional and the Policia Municipal tried to separate the two groups and calm the Spaniards. Some England fans moved into a bar facing the stadium. The bar was a favourite haunt for the pro-Franco Spanish nationalists.

Other English fans stayed on the streets and continued to sing 'Rule Britannia' and 'You'll never take Gibraltar'. A dozen mounted police officers simply rode into the crowd of about 150 England fans and scattered them; all except two who were too drunk to do anything except lie on their flags. Some England fans dashed into the bar and the singing started up again. But a mounted policeman rode right up to the door and, with the head of the horse practically inside, ordered the English out.

After the West Germany match there was a serious incident outside an underground station near the stadium. A group of England fans (including one carrying a Basque flag) were attacked by Spanish extremists who were chanting, 'Gibraltar, Español' ('Gibraltar is Spanish') and 'Muerte a los Ingleses' ('Death to the English'). Mike Buckley, an eighteen-year-old printer from Derbyshire, was stabbed near the heart by a Spaniard. Later that evening gangs of Spanish youths wearing the uniform of Fuerza Nueva beat up and stabbed three England supporters who were sleeping in a park near the Bernabéu Stadium. All three were seriously injured.

A small group of hardcore England fans saw this as a direct challenge.

'This is war,' they said.

'Bring it on.'

'We'll take it and give it back.'

There was a real sense that going on to the attack was a patriotic response, an honourable way to demonstrate that Margaret Thatcher was correct about the British. This was an era for Britain to be great again, to stand up and show the essential qualities that had been repressed by earlier weak governments; to see what the British could achieve in the world. For British read English.

For the hardcore fans this was a big moment to be supporting England – at the height of the conflict against the infidels from Spain and Argentina. These fans thought the Spanish-speaking pretenders were cowards – look at the way they dive around on the pitch and feign injury – whereas the English (players and fans) were honourable and strong.

By the end of the tournament even the British press were unanimous in their condemnation of the Spanish authorities. For once there was some sympathy in Britain for the England hooligans. But the England fans found some novel ways to insult their hosts, thus eroding any remaining Spanish sympathy. Four English fans were arrested on the balcony of a hostel in Madrid's Bárbara de Braganza quarter, completely nude and cleaning their genitals with a Spanish flag. The next day police arrived to tear down any England flags that were still flying from windows in the city's central district.

The Bernabéu Stadium was an ugly place to be for Spain v England. The England fans complained that the police kicked them, and objects were thrown at them from above. And the football was woeful. The second stage of the competition had a weird arrangement of four groups of three, the four winners going through to the semi-finals. England drew 0–0 with West Germany and 0–0 with Spain, and West Germany progressed by beating Spain. The tournament was over for England and their fans.

Paris, twenty months later. France v England in a European Championship qualifier at the Parc des Princes. A group of England fans have gathered in the upper tier. They are predominantly from southern English clubs, especially Chelsea and Millwall.

There has been serious trouble inside and outside the stadium. Now the elite French riot-control police, the CRS (Compagnies Républicaines de Sécurité), have gathered behind the England fans, looking down on possible troublemakers. Hundreds of riot police are there, wearing shields and visors, carrying sticks, armed to the hilt, taking up a classic advantageous position at the top of the slope.

Among the England fans is a big, brawny Millwall man in his late twenties, wearing T-shirt, trousers, trainers and tattoos. He turns round, looks up at the CRS, stands up and addresses the England fans.

'Come on, lads,' he shouts. 'We can do these. They're fuckin' nothing. They're only fuckin' French.'

Here was the English attitude in a nutshell. Here was how England fans defined the 1980s in terms of national character and fan behaviour.

When the fans left the Parc des Princes that evening, after France's 2–0 victory, hundreds of riot police were arranged in great curves at the visitors' exits, gleaming groups of technological warriors, waiting for the fans to come out.

'Look at this,' said one fan. 'It's fuckin' amazing. It's like *Star Wars* here.'

It was not only England fans against the rest of the world but also England against Outer Space. Being English, among English fans abroad, felt incredibly powerful. Outnumbered, with their backs against the wall and assailed from all sides, being English abroad was an attractive possibility. By his actions one lone Millwall fan could demonstrate what was unique about the English.

The English are loyal.

The English are brave.

The English never run.

The English stick together.

The English stand their ground.

The English have done it all before.

The English have a great history and heritage of being English.

The opposition don't have the staying-power of the English. The opposition may look more sophisticated and learned, but they haven't got what we have. The opposition will bend in the end. Lots of glorious battles lie ahead.

27

CHESTER'S SIX-A-SIDE TEAM

'COME FRIDAY NIGHT THEY TAKE their business hat off and they put their football one on, and emotionally the heart rules the head,' said insolvency expert Martin Spencer. 'They have pressure from fans, they have pressure from managers, that they must be successful, and therefore clubs have gone into the transfer market, usually via the manager, and have bought a £1-million player. In no way would those directors have gone willy-nilly into the industrial market and bought a £1-million machine in the hope that six months down the road they'll be able to sell one of their second-hand machines. That is effectively what they have done; they have been indiscriminate in their buying and sometimes in their selling.'

Martin Spencer was talking about football-club directors. In 1982–3 the banks decided that they wanted overdrafts settled and many English clubs were pushed to the brink of closure. The Football League was in financial crisis and there was plenty of insolvency work available for the likes of Spencer. The ninety-two League clubs owed around £37 million. Suddenly professional football was more about balance sheets than team sheets.

It was time to send for Sir Norman Chester again. On 18 October 1982 the Football League Management Committee commissioned Chester 'to review the structure of the League's championships and cup competitions and to make recommendations as to future viability'.

This time Chester ran a six-a-side team. He worked with two First Division chairmen, one Fourth Division chairman, a former PFA secretary and a representative from the Committee of London Clearing Bankers. They collected information from many sources. Chester was soon asking himself one key question: What would it take to stop the ambitious top clubs breaking away from the rest of the Football League?

*   *   *

Aggregate Football League attendances had fallen from 41.3 million (in 1948–9) to 24.6 million (in 1979–80) and then, more dramatically, to 20 million (in 1981–2). But the fall was partly offset by the increasingly popular Milk Cup competition (1.9 million spectators in 1981–2).

There were lots of reasons for the decline. One factor was the economic recession triggered by the 1979 General Election. Unemployment rose to three million by 1982, after being around 1.3 million for most of the 1970s.

'We feel that the product on the field is just as exciting now, but spectators find it extremely difficult to find sufficient cash to support their teams, week in and week out,' one club's chief executive told Chester. But others disagreed. Some felt that part of the problem was defensive football.

Another reason given for tumbling attendances was a fall in urban population as people moved from built-up football hotbeds to suburbs. Fulham chairman Ernie Clay claimed that fewer than 8 per cent of his club's fans came from within six miles of the ground. Other negatives included obscene language, fear of hooliganism, the unwillingness of liberated women to accept their men's football passion, and the continuing growth of competing leisure interests.

The most compelling leisure alternative was now television, especially after colour arrived in 1968. Monday workplace discussions in England had changed from 'Did you go down the County Ground on Saturday?' to 'Did you see *The Morecambe and Wise Show* on Saturday?' or even 'Did you see that Luther Blissett goal on *Match of the Day*?' A BBC survey showed that adults averaged sixteen hours of television viewing a week, and children and OAPs watched over twenty hours of programmes. Some fifteen million people regularly watched televised football. Sir Norman Chester described the impact of television as 'probably the most remarkable social change of the century'.

Clubs found it hard to reduce wage bills because football was so labour-intensive. British Leyland-style tactics wouldn't work – the team couldn't be reduced to seven men, or players be replaced by robots. In fact total club wage bills *rose* by 45 per cent between 1979–80 and 1980–1 (compared with a 20 per cent rise in general prices). After freedom of contract was introduced in April 1978 – transfers were still subject to fees (either agreed by the clubs or fixed by a tribunal) – clubs found it difficult to extricate themselves from expensive deals. In February 1982 Fourth Division Bristol City, £1.5 million in debt, was saved from extinction with only a few minutes to spare when eight players agreed to waive their contracts (worth £390,000 on paper) and accept £70,000 in lieu. The Ashton Gate Eight had all signed long-term deals (including one eleven-year contract) during City's First Division days in the late 1970s.

Transfer expenditure fell from £32.8 million (in 1979–80) to £22 million (in 1981–2). In the 1970s clubs would spend money on new players rather than pay tax on profits, but the losses of the early eighties halted those thoughts. In the summer of 1982 about 400 professional players were released into unemployment. One player grew so fed up with life on the dole that he offered his services to local farmers as a scarecrow.

The media hyped on about Kevin Keegan's alleged £3,000-a-week deal at Newcastle and Alan Simonsen's £1,500 a week at Charlton Athletic. At the other end of the scale, however, Wolves started the 1982–3 season with a sixteen-year-old midfielder who was on £25 a week and an eighteen-year-old striker on a Youth Opportunities Scheme. At one Fourth Division club players paid for their own boots and washed their own kit.

A more representative example was John Turner, Chesterfield's 27-year-old goalkeeper, a professional for nearly ten years. Turner was on a basic wage of £145 per week, a £2,000 loyalty bonus for seeing out the season, a £1,500 transfer fee instalment, £34 for each win, £17 for each draw and a spectator bonus of £1 per 1,000 fans. In 1981–2 Turner earned £14,500, well above the Third Division average.

The top First Division clubs wanted fewer midweek fixtures, a 75 per cent share of television money for First Division clubs, separate sponsorship for the First Division and retention of gate receipts by the home clubs.

'The First Division clubs are becoming increasingly intolerant of a situation where they are required to subsidise clubs in the lower divisions at a time when they have financial problems of far greater magnitude than the clubs in receipt of these subsidies,' Everton chairman Phil Carter told Sir Norman Chester.

Carter thought it was impossible to reconcile the ambitions and aspirations of ninety-two clubs of such widely varying potential. He believed that each division should be independent, with its own management board, its own issues to vote on and its own sponsorship deals. In Carter's view only the fixture-copyright money should be distributed equally as this was the only genuine case of each club contributing equally. The top clubs had requested a feasibility study for a Super (or Premier) League.

Chester penned a private note: 'The top clubs know from conversations in the advertising and entertainment world that if they were free agents they would be likely to secure for themselves a much higher revenue than if they are treated as but part of ninety-two clubs. This is the issue which, if not settled amicably in the near future, could split the League.'

Chester's main idea for the survival of Third and Fourth Division clubs was for their players to become semi-professionals. One model was the Alliance Premier League, where players received an average £65 per week basic wage, plus bonuses for wins (about £15) and League position. Another model was rugby league, where part-time Hull RFC had a similar income to Hull City but only 30 per cent of the wage bill. But Chester also knew that the bigger Third Division clubs – Portsmouth, Bristol Rovers, Sheffield United, and their like – would keep full-time squads and that smaller Third Division clubs might overspend in an attempt to keep up.

Chester still favoured regionalisation. Although travel accounted for only about 7 per cent of expenses, most lower-level chairmen agreed with the York City chairman's appraisal of the 1982–3 fixture list: 'It is surely better for York to play Doncaster and Torquay to play Exeter in a regionalised Third Division, than for Torquay to come to York, and Exeter to go to Doncaster.'

Hereford United did day trips by coach to Hartlepool and Torquay, eating sandwiches on the way there and fish and chips on the return, but their cut-price British Rail day-return deal to play at Blackpool worked out badly; the players had to stand on the train from Crewe to Blackpool and Hereford lost 5–1. The Football League Executive Staffs' Association polled its members and found that only 28 per cent believed that the existing structure was right for the Third and Fourth Divisions. A majority (54 per cent) wanted three regional divisions and 16 per cent favoured four regional divisions.

The Chester Committee also believed in establishing a promotion–relegation link between the Football League and the non-League pyramid, but this wasn't a straightforward issue. Crewe Alexandra had sought re-election in five of the last eight seasons but the club's directors were well respected for their financial acumen, having sensibly resisted outlay on players in favour of balancing the books. Had they faced possible relegation into non-League football, Crewe might have gone under by gambling on new players.

Was Crewe Alexandra a better role model than Bristol City?

Should financial success be rewarded as well as playing success?

Sir Norman Chester heard from half the club chairmen. Most wrote discreetly to the Oxford don. One First Division chairman expressed his concern that a vocal minority with the support of the media might get too much attention. Sure enough, two chairmen made their opinions known through the press before sending Chester a note with their cuttings file. Chester doodled 'megalomaniac' across one note. Another chairman suggested that the League and major clearing banks should jointly launch a finance company to shore up clubs. Various people suggested moving the season to the summer, when stadiums were more comfortable, catering receipts were higher and the grass grew better. Another chairman thought that all of the League's travel expenses should be pooled together and then paid in equal shares so that Plymouth, Carlisle and Middlesbrough weren't disadvantaged through location.

Most clubs had increased prices – gate receipts hadn't fallen in the same way as attendances had – but several chairmen still thought that football was being sold too cheaply. 'A packet of cigarettes now costs £1,' said Portsmouth chairman John Deacon, 'which means to say that three packets of cigarettes per fortnight would cover the cost of an entrance to a football match.'

'We have a sensible bonus scheme linked to results and also loyalty, and loyalty in that context means a player who stays with us for a considerable number of years,' said Cambridge United chairman David Ruston, a senior partner in an accountancy firm, one of many who felt that clubs needed to cut the cloth accordingly. 'Part of the trouble within the clubs is, in my opinion, due to the fact that the paid management has little experience outside football, and is not, therefore, aware of the harsh business world outside.'

Professional football's other consideration was how to generate new capital. It could come from issuing more shares, listing on the Stock Exchange as a public company (as Tottenham Hotspur eventually did in September 1983), increasing sponsorship money or finding more appropriate benefactors. Preston North End rounded up nineteen new directors each willing to put £12,500 into the club. Preston also used their Deepdale ground for firework displays, pop concerts and Country & Western festivals. Bristol City staged a Rolling Stones concert at Ashton Gate and Hereford United literally took the bull by the horns at one match and raffled a Herefordshire bull for £11,500.

Under these financial strains boardroom continuity was breaking up. The male preserve was still intact – only two female directors on ninety-two football-club boards in 1983 – but there were fewer long-serving chairmen.

Local businessmen gave way to *national* businessmen. Chelsea chairman Ken Bates had previously been associated with two northern League clubs (Oldham Athletic and Wigan Athletic).

'The dynasties are coming to an end,' said Martin Spencer. 'And you're going to see more of the likes of the Robert Maxwells coming into football, who've perhaps been very successful in their business life.'

A few ideas from the general public were particularly inventive. One man suggested converting lower-division clubs into American-style 'farm' or 'feeder' clubs. Another had a plan to introduce a football charge card which could be used for tickets, travel costs, goods, meals in the club restaurant and so on. Several wrote in with suggestions for curbing defensive football. Following the introduction in 1981 of three points for a win, it dawned on people that the points system could be changed. One new idea was to reward teams who won by two or more goals with more points. Another was to allocate points for the first-half score, the second-half score and the final score.

The media often incorrectly reported that the Football League ignored Chester's 1983 *Report of the Committee of Enquiry into Structure and Finance*. In fact only three of Chester's eighteen recommendations were rejected at the next League management committee meeting, on 26 April 1983. In several cases the committee agreed the general idea but not the detail. When writing to David Lacey of the *Guardian* to congratulate the journalist on his 'very good coverage' of the report, Chester said pointedly, 'I fear however that some of the media are more concerned at encouraging division and confrontation than achieving something.'

Among the Chester recommendations adopted immediately was one stating that each Football League club should keep its home-match receipts. In the years to come some football historians would see this as a defining moment, a tipping-point towards the strengthening of the top clubs.

Traditionally, home clubs had collected gate receipts before deducting expenses (police, gatemen, floodlighting and so on), and paying a 4 per cent levy to the Football League (to cover the League's administrative costs). Clubs had also paid a set amount to away clubs – 30p per adult and 15p per child (or OAP) in 1982. Larger clubs argued that keeping home receipts would give all clubs more control over pricing policies (especially as the League's minimum admission charges had been abolished in 1981). But the new policy favoured clubs with higher attendances.

Chester knew that something radical had to happen for the top clubs to stay in the League, but the League's decision-making process needed to change first. As few as six First or Second Division votes could block a motion for change, so almost any plan was doomed. Chester recommended a 60 per cent majority vote instead of the existing 75 per cent majority.

He himself favoured a League comprised of a twenty-club First Division, a twenty-two-club (or twenty-four-club) Second Division, and a twenty-two-club (or twenty-four-club) Third Division, thus reducing the Football League to sixty-four or sixty-eight clubs. Excluded clubs would join Alliance Premier League clubs in semi-professional feeder leagues. One can imagine Chester thumbing through the list of ninety-two clubs and rejecting twenty-eight which had no First Division experience or no major population centre.

The sixty-four-club or sixty-eight-club League never materialised. The big clubs, briefly appeased by some of the other changes, continued to think about their own future. They felt they had to either cut off the dead wood at the bottom or escape into a league of their own.

By 1985 the Football League could say that they had adopted many recommendations from one Chester report or the other, including the raising of the maximum dividend on club shares, the modernisation of the players' pension arrangements, improvements to the status of match officials, the introduction of Milk Cup seeding, abolition of the payment to visiting clubs, curbs on transfer fees, the use of grounds for other activities, improvements in disciplinary procedures, commercial sponsorship at local and national level, vocational and education schemes for young players, automatic promotion for Alliance Premier League winners (if they had satisfactory facilities) and allowing directors to be remunerated. The second paid director in the country was Sheffield United's Derek Dooley, who, after his leg amputation, had spent eight years working at Gunstone Bakery, eight years as manager of Sheffield Wednesday's development fund, three years as Wednesday team manager and then a sustained period as Sheffield United's commercial manager.

The Football League accepted Chester's recommendation for advertising campaigns and market research on kick-off times and preferred match days. The J. Walter Thompson agency's 'We'll be there' advertisement was aimed at attracting back armchair fans and enticing fair-weather fans more often. The First Division clubs were eventually granted 50 per cent of the League's sponsorship money (plus whatever they could raise themselves).

League football had always been both a business and a sport, but in the early 1980s the balance was shifting sharply towards the former. Chester argued that, at the top end, football had to place itself within the entertainment industry, define its product more clearly, create the correct image and compete with television, DIY and gardening. After the second Chester Report the Football League would never again be the fraternal, self-supporting conservative body that it had been set up to be by the nineteenth-century Methodist football enthusiasts. The market was finally coming to English football.

28

FIRE AND RAIN

B Y 11 MAY 1985 BRADFORD City had already secured the Division Three championship. They would return to Division Two after an absence of forty-eight years. The final day of the season started as a day of celebration. A group of majorettes performed in a pre-match carnival atmosphere. The players brought out placards with messages of thanks to supporters. The championship trophy, presented to 23-year-old Bradford City captain Peter Jackson, was the club's first major trophy for fifty-six years (unless you count the West Riding Cup). And then came the game.

Bradford City v Lincoln City at Valley Parade.

By 11 May 1985 Birmingham City had already achieved promotion to the First Division. They had a slim chance of winning the Second Division championship – if they beat Leeds United and Oxford United lost. But that wasn't the issue. The main talking point, as people made their way in sunshine to the St Andrews ground, was that something big would surely happen. Lots of Leeds United fans packed into the open away-end terrace, the Birmingham City hooligans were up for it and the atmosphere sizzled with testosterone and adrenalin.

Birmingham City v Leeds United at St Andrews.

During that spring Leeds United followers could sense a climax on the season's last day. People in the city counted down the Second Division fixtures from a distance of months away. Yes, there would be a big event at Birmingham. Leeds United FC feared it, the West Midlands Police force geared up for it and Leeds United fans anticipated it.

There were two main influential contingents of Leeds United fans. One group, the Kippax lads, were tough, older, working-class men who had served their time following Leeds. Their heart was in the club and they now operated to a strict code of spectating – enjoy your drink but stay clear of trouble unless no other option was available. The other main group was a much larger collection of younger, wilder Leeds fans – the Leeds Service Crew and their admirers. These boys didn't accept the traditional structure of hooligan behaviour. They were out to party.

The Kippax lads recruited heavily among ex-miners who had a strong, Labour collective tradition. They liked anything Yorkshire (especially Yorkshire cricket) and they were great supporters of Arthur Scargill, leader of the National Union of Mineworkers, through a bitter strike. The Kippax were hard, proud men who would give as good as they got if someone attacked them. But they would never do what the younger group now routinely threatened at Leeds away matches – attack the police for fun, disrupt a match or damage a stadium.

On away grounds, as the 1984–5 season careered on, the Leeds Service Crew could look around and see a couple of thousand others just like them. There were no black faces in this hostile crowd, few females and very few stabilising older people. These young lads favoured designer labels – Stone Island, Ellesse and Burberry – and they went to matches expecting to start trouble. They felt powerful and beyond the law.

Whereas the older Kippax fans had watched Leeds United in the Don Revie glory years, these younger fans got no satisfaction from this relatively poor Leeds United team. Chances of promotion to the First Division slipped away as the 1984–5 season edged towards the fateful last fixture at Birmingham City. The younger Leeds fans tested their superiority *off the pitch*.

'We'll make everyone afraid of us.'

'We'll have a great afternoon – win, lose or draw.'

'*Wherever* we go.'

Their aim was mayhem, and they wanted it most weeks. Their numbers swelled as their reputation grew. Their antics attracted more and more people from outside Leeds, especially to away matches (as had happened with Manchester United fixtures in their 1974–5 Second Division season). These younger Leeds United fans could easily swamp opposing fans in Huddersfield, Barnsley and even Sheffield.

The Kippax fans were concerned that their beloved Leeds United might be thrown out of the Football League if these younger fans created a major violent event on the season's final day. The Kippax lads thought that the football establishment already hated Leeds because of Revie's snub of the England manager's job, the gamesmanship allegations in the early 1970s and their own big hooligan moments, especially the rumpus at the 1975

European Cup Final in Paris. But the Kippax lads were older and wiser now, talking like old Mafia bosses: 'These young guys! There's no honour any more. They don't respect football. They don't drink or fight in the right kind of way. They're just wild and crazy. And they're all high on drugs half the time, sniffing amyl nitrate and God knows what in the toilets.'

Over 5,000 Leeds United fans were at Birmingham. After a few minutes of the match some Service Crew lads wrecked a refreshment stall at the Tilton Road end. Shortly before half-time, when Martin Kuhl scored for Birmingham City, trouble escalated. Soon it was raining placards, rocks, chunks of wood and bottles. People at the front tried to protect themselves. Pieces of advertising board landed on the pitch. A kettle from the wrecked tea-hut was thrown at the police.

It was clearly an attempt to stop the match. The Service Crew were challenging the West Midlands police: 'Come on, then, see if you can keep us under control.'

The referee took the players off the field and the Leeds United fans let out a spontaneous celebratory roar. Birmingham were 1–0 up, but Leeds United fans controlled the game.

Police came on the pitch and repeatedly charged the twelve-foot fence. Sixteen mounted policemen oversaw the two ends, also blocking Birmingham fans who had climbed their fence. The Kippax fans were worried.

'This has gone too far,' they said.

'The police are scared shitless. *We* need to sort it out.'

'And get the match restarted.'

'Or we'll get thrown out of the League.'

Four or five Kippax fans made their way to the front of the terrace and somehow got on to the pitch. The throwing stopped almost immediately. The Kippax fans carried pieces of board off the pitch. The West Midlands police looked on, intrigued.

The teams were off the field for thirty-three minutes.

Meanwhile, at half-time on that same day at a South Yorkshire First Division ground, a journalist came off the phone and spoke to his colleagues in the press box.

'There's a fire at Valley Parade,' he told everyone, deadpan. 'It's done three quid's worth of damage.'

Everybody laughed.

*   *   *

In the Bradford City press box, forty miles away, it was no joke. A fire had broken out in G Block of the old wooden stand.

Sports broadcasters Tony Delahunte and Mickey Bullock were covering the Bradford City v Lincoln City match for BBC Pennine Radio. Spectators spilled on to the pitch from the main stand and, as at Birmingham, the referee stopped the match just before half-time.

Seemingly oblivious to the flames coming his way, Delahunte did what all good journalists are trained to do: he continued working. He spoke exceedingly quickly and dramatically to his listeners, his words accelerating as the flames became a wall of fire. It was an extraordinary performance. In the space of seventy-two breathless seconds, this is what he said:

And we're on fire here at Valley Parade. The whole end of the stand on one side is actually in flames now. I can see the orange of the flames. The game is actually stopped here at Valley Parade. Before that there was a certain amount of shaking of fists and a bit of a hoo-ha at that far end. And they're running out of the ground now from that far end at this moment, and I'm hoping that the police – I can see some policemen's helmets over there – can control this. It looks like there could be a situation of panic, but all the time people are spilling on to the pitch and we can see the flames going up into the air there now. We're getting reports outside that that steam [smoke] is going over. People are running around, they're running around beside us, they're running around all round us. People are saying, 'Get on to that pitch!' People are all the time spilling on to the pitch. The game is stopped. Mickey Bullock, you're big, you can see above people, can you see? [voice of Bullock: It's terrible, the whole stand is on fire, Tony, it's an absolute . . . it's spreading fast, there's going to be problems for 'em, Tony.] Let's get all those people out of there, let's get those people, just take your time, don't rush, go down there, take your time, don't pull on the wires, keep the electric open, take your time, don't rush, don't push, watch for the kiddies. People are coming round us, you can hear the heat, there's smoke coming everywhere. We are going to have to disconnect very shortly, because it really is flaming all the time. We're taking a break, we're getting out of there . . .

But not everyone in the 11,076 crowd was able to escape.

*   *   *

About forty minutes into the Bradford City–Lincoln City match a spectator in Row I or J, between seats 141 and 143, dropped a lighted match or cigarette through a gap in the wooden floorboards. The tiny flame dropped into twenty years' worth of debris and a fire started. The debris had been identified as a fire hazard in letters to the club from the Health & Safety Executive (June 1981) and the local council (July 1984). Only First and Second Division clubs were *required* to have a local-authority safety certificate. Bradford City were still a Third Division club on the day of the match.

'So it was not the wood that was to blame, or even the fag end,' wrote Simon Inglis, a leading authority on football grounds. 'It was complacency. It was neglect. It was the systemic failure of an industry that had lost its way.'

There were 144 police officers on duty at Bradford, and most arrived expecting the possibility of public disorder rather than an inferno. In fact the pre-match police briefing contained no mention of how to evacuate the stand. The Health & Safety Executive pointed out that the target for evacuating the stand should have been inside two and a half minutes.

Spectators in the stand reacted slowly to the smoke. Most were concentrating on the match. Some set off for the half-time refreshment queue. Then came the reality; people had to move quickly. There was no dedicated person in charge, and fire extinguishers were hidden away because fans had sometimes used them as missiles.

Paul Firth's book on the Bradford City fire is called *Four Minutes to Hell*. It took only four minutes and a few seconds for the whole of the 4,000-capacity stand to catch fire. Some spectators tried to find their way out of the back of the stand. It made sense to come out the way they came in. But the turnstile doors only operated one way and the gates needed a bolt to be slipped or a bar lifted off. Most of the deaths occurred at the back of the stand.

Going forward wasn't easy either. There was a drop of about four feet from the seated area to the paddock. Then there was a climb of about five feet to get over the wall and on to the pitch.

All of this happened in an atmosphere of raging flames, white heat, grey smoke, pale smoke and black smoke (from the burning asphalt in the roof). The intense heat drove people back. Temperatures reached 900° Centigrade in places. It was so hot that it burned the pitch up to twenty-two yards from the actual fire, melted plastic cups in the distance and spontaneously lit the synthetic fibres covering people's bodies. The stand was so starved of oxygen that some people had to duck down to gasp for their next breath.

Some people on the pitch helped others over the pitch-side wall. John Hawley, a Bradford City player, leaned over, lifted people up and hoisted them over. Then people had to move back from the pitch edge as the heat was too much. Some climbed over the pitch-side wall with their hair or clothes on fire. Some helped by *throwing* others over the wall. The fire brigade, called to Valley Parade at 3.43pm, took only four minutes to arrive. In those four minutes, however, the fire had gripped the entire stand. There was little the fire-fighters could do.

At Birmingham City, meanwhile, the authorities had their own problems. The referee and the police could see there was now no danger of anyone being hit by boards – the Kippax had dealt with that – so the players returned and the match continued in an eerie atmosphere. But Leeds fans anticipated more excitement afterwards.

Birmingham City won the match 1–0.

By now the West Midlands police had donned their serious riot gear. Police forces around the country had an informal league table – one force would make fun of another if they were turned over by fans – and the West Midlands police were supposed to be notoriously tough. The police were banjaxed. The police were angry. The police wanted to punish some Leeds United fans. The batons were ready.

It was difficult for the police. They feared more serious incidents inside the ground, but they were also wary of trouble escalating outside the ground. They had to police the departure of Leeds fans from the stadium and transfer officers outside as soon as possible in order to police the streets. They charged towards the Leeds supporters in order to move them towards the exits.

At the top of the open banked terrace was a high wall one brick thick and a series of narrow exits to stairwells. When the police came forward the Leeds fans retreated, but they couldn't all get out. The back perimeter wall collapsed under the pressure and some people fell down a level on to a small car park.

Fifteen-year-old Ian Hanbridge from Northampton died of severe head injuries. He was attending his first professional match. PC Corrigan went to hospital in the same ambulance with a fractured leg and broken bones in his back. Spectators and police near the collapsed wall helped each other to clear the rubble and help the injured. The police corralled off the area and it was clear to more distant spectators that something bad had happened. Immediately there were a lot of rumours.

'The police have beaten up people.'

'There's lots of injuries.'

'A wall's collapsed.'

Some Leeds United fans, high with excitement, grew even wilder. They jumped up and down and shouted.

'It's goin' off.'

'It's fuckin' goin' off.'

'In the name of football, please go home,' pleaded the stadium announcer.

It was chaotic outside the Birmingham City ground. Sirens wailed. Supporters yelled war-cries. Rival fans chased one another and threw bricks. A police horse was wrestled to the concrete by fans. Police barked orders and swung batons.

'Fuck off out of here.'

'Fuck off.'

The streets were an emotional whirlpool as the 25,000 crowd left the stadium. Exhilaration, pride, excitement and fear.

Later, on a coach going home to Yorkshire, the deflated Kippax crowd were pessimistic.

'We're done for.'

'They're bound to chuck us out of the League.'

'This is a really bad incident.'

'It'll be everywhere in the papers.'

In fact the disturbances at Birmingham were hardly covered in the press. Something else had happened, something much worse.

'There's been some trouble at Bradford,' said a Kippax lad as they travelled back.

'Who was playing there?'

Meaning, whose hooligans had tried to outdo Leeds?

So many assumptions.

Fifty-six people were killed in the Bradford City fire and more than 250 were injured in a blaze that spread faster than people could run. The liability was shared among a number of parties, but Bradford City chairman Stafford Heginbotham later accepted that the club was culpable. Considering the number of wooden stands at football grounds around the country, and the number of *off-peak* fires, it was amazing that no supporters had died in a fire at a League match before. So much more could have been done to improve safety, but professional football was poorly financed and poorly run. About eighty of the ninety-two Football League clubs were technically insolvent.

Tony Delahunte's car, parked at the back of the stand, was completely destroyed by the heat. The Pennine Radio reporter had a burned face. One of the most common injuries, though, was burns on the back of the hands, as people instinctively put their hands up to protect their faces. By Sunday ten per cent of the country's plastic surgeons were on their way to Bradford. Eighty patients were admitted for surgery, and the operations and grafts were immensely successful. The University of Bradford established a Plastic Surgery & Burns Research Unit.

At Birmingham one young man died and eighteen police officers and fifty fans required hospital treatment. Many others were given first aid at the ground, and 125 spectators were arrested. It proved a watershed for hooliganism. The police became more committed to what became known as 'intelligence-led policing', attempting to infiltrate the core Leeds United hooligans and gather evidence about their activities. They later successfully prosecuted a group of Service Crew members and the courts imposed stiff sentences of up to ten years.

In the week after the Leeds United match the *Birmingham Evening Mail* postbag was full of suggestions. H. Alexander of Acocks Green said that a Minister of Sport was not needed when there was no sport ('a Minister of War would be more appropriate'). Two letter-writers called for the Football League to be stopped, one called for the army to be brought in and another proposed sending convicted hooligans in chains to a remote uninhabited Scottish island. E. H. Collard of Great Barr linked the two tragedies: 'It is more than possible that the terrible fire at Bradford's football ground could have been put out in its infancy if water cannons had been erected to prevent hooliganism.'

Bradford and Birmingham were connected because they happened on the same day. However, they were also connected by the idea that awful facilities were contributing to nasty attitudes and dangerous settings. The deaths were caused by a wooden stand at Bradford and a crumbling wall at Birmingham.

An eerie footnote to this story of neglect and disorder followed in September 1986. While Valley Parade was being rebuilt, Bradford City played Leeds United at Odsal Stadium. Visiting Leeds United fans turned over a chip kiosk and set it alight. Fans spilled on to the pitch and many were in tears at the awful symbolism of this act.

'We've had this terrible fire at Valley Parade and now Leeds fans have done this,' said one. 'When will it all end?'

29

'CORRUPT TO THE POINT OF MURDER'

THE KENNEDY BROTHERS, KEITH AND Alan, grew up in Shiney Row, a village six miles from Sunderland and ten miles from Newcastle. Their father took them to watch Newcastle United one week and Sunderland the next. Both Keith and Alan played for Newcastle United before Keith left for a football career at Bury and Alan moved to Liverpool, where he played mainly under Bob Paisley. As a young man Paisley had often visited the fish-and-chip shop where Keith and Alan's mum worked. At Anfield Alan grew to like the playing success and the players' drinking culture, but he wasn't so keen on the constant flights to and from mainland Europe, especially the take-offs and landings. The Kopites affectionately nicknamed him 'Barney Rubble' after a character in *The Flintstones*.

Alan Kennedy played in two European Cup Finals and, from left back, decided the outcome each time. In 1981 his brother Keith watched from the stands in Paris as Alan, sprinting through from a deep position, collected a throw-in and beat the Real Madrid goalkeeper at the near post with a left-foot shot. A delirious Alan ran off towards the perimeter moat and finished his celebration yards behind the goal, while Keith finished his celebration three rows in front of his seat in the stands. In 1984 Keith watched incredulously on his home television, the hairs on the back of his neck standing up as Alan walked up to take the decisive penalty in the shoot-out against AS Roma. As Alan ran in Keith had everything crossed, and when his younger brother calmly placed the ball safely several yards past the goalkeeper's right hand, the house phone started ringing. Keith was still shaking when he got to his local pub.

Alan Kennedy had hopes of playing in a third European Cup Final but he was carrying an injury when Liverpool met Juventus in the final in Brussels. He found himself with an unenviable role in the drama that was to come. The date was Wednesday 29 May 1985.

*   *   *

When Liverpool manager Joe Fagan announced his team to play Juventus at the Heysel Stadium, Alan Kennedy was devastated. He wasn't too surprised that young Jim Beglin was retained at left back, but he was dismayed to find himself not listed among the substitutes. Nevertheless he joined the other Liverpool players on the pitch long before the match. They went to the Liverpool fans and gave them a clap. Kennedy looked at the rickety fence separating Liverpool and Juventus fans. That doesn't look secure, he thought.

The players were also surprised to see Juventus fans in one particular segment (Block Z). This was supposed to be a neutral area but Juve fans living in Brussels had snapped up tickets.

'I thought this would be all Liverpool fans,' one Liverpool player said.

'There could be trouble here.'

Kennedy watched the ground fill up. Many Liverpool supporters had been on the ale all day, so the atmosphere was wild. Some remembered the knife attacks on Liverpool fans in Rome after the 1984 Final.

'Fuckin' Italians!' the Liverpool fans shouted.

Bricks started flying. The crumbling stadium offered plenty of ammunition and some Liverpool fans clearly wanted to fight.

While the players changed, Alan Kennedy walked around in his suit. He wandered outside and wandered inside. His was always a difficult role for a professional footballer – neither part of the team nor part of the crowd – but it was shortly to become even more difficult for him.

When he walked outside he could see things were getting nasty in the crowd. There was trouble between Juventus fans and the police, and Liverpool fans rattled the fence between Block Y and Block Z.

Stop it, Kennedy thought. Stop it.

He was in the dressing-room around 7.30pm when everyone heard a menacing low, rumbling noise.

'What the fuck was that?' someone asked.

Alan Kennedy was sent out to see what had happened.

A tragedy had occurred. Liverpool fans had broken through the wire fence and charged across at Juventus fans. A wall collapsed at the edge of the far end of Block Z and bodies spilled on to the track. The wall was not embedded in mortar or fixed to the concrete wall. The stadium was a crumbling wreck.

Kennedy saw people falling over and could do nothing about it. He became a go-between. He went to see the players' wives in the stand.

'Are you all right?' he asked them.

'Yes,' they said, but they were being hassled by Juventus supporters nearby.

'Are the players all right?' the wives asked.

'Yeah, the game's going to start in half an hour or so.'

They kept saying that.

Kennedy went back towards the dressing-room. On the way he saw fans and officials bring out bodies, lay them under the stand and cover them with black-and-white Juventus flags. Crushed and suffocated bodies. He couldn't believe that those same people, ten minutes ago, were alive and waiting to watch a game.

Almost all the victims were Juventus fans, but Kennedy found one Liverpool supporter on a stretcher. The Italians were spitting on the fan, cursing him for what had happened, whatever it was. Kennedy kept his mouth shut, worried that he would be lynched. His suit was covered in spittle and more.

'The game's going to start in half an hour or so,' people kept saying.

Should the game be played, under these circumstances? Kennedy asked himself. There was a disaster scene near the dressing-rooms. Most Liverpool players didn't want to know exactly what was happening – they wanted to stay focused for the game – but others asked him directly ('Why the delay?'). What should he tell them?

'Yeah, one or two things have happened, but don't worry about it,' Kennedy said.

More messages came through.

'Another one's died.'

'Another one's been carried out dead.'

'Look, it's really bad,' Kennedy said.

'The game's going to start in half an hour or so.'

Kennedy continued to do his tour of the stand, the pitch, the tunnel area, the security workers and the dressing-rooms, where he occasionally stopped off to play a hand of cards with the players. The Liverpool lads needed distractions but it was hard to take their minds off such an unfolding tragedy. The card games lasted only a few minutes.

'When's the match going to start?' the players asked.

'Another half an hour.'

'What's happening?'

'We're not quite sure.'

'We've got to go out and do a job.'

Kennedy went for another recce. He saw the blue faces of the dead as they were carried away.

Meanwhile the shell-shocked Brussels chief of police was deciding that the match should still be played because it would help to control an angry crowd. There were TV schedules to fulfil across Europe, and UEFA and sponsors to satisfy. The kick-off eventually took place two hours after the scheduled time. Kennedy sat on the Liverpool bench, unable to think of anything except the bodies he had seen taken from the carnage. Later, when he reflected on events, he even wondered if the match had been rigged so that Juventus would win. You could tell that most of the Liverpool players knew about the deaths from the way they played. Juventus won 1-0 through a dubious penalty-kick and celebrated like there had been no disaster. It was a weird match to watch, probably even weirder to play in.

The atmosphere afterwards was hostile towards the official Liverpool party. The players were ringed by about 300 police, and the team bus was stoned. None of the players spoke. In their hotel they maintained their silence. They were told to stay in the building as they couldn't be guaranteed safety outside. The players couldn't wait to get back home.

Then the analysis began.

Thirty-nine people died and 580 were injured in the Heysel Stadium disaster. The dead were thirty-two Italians, four French, two Belgians and an Irishman. A combination of poor facilities, inadequate policing, heavy drinking, English hooliganism and 'revenge for 1984' had contributed to the fatalities. The ensuring Popplewell Inquiry reported that British fans were primarily to blame and match organisers secondarily. Popplewell's solution to the problem was better policing, CCTV, controls on alcohol, more seating at grounds, more security and stiffer penalties.

Normally you wouldn't have expected *Liverpool* fans to be implicated. Liverpool fans had a rough-and-ready code of practice at home and abroad. Robbing and fighting back were acceptable, but the match itself was usually sacrosanct. Missile-throwing and stadium riots were usually off-limits as they could disturb the football.

Rumours circulated. They always do with disasters. At Heysel there was speculation that the National Front had infiltrated the Liverpool fans.

'I heard some London voices,' someone said.

'It can't be our people,' said a Scouser. 'It must be National Front guys from London.'

'Look at Liverpool's record: we don't do things like this.'

'It was the police's fault.'

'It's *their* fault, for putting us next to Juventus fans.'

It took the city of Liverpool some time to acknowledge that their fans were to blame. Over the next few days the whole city was shocked. Liverpudlians grieved for the loss of life, but they also grieved for the city's pride because football had been one of Liverpool's last remaining sources of excellence. Disorder and xenophobia had become so routine in English football that some Liverpool supporters were saying, '*They* should know what kind of people we are. If you don't control us properly we'll do this. Putting us next to Italians was provocation in itself.'

Other Liverpool fans sat around in pubs and stared into their pints.

'This isn't working.'

'Yeah, I want out of this now.'

'It's not worth people getting killed.'

Rogan Taylor was deeply affected by the Heysel tragedy, but he hadn't even been there. A Liverpool fan, he had settled down to watch the match on television with his wife and three daughters, a bottle of champagne in the fridge. When the disaster unfolded, Taylor decided he would write something about the event.

Having completed a degree in Comparative Religion at Lancaster University, he was now doing a PhD in psychoanalysis and shamanism. His specialist interest was how public entertainment transmitted meaning to people's lives – 'What does it mean when a primitive religious performer, like a Siberian shaman, performs a particular trick?' Heysel left him with lots of questions. In the week after the disaster Taylor took in a lot of information as the media asked their questions.

'Whose fault was it?'

'Who sold the tickets?'

'Why did the fans want to fight?'

'Why couldn't the police control it?'

But Taylor was struck more by the missing questions.

'What does this disaster *mean*?'

'What can we learn from the stark image of dead football fans with purple faces on a green football pitch?'

'Why are these people in the place they love to be and yet they are dead?'

'What does it say about the ultimate relationship in football – that between those who play and those who watch?'

'What does it say about other relationships in football?'

Taylor let his thoughts cook for over two months. When he started writing his piece, on the Saturday before the start of the 1985–6 season, it was a nadir for English football. That season aggregate League attendances dropped to 41.5 per cent of the 1948–9 figure, English club teams had been banned from European competitions and a television deal had not been agreed. Taylor began writing about how the great connection between spectators and performers had declined into a network of dysfunctional relationships. The problem showed in hooliganism but it also showed in mismanagement and poor administration. There was a major dysfunction between those who organised and administered the game and those who watched it. That was what purple faces on a green pitch really meant.

In the course of writing his article Taylor phoned a fellow Kopite, Peter Garrett, for some information.

'What's the punch-line of your piece?' Garrett asked.

'Well, the punch-line is that there is no dialogue. There is no recognition of the value of the great silent majority of supporters. We see how the policing is poor, the transport systems fail and the farcical ticketing system creates a black market that is guaranteed to desegregate fans. We know as much about it as anybody because we do it twice a week. Why aren't they asking us?'

'Listen, I'll come round tomorrow,' Garrett said.

The next day, a Sunday, Garrett arrived with three other people, including an Everton fan.

'What are we going to do?' Garrett asked.

'Do?' Taylor said, puzzled. 'I'm just writing a piece, Pete, I'm not going to *do* anything.'

'No, we've got to do something. It's the proper thing to do.'

By a weird coincidence Taylor was reading chapter seven of William Empson's book *Seven Types of Ambiguity*, a chapter on Faust called 'The Proper Thing to Do'. The chapter argues the need for direct experience rather than secondary experience.

'We should do something,' Garrett continued. 'We're Liverpool fans. We're responsible. We weren't fighting on the terraces ourselves, but we are responsible here. We should act. We should organise. It's the proper thing to do.'

It's the proper thing to do. He's right, Taylor thought. The greatest tribute you can pay to an event or a person is to change, and that's the hardest thing to do. You can't bring the dead back to life but you can change. This small group formed the Football Supporters' Association (FSA). Taylor sent his piece as a letter to the *Guardian* and it appeared with an address for the new organisation. On the Friday three of the group appeared on BBC's *Newsnight*. Hundreds of letters arrived, many including cheques or cash.

The FSA was organised in regional groups and the founders travelled around the country to promote it. This was a campaigning organisation at a time when fanzines were blossoming and radio phone-ins were starting.

'This is about football and its fans, whoever you support,' they said. 'Once we take the ninety minutes away, we share much more than what divides us. Has anybody ever asked you whether a three o'clock kick-off suits you? You could have got Liverpool and Juventus fans together in an ale-house and made a better job of planning that European Cup Final.'

During the 1985–6 season Liverpool City Council commissioned research into local young people's attitudes towards football. It threw up some alarming findings, especially among those who didn't attend matches.

'Football is a boring game,' said an eleven-year-old girl. 'All they do is run around kicking a ball and that makes the players famous. Anyone can run about and kick a ball. People take football too serious. If their team loses they beat up innocent people and smash windows. It's causing a lot of trouble. It should be banned.'

'I think football is good without violence,' said a ten-year-old Liverpool boy. 'I think vandalism spoils a good game. I think fences should have electricity through them and machine guns.'

'Yes, like many people, I am going to talk about Heysel,' said a fourteen-year-old girl. 'It was disgusting the ways fans fought like that. It was degrading. It made me feel ashamed to be a Scouser ... Now if you go abroad, and you voice out where you come from, you can't say it with pride like you should be able to. You have to sort of mutter it because of the shame and the guilt we carry.'

'If we look ahead, the way the present system of generations is going, by the year 2000 the people will be like something portrayed in films like *Mad Max* where people have to fight just to stay alive,' said a fifteen-year-old boy. 'So, something must clearly be done to break this run of bad things and show the new generations that violence can be done away with.'

A *Financial Times* editorial also called for drastic measures. Professional football was compared to barbaric sports such as cock-fighting and called 'corrupt to the point of murder'. The *Financial Times* wanted clubs with errant supporters to have their grounds closed (for a period or permanently) and the clubs removed from the Football League.

*　　*　　*

At the end of the 1985–6 season the FSA wrote a report on the 1986 Everton–Liverpool FA Cup Final. It was the Final that five or six generations of Liverpudlians had wished for. But the FA still allocated only a small proportion of the tickets to the clubs, and used the rest to reward county FA stalwarts for their unpaid work. Tickets ended up on the black market. At Wembley, on the day, fans with rubber suckers were doing Spiderman impersonations outside the stadium, scallies were climbing Wembley like it was the north face of the Eiger and grown men without tickets were crying on the Wembley steps. It was like a medieval siege.

The Metropolitan Police and Wembley Stadium wrote to thank the FSA for its report and said they would study it and organise meetings. The FA secretary, Ted Croker, wrote a curt letter saying that he hadn't been able to get a ticket for the 1946 FA Cup Final when his brother was a Charlton Athletic player. The FA ignored the FSA report. The FSA then realised where the problems in football really were.

30

'WHAT STUDS WILL IT TAKE?'

HAVE YOU HEARD THE STORY about the amorous young cleaner at a professional football club? She has worked at the same club for a few years, so her face is familiar to all the players and other parts of her anatomy are known to some.

The cleaner is an attractive woman, especially after a good result. The players are so comfortable around her that they invite her into the dressing-room immediately after the match – or after training – so she can get her work done and finish early. While the dirty kit is being collected, the cleaner begins sweeping up the debris: discarded Elastoplasts; muddied bandages and cotton wool; tie-ups and broken laces; empty liniment bottles; Vaseline jars and Vic Vapour Rub; chewing gum and sweet-wrappers; dirty blades of grass; and clods of mud with patterns of studs.

'Hey, I thought I was the only sweeper in this team,' a player tells her.

The cleaner continues discreetly with her work as the players go in and out of the showers. She knows to keep her head down. She pushes her broom around, past the feet of several players, her eyes never straying above waist level. Then she stops at one player, smiles and, without looking any higher than his groin, says, 'You must be the new signing.'

This is a mythical tale born of grains of truth – you might hear different versions told in different clubs – but it tells us something about dressing-room culture. In the men's game the changing-room can be a cruel arena. Women are just a footnote to the room's main function – to bond players to one another through banter, pranks, stories and shared experiences which, in turn, produce more stories.

Before the match, when players walk into a dressing-room they may find familiar or unfamiliar territory. If it is a player's first match for a new club, everything is unknown and the newcomer may have to work out which part of the dressing-room doesn't intrude on someone else's regular space.

If it is the club's first visit to a particular ground, there will be first impressions.

'What a pokey place.'

'Not sure we'll all get in here, lads.'

'We'll be pickin' each other's noses.'

'Hey, Clarkey, you'll have to change outside.'

'Where's the showers?'

'Is there a bar?'

As soon as players arrive in the dressing-room they look for a running gag to suit an afternoon of teasing.

'Hey, lads, Barney's wearing a tie. Have you come straight from court, Barney?'

'Take that shirt off, Smudger. It's like being on an LSD trip.'

'Oh, yeah? That broom in the corner's got more style than your haircut.'

Then it comes to choice of footwear.

'Have you seen the pitch?'

'Grass is a bit long.'

'What studs will it take?'

'Doesn't matter. I've only got one pair of boots.'

In local football, mouldy boots emerge from a plastic bag, the smell reminding their owner that he forgot to clean them last time out.

At some point the manager will announce (or confirm) the team. Everyone will refer to players by nicknames. Some players change quickly, others more slowly. Some rush in at the last minute, others make a day of it. They often wear 'lucky clothes' and follow a changing ritual that suits their superstitious nature. Maybe they always put on their right football boot before the left one. Perhaps their shorts go on last. The slightest delay can disturb a player's whole pre-match routine.

'Anyone got a spare lace?'

'Any scissors?'

Hands are clammy with perspiration. Queasiness may lead to retching. Images of the forthcoming match appear. The players distract themselves with talk about local events.

'What did you get up to last night?'

'We ended up at Stax. The women were all running after me.'

'Well, we know you can't run very fast.'

The lads talk about new places for clubbing and pubbing, who they've met around town and recent adventures. Then it is time for business.

'We've got to change shirts today, lads,' the manager says. 'The opposition are wearing blue. We'll swap with a team on another pitch.'

'Don't get red, Boss. I hate red.'

'Swap with Athletic, Boss. They wear the Brazil kit.'

Some players are oblivious to all this, listening to music through headphones or disappearing into a world of their own. Dressing-rooms can be contemplative places as players prepare themselves in their own way. Some teams talk tactics; others don't. The mood will vary depending on the importance of the match.

A few players will get out footballs and release some nervous tension. Two share a ritual of ten headers in a confined space. Another kicks a ball back and forth against a wall. One plays keepie-uppie, trying to reach a certain number before he feels ready. And a crazy defender jumps up to head a girder. Sometimes clothes are caught up in all this activity and trousers fly off the pegs.

Then comes the highlight – the gaffer's team-talk. The players don't necessarily look at the manager because a little eye contact can be a dangerous thing in their world. Here are some snippets:

'OK, lads, damage limitation; if you win the toss, try to kick the same way as them.'

'No fuckin' swearing at this referee. Just fuckin' walk away.'

'Everyone play better than their opposite number and we'll win.'

'Remember, lads, if we score first, we're one–nil up.'

'I don't want to see anyone fannying a tackle. Get the fifty-fifty balls. Get the forty-sixties too.'

'Just go out and enjoy it.'

At some local grounds the referee will change with the players. Ideally, though, the officials have their own separate room. On council pitches a group of referees will change together. They will go through their equipment check – notebook, pencil, flags, whistles, coin, red cards, yellow cards, two watches and so on – and may share advice about how to handle players and teams.

In the classier joints a bell or a buzzer will sound to indicate that it is time to take to the field. The players may shake hands or hug one another. They jostle for positions that satisfy superstitions. One might want to go out second; three might want to go out last. Another wants to touch every piece of wood in the room. The players get behind their captain and hope he knows the way. It isn't always straightforward, especially if they are changing in a pub a few hundred yards from the ground.

Often, at grassroots level, players leave the dressing-room in ones and twos. Ideally the captain leads out his team in a line of togetherness. The last man out of the dressing-room will follow the clatter of boots as he leaves the building and heads for the main stage. Tension is at its peak now, butterflies coursing through the body as nervousness is about to give way to essential activity.

Someone will stay behind to make sure the dressing-room is locked and that valuables – watches, jewellery, money, fags – are safe. The minder may also be trusted with someone's false teeth, the badges of courage which leave players with toothless grins on the pitch. Soccer players see sensible gumshields as protection only for 'the posh rugby-union bods'.

The minder locks the dressing-room door and trudges away to watch the match.

On the pitch, football is a physical experience, either intrinsically (as a player) or vicariously (as a spectator). The game is bodily satisfying within a natural context – wind in the hair, rain on the face, sun at the back, mud on the legs, chill on the hands, spittle through the air and so on. On a bright and still English September morning the ball rolls through a coat of dew and leaves its mark. On a windy November day a midfield player intuitively calculates an equation for the weight of a forward pass. During January feet squelch across a quagmire of a pitch. On a hard, bumpy April ground players suspiciously study the geometry of the bouncing ball. Football confirms our essential corporeal and mental being. When we play the game we are definitely alive and kicking.

Adrenalin flows through players' bodies. When they feel in control of themselves for the standard required, when their perceived skills are compatible with the challenge ahead, players experience a natural buzz. They concentrate and focus. They see no further than the next pass, the next tackle or the next shot. The flow reaches its zenith when the team scores a goal. Scoring an important goal can be as good as – if not better than – having sex. It is a moment of self-actualisation.

Football, like sex, offers players a biology lesson. Footballers discover what their bodies can do. They sense the confidence or fear in their limbs. The game is a benchmark for well-being or injury. As a footballer you learn about muscles and bones and ligaments and joints and a lot more. Football examines the whole body. Ask any stiff player the day after the first match following a long lay-off.

During the half-time interval there are three main concerns. One is fluid intake, but a good organiser will be ready with sports drinks, bottled water, tea or orange slices. A second concern is checking and treating injuries, especially if a substitution may be required. The third is a team-talk. It isn't always easy to get players together, especially if one of them is outside talking to his girlfriend and another is on the phone to his bookmaker. Very occasionally a dreamy player will follow the opposition into *their* dressing-room, forgetting that his own team has changed shirts because of a colour clash.

'Come on, lads, get yourself sorted, let's have a few words,' the manager says.

A sophisticated manager may use different techniques for different players. He may insult the ability of one player in order to provoke a response, put his arm round another under-performer and tell him how good he is, and simply joke around with a third. Team-talks make less difference than managers and journalists suppose. Here are a few gems:

'Remember we've got the wind behind us in the second half. Have a pop at goal from distance and don't over-hit them long balls.'

'I've been sick twice in the first half just from watching you lot. I can't decide whether to resign now or after the match.'

'Come on, lads, stop this number seven. All this lot can do is score.'

'You showed good character to pull a goal back. Get another and we're back in this.'

Playing the game requires intelligence. Top footballers have great self-awareness. Players need suitable body–mind co-ordination. In the space of a tenth of a second a player can take a stride, scan the pitch to see the location of others, fake a move to hoodwink an opponent and touch the ball. 'The boys are all mad footballers, and when they're playing out in the playground, they are very, very mature,' said an East Anglian teacher interviewed by Mary Chamberlain for *Fenwomen*. 'It's surprising, it never ceases to amaze me when I see them playing football, how much they do think.'

Individual skills can be stunning, but it is teamwork that delivers results, and the English are especially celebrated for their communalism.

Teamwork brings discipline, pride and belonging. Football's togetherness builds confidence and a determination to beat the odds. There is little more satisfying in life than setting targets, working hard, establishing a training routine, overcoming problems, not giving up, achieving something worthwhile and sharing the eventual success. Only teamwork offers the rewards of a successful set of interactions, known in football circles as 'a move'. The ball and players go exactly where they should, and an aesthetic ideal becomes real. Players take the ball in their stride, progress is made and camaraderie follows. One player gives a thumbs-up, another shouts, 'Good ball', a third mimes a hand-clap and a team-mate fifty yards away shouts, 'Quality' even though he knows he is playing in the Medway Messenger Sunday Football League Division Five.

Teamwork helps players to transcend tiredness and overcome the superior individual skills of opponents. Players urge each other on ('Keep going, let's pick it up again'). Football nurtures the strength of character that sees you through other setbacks – illness, injury, job loss – because determination is an essential component.

The pitch has changed from being a relatively quiet place in the 1920s to the rowdy playground of modern times. As one old man said, watching a local match, 'It's like the House of Commons, with all the yapping that goes on.' Players yell advice and criticism to aid combination:

'Man on.'

'Easy ball.'

'Knock it on.'

'Stay with nine.'

'Goalkeeper's ball.'

'Give him some options.'

Some players will be in the twilight of their career. As their body declines they desperately hang on to their identity as a footballer. Top players need to live on the edge. They need a taste of excitement. In the same way that binge-drinkers and sky-divers put themselves into chaotic situations that they think they can handle, so footballers try to retain enough control to deal with the potential chaos of the pitch. They are on show, exposed, out on the stage, but they think they can still do it, and the collective nature of football helps them cope. The football pitch is still a sanctuary from life's everyday problems.

Playing football, at any level, always promises moments of self-realisation. You are there to meet the ball with your forehead or foot. The ball loops high and drops just under the crossbar and just inside the post, sweetly rustling the netting before dropping to the grass inside the goal.

You have done it. It is your individual action. It is your goal. *You* have changed the game.

And then the other players join in.

'What about my cross?'

'I won us the ball.'

'It was my decoy run; I took their big defender away.'

And then in comes the coach.

'See what happens when you get the crosses in early?' he adds. 'Finally you've listened.'

Here it is in a nutshell. Your team has made something happen. It is a combination of your individual skills, your team-mates' willingness to collude and your coach's role. Being a player, at any level, symbolises some of the great philosophical, economic, political and military debates in history – free will versus determinism, the system and the individual, socialism against capitalism, attack or defence, managers and workers, ego and id, yin and yang, graft and craft, creatives and water-carriers, warriors and worriers, coached responses and intuition, nature versus nurture and so on.

It's all in there somewhere when you are playing the game.

After the full-time whistle the dressing-room mood varies according to the result. Defeated players may sit silently, staring at the floor, lacking the energy to move. Eventually a boot goes down with a bang, a shirt hits the floor and a voice starts up.

'How did we get beat by a rubbish team like *them*?'

This is an emotive part of the dressing-room's day. Arguments can break out. Cups of tea may be thrown. Dressing-rooms may be damaged. The banter may turn into a barney.

'It was the defence's fault.'

'Piss off! Three–*nil*. Who scored the *nil*? What was happening at your end?'

'Defence's fault.'

'Oh, yeah. What about that one you missed? You could have blown it in.'

'It bobbled.'

'*Bobbled*? Half a yard out?'

And so it starts. Unless someone stops it.

Sometimes players are literally knocked into line.

A winning dressing-room is a much happier, noisier place. The banter is sharper. People laugh and smile at very little, and no one takes offence. No one wants to dash home.

'Where does that put us in the league?'

'Anyone hear the Rovers result?'

'I can't wait to tell Jonah our score.'

'Hey, Birchy, that was hilarious when that ball smacked you in the gob.'

'Yeah, I wondered why the ball was getting bigger and then it hit me.'

The pranksters are already at work. A shoe disappears from the dressing-room and ends up in a muddy centre-circle. A half-dressed player may get a dousing with the groundsman's hose. An experienced team-mate, knowing he is about to get hosed, deliberately puts on someone else's clothes.

Dressing-room banter is the working class's equivalent of the public school's cold showers. It works on the principle that what doesn't destroy you makes you stronger. It is supposedly character-building and creates team solidarity. You don't survive in football unless you are 'one of the lads'. You need a role in the dressing-room, even if it is only as the butt of jokes. A young scapegoat might be sent to the hardware store for some elbow grease or a long weight.

'My mum rears budgerigars,' one eager young player told his team-mates in the dressing-room. 'Would any of your kids like one for Christmas?'

'Nah, we'll be having turkey this year.'

'Anyone not paid their subs, lads?' the secretary asks, while looking at one player in particular.

'Can I give it you next week? I've got no change.'

What do you do about the really good player who doesn't pay his subscription fees? Do you subsidise him?

'Who are we playing next week?'

'The Town Hall. Away.'

'Will we get a civic reception after the match?'

'See ya.'

'Cheers.'

'An' get yer hair cut, ye bald git.'

'Hey, Barney, put your tie back on. Your solicitor won't recognise you.'

Finally, three or four hours after first arriving, the players have all left. The manager looks around the room, sees the mess and thinks, I'm glad I don't have to clean up after this lot.

One day, after a home match, a group of professional players locked their cleaner in a skip and set off home. The cleaner had to wait for the groundsman to free her a couple of hours later.

These footballers do like their little jokes, don't they?

And their stories.

3 1

MEMBERS ONLY

T HE TROUBLE STARTED AROUND LUNCHTIME on Wednesday 13
March 1985. Many Millwall fans arrived early in Luton. Supposedly
they were there to watch an evening FA Cup sixth-round tie – First Division
Luton Town and Third Division Millwall – but their real purpose was to
take over what they saw as a country-boy club in a country-boy town. They
expected television coverage. A day in the hooligan limelight was too good
an opportunity to be missed.

Luton was the perfect place for away-fan violence. Luton wasn't like
Ipswich or Watford, where there was no prospect of local aggression. Luton
was always a good hooligan outing. All the London hoolies knew that.
So bring on the Luton firms, these London guys said. Roll out your lads
from Bury Park Youth Posse, let's sort out Men in Gear and bring on the
fuckin' Boys of Luton Town. Let's take on the police if they want it, bring
on everyone else and we'll take over this fuckin' town in the sticks. And, for
fuck's sake, who could blame us: the match ain't even all-ticket!

Bolstered by mates and assorted crazies from other London clubs, Millwall
fans travelled forty miles to Luton, and started arriving six hours before the
match. Luton Town's ground, Kenilworth Road, was about a mile from the
railway station and the town centre, so it was difficult to police the journey
to the ground and the pubs en route. It was a long day for the locals.

Luton Town's true place in the post-war era was around twelfth or thirteenth
in Division Two. The team had actually occupied one of these two positions
at the end of eight seasons between 1946 and 1978. In the mid-1980s Luton
Town entered one of their best-ever periods, one to match the late 1950s,
when the club had once finished eighth in the First Division (1957–8) and
reached the FA Cup Final (1959).

Each club has a rough position in the League hierarchy, a moving average which changes slowly. This underlying placing is determined by a number of factors: population size; the economic well-being of the local area (including net migration); the scale of the hinterland; the importance of soccer as a pastime to the area (especially when compared with other sports); the proximity to a traditional hotbed of masculine, working-class culture (e.g. coalmining, steelworks); and the location (and relative success) of any nearby clubs. This average position can fluctuate twenty to thirty places when a peculiar set of circumstances take hold – a wealthy benefactor, the manager's talents, a scouting system or a change in the quality of the players. Burnley (in 1960) and Suffolk's Ipswich Town (in 1962) each overachieved to win the League Championship.

Some people also believe in a trade cycle. Each club has peaks and troughs. The cycle might last ten, fifteen or twenty years, or, in the case of the Sheffield clubs in the 1950s, one or two seasons. In times of adversity, on a day when another home defeat seems likely, fathers on the terraces have turned to their offspring and said convincingly, 'Don't worry, son, they'll come again.'

In the eighties Luton was the twenty-fifth largest town in England and Wales. The football club took its nickname, the Hatters, from the town's traditional straw and fashion hat trade. Other industries included cars, pumps, electrical goods and scientific instruments. More than half the town's jobs, though, were in shops and offices.

Luton wasn't an affluent town. Just below a quarter of Luton's houses were council-owned, over 37 per cent of households lacked access to a car and the town had one of the highest crime rates in southern England. Luton's 11 per cent unemployment rate was higher among the town's Asians, who comprised 14 per cent of its population. Many of the Asians lived near the Kenilworth Road football ground. They were not interested in the club (and the club was not interested in them). Part of the difficulty of the Luton–Millwall match was the way that visiting Millwall fans treated the local people, especially the shopkeepers.

In the hooligan-ridden mid-1980s the fractious relationships between clubs and their neighbours had to be resolved or transformed into something else. Property prices around football stadiums had hit rock bottom, so these areas had attracted new minority communities. Windows had to be boarded up, police and hooligans occupied the streets and fans pissed in gardens (or worse).

On 13 March 1985 Luton Town v Millwall took place in the streets as well as the stadium. Bricks were thrown at cars, houses and shops, and £10,000 worth of damage was caused outside the ground. Luton Town FC had stopped serving alcohol at the ground in 1979, but many Millwall followers arrived in town drunk. The local Asians didn't understand why aggressive-looking burly white strangers kept appearing in their neighbourhoods to abuse them, rob them and make their lives a misery. The crisis between football clubs and their minority communities was starkly revealed in places such as Bradford, Derby and Luton.

Luton Town later claimed that nearly 2,000 spectators entered the ground illegally after exit doors and turnstiles had been broken down. 'At 7.10pm, police and stewards alike were swept aside as hundreds of visiting supporters scaled the fences behind the goal and raced down the pitch to the Oak Road end,' recorded the *Luton News*.

Amazingly the match started on time. After fifteen minutes of play, however, Millwall fans spilled over on to the pitch again. The referee, a police inspector, took the players off. There was a twenty-five-minute delay while fans were relocated.

After thirty minutes' play Luton Town scored what proved to be the winning goal. Millwall fans started to rip up seats and throw them around. Among the missiles thrown at Luton goalkeeper Les Sealey were a coin, a bottle, a firework and a six-inch knife. A massive pitch invasion followed and for once it was the police on the run. Forty-seven people were injured, including thirty-three police officers (out of the 360 officers present). Seven hundred seats were ripped out of the Bobbers family stand and an estimated £20,000 worth of damage was done inside the ground. Fires were lit on the Kenilworth Road terraces.

Television footage of Millwall fans chasing the police across the Kenilworth Road pitch made the national news. Hooligans called it 'running the police'. In hooligan circles this was a fantastic triumph.

Television viewers and BBC commentators such as Jimmy Hill reacted angrily. It wasn't only the pitch invasion and the violence – all that had been seen before in the English game, if not always on this scale – it was also because Millwall fans had rousted the local police. That was the enduring image.

Around the country, people reacted angrily to the television images. They joined Jimmy Hill in asking questions.

What are we going to do with Millwall?

What can we do with these hooligans?

Isn't it time for some harsh measures?

         *   *   *

Margaret Thatcher's Conservative government had a strong law-and-order agenda. That was partly why they were voted in. After the Millwall television scenes the Prime Minister became involved, but she had no understanding of football. Having been brought up in Grantham and attended university in Oxford, she had never been based within twenty miles of a Football League club during her formative years. She hated the game. The only time football came up on her political radar was when the Home Office received reports of English fans causing disturbances. All these dreadful hooligans needed to be brought to book.

The Tories were tackling the miners' strike by strong policing methods, so TV pictures of police officers running from hooligans were utterly unacceptable. Thatcher was riled. Here she was, trying to manage all kinds of political and social disorder problems, and her police force had been made to take to its heels by a bunch of thugs from south-east London. This was an era when local police forces were losing some of their independence. Policing was being assimilated into political power. The government was issuing instructions.

Thatcher's administration had no spokesperson on football. The Minister of Sport, Neil Macfarlane, was never sympathetic towards the game. The only major Conservative figure to display any deep football interest was Kenneth Clarke, a Nottingham Forest supporter. Maybe other politicians hid their colours. Football, in the 1980s, was not a vote-winner.

Parliament discussed the Luton incident the next day. Everyone agreed that the Cup tie should have been all-ticket. Graham Bright (Conservative, Luton South) called for Macfarlane to 'urge magistrates to really dish out some jolly good punishment to those arrested yesterday'. John Carlisle (Conservative, Luton North) said, 'My constituents demand nothing less than revenge on those who inflicted that damage.' And Joe Ashton (Bassetlaw, Labour) asked, 'Why is it that the National Coal Board did not have to pay for policing but the clubs do have to pay for policing inside their grounds?'

Two weeks later the FA and the Football League met Margaret Thatcher at Downing Street. They were told to report within six weeks on how to deal with hooligans. Twenty-nine Millwall fans went before Luton magistrates, but hundreds more were involved in the trouble. Many went home unpunished with tales of a great night-out in Bedfordshire. Damage on the trains back to London was estimated at £45,000.

The FA fined Millwall FC £7,500. They also ordered Luton Town to put up more fencing, even though some fans already called Kenilworth Road 'Colditz' because the view of the pitch was so marred by fences and gates.

Margaret Thatcher felt that the answer to the hooliganism problem was a national membership scheme for fans. Football supporters called it a registration scheme. Football administrators had to act quickly if they wanted to keep the metaphorical Thatcher handbag off the back of their heads.

The chairman of Luton Town, David Evans, had taken over in November 1984 after serving seven years on the club board. He was the former head of an international cleaning and refuse-disposal firm and the prospective Conservative candidate for Welwyn & Hatfield. He was a Thatcherite, but one with his own voice. Evans saw a lot wrong with football that he could put right. He set about putting the idea of a membership scheme into practice, albeit in his own way.

Evans realised that Luton people were fed up with living in a hooligan hotspot. Here was a great chance to experiment. Margaret Thatcher would definitely approve and FA secretary Ted Croker showed little sympathy for the travelling fan. Evans wanted to make Kenilworth Road a safer place for fathers and sons. He didn't want to see away fans being frog-marched under police escort between Luton railway station and Kenilworth Road. He didn't want a society that relied on CCTV cameras, dogs, horses and abundant police. He wanted away fans banned.

'The away-fan era is coming to a close,' he told radio listeners in December 1984. 'Fans will go to their home ground to watch away matches on video screens.'

The Police Federation had already tried to generate support for a ban on visiting fans. Leslie Curtin, the Federation's chairman, had requested that the Minister of Transport tell British Rail's new chairman to 'stop sending trainloads of marauding thugs from one part of the country to another'. But some police officers were worried about the details of a football membership scheme. They feared chaos outside the stadium if people lost registration cards or away fans turned up unannounced. What happens if 2,000 shut-out fans set off for the town centre?

The English football tradition was that you turned up, paid your cash, slipped through a turnstile and made your own way to your spot in the ground. There was no hint of planning except for the very occasional all-ticket match. This 'turn-up-and-pay' approach was part of the democratic nature of the game, and it helped to maximise attendances. The membership scheme suited the political thinking rather than the clubs. The authorities thought that a lot could be solved by electronic wizardry.

The Luton Town scheme was eventually introduced in August 1986. The club defined a membership catchment area which included Bedford, Milton Keynes, Aylesbury, Stevenage and St Albans. (Applications from outside the area were accepted if proof of support for Luton Town was provided.) Fans completed a membership form and agreed to a number of conditions, one of which was being a Luton Town supporter. Plastic membership cards with a magnetic code were posted to successful applicants. At the ground fans had to insert their card into a security scanner and, when the green light flashed, they moved forward towards the cash turnstile.

Barcodes and scanners were state-of-the-art technology. The computer-controlled turnstile cost £49,000 to develop and the whole project cost £250,000. The first home game of the 1986–7 season, on a miserably wet August night, was blighted by the water-induced breakdown of two turnstiles and long delays outside the ground. The start was not so much hi-tech as high tide, but the scheme worked well when it settled down. In the first seven months 137 people had their membership cards withdrawn.

Bedfordshire police and club officials began a publicity campaign to deter away fans from travelling to Luton. They targeted the away club's programme editor, their local media, coach companies and British Rail. When Arsenal visited, only twenty-five Gunners fans arrived in Luton.

Kenilworth Road was virtually free of hooliganism. The only trouble came when the mischievous Chelsea chairman, Ken Bates, randomly distributed sixty-eight complimentary tickets to Chelsea fans. Otherwise the home-only scheme was a resounding success. In 1986–7 Luton Town home matches had no reports of arrests or football-related criminal damage in the town (something unheard of at the time). But eighteen Luton Town fans were arrested on away trips and twenty-eight Luton fans ejected from away grounds.

There were obvious drawbacks, however. Luton Town's home attendances fell by 7 per cent on the previous season, despite the sixth-place finish in the First Division and a superb home record. And, in September 1986, the Football League expelled Luton Town from their Littlewoods Cup competition because the rules required visiting clubs to receive 25 per cent of advanced match tickets.

The members' scheme helped to reduce the club's policing costs. During the previous season, 1985–6, the average number of police officers on duty for a home match was 169 and the policing costs of £296 per thousand spectators were the highest in the First Division. By the last matches of the 1986–7 season only about twenty police officers were needed. The estimated saving on police officers was £70,000 a year.

Luton supporters changed their habits in the 1986–7 season. There were no more 'You're gonna get your fuckin' head kicked in' chants directed at opposing fans and no more danger spots for home fans to avoid. Fences and cages were removed and a dry moat now separated the terraces from the pitch. Home fans felt more comfortable when travelling to home matches, and they mingled outside the ground. The St John Ambulance dealt with far fewer casualties. The local residents and shopkeepers felt far safer. Relationships between Luton Town fans and local non-supporters improved. One local store manager claimed that Saturday takings had risen 14 per cent on previous seasons as shoppers once again stayed in town after 4.30pm. The principal of a secretarial college near the ground was delighted that there was less rowdyism, no more harassment of her girls and no longer any need to cancel courses or lock in students.

On the debit side, however, Luton Town fans began to sense that something was missing, and fans elsewhere joked about Neil Armstrong's first words when he stepped on to the moon: 'It's just like Luton Town, there's no atmosphere.'

'When you go [to football] and there's a rubbish match but there's a good atmosphere at that match, then you'll go back again,' said a Luton fan in his twenties. 'When I went when I was about seven or eight, the football didn't hold your attention for ninety minutes. You remembered the crowd and the atmosphere. That's what drew us back the following week – being part of the crowd. If you went to a football match and there wasn't an atmosphere, then, for a lot of people, us included, you may as well sit in the front room and watch football on the television. But you're not going to have that involvement. That's what people go to matches for.'

Atmosphere at football equals passion, identity and belonging. Identifying against visiting fans means more commitment to your own team and to fellow supporters. Sometimes this went too far, of course, but mainly the rivalry at matches added to the buzz of attending a collective event. Without it football began to feel like a rehearsed form of entertainment, like a theatre show or a television performance.

A more general survey of avid football fans in England found that about a quarter of them thought that Luton's scheme 'ought to be given a chance' but over 68 per cent wanted to see Luton forced to abandon their scheme. Very few felt that membership schemes could solve hooliganism. It also became clear that what worked for Luton might not work for bigger clubs, especially those with fans scattered around the country.

As the 1986–7 season wore on, Luton Town fans became increasingly unpopular at other grounds. This national unpopularity and the lost revenue from away fans eventually forced Luton Town to reverse the away-fan ban. The cure proved worse than the disease. But its success in dealing with hooliganism and its Conservative Party support meant that the membership idea stayed on the national agenda. After serious problems involving England fans in Germany during the 1988 European Championships, the British government prepared a bill outlining a national membership scheme for all football fans. It was bitterly opposed by supporters' groups, who organised demonstrations and petitions. These groups argued that the scheme failed to discriminate between hooligans and *orderly* away supporters, and there were still fears of chaos outside stadiums and at turnstiles. Also, it wasn't a real membership scheme as it failed to offer any benefits. It was really an identity scheme, and the British had traditionally opposed identity cards.

32

'SOCCER ON THE RATES'

O NE DAY IN 1987 LABOUR Councillor David Helliwell sat on a bar stool in the White Swan Hotel near the Town Hall in Halifax. He told a football researcher about his amazing vision for the future of professional football. His local club, Halifax Town, was now a community club, more responsible to the town's people.

'The club belongs to the authority,' Helliwell said, 'and the players are employees of the authority. We seek not to make a loss but if there is a loss it is underwritten, just like any other council service which makes a loss. But it might not make a loss. The civic theatre doesn't, the leisure centre doesn't, so why should the football club? If it doesn't break even, I see nothing fundamentally wrong in subsidising such a service, given the importance of the team to the town. We subsidise car-parking to the tune of £150,000 a year.'

In Helliwell's plan Halifax Town players would visit schools and youth groups. They could coach kids and teach good behaviour and health. They could present trophies and get involved with the supporters' club. They could give something back to the town. Helliwell's dream was to make his local football club a valuable resource for local people.

Helliwell disliked the existing model for small football clubs. Success was seen to be synonymous with League table position, and that branded most clubs failures. Halifax Town had never won a divisional championship since they were formed (in 1911) and had been promoted once. Football had to be about something other than winning matches.

David Helliwell was deputy leader of Calderdale Council. The White Swan in Princess Street was his bolt-hole, away from disbelievers and cynics, and he was very articulate.

'Football has failed promotionally and socially,' he pronounced. 'We've got a chance here to do something different. Calderdale Council subsidises opera to the tune of about £50,000 a year in Leeds for a very small group of middle-class people to go and see people in ridiculous costumes singing in German! If we can afford £50,000 for that, we can certainly afford £50,000 a year if we have to pay subsidy to football.'

In his vision the new Halifax Town would have elected directors and a democratic membership – like FC Barcelona. The supporters would vote. It sounded idealistic but surely it was better than the alternative. Without the council's intervention Halifax Town would have been extinct.

In September 1986 the club was given six months to pay off a £70,000 tax debt or risk closure. The following month the *Daily Telegraph* ran a story claiming that the club could be forced into liquidation with debts of £250,000. A fortnight later a partner in the accountancy firm Peat, Marwick & Mitchell told the club's directors that they had been breaking the law for at least nineteen months by trading while insolvent. The size of the debt was over £425,000.

Halifax Town's only assets were the stadium lease (with 120 years to run), the floodlights, a few fixtures and fittings, stocks and the players' contracts. The Shay was a ramshackle stadium, built in an enormous natural bowl. Behind the goal there were grassy banks and overgrown areas. At the famous Bus Garage end the buses could be seen revving up, high above the pitch, and even diehard Halifax Town fans eyed them longingly when Northampton Town scored six at the Shay in September 1986. The Shay had once held 36,885 for a 1953 FA Cup tie against Tottenham Hotspur, but its capacity was now below 3,000 (the smallest in the League). Developers hovered.

On 7 January 1987 Halifax Town became the first football club in the country (and possibly the first *company* in England) to apply to a judge for the appointment of an administrator under the 1986 Insolvency Act. This new law meant that the club didn't have to go into liquidation. They could have a period where an administrator was in charge, costs were drastically cut and all ways of paying the existing debts were considered.

David Helliwell was unimpressed with the paternalistic efforts of local businessmen to run a small football club. He thought football clubs were merely a virility symbol to them. Stand back, he thought, and make way for Calderdale Council. The important asset was the thirteen acres of land that included the Shay. Only five years earlier the council had granted the club a 125-year lease and Helliwell was concerned that the lease could be sold to asset-strippers under the insolvency agreement.

In 1987 Calderdale Council had a Labour and Liberal Democrat majority. Enough influential Liberal Democrats understood Helliwell's land-issue argument, so the scheme to run Halifax Town was passed by one vote. The Council bought back the unused years of the Shay's lease for its commercial value (£150,000). They paid off club debts of £160,000 and handed over £50,000 for running expenses. The money was found through the Manpower Services Commission, the Football Trust, the Sports Council, the sale of land and the transfer of players. The Council had saved the club by paying about £400,000 for land that was worth an estimated £3.2 million. Ground improvements soon followed and a stand was purchased from Scunthorpe United.

The Council's ownership of Halifax Town lasted just over four years. David Helliwell had a great vision but he was dogged by local opposition. To start with, Halifax was a rugby-league town. And Halifax RLFC was going through an unusually successful period with a Challenge Cup win and five-figure attendances. On average only 1,406 went to the Shay to watch lowly Halifax Town play at home on windy, damp Friday nights.

A second source of opposition was Halifax Town's Billy Ayre, a young football-club manager not long out of a Fourth Division playing career with Hartlepool United (as the club had been known since 1977), Halifax Town and Mansfield Town. Ayre was not only manager, he was assistant manager, coach, trainer, scout and, with an HGV licence, he was ready to drive the team bus at anytime. Ayre worked from 8am to 11pm most days, took a day off every few months and took two separate weeks of holiday a year, all without a contract.

Billy Ayre negotiated players' contracts according to an overall budget, but Halifax Town's directors had been optimistic in the early 1980s. Even at this level they were likely to over-fund managers in the *hope* of better results, bigger gates and a possible Cup run. Ayre could deal with all of that, but the idea of turning Halifax Town players into part-timers with other duties ran contrary to his impression of what a *full-time* professional club should be.

Ayre felt that the council were putting obstacles in his path. The club had lost its boardroom, manager's office, physiotherapy room and store room. The council had taken over bar rights and advertising signs and stopped the team from training on the pitch. The manager was a proud football man and he thought his authority was being undermined. He wanted to be measured in the same way as other League managers, by match results, and here was this Councillor Helliwell saying that results were not the be-all and end-all of football. Ayre didn't fancy rival managers giving him merciless banter about his council set-up ('Here comes the Socialist Republic of Halifax'), the female politician on his board of directors ('Have you brought your girlfriend, Billy?') and having to collect keys to the Shay from the council on match days ('Are you not twenty-one yet, son?'). In February 1988 the *Halifax Courier* claimed that Ayre was on the verge of resigning because he felt his job had become impossible since Calderdale Council had taken over the club.

The local newspaper was another source of opposition. When the Council took over the insolvent Halifax Town, the *Courier* ran damaging stories: 'Ratepayers' Money Used to Foot Bill', 'Soccer on the Rates' and 'Shirt Deal Costs Ratepayers £2,000.'

On 26 August 1987 the *Courier* printed a letter from a former Halifax Town director saying that 'Calderdale Council by listening to and accepting Councillor Helliwell's scatterbrained idea, has not rescued the club but ruined the club'. A year later another letter-writer, Stanley Solomon, head of a local news agency and an associate of the *Courier*'s editor, said, 'To allow the councillors of Calderdale to continue to meddle in the club's affairs will in the long run lead to disaster.'

Helliwell sensed that local people didn't understand his grand scheme. The *Courier* was a real hindrance to him getting his ideas across.

'I became Public Enemy Number One here,' Helliwell said years later. 'It is hard to emphasise how vilified I was by the local press. So much so that I still bear the scars. Some years ago I met the old *Courier* editor, Edward Riley, in town and he tried to talk to me. And I said to his face, "Don't you ever fucking speak to me again – and I mean it." It was personal animus and quite awful stuff from the *Courier*.'

One day at the turn of the decade Helliwell went on to the pitch to receive a large Football Trust cheque on behalf of the club. He thought Halifax fans might be mildly interested, but instead some spectators booed and others remained indifferent. I saved this club, he thought to himself, I made it possible for you to turn up to watch today. I did it for some ideal and you're booing me now because you've read something that suggests I'm your enemy!

This was a defining moment for David Helliwell. He realised that his municipal-ownership idea simply had no currency in the town. It was not going to work. Local people would never understand what he was trying to do. Why don't we just let local entrepreneurs take over this club, he thought? In June 1991 the Council sold their shares to a local business consortium.

A final reason for the scheme's failure was that Helliwell's brand of municipal socialism was at odds with Britain's Thatcherism of the 1980s. The prevailing neo-liberal argument was that sports clubs were businesses and if they couldn't cover their costs they deserved to go out of business. Local authorities were stripped of many of their local powers, rates were capped in certain councils (including Calderdale in 1990), cuts came from above and policies were squeezed. There was government talk about *local* responsibility, *local* involvement and *local* democratisation, but, to people like David Helliwell, it felt like another kind of *central* totalitarianism, another form of *central* managerialism. The political climate had changed quickly. As recently as 1980 the Young Socialists had voted to nationalise football at their annual conference.

Deep divisions opened up. Coalminers went on strike to save their industry and councils went to war with the government in places like Sheffield, Liverpool and Lambeth. In Halifax David Helliwell looked for an alternative because Thatcher's free-running capitalism seemed so cruel and selfish to him. He saw football as the people's game; gathering together 4,000 or 40,000 people on a Saturday was an act of democracy, subverted only by people in the boardroom. Eventually, however, he realised that public ownership wouldn't work in a town like Halifax. Indeed, years later, fans couldn't remember being offered membership of the club.

'People couldn't get away from the idea of a boardroom and a boss, the idea of how their workplace was run,' Helliwell reflected years after the event. 'They couldn't get beyond the idea of the local businessman having control and that their job was to grumble at him or demonstrate in front of the stands. They could never understand that this could be a different model where *they* ran the team, where *they* could become a director. So they never embraced it. They saw it as "soccer on the rates". They didn't think it was the Council's job to run football. It was the local butcher's job, or the pieman's, or the local garage bloke.'

Helliwell had a year as Leader of Calderdale Council in the early 1990s but he resigned over another funding issue. He stayed with the Council until 1994 and later became involved in a local oils business. His great vision had been to realise that smaller professional football clubs could not continue as mini-versions of the Evertons and Arsenals. Like Sir Norman Chester, Helliwell knew that the small clubs had to change to survive. But his plans for football democratisation were hatched in the wrong place at the wrong time. His county-council background and his work in London with the Association of Metropolitan Authorities meant that he was trying to introduce metropolitan thinking into Halifax's conservative provincial setting. When community democracy eventually came to small clubs, about ten years later, it would be via supporters' trusts rather than the mechanism of municipal socialism.

PART FIVE

INTRODUCTION TO PART FIVE

The Hillsborough disaster, in April 1989, radically changed professional football in England. This terrible tragedy was the game's lowest point. Lord Justice Taylor's subsequent inquiry set out guidelines for safety, and clubs began to improve stadiums. From the Hillsborough nadir the game began to rise again. It took off in new directions with a radically different infrastructure.

Hillsborough was an appalling catastrophe, but it also demonstrated people's deep commitment to football. The public grieving highlighted the role of football grounds as shrines and as emblems of togetherness and solidarity for local communities. But those stadiums had to be modernised.

'The standard half-time experience at the average English soccer club, in 1989, was of a ten-minute wait in line for a tepid and tasteless cup of tea in a polystyrene cup, for the English meat pie (a food item which would not be offered, in most countries in continental Europe, to a dog),' wrote the sociologist Ian Taylor in 1991. Taylor was also a Sheffield Wednesday fan. He saw Hillsborough as an inevitable consequence of poor resources and the law-and-order rhetoric applied to soccer during the seventies and eighties. The disaster was clearly caused by the way fans had been treated – the lack of responsible management of the crowd by the police and the building of dangerous cages to house terrace supporters.

The revival of the English game began in 1990 when the England national team was reborn during the World Cup Finals in Italy. After the five-year Europe ban on English clubs this was a welcome opportunity to re-establish international pride. Some fans of top clubs, denied their routine European football trips, had switched to following England abroad. As England reached the semi-finals, in a tournament dominated by TV images of wonderful stadiums and operatic drama, football suddenly became a mainstream cultural highlight again. This time, in contrast to 1966, the business acumen in and around the game was sufficient to hold on to new consumers.

In the period after Hillsborough there was a power struggle between the FA, the Football League and the PFA. A new league, the FA Premier League, was born (albeit in astonishing circumstances). In a new age of satellite technology television-company executives understood football's global market potential. The TV companies and sponsors invested money, and clubs were able to provide more attractive stadium facilities. The game became glamorous again.

The new wave of football interest had some unanticipated consequences. Many traditional spectators were lost to the game because of rising ticket prices, stadium relocation, the new all-seater regulations or up-market club policies. Many of these excluded fans were not hooligans. They were dyed-in-the-wool committed supporters who felt themselves squeezed out by arrivistes who lacked the same commitment. The clubs were set on making the game as peaceful as it had to be to succeed in the new free-market era, but they also realised that they had to try to repair their relations with excluded locals through community projects.

In his bestselling book of the time, *Fever Pitch*, Nick Hornby brilliantly captured the tension between the new and the old. In the new football world he missed some of the really big, atmospheric crowds on Arsenal's North Bank, and he rued the higher admission prices and the introduction of bond schemes. But he could also see why the clubs had tired of their traditional, problematic fan base. Hornby saw his own life events as synonymous with match events. He showed how football could provoke memories, fantasies, daydreams and connections with others. Large crowds offered belonging and anonymity. In the midst of so much disaster and doubt Hornby and others showed that an obsession with football could become fashionable again.

33

'AMEN TO THE KOP'

JIM POLICED THE ANFIELD KOP in Liverpool for many years after the Second World War. The Kopites knew him as 'the Walrus' because he had a big white moustache. One day Jim confiscated a ball which had come on the pitch after a chaotic game of head-the-ball at the front of the Kop. A little girl was lifted over the fence by fans. She walked up to Jim and said, 'Excuse me, Mr Walrus, can I have my ball?'

Jim enjoyed seeing the same people in the same places every other Saturday. He found the early post-war Kop a respectable place with a lot of ex-servicemen in the crowd. Spectators usually gathered in an orderly manner outside the ground, and, if necessary, a mounted policeman could turn the queues into the shape of a corkscrew or a snake. Inside the ground very little police control was needed. Occasionally Jim stopped a shenanigan, but he knew how to approach Scousers. He recognised that he shouldn't bully them or talk down to them. Scousers were generally a gregarious bunch who liked to please – unless you upset them.

On some days Jim found the crowd more entertaining than the players. The Kop was better than theatre. Sometimes the noise gave him shivers up and down his legs. Then he would have to walk to the other end of the ground and back to recover the feeling in his limbs.

Policemen like Jim were known to be tender-hearted and sport-loving. They were operating on private land but they had their normal powers of arrest. Such powers were rarely needed in the 1940s and 1950s, when the police were more like crowd stewards and the major problems were petty theft and forged tickets. But Jim looked daggers at the Anfield Kop in the mid-sixties when they sang, 'Ee, aye, addio, the Sergeant is a queer.' By 1967 he had a new nickname – Sergeant Pepper.

Into the 1960s the main spectator problems occurred outside the ground, where more and more cars mixed with pedestrians. For most of Jim's career crowd trouble was something unknown. Then one day a big 'drunk and incapable' man collapsed in the crowd. Four young policemen climbed in to get him out, and their helmets fell off. Jim collected three helmets from nearby spectators. He walked around the track with the helmets.

'What's the collection for, Sarge?' shouted one wag.

'It's for big Jim's benevolent fund,' Jim shouted back.

He was showered with pennies. A press photographer took the picture and it appeared in a newspaper with an appropriate headline ('Sergeant Does a Hat-Trick'). But other papers picked it up with different slants:

'Hooliganism Strikes Again' and 'Helmets After Battle'.

Assumptions were changing.

By the late 1970s the police planned matches as if they were military operations. They introduced Police Support Units and paramilitary riot gear, and used pre-emptive policing methods that targeted the most likely troublemakers (usually previous offenders). By the early 1980s it became more common to hear police dogs barking on railway stations on match days and see mobile cameras panning the streets. Stadium-seat design improved so that broken seats couldn't be used as weapons, local police combed streets near the football ground to purge any dangerous items and possible ambush spots were logged. Big-club fans were introduced to closed-circuit television cameras (CCTV) and perimeter fencing was erected at all large clubs except Arsenal and West Ham United. Rival fans were segregated and penning arrangements introduced in most major English stadiums. Fans made lazy comparisons with Colditz and Hereford Cattle Market, but the authorities lauded these stadiums as 'modern'. The police thought of unruly young fans as 'toe-rags', 'yobs' or 'animals'.

In 1989 the National Football Intelligence Unit was set up to identify persistent hooligan criminals. Whereas some football managers provided their players with dossiers on opponents, Chief Inspector Bryan Drew and his colleagues fed information to local Police Support Units about their next hooligan opponents. The consensual 1950s had given way to the confrontational 1980s, and one outcome was the Hillsborough disaster.

'Look, can't you see what's going on?' Liverpool fan Trevor Hicks shouted across at a senior South Yorkshire policeman. 'There's trouble down there. It's not a pitch invasion. For Christ's sake give them a hand.'

Hicks stood at the Leppings Lane end of Sheffield Wednesday's Hillsborough Stadium. He wore a leather jacket and jeans. He stood level with the police control box in one of the outside pens, and there was room to sit down. But the *central* pens contained far too many Liverpool supporters. That was obvious to Hicks.

'If I had my fuckin' suit on you'd take notice of me, but because I've got my leather jacket on I'm just a bloody football supporter,' Hicks shouted. 'Can't you see there's a problem? You must be able to fuckin' see.'

Hicks could see that the people in pen three were being crushed, and he knew his two teenage daughters were in there somewhere. He had become separated from them when he went to buy a programme. He knew that the Liverpool fans climbing the perimeter fence to get on to the pitch were trying to escape the crush. Hicks thought the police must be able to work that out. Yet the police were backing away into a restraining position on the pitch. They weren't helping the fans. Surely the men in the police control box watching the CCTV footage could see that Liverpool fans were in trouble? The box was close enough to the crushing.

'Can't you see what's going on?' Hicks shouted again. He was a pillar of the community, the managing director of a company working for a household name in security. He had worked closely with the police for seven years. He respected them, understood the difficulties of their job and sympathised with them for the pressures on their family life. You might say Trevor Hicks was an Establishment man. Until now.

The senior policeman looked at Hicks with contempt. 'Shut your fucking prattle,' he said.

Hicks grew desolate with concern. He now really feared for the safety of his two daughters. He couldn't believe that the police weren't helping. He knew this was a serious incident.

The date was Saturday 15 April 1989.

Liverpool v Nottingham Forest in an FA Cup semi-final.

The time was moving very slowly towards three o'clock.

And it felt like the police and spectators were on opposite sides.

In all, there were 1,122 police officers on duty on the day of the Hillsborough disaster, about one for every forty-five fans. The numbers included thirty-four mounted police from Liverpool and Nottingham, brought in to assist in marshalling their respective fans. About 38 per cent of South Yorkshire's total police force was at the match. The Hillsborough disaster ultimately claimed the lives of ninety-six Liverpool fans as a result of crushing on the Leppings Lane terraces.

*   *   *

Reading the survivors' stories is to trace a journey to hell and back. Yet the day had started so brightly. Fans with tickets set off in sunshine to watch a gala event. At the ground most got in without any trouble. In the tight area outside the Leppings Lane terraces, however, crowds became wedged and the stewarding seemed inefficient. Eventually, with fans fearing for their safety, Chief Superintendent David Duckenfield ordered the opening of the gates at that end of the stadium and people rushed in without guidance. The signposting was notoriously bad. Almost all the onrushers careered towards the tunnel leading to the already full central pens, and suddenly the smell of death was in the air. Many people in the overcrowded areas couldn't lift their arms from their sides. Some managed to climb to the seated area above. Others scaled the perimeter fence. The match was halted six minutes after kick-off.

The police officers got word of trouble among the Liverpool spectators and almost all of them assumed that this meant hooliganism. After all, this was a police force that had taken a notoriously hard line against the striking coalminers and was used to fighting the public. But why would fans invade the pitch six minutes after the start of a much-awaited FA Cup semi-final?

The referee got the players off the pitch. An ambulance arrived and the paramedics assessed the scene. Some fans tried to help. Doctors in the crowd did what they could. Advertising hoardings were used as stretchers. Most spectators watched helplessly. The police, still in restraining mode, formed a human phalanx across the halfway-line as if to keep apart rival fans.

The club gymnasium was converted into a makeshift mortuary and a casualty station for the injured. When the stadium was eventually evacuated many shocked fans were invited into local houses to use the phone or have a cup of tea. Others searched for phone boxes and queued to tell their family they were safe. People ran around between the stadium, the hospital and the mortuary, trying to find the missing. In the makeshift mortuary the police showed worried fans Polaroid photographs of the dead. If a dead person was identified, the police took statements from the relatives, asking them if the deceased 'liked a drink'. The dead were tested for blood-alcohol levels. It was clear from the start where the police were locating the blame.

The Leppings Lane terraces were left covered with debris – spectacles, shoes, coats, newspapers, programmes . . . and Trevor Hicks's radio.

The Hillsborough disaster was an immediate media story. TV cameras were present at the match, so images flew round the world almost instantaneously.

Meanwhile the charge nurse of a nearby Sheffield hospital, on his tea break and far away from any television or radio, had to rely on a garbled phone message that could have meant a car crash in the Hillsborough area for all he knew. He prepared for a major incident anyway. He phoned his boss and opened all the emergency cupboards.

At five o'clock BBC Radio 2 announced the start of *Sports Report*. For the only time in the programme's history, no music was played. This was a sombre occasion. Peter Jones reported from Hillsborough and listeners cried in their homes. In Sheffield the sun was still shining.

Later that evening the BBC's *Match of the Day* showed no football. Desmond Lynam's script was respectful. The television images were stark and scary. Of all the day's participants only the media people, accustomed to their clock culture, had a sense of time. For Trevor and Jenni Hicks, running around trying to find their girls and each other, the only sense of time was 'daylight' and 'darkness'. Their two daughters, Vickie and Sarah, had died in the crush.

The causes of the disaster involved presumptions about how spectators *might* behave at a football match. Policies put in place to curb hooliganism – pitch fencing, segregation of fans, CCTV cameras, pens, PSUs, attitudes to members of the public – somehow conspired with police mistakes to kill ninety-six Liverpool football fans. As Lord Justice Taylor wrote in his report after his inquiry, 'The main reason for the disaster was the failure of police control.' The crowd outside the Leppings Lane end of the stadium grew uncontrollably large. After the catastrophic decision to open the gates, spectators were not shepherded to the empty outside pens and the police reacted very slowly to the obvious over-crowding in the central pens.

'The lack of vigilant monitoring caused a sluggish reaction and response when the crush occurred,' said Taylor, who heard a succession of police officers say that they had expected fans to 'find their own level'. The Hillsborough disaster was one of a number of English disasters caused by the lack of concern for safety in the late 1980s.

Attitudes at football matches had changed enormously since the 1950s, when the Bolton disaster was still fresh in people's minds and football fans looked after one another in public space with a sense of collective engagement. In the 1980s public space seemed less valued. Rival fans fought one another and the police fought rival fans. It reached a point where potential hooliganism was all the police could see. And yet many people had suffered crushing injuries in the past. One example was in January 1983, when Luton Town played Manchester United. Lord Hatch of Lusby wrote to Baron Hill of Luton to say that people were injured in an overcrowded part of the ground and it could have been much worse. 'I talked with the police sergeant in charge at the end of the match and he entirely agreed that the situation had been dangerous throughout the game,' he said.

After hearing evidence about Hillsborough, Lord Justice Taylor defended the Liverpool fans, saying that 'the great majority were not drunk nor even the worse for drink' and 'there was not a very significant body of ticketless fans in the crowd'. According to Taylor, 'some officers, seeking to rationalise their loss of control, over-estimated the drunken element in the crowd'.

As ever, the press came up with spurious theories that stuck. Just as the *Star* had claimed that a firecracker had started the 1985 Bradford City fire, so the *Sun* laid the blame at the feet of Liverpool fans and published false accounts of looting and fans urinating on the dead. Sales of the *Sun* dipped sharply on Merseyside and never recovered.

Three newspaper columnists were censured for writing erroneous stories and families of the Hillsborough victims were harassed by members of the media. Tabloid newspapers published disturbing photographs of dying fans and one journalist tried to sneak into a hospital by posing as a social worker.

On the evening of 15 April 1989 a few stunned fans tied Liverpool and Everton scarves to the Shankly Gates at Anfield. On Sunday morning Liverpool chief executive Peter Robinson opened the gates to the ground; he realised that people would gain some comfort from seeing Anfield as a shrine. Over the next few days thousands of people queued to file in and pay their respects. They left tokens of sympathy on the Kop terracing – hats, scarves, flags, teddy bears, photographs, jackets, flowers, badges and all sorts of other memory-evoking objects. These soon spread to cover the pitch. Bob Gill, secretary of the Liverpool supporters' club, later had the onerous task of clearing the stadium of these treasured possessions.

Condolence books in Sheffield and Liverpool collected around 7,000 messages and signatures. Mike Brennan of Warwick University studied the entries and found they could be religious, quasi-religious (e.g. referring to Bill Shankly's immortality), communications with the dead, references to the afterlife or a celebration of community or carnival. Brennan found that multiple losses could co-exist in the aftermath. People vicariously process unacknowledged or unresolved grief. The menfolk of Brennan's city (Sheffield) had experienced enormous loss of work identity and masculinity as a result of 70,000 steel redundancies between 1979 and 1986. Modern society needed rituals to deal with such major social change. Culled industries, such as steel and coalmining, didn't get the mass funerals they deserved, and the repressed grief came out following Hillsborough. The same was true in Liverpool.

Liverpool FC ensured that someone would represent the club at every funeral. Many players went to a dozen or more and their wives were very supportive. Liverpool manager Kenny Dalglish and his wife Marina were both very strong. But the trauma of Hillsborough caught up with these key Liverpool people later. The club became a sad place, wreathed in a sense of loss.

In the midst of the mourning there was some more football to play. The FA finally decided that the 1988–9 FA Cup competition should continue. Liverpool won the semi-final rematch (at Old Trafford) and beat Everton 3–2 after extra time to win the Final. Then, favourites to win the League too, Liverpool lost the title on goals scored when a stoppage-time goal by Michael Thomas gave Arsenal a dramatic 2–0 win at Anfield in the season's last match. Arsenal fans celebrated wildly while Kopites sat down and watched. There was more to life and death than football.

Millions of people were troubled by the Hillsborough disaster. Five years later police officers were still resigning at a rate of three a month because of that day's trauma. Some suicides could be attributed to the event. Survivors were troubled by guilt – 'How come children died and I didn't?' – and some felt that they had killed others in the crush even though they clearly had not. Many felt they could have done more to help.

The House of Lords eventually ruled that relatives of the dead fans were not entitled to compensation unless they had a close emotional relationship with the victim and were at the game. But police officers were granted compensation for suffering post-traumatic stress while working. Overall, Hillsborough produced a mass case of post-traumatic stress – anger and guilt, flashbacks, depression, altered sleep, nightmares, increased drinking and smoking, fatigue and energy loss. Almost everyone on Merseyside knew someone who knew someone who had died. Around the country many people could identify with the deceased fans because they too had once set out on a sunny day to see a football match.

The Hillsborough tragedy and the Council takeover at Halifax Town were symbols of how the English game had to change. The message at

Halifax was how the *smaller* professional clubs had to adapt in order to bond with local communities. The message from Hillsborough was about how the *bigger* clubs and policing had to be altered to make stadiums safe. Lord Justice Taylor reported that stadiums needed to be modernised, football's leadership needed to be more effective, spectators should be involved in decision-making and police strategies changed. Delays to kick-offs were encouraged in cases where the police saw that there were turnstile hold-ups and the possibility of people stampeding the entrances. The Football Spectators Act 1989 was kept on the statute books but the Tory idea of membership cards was not taken up. CCTV footage in grounds would now be monitored for safety reasons as well as for public-order purposes. Changes were made to emergency-service response. The police would now take responsibility for hooliganism, but clubs would deal with issues of fan management and crowd safety. The Football Offences Act 1991 introduced new offences – entering the pitch without good reason and chanting obscene or racist abuse.

As the killer perimeter fences started to be removed, football-fan leaders said that anyone who intruded on to the field would now be climbing over the bodies of the Hillsborough dead. By 1992, however, only half of the ninety-two League clubs had jettisoned *all* perimeter fencing. Larger clubs made plans to turn terraces into seated areas because Lord Justice Taylor reported that 'seating does more to achieve those [safety] objectives than any other single measure'. Taylor recommended that no spectator should be more than fourteen seats from a gangway.

More family sections were introduced into grounds. Ticket prices rose and stadium conditions became more gentrified (better food, improved toilets, corporate boxes and so on). It took some time to work out a consistent interpretation of the new regulations – when should a person be arrested for racial abuse, for instance? – and issues of desegregation, suitable stadium language and bans for troublemakers proved contentious.

The basic enmity between police and some spectators remained. In fact it increased a little with news of rising police costs and police input into fixture scheduling, kick-off times and ticketing arrangements. However, the police became more likely to view football fans as *citizens* rather than as animals or hooligans. At Preston North End special constables made a point of chatting to away fans before matches, the police met with supporters' organisations to improve relations and Preston's police football liaison officer wrote a regular column in the club's match programme.

Eventually there emerged a clearer demarcation of lines of responsibility between stewards and the police. Stewards were employed by the club to search supporters entering the stadium, make sure all fans had seats, enforce ground regulations and ensure spectator safety. The police had the job of enforcing the law, keeping the peace and providing a deterrent. They might be called on to arrest drunken spectators in the stadium, enforce exclusion orders, prevent theft and obtain intelligence.

At the time of the Hillsborough disaster 'Walrus' Jim had been retired from the police for more than a decade. He understood that the Anfield Kop would become an all-seater stand within a few years. Bigger brains than mine are sorting this one out, he thought, but it would be a shame if it breaks up the Kop choir and scuppers the general camaraderie. Jim was sorry to see the terraces go. The Kop was a spectacle and a shrine. Look at how many fans' ashes had been buried in front of it.

'Amen to the Kop,' Jim said in 1994, when the seating was installed. 'And to all who stood on it.'

34

DON'T TRUST THE PRESS

'EITHER WAY, WHETHER YOU TALK to them or you don't talk to them, they slaughter you,' said one established England international when asked about newspaper reporters in 1991. 'So you try and be fair, and you try and be nice to them. And there are certain ones that stitch you up and you don't speak to them again. With me they get one chance. If they blow it, they're history. But the sad thing is, now, you speak to one [reporter] and it gets passed round. But by the time it's got passed round six people it's totally different. That's the sad thing, and that's what's annoying about it. At the end of the day I've got maybe one or two people in the North-West that I can trust and I'll speak to them, and if they pass it on then that's unlucky. That's a chance you take.'

In the early 1990s England international players saw the media in two ways. On the credit side the intense coverage of high-level football provided free publicity for the sport and created enormous public interest, and players recognised that some journalists reported football reasonably. On the debit side some newspapers and television stations sought sensationalism and were not really bothered about football as a game. England players often saw the press as too negative towards the national team. It felt like some journalists wanted England to fail, with the headlines already written.

'You're not going to control the media,' said one veteran international. 'They are an independent organisation and they are only interested in one thing – selling newspapers – and the more days they can get out of a story, the better. A reasonable amount of co-operation goes on but at the end of the day a lot of journalists themselves say, "Look, we don't want to write what we write but we're told to write it." You can't control editors and newspaper owners.'

In the late 1980s a big change had occurred. Football stories shifted from the sports pages to the news pages.

'When I started with England, the relationship with the press was very good,' said one experienced international. 'You could stand and have a couple of half-lagers with them, have a little chit-chat, and nothing would ever be mentioned in the papers about what you've been talking about. Then for some reason, about six years ago [1985], it changed. You'd be talking to them and all of a sudden you'd see it in the paper.

'It is to the point where they don't just want to know about football. Because they build you up to being a star in the society then they think that the public have a right to know everything that you're doing in your private life. I don't think this is the case in Italy and America. They don't treat the sportsmen like that. I mean, people can criticise me as much as they want as far as on the football field is concerned, but I don't see what right the public have in knowing that I drive a Mercedes or what car I've ordered. You get press phoning you up, saying, "I hear you're jumping up on a waiting-list for this car," and all that.'

Every English footballer dreams of playing for his country; not many get the chance. Opportunities were particularly scarce if you were a midfield player in the late 1980s. Then you had to covet one of the positions filled by the contrasting talents of Bryan Robson, Peter Reid and Glenn Hoddle.

Towards the end of the decade, however, the call came for another midfielder to join the England squad. He was an established player in his early twenties. Despite the big-time pressures involved, he felt that the game should be fun, and he was always happiest when he played with a smile on his face.

When he got the England call he drove south in a sponsored car with his name on the side. When he reached the hotel rendezvous he noticed that no other car carried a player's name. He walked into the hotel. The other players were having dinner. All the big names were there. Shilts. Terry Butcher. Hoddle. Robbo. Reidy. Gary Lineker.

The newcomer sat at the end of the table and waited.

The first person to approach him was Bryan Robson, the team captain.

'Welcome to the squad,' Robson said. 'I've not met you before.'

Robson introduced him to everyone.

An England international cap is a peak achievement confirming excellence, national identity and family roots. This midfielder had started playing competitively at nine. He had first turned out in his older brother's team, playing with boys two years older. Having an older brother accelerates many players' sporting careers.

At thirteen he couldn't get enough of football. He ran around the roads for extra training and often played five games a week, including two on Sundays. On Saturdays he stood on the terraces at his local club, eating a meat pie and drinking Bovril. He wasted his examinations and left school a month before his sixteenth birthday to become an apprentice footballer. He went back to college a year later and did his English O level.

As part of his football apprenticeship at a lower-league club he brushed the grass off the pitch after the groundsman had been over it with a Flymo. At the start of a season he painted the goalposts white and painted the boundary walls in the team's colours (because his club didn't have enough advertising boards). He swept the litter off the terracing after matches, and sometimes he came away a few pounds richer after picking up all the small coins. At sixteen he was paid £14 per week, at seventeen it was £16. His first-ever professional contract was £80 per week for two years. He made his debut for the reserves at fourteen and played in the first team at sixteen. On the day of his senior debut the manager let him carry the kit and lay it out for everyone before telling him he was playing.

In the late 1980s and early 1990s about half of full England internationals were groomed through the under-age international teams. From as young as fifteen, for some, their England apprenticeship included new experiences: training camps; coping with jet-lag; adapting to the added expectations and pressures; blending in quickly with team-mates who were relative strangers; following a code of behaviour in hotels, press conferences and National Anthem line-ups; and so on.

The players had to be very adaptable to cope at *full* international level. They were representing their country, not their club, and failure was like letting down the nation. They were treated as national public property. England's training was scrutinised by every newspaper and TV network. Each international match seemed like a Cup Final.

On the field international football was more like chess than the typical biff-and-bang English club game. If you lost the ball your team might not see it again for several minutes. In one of his first international matches our chunky midfielder came on for twenty minutes as a substitute. It was the quickest twenty minutes he'd ever played in his life. He didn't see the ball at all. The opponents seemed so skilful, passing the ball between themselves, and he came off the pitch dripping with sweat. You've got a lot to learn, he told himself.

It was mentally tiring. One player thought that international games needed more concentration because you were playing with relative strangers. Another player thought that international matches were cagier and less physical than top English matches. You had to be more patient. At one point on the pitch you could turn with the ball and have fifteen clear yards of daylight, but the marking was fiercely tight in critical zones, especially near the penalty areas. You had to be ready for a sudden shift in the pace of the game. Some people thought that it took a dozen games to get used to international football. European club football was a useful stepping-stone between the two.

People say that it must be a great life, travelling all over the world to play sport, but England players don't do much sightseeing. They fly out on the Monday for a Wednesday match, sleep the travel out of their bodies, train, rest, eat, sleep again, go to the stadium, play the match and then fly home immediately.

During the 1990 World Cup Finals England players saw a bit more of the host country (Italy), but most were careful about leaving their hotel. If they walked down the street, it was too easy for England fans to recognise them and that brought additional responsibility and risk. Arsenal players were worried about meeting Tottenham fans, and Manchester United players were concerned about running into Merseysiders. On the other hand England players appreciated having their fans behind them.

International footballers have to pass a lot of time before and after matches. They hang around in hotels, dressing-rooms or transport vehicles. The higher the class of football, the more hours to kill. A local player may be able to leave home at one o'clock on a match day and be home by five-thirty. An international player may be away for three or four days. For big tournaments, like the 1990 World Cup Finals, the trip lasts several weeks.

In Italy the England lads stopped training at 1pm and had nothing to do between 2pm and dinner at 7pm. It wasn't easy to understand the Italian television stations and there were no satellite channels available.

'The average boredom level of a footballer isn't too high,' said one player, a man who had anticipated going to university before football intervened.

The England players took two or three dozen videos with them to Italy, but they had probably seen them all twice by the time the tournament started. The hotel complex had a golf course, a driving range, pool tables, tennis courts, a swimming pool and training facilities, but golf and tennis were restricted because the training was planned so precisely that any extra activity could detract from fitness. The weather was superb, but time in the sun was rationed.

'A lot of people think that it's a good life, being in a hotel,' said one 1990 England World Cup player, 'but I can assure you that it's boring, especially when you have got a ten-year-old lad, a seven-year-old daughter, and the wife's not there as well. It's hard work because I thoroughly enjoy having the family around me.'

The further England went in the tournament, the longer between matches and the greater the chances of being bored. Meanwhile the more predatory members of the British media watched and waited.

Before the 1990 World Cup Finals most England players thought that the British press would seek 'the big scandal', even when one didn't exist. Paul Gascoigne was a good bet for a story.

Gascoigne was twenty-three at the time. He was a complicated man-child who had suffered a number of personal tragedies and unfairly blamed himself for most of them. Gascoigne had moments of despair, panic attacks, nervous twitches and obsessive-compulsive disorder. When bored and hyperactive he engaged in crazy stunts and dangerous pranks. He was a vulnerable man who needed sympathy but got publicity instead.

When Gascoigne joined the England squad at Luton, three weeks before the 1990 World Cup Finals, he found that he had left his passport behind. His friend, Jimmy 'Five Bellies' Gardner, drove to and from Newcastle to collect the passport while Gascoigne waited in the hotel bar. Forest's Neil Webb stayed with him because he knew that the British news reporters in the foyer were looking for a Gazza faux pas. Reporters joined the two players for a drink, after Webb had checked that it was off the record. But the story was a big one: 'It's 4am and Gazza Is Training in the Bar.'

'Gascoigne tackled pints of lager during a relaxing six hours that ended as dawn broke,' wrote John Coles of the *Daily Express*, 'just four hours away from the squad's departure for Italy.'

The game of Chinese whispers was under way.

Gazza 'in bar brawl', reported the *Daily Star*.

'Gazza Held by Cops,' said the *Daily Sport*.

Top-class professionals try to let the stories wash over them.

'Funny enough, it has been more painful for me to see the reaction of my parents and my wife than it is for me,' said one England international. 'It's never bothered me really. There might have been times when I was younger where you got a bit down and somebody has criticised you, but it used to fire me up, and I used to use that as a springboard to go out and play even better. But it hurts me to see my family worrying and letting it affect them.'

Footballers don't trust the press. After the stories published early in the 1990 tournament, England players stopped talking to reporters. This was an irony, though, because some players had newspaper columns themselves. One was under contract with the *Daily Star*, two were with the *Sun* and two more were with the *Daily Mirror*.

When Bobby Robson's England team surprised many people by reaching the 1990 World Cup semi-final, losing a penalty shoot-out to West Germany, the newspapers resurrected two world wars:

'The Kaiser Puts Troops on Full Alert.'
'Bash the Bosch.'
'Herr We Go.'
'Nobble the Jerryatrics.'
'Out by a Herr's Breath.'
'Kr-out.'

Graham Taylor took over as England manager in July 1990. Terry Butcher and Peter Shilton had just retired from international football, Bryan Robson was already thirty-three years old and injuries excluded Paul Gascoigne from all except three internationals in the next three seasons. There were ritualistic 'Taylor out' newspaper articles in his first year, even though Taylor's England team was undefeated during that time. England qualified for the 1992 European Championships from a group containing Poland, the Republic of Ireland and Turkey.

Graham Taylor understood the press because his father had been a journalist in Scunthorpe. Times had changed, however, since Taylor's childhood, when there was one local newspaper and no local radio. By the early 1990s there were over a hundred local and national daily newspapers, nearly a hundred radio stations, over twenty Sunday newspapers and an increasing number of commercial TV channels. Taylor understood that many reporters now needed a story every day. He introduced a European system for press contacts whereby journalists could ask for four England players for interview. Before they went out to face the press the manager attended a session with them where questions were fired at the players.

The main problem, according to the players, was that the press could do anything they wanted, with no comeback.

'They can ruin people's lives and their playing careers,' said one international player. 'They build you up to knock you down. You only realise all this as you get older. I've been stitched up a few times in the last few months and it won't happen again because I won't speak to them again. I'm still learning really.'

'Graham Taylor's got things so well organised,' said a more experienced player. 'There was a slight problem when Bobby Robson was in charge of the plane. He had the press sitting at the back, and we were always at the front, so they could always see what we were doing. I mean, if you come back from a good win, where the boys are having a few, they're seeing everything you're doing. So now Graham Taylor's swapped it round. We sit at the back and if the press want to see anything they've got to be looking round. So you can see them looking at you, so you know to steady down and not be stupid or whatever.'

When interviewed during the 1991–2 season these elite footballers were preparing for the 1992 European Championships in Sweden. They were intelligent individuals who had tremendous body awareness, a keen eye for detail and minds that were hungry for knowledge about football and all its trimmings. Four had A levels and three had spent a year at college. Two had trained as electricians before taking a drop in wages to become footballers. This cohort of England players were much more likely to vote Conservative than Labour (responding particularly to tax issues) and their favourite newspaper was the *Daily Express*.

'The *Sun* is quite a popular paper with the footballers as well, in respect of they pay the most money for interviews, so they generally get the information before anyone else gets it,' said one England international player. 'I wouldn't buy it, I'd borrow it. The actual match reports in the *Sun* are not close to my heart, to say the least.'

Graham Taylor knew how difficult it was to win a major tournament with an England team. As well as all the traditional 'club v country' tensions, major tournaments were held during the English close season in unfamiliar weather conditions after a gruelling season.

'Last year I played fifty-nine, sixty competitive games, and that's nothing to do with pre-season or anything,' said one England player. 'That is a frightening amount of games. There is a big call for them to cut the League games down. When you actually sit down after a game and you think how tired you are and you think, "I've got a game tomorrow, and I shouldn't have played Saturday, and now the chances of me playing tomorrow are quite slim." And the pressure on your body to get yourself into the physical state to play for another ninety minutes!'

One of the biggest problems, given the arduous English schedule, was just getting players to international matches. Graham Taylor would often find that eight or nine proven internationals could be absent from an international squad. He was critical of a system that produced so many injured players. As the clubs paid the wages they could be protective of players with minor injuries, and withdrawals from international squads were commonplace.

The British press's treatment of Graham Taylor was particularly vitriolic. 'Swedes 2 Turnips 1' was one headline after England's exit from the European Championships. The next day the same newspaper published a strange caricature of Taylor as half man and half vegetable. Newspaper abuse had always been part of the England manager's job – even Sir Alf Ramsey had it – but now it had shifted to personal criticism and harassment.

When England lost 2–0 to the USA in June 1993 the media camped outside Taylor's house in England. His wife returned home to look after her wheelchair-bound mother but couldn't get into the driveway as the media people were occupying it.

One journalist approached her for an interview.

'I don't do interviews,' she said.

'About fuckin' time you did,' one reporter replied.

After this Taylor wondered whether the job was worth it. At times he had to take legal advice because of the media pressure he and his family were under. When Taylor resigned in November 1993, having failed to guide England to the 1994 World Cup Finals, he couldn't get into his home for two days for journalists. His parents answered a knock on their door to find a television camera aimed at their faces and someone asking questions. Taylor's parents were in their seventies.

What is going on here? Graham Taylor asked himself. Does getting the story beat everything? Is it that important that it doesn't matter who you upset or who you hurt?

When he agreed to being filmed for a TV documentary, Taylor thought it would tell the story of England's qualification for the World Cup Finals.

Only part way through did he realise that England might not qualify. The eventual film vilified him, featuring his touchline emotions and most of his swearwords from the previous year.

'Graham was great to the press,' said Republic of Ireland manager Jack Charlton shortly after Taylor had left the FA. 'In fact Graham said far too much. Graham would take twenty minutes to explain something. He could have done it in a minute, but he wanted the people to understand what he was trying to do and the way he was doing it, and in doing that he gave them more and more ammunition to fire back at him. You cannot have a good relationship with the English media. You can try and do your best for them, but you can't trust them.'

Being an England manager or playing for England seems like the greatest honour in the world, so why can't everyone deliver? Well, one reason is the intense media pressure. The media is part of the England-team story. Managers may be correct in thinking that relaxation improves performance, but England players will get little help there from the press.

35

A WHOLE NEW BALL GAME

G RAHAM KELLY WAS SOMETHING OF a Renaissance man of football. Not only did he become a top football administrator, but he trained with Accrington Stanley as a teenager footballer, kept goal for Blackpool's A team and made his Wembley Stadium debut as a 51-year-old, bustling centre forward for the Football Trust. Like a lot of football men, he could play golf to a single-figure handicap; unlike most of them, though, he was also an experienced local referee. In his fifties Kelly ran half-marathons and even a marathon, thus emulating boyhood heroes like Stan Mortensen and Stan Matthews, who endlessly lapped the field in training. More than anything, though, Kelly understood football's rules and regulations. His football career was unprecedented. He was Football League secretary (1979–88) and Football Association chief executive (1988–98). In his heart, Kelly was simply a football fan. He wanted the best for the game.

After leaving school Kelly spent four years at Barclays Bank before joining the Football League as a junior clerk. He studied for chartered secretary qualifications and was appointed assistant secretary in 1973, succeeding Alan Hardaker as secretary six years later. In the early 1980s Kelly knew that the League's future was clouded by poor finances, crowd violence and outdated facilities. He worked closely with Sir Norman Chester and told Football League insiders that the Oxford don was a clever man who understood the game only too well. But if Chester couldn't unite his committee of six, what chance was there of all ninety-two League clubs acting together?

Graham Kelly also knew that Margaret Thatcher's proposed membership-card scheme wouldn't solve professional football's fan problems. He saw a power struggle developing between the government, the Football League management committee, the chairmen of the top League clubs, the Football Association, the Professional Footballers' Association, the television companies and, a long way behind, the supporters' associations. Throw in a few mavericks like Oxford United chairman Robert Maxwell and Chelsea chairman Ken Bates, and you get a sense of Kelly's problems as Football League secretary in the late 1980s.

Kelly was long familiar with the term Super League; it had been around longer than the 1983 Chester Report. But the first substantial Super League story came out in October 1985. The First Division clubs threatened to break away from the rest of the League if their demands were not met. The top chairmen were briefly appeased by a 50 per cent share of the television money going to First Division clubs, but the League's four divisions were soon divided by far more than promotion and relegation. And no one knew that more than Graham Kelly.

Throughout the 1980s Kelly frequently sat across a table from FA secretary Ted Croker and thought, Well, maybe the grass *is* greener on the other side, maybe I can do a job there someday. When Croker left the FA in 1988 Kelly applied for the post.

The FA chief executive (previously FA secretary) had more influence on the national game than the Football League secretary. His brief included the development of coaching, the international arena, the future of refereeing and the grassroots game. The Football League secretary was confined to running a specific competition full of tetchy professional clubs who were mere members of the FA. The Football Association job was more wide-ranging, challenging and appealing for the ambitious Kelly. He was appointed in September 1988.

Kelly's unique job move – from the professional enclosure to the governance side of the sport – contributed to an astonishing course of events that led to the formation of a new league, to be called the FA Premier League. In football it was normally difficult to get committee action. People could be selective in what they followed up, voting systems were arcane, agendas were unstructured and meetings sometimes drifted off into anecdotes and name-dropping. But a major change took place during the 1990–1 season. In the wake of the Hillsborough disaster and the Taylor Report, a small group of people took an initiative. Kelly was a pivotal figure.

In October 1990 the Football League published *One Game, One Team, One Voice – Managing Football's Future*. It was a discussion document aimed at a power share between the Football League and the FA at club and national level. This proposal was designed to satisfy Lord Justice Taylor's call for common leadership in football. But the League's idea went down badly at FA headquarters. The FA was already English football's governing body. The professional clubs were ultimately under its control. The FA simply needed a plan of its own.

Graham Kelly responded by asking Charles Hughes, the FA's director of coaching and education, to co-ordinate a new FA document, *The Blueprint for the Future of Football*, which would establish more sophisticated planning in the game at both the local and the professional level.

On 6 December 1990 Arsenal vice-chairman David Dein and Liverpool's new chairman Noel White visited FA chairman Sir Bert Millichip and Graham Kelly. White and Dein were clearly concerned about the Football League's ability to come up with an acceptable television contract for 1992 at a time when clubs needed to fund stadium changes following the Taylor Report. Kelly learned that the visitors were considering a breakaway league, but there was one major obstacle.

'We're worried about Regulation 10,' White and Dein told Kelly. Regulation 10 was the requirement for clubs to give three years' notice to quit the Football League. Ironically Kelly had been involved in the regulation's introduction in the late 1980s.

'Leave it with me,' Kelly replied. He went away to discuss the matter with the FA's *Blueprint* team. A vision of an FA Premier League arose.

Kelly was concerned about the FA's position if the Football League's top clubs broke away and established a completely independent, market-driven league. The new league would have its own sponsor, it might shackle the England players and the FA could be seriously weakened.

What were the alternatives?

In January 1991, as the FA's *Blueprint* discussions continued, Kelly, Millichip and Hughes talked with Saatchi & Saatchi's Alex Fynn, who had previously been involved in estimating the real value of football's television contract. Together these men formed a tight-knit group. They were sworn to secrecy about the new FA Premier League.

As the *Blueprint* document developed, the FA's commercial strategy became clearer. The England team, the new FA Premier League and the FA Cup competition would be at the top of the English football pyramid. Not only would this enhance the England's team prospects and end the League–FA power battle, but it would raise commercial income for stadium improvements, grassroots football and all the rest. According to the eventual *Blueprint*, this pyramid elite would guarantee income of £112 million to run the whole of the sport. Graham Kelly was later challenged many times about how that figure came about, but always refused to justify it on the grounds of commercial confidentiality. The figure was Fynn's estimate.

Late in 1990 Kelly phoned Rick Parry, an Arthur Young management consultant in Manchester. The two men had worked together on one of Parry's earlier consultancies, in 1988, when the Football League clubs were tearing one another apart over television money.

Kelly knew that Parry was a football fan and a moderniser. Parry had just come to the end of his work on Manchester's 1992 Olympic bid, so he was happy to work for the FA on a Premier League outline. Parry already knew not to be surprised at anything that happened in football. He thought that the job would be two months of good fun and nothing would materialise.

Parry joined the FA *Blueprint*'s inner circle. He felt that the Premier League idea was shoehorned into the *Blueprint* as a response to the emerging power struggle between the Football League and the FA. White and Dein's discussions with Millichip and Kelly were just a happy coincidence.

The FA and the big-club chairmen liked Rick Parry's work on the Premier League plan. The FA now had its own programme for change.

In April 1991 the FA announced that its forthcoming *Blueprint* would outline the formation of the FA Premier League. This took almost everyone by surprise, including some of the *Blueprint*'s own committee members and contributors. It was an incredible moment in the history of English football. Historically the FA had always been the guardian of the game's morality and discipline, an anti-commercial body that had even stopped ex-professional players from holding office within the FA. Now the FA was opening its doors to the ultra-professionals. The FA would be running the game's biggest professional league.

The announcement was made possible by a special FA Council meeting on 8 April 1991. The FA Premier League was accepted in principle there, and the Football League's Regulation 10 was disallowed on the grounds that it was considered incompatible with the free movement and progress of clubs as envisaged by Sanction Regulation 24.

The FA's prototype was an eighteen-club FA Premier League. It would clear space for European club matches and England fixtures, bring the top

English League closer to the other European national leagues and reduce the burn-out experienced by top players. But when Bert Millichip met the prospective FA Premier League clubs the next month, he said that the size of the league was up to the clubs themselves. A big mistake. The chairmen settled on twenty-two clubs in the first instance.

When the FA's *The Blueprint for the Future of Football* was finally published, on 20 June 1991, media interest was monopolised by the single paragraph unveiling 'a Premier League within the administration of the Football Association'. Kelly tried but failed to interest the media in other *Blueprint* issues, such as fans, referees, community roots, player development, sports medicine and the plan for an International Sports Institute.

And so it would continue.

The FA Premier League was here to dominate the media interest.

One desperate low point came when Football League president Bill Fox reacted to the possible loss of the League's most powerful clubs by threatening to disaffiliate the League from the FA, thus raising the possibility of football anarchy. The only real ray of hope for the Football League came when the PFA's own blueprint, *For the Good of the Game*, proposed a power-sharing arrangement between the League, the FA and the PFA. The PFA also pointed out that a number of England international players – David Seaman, David Platt, Geoff Thomas and Lee Sharpe – had started their League careers in the Fourth Division. But Graham Kelly knew it was too late. The top players were not going to revolt against the new deal. They were happy with the idea of a new league that offered bigger financial rewards, fewer matches and less player burn-out.

Shortly before the final deal was agreed Football League chief executive Arthur Sandford asked the FA to take over *all* the League clubs. The idea was dismissed as unrealistic and distasteful. As Football League assistant secretary Andy Williamson said darkly, 'It's like a rape victim asking the rapist to marry her.'

On 31 July 1991 Mr Justice Rose concluded that the FA *did* have the constitutional power to set up its own Premier League, so the Football League's cause was finally lost. On 23 September 1991 the FA, Division One and the Football League finally signed documents committing all to the new FA Premier League, with a smaller, poorer Football League left in its wake.

*   *   *

Graham Kelly soon found out that the FA's new plan faced a challenge from within. The FA Council argued against the new alliance. They didn't want twenty FA Premier League representatives on their Council – they settled on five – and the idea of a sponsored 'FA *Carling* Premier League' rankled.

At the second FA Council meeting after the approval, Kelly realised that the FA was not up to handling this momentous opportunity. The FA wasn't a forward-looking business with a compact board of directors capable of managing such a gift horse. Later Kelly felt he should have envisaged this sort of resistance. Legal challenges or risk-taking behaviour were just not in the FA's make-up. But Kelly had no choice over the timing. White and Dein were making breakaway noises, satellite television companies were steaming over the horizon with big money and the 1992 football contract needed sorting. Kelly couldn't tell ITV's Greg Dyke and BSkyB's Rupert Murdoch to go away for ten years and come back when the FA had restructured for the modern era. This golden opportunity to secure English football's future was happening *now*.

Kelly's vision quickly ran away from him. By June 1991 he already sensed that the Premier League was becoming something else. Kelly thought he was reining in the top clubs for the FA, but in fact he was freeing them to form their own favoured economic structure.

The various supporters' associations responded to the FA *Blueprint* with their own plans. The Football Supporters' Association blueprint contained one prescient section: 'If the events of 1991 demonstrate anything, it is that there can be no such thing as a hard and fast blueprint for the future of football. There are too many competing and conflicting interests, too many compromises to be made and too many people unwilling to do as they are told by the *Blueprint*'s authors.'

By the end of 1992 only twenty-four of the FA *Blueprint*'s eighty-eight major recommendations had been implemented.

The FA Premier League was the first European sports league to be developed by and for television. The inaugural FA Premier League television contract was a contest between Dyke's ITV and Murdoch's BSkyB. Dyke felt that football must be better off with audiences of eight million (with ITV) rather than BSkyB's putative half a million, and that ITV could compete financially. But Murdoch put a lot of time and cash aside to woo the Premier League.

He realised that clubs were concerned about over-exposure on TV and that the more affluent consumers were willing to pay (through income or credit) to fund their leisure pursuits. This was the era of home ownership (65 per cent in 1990, compared with 53 per cent in 1980), home comforts (75 per cent had central heating in 1990), home videos, home gyms – and, quite likely, home subscription satellite football. BSkyB recognised that there were sufficient affluent working-class and middle-class consumers to produce the necessary profit. Many people had been captivated by England's success at the 1990 World Cup finals.

The deal went Murdoch's way. Alan Sugar, who had taken over as chairman of Tottenham Hotspur, backed the BSkyB bid. Sugar's company had a deal with BSkyB to produce TV satellite dishes, but he had declared a conflict of interests and, in modern thinking, that made his involvement OK. The BBC had contributed to the ITV bid in order to guarantee their *Match of the Day* highlights programme but they pulled out in the final few days. Greg Dyke pointed out that BBC head Marmaduke Hussey had once worked for Rupert Murdoch, and Dyke complained that ITV had been left out of the auction towards the end.

The core *Blueprint* idea that all the income and commercial properties of the FA and the FA Premier League should be centralised (as a means of supporting the England team and the wider game) was soon ditched by the FA Premier League clubs. They refused to pool their sponsorships with the FA. They also refused to have an FA director on the Premier League board. Graham Kelly was not that surprised. The German model, with the Bundesliga integral to the German FA, was never likely to suit the big clubs in England. The historical division between the FA types and the professional League men remained. In the end the FA took a 'special share' in the Premier League, with rights of veto on certain questions. The upshot was that from then on the FA and the Premier League negotiated their own sponsorship and TV deals and each kept its own income. This was now far from Graham Kelly's vision of the FA Premier League. The FA would have little input into the Premier League, the England team wouldn't really benefit from the new arrangements and the clubs would continue to win the club v country battle.

Rick Parry was appointed chief executive of the new FA Premier League. Parry was very good at his job. He introduced some strategic thinking and brought a rare sense of coolness to an emotionally charged environment of unruly chairman. The new League was more consensual than the old one, and it was easier to agree a constitution and a formula for sharing TV income. It was one club one vote and there were no committees. Parry felt it was a streamlined organisation that could make decisions more easily than the old set-up. Graham Kelly could only look on with envy. As the FA and the Premier League drifted apart, Parry allied himself totally to the clubs. His office was in Manchester, thus retaining the old geographical separation between the FA and the major professional league.

Although the new Premier League was criticised by fans and UEFA for taking live television coverage away from the terrestrial channels, it proved a good business deal. The new policy of more live games, shown to a restricted audience, minimised the impact on attendances and seemed to market the sport more effectively. In fact attendances rose. Ticket prices rose too, but Parry blamed that on the cost of stadium improvements required by the Taylor Report.

Graham Kelly's hopes of the FA leading a united sport were now dashed. The old First Division was independently running itself. The FA's involvement in negotiating this change stemmed from its own ambition and a coincidence of mutual interests at a particular time. Even if the FA Council had backed Kelly, the odds were that the Premier League clubs would still have run the new league. British society was no longer a centrally regulated 'one-nation' model of administration based on paternalistic FA lines. It was now market-driven. Therefore English professional football could no longer have small clubs and large clubs sharing a philosophy of equal interests. But there was an irony here. In order to become deregulated the top clubs first had to go to the regulator (the FA), via Kelly, to have Regulation 10 removed. Kelly, a decent man with football at heart, was a cog in the origination of the Premier League. He was a means to an end rather than the instigator of a strategic plan that would safeguard the FA's position. In future years Kelly would reflect on how far the game had come from the likes of Tom Finney, the Preston plumber, and Sam Pilkington, the Accrington fent merchant, and wonder at his own role in it. At the end of it all he was left with some key questions:

Are these new football-club owners involved more to make a profit rather than to reinvest?

When did that sort of profiteering start?

Where exactly was the turning-point?

Did it come with the arrival of Alan Sugar, Martin Edwards or Doug Ellis?

Why did the FA remove the limits on paid directors in the early 1980s?
Did that decision open the door for asset-strippers?
Did anyone ever make money out of post-war football?
Do people actually *like* their footballers today?

We are left with a question of our own: If Kelly himself, with all his experience, has so few answers, what chance do the rest of us have of solving the enduring power struggle between the FA and England's major professional league?

36

LOOKING AFTER THE LOCALS

BILLY HAD PLAYED PROFESSIONAL FOOTBALL at the top level. When coaching youngsters he sensed that he was a natural communicator. In the early 1990s he worked as a community officer at a successful Premier League club. Other than his FA coaching badge, however, he had no formal training for his role, not even an induction day. But professional football taught you to get on with the job.

As a community officer Billy wanted to make his club the focal point of the local community. He concentrated on reaching a wide spectrum of people – from school-age kids to senior citizens, not forgetting disabled people and children with special needs. He regularly worked with organisations for the deaf and the blind and he coached in black neighbourhoods, but he found it difficult to make good contacts among Asians.

Billy's role was to restore something that had once been indigenous – a strong relationship between the football club and its local community. He organised tea-dances for the oldies, worked with a local anti-drug initiative, ran coaching courses in deprived areas and arranged soccer camps, keeping his eyes open for talented footballers aged nine and upwards. His Saturday Club schoolchildren were given a grand tour of the stadium, lunch and seats at the match, and he planned to set up a five-a-side competition for females. He also developed some sponsorship ideas with Pizza Hut. In the main Billy concentrated on football projects, but he was open to ideas for other sports.

He had a joint project with the local probation service, coaching young offenders for five or six weeks before they played in a representative match against young offenders from another city. The project helped the young men to develop self-discipline, confidence and teamwork. Billy was respected by the lads because he was an ex-pro. He taught them to play with pride and keep their heads up. Even gnarled probation officers experienced a warm glow when they saw Billy at work with the young offenders.

Billy was also involved with the 'Learning through Football' project developed by Jean Evans and her colleagues in Birmingham. Schoolteachers had recently discovered that they could design their mathematics lessons around the geometry of the football pitch ('What's the circumference of the centre-circle?') and football-club issues ('How do you calculate the number of police needed for this crowd size?'). Football was also a conduit for history, geography, social studies and many other subjects. Initially Billy had problems getting a room for thirty kids – his club's stadium was now run as a business and he had to compete with seminars, conferences and job clubs – but the club eventually dedicated a classroom. The club also assigned an area of the new stand as a 'Community Corner' for locals, who received free match tickets.

All over England in the early 1990s Billy and other community officers were fronting schemes with enthusiasm and fortitude. They worked long, unsociable hours for a modest salary, with poor resources and uncertain funding, all to stay inside the game. The schemes relied on the strong personalities of these community officers and the support that they had from their management committees, their clubs and unemployed assistants. No other country in the world had a national scheme like this.

Flashback to 1976 Young Lincoln City manager Graham Taylor understood the role of football in the community. He brokered interaction between players and the crowd. Before a match City players kicked balls to spectators and fans threw them back for the players to control or the goalkeeper to save. Taylor went on the Tannoy half an hour before a home game, talked about the last match and explained what he was looking for in this one. He insisted that Lincoln City players live within ten miles of the ground. He told them to go into schools and visit the community. He wanted football to mean to others what it had meant to him as a lad. Graham Taylor felt that football clubs had been distancing themselves from fans since the early 1960s, when the maximum wage was removed and nightclubs became fashionable.

Flashback to 1978 Denis Howell, Minister of Sport in Jim Callaghan's Labour government, suddenly discovered an unused pot of money in the Department of Environment kitty. He used it for football-in-the-community schemes. By March 1979 twenty-nine professional clubs had received grants. At Ipswich a £48,500 project saw the construction of a shale all-weather pitch with floodlights, brick changing-rooms and showers. Sited across the road from the Ipswich Town ground, it provided a focus for a local football league (with eighty teams), coaching courses, meet-the-ref sessions, sports film shows and coaching for unemployed teenagers. The Ipswich scheme worked well, helped by additional contributions from the local authority (£10,144) and the club (£2,000). In general, though, these early community schemes were hastily put together, there was no follow-up money and in some cases they showed no real commitment to community use.

In the 1990s Alan was the community officer at a Midlands club. He had spent fifteen years as a professional player with seven clubs and he was a full-badge FA coach. For the last eight years of his professional playing career Alan had also worked as a volunteer in a variety of community settings, including caring for the disabled and working with drug users. After retiring from the game he worked in a local-authority social services department and helped to run a children's home and a secure hostel.

Raised in an inner-city area himself, Alan felt that all professional football clubs should have a welfare officer who could support the uncertain but talented young players who were lost to the game. He saw 'caring' as the central notion of his community-officer role. He was willing to search for 'difficult to reach' groups, particularly vulnerable adults. Whatever the problem, he would try to respond. He was shocked to discover that he was the only community officer to have a social-work background.

Alan felt compelled to involve himself in rehabilitation programmes for drug users, crime-prevention panels and mediation schemes. When he went to work with juvenile offenders he was looking to create a long-term project, so that it wasn't just about an hour's one-off coaching. For example, Alan arranged for members of the 200-strong senior citizens' group to visit young men in prisons and act as surrogate parental support. Alan felt that his best work happened when he was a facilitator, either by launching activities which others could run or by putting diverse community groups in contact with one another.

Alan worked with an assistant, Josh, who held a preliminary FA coaching badge and worked on holiday courses and other projects. Josh was a young black coach from the inner city at a time when there were few black coaches. Josh enthused about the scheme because he saw it as far more than just football.

'I've got someone who lives across the road from me who until Alan came to pick me up didn't know I had anything to do with the club,' Josh said. 'And she said, "That's him who works at the football club!" Now, that woman can't stand football. But he's made her aware of what's going on and what's available for her as regards the community programme. That's fantastic, that! That's what a community scheme should be about.'

The community scheme ran soccer schools every half-term break and coached 25,000 kids in local schools, but the ethic was to establish a caring approach. Alan stayed clear of commercial ventures and concentrated on covering the community in a structured way that suited the area's demographics. He recruited six unemployed trainees who all believed in his ethic and were capable of venturing into the *whole* community, warts and all.

'The community programme should serve all groups,' said Josh. 'You're not missing anyone out if you deal with young adults too. Yes, they can be difficult to work with – the young offenders and that; they are people with problems. But they're your community. I have worked at other clubs and this [one] is nothing like them. I wouldn't work at any other club. At other clubs everything is soccer-based: Can we get the kids to come here and play football? Can we get into schools to coach? These are, literally, *soccer* schemes. But here you come into contact with a lot of other things. A football club can be a real community thing – like this one.'

Flashback to 1986 Six professional clubs in the North-West piloted football-in-the-community schemes, supported by the Professional Footballers' Association and the Manpower Services Commission. The clubs ranged from Manchester United (fourth in Division One) to Preston North End (twenty-third in Division Four). The schemes provided temporary employment and training for the unemployed, and set out to establish closer links with the community, especially ethnic-minority groups. The football authorities had to try things after the Heysel Stadium disaster, but it was optimistic to think that community projects would turn hooligans straight. The PFA were keen because their members could learn useful skills and develop post-playing careers in professional football. The pilot led to a national scheme and within a short time fifty ex-players were running club community projects. By 1992 every Football League club had its own community officer.

Flashback to 1987 Derby County had signed Watford's Nigel Callaghan for a fee of £140,000, but the player was now standing distraught in the Watford reception area. He didn't want to leave Watford because the club had been good to him and it had a family ethic. Graham Taylor, Watford's manager since 1977, knew that community work by players improved the club's image around the town, made the players more responsible to fans and tied the players to the club. The players had a clause in their contracts requiring them to do community activities for a few hours a week. The club also recruited a public-relations officer and a marketing manager, and made links with a local chaplain, who offered pastoral care and a confidential listening ear to all the staff. Watford also created the country's first Family Enclosure, where adults had to be accompanied by a child to gain access. Typically Graham Taylor raised £30,000 sponsorship money for a Family Terrace by running the London Marathon. Watford climbed through the divisions while remaining a community club, and attendances at Vicarage Road rose steadily from 5,000 to 20,000.

One of the early leaders in the football-in-the-community initiatives was a small lower-league club in London. By 1993 this club's community wing boasted a thriving schools coaching programme, a well-established scheme for female footballers, an educational Kick Start programme for local youths, a unique Sports Scholarship scheme, a popular voluntary coaching scheme for young offenders and a scheme for school truants aimed at developing personal and social skills. This club also had the first match-day crèche in professional football, a pensioners' club, archery at the ground and mural-painting projects. No local problem was turned away – and there were plenty of local problems. The club's inner-city neighbourhood was rife with poverty, single parenthood, unemployment, crime, drugs, racism and poor educational achievement.

Unsurprisingly this club had a significant hooliganism problem in the 1970s and early 1980s. In desperation, in 1985 a rate-capped council and a near-bankrupt football club got together to see if they could bring life back into the community. The club appointed a community officer whose background was in sports coaching and community sports work rather than professional football. At first he felt like he was doing missionary work. He saw his job as adding two things to a football club – stability and a caring attitude. The latter was quite rare; football clubs were generally ruthless organisations.

The community officer soon realised that his scheme needed an informal approach in order to attract local people. Soccer schools had to be free of charge and free of formality. Kids were allowed to come when they liked rather than attend the whole course, and they could wear what they wanted. The first rule of coaching was never to throw a kid out of a coaching session.

'You have to have different ways of disciplining people – like a sin-bin, for example,' said the community officer. 'We do it like this because the ones who are causing you problems are likely to be the ones you want in your soccer schools. They're the ones who will get the club philosophy over to everyone else. Kick 'em out and it's an easy option for you, and, as a coach, you've got no challenge.'

This community officer cited the example of an FA soccer-schools course where swearing was banned and there were rules about kit.

'If I had those rules in my soccer schools I wouldn't have five people on them!' the community officer said. 'No swearing! Now, that's not constructive to people, having rules like that.'

This community officer realised that he had to befriend the youngsters; to be seen as a figure of authority was counter-productive. It needed a more subtle approach.

'Football is a language,' he said. 'It's no different to music, no different to art. The message we're conveying is from a professional club. Our kids here are more likely to listen to a football club than to a teacher, a social worker or a probation officer. It [the football club] is dealing with problems that these people are dealing with all the time – the problems of violence, problems of self-discipline and so on. A skilled coach can begin dealing with problems like these on the spot. When we set up sessions you can pretty much guarantee that during the week something will occur during that session, and the coaches know they have to deal with that because what happens in these sessions will also happen outside, on the streets, after school, whatever.'

By the mid-1990s the idea that community projects would curb spectator hooliganism was passé. After the establishment of the Premier League in 1992 the larger clubs found that community work was necessary for other reasons. It could deflect accusations that they were pricing out local fans or cutting off effective links with poorer local communities. Of course, community work was essentially a good thing, but top clubs soon learned that it also helped their corporate image and identity. Even clubs with full stadiums could use their community schemes to assuage people who were excluded by ticket price or the feeling that they were of the wrong ethnic origin. It was the top clubs' way of being global entities *and* locally grounded. Clubs began to offer their traditional core customers and core supporters another kind of service – community access. This new product became loaded with responsibilities and duties about delivering, and its value could be measured by the relative cost of the local authorities or other agencies doing similar work.

This development was a long way from Billy's early enthusiasm or Alan's idealism in the early 1990s. By the new century football community work was a much more considered activity than a youthful Graham Taylor kicking balls into the crowd at Sincil Bank, Lincoln. But everything in modern football carries multiple meanings. Spending an afternoon playing small-sided games that are 'being delivered by coaches from the local professional club' can still spark a young kid's dream.

37

MOVING GROUNDS

S TUART CLARKE TOOK HIS FIRST football photograph at Vicarage
Road, Watford, in the mid-1970s. That day he played truant from
Saturday lessons at his grammar school, caught the train, walked to the
Watford ground and snuck his Instamatic camera through the turnstile. He
had all day Sunday to think up an excuse for missing school.

As a young boy, watching Watford alongside his father and brother,
Clarke spent half the time studying the people. He was fascinated by the
crowd. At home he drew pictures of stadiums and spectators. Out and about
he took photographs with classic cameras. When he began hitch-hiking he
found that the fate of football teams was a guaranteed starting point for
conversation.

After the Hillsborough disaster Clarke realised that something of national
importance was decaying or dying. During the early 1990s professional
clubs were undoubtedly in a sad financial state, but Clarke saw beauty in the
squalor of the grounds he visited. He decided to capture some of football's
former glories before they became the ruins of Rome. He started work on a
photographic collection called *The Homes of Football*.

After slipping through a crack in the gate and bypassing the ticket office at
the new Wycombe Wanderers ground ('a bit like an industrial unit'), he took
a famous picture of BBC commentator John Motson talking live to camera
in a blizzard. At Blackburn his shot of a man waving a crutch to celebrate a
Manchester City goal (and the club's second successive promotion) portrayed
football's healing powers. And 'Sunset over Springfield Park', taken at Wigan
Athletic's unfashionable ground, preserved a stereotypical sunset scene with
blurred figures that seemed to represent ghostly generations of dreamy fans.
The image was made all the more poignant by Wigan's later departure from
Springfield Park (in 1999) and their propulsion towards the FA Premier
League.

Realising that he was on to something, Clarke travelled around the homes of football, from one fascinating place to another, capturing images of character and substance. He understood that fans found real meaning in the detail of football grounds: the first sight of the floodlight pylon or a grandstand roof; the fanzine-sellers outside the stadium; a 'Players and Officials Only' sign; a coach with the visiting team's name on the side; a rickety tea-hut; the half-time scoreboard; a coracle outside Shrewsbury Town's Gay Meadow ground (to collect the ball when it went in the river); a Bradford City staircase painted yellow to symbolise safety; a rolled-up match-day programme in a clenched fist; a distant view of hospitality boxes; and even football graffiti. He discovered that each ground had something distinctive. He loved the slightly scary walk to Burnley's Turf Moor, with the occasional view of the Pennines, the sun low on the Towneley-side streets as queues formed in the chip shop. He was particularly pleased when he took his *Looking Up* picture of fans at Sunderland. It captured generations together, a thousand mouths ajar, heroic and wondrous people in red-and-white-striped shirts, somehow affirming football's post-Hillsborough meaning. Stuart Clarke built up a rich body of photographic art that portrayed the English national spirit through England's national sport.

Geographers use the concept of topophilia to describe the love of place. Football fans, as much as anybody, have strong emotional ties to the built environment. Regular visitors to a football ground grow to appreciate the quirks of familiar surroundings. They accept defects and discomforts, rather like the stereotypical old man who sits in his favourite chair (despite its faulty springs) with pipe, slippers and newspaper at hand, perfectly content even though he knows that the house needs decorating and the roof leaks. By the early 1990s the average English top-division stadium was the old man of Europe, eighty-eight years old, far older than the average stadium in Germany (forty-eight) and Italy (thirty-seven).

Like an old man's home, a football ground can represent a castle, a theatre, a fortress, a refuge, a shrine, a cathedral, a site for a political rally or a tourist resort. A stadium is literally *our home ground*. It is a sacred place where feelings can be shown and you can be yourself. It is a therapy centre. It is a place for intimacy.

'You are close to the public,' said the French player Eric Cantona in the early 1990s, comparing English grounds with those in other European countries. 'It is warmer. There is room for love.'

Very different to topophilia is topophobia – the fear of a place. Some rival grounds scare fans. At times, during the hooliganism era, home grounds did too. Some grounds felt like prisons. Fences and walls were built, dangerous objects were confiscated, CCTV footage recorded your every move and police supervision matched that of prison warders. But the rump of fans still thought of their stadium as home. It still gave them an uplifting feeling on arrival. They enjoyed the smells of grilled food, the sounds of the Tannoy system and the visual pleasures of a green canvas dotted with colours.

Some fans have visited their football ground more times than they have visited a close relative (or even a workplace). They understand the impact of the weather on the pitch, the angle of the sun in different seasons, the wind direction, and they can guess the attendance by a mere glance at a few telling areas of the ground.

Stuart Clarke intuitively understood this culture. Football grounds were Dickensian and dilapidated, but they were also soaked in meaningful history. Southend United's Roots Hall had subsiding terraces built over a rubbish tip, three stands clad in asbestos and crush barriers that could be shaken loose, but it was still home, and some fans had been going there since it opened in 1955. Teams, managers, directors and players come and go, the kit changes from time to time, but a club's football ground remained a constant – until the early 1990s, that is, when the homes of football began to change radically.

In his report on the Hillsborough disaster Lord Justice Taylor stipulated that all Football League grounds should be all-seaters for safety reasons. In March 1990 Chancellor of the Exchequer John Major reduced the pools' companies' spot-the-ball duty from 42.5 per cent to 40 per cent (despite resistance from Treasury staff who thought that football was awash with money) with the proviso that the difference went to the Football Trust for grant aids to help upgrade major stadiums. The Taylor proposal was soon limited to the top two English divisions (and the Scottish Premier League). By the end of August 1996 the Football Trust, having received £127 million from the betting companies, had committed £144 million to the clubs (with £114 million already paid) and the total ground-improvement cost to the clubs was estimated at £455 million. But the launch of a National Lottery in November 1994 dramatically reduced the Trust's spot-the-ball income.

Stadium modernisation was a great opportunity for the building industry (and profiteers inside and outside football). In the early 1990s football was as much about Alfred McAlpine, Taylor Woodrow and Norwest Holst as it was about Gary McAllister, Chris Woods and Nigel Clough. Football was regularly featured on the business and property pages of national newspapers and in magazines such as *The Economist* and *Construction News*. Newspapers ran speculative stories that simply petered out, including Arsenal's supposed takeover of Wembley Stadium, Wimbledon's emigration to Ireland and Coventry City's move fifteen miles east for a possible ground-share with Leicester City.

Between 1988 and 2007 twenty-four of 102 League clubs moved grounds, mainly as a result of the Taylor Inquiry. Key factors were the financial value of the current stadium's land (especially if it was centrally located in an expanding town or city), the opportunities for developing a cheaper site elsewhere and the chances of getting planning permission for that alternative site. Some clubs decided to stay, raising development money by selling adjoining land for housing (e.g. Brentford) or a supermarket (e.g. Crystal Palace). Blackburn Rovers planned a £12-million redevelopment of three sides of their existing ground but it meant buying several terraced houses on Nuttall Street and mills at either end of the ground. Other clubs wanted to move in order to raise their capacity. In 1997 Sunderland left the long-neglected Roker Park (capacity 22,700) for the Stadium of Light (capacity 41,600). Stuart Clarke photographed them all in flux and even held a show at the Royal Institute of British Architects.

Moving grounds was a great opportunity to rethink the strategy of stadium design. It raised the question of business partnerships and more effective ways of using outdoor and indoor space. Clubs looked to share new stadiums with other sports clubs, and multi-purpose ideas included golf driving ranges, five-a-side pitches, bowling alleys, conference centres, health spas, squash courts, offices, hotels and multiplex cinemas. It was also a chance to think about facilities for disabled spectators.

The symbolic meaning of football grounds is never more powerful and poignant than just before a club moves to a different stadium. After the last match at the old stadium, fans hang around, sifting through their memory bank as if it were a card-index file, feeling the tears well up, perhaps even remembering a friend whose ashes have been scattered on the pitch. When Brasenose College evicted Oxford City from the White House Ground in 1988, former City goalkeeper Alf Jefferies made a special journey to the ground, stood in both goal-mouths and thought of all the wonderful times he had had there over forty years earlier.

A stadium closure usually heralded a memorabilia sale. At Leicester City fans could buy giant polystyrene figures of ex-manager Martin O'Neill and former players. At Millwall the ground was thrown open to the public and bids were taken for eleven sets of gates, thirty-seven turnstiles, fifty-three stadium signs, pieces of carpet, a selection of club crests and a few wooden programme-selling booths. Patches of turf and plastic seats were available, but most of the Millwall seating was sold to Peterborough United. On the day of the sale many fans just stood and stared at the site. A lot took photographs.

Millwall's new stadium, the New Den, took only fifty-seven weeks to build. It cost over £15 million, and the money came from the Football Trust (£2.6 million), Lewisham Council (£2.6 million), the sale of the old ground for housing (£5 million), the stadium's new management company (£1 million), the FA (£250,000) and an underwritten rights issue (£4 million). The arena was also designed as a concert venue. At Huddersfield Town's futuristic new home, the McAlpine Stadium, two REM concerts brought money into the whole town.

Most new stadiums met with complaints about parking and traffic snarl-ups until fans established a new match-day routine. A national organisation, the Federation of Stadium Communities (FSC), lobbied on issues of planning applications, parking for residents and general disruption. For instance, higher stands could block the sun from houses or gardens.

Another issue was a new stadium's name. The choices were sententious words from the English language (Pride Park in Derby), a traditional name off the map (Glanford Park in Scunthorpe), or a sponsor (the Britannia Stadium in Stoke). One trend was to commemorate club stalwarts in the naming of stands (e.g. the Tom Finney Stand at Preston). The Madejski Stadium at Reading and the Kassam Stadium at Oxford United were named after club chairmen. And, as Peter Corrigan wryly pointed out in the *Observer*, Bolton's Reebok Stadium was named after one of the club's trainers.

Fans were concerned about production-line stadiums which added to clone-town feelings. Some fans saw them as part of an English trend towards placelessness. The 1996–7 Premier League fans' survey found that 60 per cent of spectators rued the lack of atmosphere in all-seater stadiums. The League investigated further and recommended attracting more away-team fans and creating 'atmosphere areas' around the ground. Bands were encouraged and amplifiers put in the stands. There were periodic campaigns for some terracing to be restored, but football's impetus was towards the future. Photographer Stuart Clarke had captured the disappearing past at a critical time.

Once a club became homeless it was a long and difficult road back, as Bristol Rovers, Charlton Athletic, Wimbledon and Brighton all found in the 1990s. Brighton shared Gillingham's ground, seventy miles away, before renting the Withdean Stadium athletics facility in Brighton. Bristol Rovers spent ten years in Bath, fifteen miles away, before agreeing a ground-share deal with Bristol Rugby Club.

The most distinctive period of homelessness befell the England national team between 2001 and 2007. Wembley Stadium, tatty and debt-ridden, had been the subject of a £170-million rebuilding plan (in 1996), a £210-million plan (in 1997) and a £245-million plan (in 1998). The last of these meant the FA would contribute £125 million in loans and the remainder would come through the National Lottery. Wembley Stadium was in private hands, but it was sold to a public trust – for £103 million in April 1998 – so that the project could qualify for lottery funding.

London fought off competition for the national stadium from Bradford, Sheffield, Birmingham and Manchester. The FA always wanted to rebuild Wembley rather than move elsewhere, even though staying in north London made little sense. When offered three site choices in 2001, active fans preferred a national stadium in Birmingham (60 per cent) to one at Wembley (29 per cent) or Coventry (11 per cent). According to fans, a Midlands venue would even up the travel time for England followers, attract more interest, improve the atmosphere at matches and provide better value for money. But most fans couldn't see the need for a national stadium when so many good club grounds were available.

'Wembley was a ghastly dump in the middle of a ghastly city,' said one forty-year-old female Leeds United fan. 'Anywhere would be better – the toilets were a disgrace, the view was appalling, the travel difficult. Anywhere but Wembley.'

'The nostalgia around Wembley is fuelled by the southern press who don't like to travel to games,' said a Liverpool fan in his thirties. 'I feel wherever the national stadium is built some matches should still be staged around the country.'

'I consider the whole affair to have been handled terribly,' said a Newcastle United fan. 'Those in supposed authority have made English football appear in the hands of idiots. We now need positive action with those responsible showing strong leadership. I am sure if the fans are listened to, Wembley will soon be forgotten and either Birmingham or Coventry given priority.'

The main arguments in favour of Wembley were its tradition, its location in the capital city (with so many tourist attractions) and London's prestige throughout the world.

'I believe strongly that a national stadium should be in the nation's capital,' said a female Chelsea supporter in her twenties. 'Wembley is historically the home of football and should remain so. Even northern fans loved coming to London as it made matches an occasion.'

'Wembley is the home of football, always has been, always should be,' said a Sheffield United fan. 'Wembley is traditional, and where our greatest sporting moment took place.'

Wembley was a good example of the problems of moving grounds. Lots of interests came into play. The fans didn't get what they wanted, the rebuilding took nearly seven years and estimates of the total cost varied from £750 million to £1 billion, depending on what you included.

Stuart Clarke succeeded in getting his photographic art approved by England's football-resistant museum and art-gallery curators – his *Homes of Football* project was on tour for fifteen years – but he was only one of a number of artists, writers and musicians who captured football's essence in the 1990s. As John Gausted, founder of the Sportspages bookshops, said at the start of the decade, 'Football has rediscovered its history.'

Football became a conduit for creativity. The sculptor Tom Maley produced statues of Wilf Mannion and Jackie Milburn, North-East heroes of the 1940s and 1950s. Opera singers sang about football or sang to football audiences. Dance troupes were turning footballers' movements into an art form. At the New Victoria Theatre in the Potteries, the play *C'mon Stan* dramatically reprised Blackpool's fourth goal in the 1953 FA Cup Final, acted in slow-motion (forwards and backwards), and there were television shows such as *The Manageress* (Channel 4) and *Standing Room Only* (BBC2). Popular music unveiled 'Fog on the Tyne' by Paul Gascoigne and a production line of FA Cup Final songs. *The Fast Show* featured Ron Manager, an incoherent nostalgic professional, and Roger, a nouveau football fan who knew nothing about football. The Philosophy Football company produced T-shirts and literature that commemorated the game's intellectual place. And the Association of Football Statisticians went from strength to strength.

Football literature blossomed. Fanzines filled a gap by giving intelligent and informed opinion by biased and committed fans. Nick Hornby's *Fever Pitch* captured the complex intensity of a fan's relationship with his club. Books on hooliganism created a new sub-genre, featuring not only past violence but also the togetherness, sense of ownership and loyalty to your club. A Derby company, Breedon Books, produced a 'Complete Record' series with team, goalscorer and attendance details of every game in a club's history.

Football became fashionable in high-brow circles. Julian Barnes ended his *A History of the World in 10½ Chapters* with a fantasy about Leicester City winning the FA Cup. Literary magazines such as *Granta* and *The Times Literary Supplement* published football-related pieces, and academic papers appeared in new journals such as *Soccer and Society*. Football had grabbed the zeitgeist.

In the early 1990s English people were faced with economic recession, negative equity and repossession of homes, war in Iraq, poll tax, unemployment and redundancy. People looked to their football club for some stability. Some people rejected the immediacy of modern popular culture and reprised what they saw as the authenticity of football's past. Or else they glorified football's past because the late 1980s had been so awful for modern football. Also, the new generation enjoyed the modern facilities and interest was at its highest for years. A new ground was a new ground for anybody who wanted it to be their ground.

England hosted Euro 96 under the banner 'Football's Coming Home'. Youth culture, football, music and comedy merged as they had in the 1960s. The tournament's anthem became 'Three Lions' by Ian Broudie, Frank Skinner and David Baddiel, but the real catalyst for English sentiment was a collection of football grounds that were undergoing change. The experience within the grounds gave football meaning, whether one was bemoaning the destruction of the past or simply celebrating the present. It was where you stood or sat with a close relative, a friend or strangers, and how you collected memories that spanned a range of emotions, whether you were across the touchline from Eric Cantona at Old Trafford, with Nick Hornby at Highbury or rubbing shoulders with Stuart Clarke at one of the many emotionally moving grounds of England.

38

WHERE HAVE ALL THE PLAYERS GONE?

'I STOPPED PLAYING WHEN I WAS about thirty-eight or thirty-nine,' Tom says. 'I think the reason I didn't feel depressed is because I knew I'd really had enough by then. I was just about at the end of my tether. Coming back from Aldershot on the train, looking in the mirror, I was as white as a sheet. I thought, It's getting too much for me now.'

Tom's career as a professional footballer was over in the early 1960s.

What next?

A crowd of former professional footballers from the 1950s and 1960s gather in a football-club boardroom over thirty years later. They stand in small groups, wearing suits and ties, holding drinks, reminiscing about their playing days. Some look a little paunchy now; others seem in excellent shape. As you move around the room you can eavesdrop on their conversations.

'Looking back now, it's as if it never happened. It's been part of your life, a great part of your life, and it's great. But now it's as if it never happened.'

'When you finish is the hardest time, and I think a lot of players can't cope with it.'

'You want it to go on for ever, 'cos it's such a good life. Some people just can't handle it when they come out of the game, they can't handle it, and that happens today.'

'We were getting twelve-month contracts. It was a good living then, but it wasn't a living where you could say, "Well, if I get seven or eight years out of this, that's me, I've got enough money."'

'Two pound for a draw, four pound for a win.'

'Some of these players now, some of them getting £10,000 or £16,000 a week, and I used to kick a bloke off the park for four pound.'

'Money's spoiled it. Money rules it now.'

'I've got arthritis. That's all it is. There's just wear and tear. Just the one knee. If it's cold, it gets sore. Sometimes it's hard if I drive a lot. I think I'll have to have something done to it eventually.'

The past catches up with the present. Their playing careers slipped past like a click of the fingers, and they were left with another thirty or forty years before the next retirement.

On average a modern professional footballer's career lasts eight and a half years. In practice it can cover an unpredictable time-span between teenage years and the early forties. Most of these men feel very fortunate to have had football opportunities, but a few are bitter about what their careers might have been.

Standing in a room together they look like their working-class contemporaries. They have grey hair and a background manner, but they show a special kind of inner confidence that comes from success in a fantasy occupation. They don't regret the physical price. They have more replacement hips than others of their age. Now in their sixties and seventies, these men have spent most of their lives in jobs outside professional football, but somewhere in their minds they are all still footballers.

'If I wasn't coaching Wellingborough I'd go there anyway to watch my two sons play. It's a good laugh as well. You get the banter before the game and after the game.'

'I go shopping on Saturdays. I might go to a game. Depends. I might go to Milton Keynes shopping. I go to Coventry and the craic's brilliant. You meet a few of the old players, and you have the craic, guys you've not seen for ten, fifteen years.'

'I'm still football crazy. It's been my life. My wife will tell you. Every time there's football on the telly I want to watch it.'

Tom was nearly forty when he retired, so he took it better than most players. But he worried about doing a job outside football. What would that mean? Would he fit into another working environment? Would he be good enough? He knew he had to do well at a job somewhere. He had to get into a job and learn it. He had a family to raise.

For twelve years Tom ran a bookmaker's office. It meant working Saturdays but, let's face it, he had worked Saturdays for most of his life. It didn't bother him that he couldn't see matches. He got the job because he knew the boss. Maybe the boss thought that a former footballer might bring in a bit of trade.

Eventually Tom's boss died and the bookmaker's offices were split up. Tom decided to look for a five-day-a-week job. He liked the bookmaking business but working bank holidays was tiresome. He got a job at British Timkins, looking after five or six girls on a line that produced cups and cones for roller bearings. He worked the two-to-ten shift and the nightshift. He found it hard at first, especially going to work at 6pm. He was promoted from a semi-skilled job to a skilled position, and was a leading hand by the time he retired at sixty-five with a small pension. He then kept himself active by working Saturdays at the bookmaker's.

Ben was raised in a village pub but never drank beer himself. Brought up to a simple village life in the 1930s, he left school at fourteen and worked as an engineer at the Express Lift Company. After National Service he became a full-time professional footballer. There were no real pressures then. People went to matches and had a laugh. In the 1950s it was no great disaster if your team finished halfway down the Third Division (South) table; they still got crowds of 8,000 or 9,000.

All the normal pitfalls for young footballers, such as the bookies, snooker and drinking, Ben avoided. He lived at home and married at twenty-six. A year before he retired from football he had the idea of starting a business. He thought there was a niche for a sports shop in the town. He and a team-mate each put in £100, but after six years he bought out his team-mate. Running his sports business was hard work but it proved successful. He was a local lad, he'd played locally for thirteen years and he knew local people. He treated everybody the same way. He loved seeing customers happy and satisfied with a purchase. He particularly enjoyed watching granddads buy grandsons a pair of football boots or a cricket bat. Eventually he handed over the day-to-day running of the business to his son-in-law, but he worked one day a week into his seventies.

Ben didn't miss football too much when he retired from playing. He was too busy building up his business. At the age of seventy he thought of himself as a businessman rather than an ex-footballer.

Joe came from Scotland. During the 1960s he returned there three or four times a year. On one such trip he heard that his club were giving him a free transfer. It came as a shock. He was only twenty-nine, playing well, and had been with the club for nine years. Another year and he was due a testimonial.

Joe turned down offers from two other clubs. He didn't feel it was worth moving his family to another town. Then he thought, Christ, I haven't got a trade.

He hadn't thought about retirement before that moment.

'What are you going to do?' his wife asked him. 'You don't want to go to the two clubs that want you. If you're gonna stop here, you need to get a job.'

'What *am* I gonna do?' Joe said.

He was good at drawing and painting at school, so he decided to become a decorator. He got a job with a friend who was a painter and decorator, and played part-time in the Southern League for a year and a half. Eventually, in his late forties, Joe got back into full-time football. A former team-mate asked him to be his assistant manager. Two years later, when the receivers were called into the club, Joe was made redundant, along with the manager, the youth-team manager and nine players. This time he was shell-shocked. He went back to being a self-employed decorator and slowly built up his customer base.

Bob started playing football with his village team. He joined the army and played a lot of football. Being a professional footballer never entered his head until he completed his national service and resumed his apprenticeship in the printing trade. Then he had a trial at his local professional club and signed as a part-timer. He turned full-time after finishing his apprenticeship. He felt that he needed a trade because football could be a short life. That certainly proved true for Bob.

He was twenty-five and playing well when his leg was broken at Walsall. Bob felt that his opponent had gone over the top of the ball, a cardinal sin in the professional world. The leg was set but the pain continued, and he drank a bottle of brandy on the coach journey home. On the Tuesday his leg was reset. He was in hospital for two weeks, in plaster for eight months and in a calliper splint for another eight months. It was two seasons before he played again. He played four reserve games before the club let him go.

Bob then played part-time Southern League football but soon suffered a serious ankle-ligament injury. Again he blamed his opponent. He felt bitter for a long time and did his best to stay in football. He managed two non-League clubs. In his day job he worked for a number of printers. He saw thirty years of radical change in the printing trade, and thirty years of radical change in the football world.

* * *

Ken was sixteen when he moved from Wales to start his football career. He was very homesick. He married a local girl and they had two daughters. His football career was very successful. He enjoyed the game itself, especially the comradeship and the excitement of scoring goals. But his career also involved six transfers in fourteen years.

Towards the end he realised that he needed to make some money if he was ever to buy a house or go into business. As he approached thirty it preyed on his mind – what will I do when I finish playing football? Then his mother died and he moved back to Wales to be near his bereaved father. For five years Ken worked in the packing department of a fabric firm and played part-time football. On some away trips the team slept overnight in the coach in a lay-by and then travelled on the next morning.

Ken retired from football without a trade, qualifications or any significant savings. Family security was always an important consideration, so he eventually moved back to his wife's home town and found a job as a packer. That allowed him to settle after the continuous migration of football. He told himself that he had to swallow his pride and get on with it. You can't live on pride, can you?

Football is an unusual occupation because it generates such a distinctive professional identity. Football clubs are enveloping institutions. Daily life is structured and organised, the discipline is strong and the players are well looked after. They are driven to away games, fed at mealtimes, shown their hotel room, and their kit is usually washed for them. It is like being a child at a school full of games lessons, except that football-club managers expect their players to be totally dedicated.

Football is an excitement arena. Everything focuses around the match. There is a fervent desire to win, an uncertain outcome, the risk of injury, an unpredictable crowd and a build-up of tension. All roads lead to a stadium that is swirling with emotion and drama.

Football is also one of the few jobs where you can get paid for keeping fit. So much of a player's life is about maintaining the body. Players have to manage injuries, train hard, rest properly and sleep well. Older players risk the ever-present possibility that a bad game can signal 'He's past it'.

Around thirty, for most players, the body begins to send out messages that suggest the start of a physical decline. The flat pitches of their twenties gradually become uphill both ways and against a gale. Then one day you sprint flat out for the ball and the linesman flies past you. Some say the legs go first and the breathing goes next, but there is no typical fade. Nearly all retired players talk about reflexes slowing with age and longer recovery periods after injury. But they can compensate a little through anticipation, experience and ability to read the game ('The first yard is in the head'). Some players change their positions – from midfielder to defender, from striker to midfielder – so that they can compensate for lack of pace. Ultimately, though, there is only frustration. One time you could get there and nick the ball, and now you can't. One year you are a professional footballer, the next you are an ex-player.

To the professionals, football is more than a job. It is an all-encompassing identity, with its sense of belonging to a revered institution (the football club), camaraderie, fitness, public scrutiny, travelling and pressures from various directions. It is hard for the retired footballer to replace all of these defining aspects of the job. Some get depressed when their career finishes, especially if the end has come as a shock. Some grow up quickly at this point in their lives. Some find their marriage put to the test. Some find the excitement of match days difficult to replace. One player argued that all players end up with a vice. His was the dogs.

Similar retirement issues come up for amateur and part-time players, but there isn't the same loss of intensity for amateurs that you find among the pros. The change in daily life is less acute and there is not the same loss of fame. The non-League men may already have a wage or career to fall back on. But some people argue that it's harder for amateurs to finish playing because, lacking the pressures, they enjoy the game more than professionals and therefore miss it more.

Professional footballers often say that their occupational lifestyle allows them more time with their wives and children than people doing regular jobs. However, the wives of 1960s players point out that their men chose to spend their spare time in the company of team-mates – playing golf, watching horseracing and so on – rather than with their wife and children. The players were away a lot, especially at weekends, and a wife's life could be lonely. Often she lived some distance from close relatives, having migrated with her man. In general she married young, had children young and kept her husband's valuable feet on the ground. She cosseted him through long lay-offs and found ways of dealing with women who chatted him up. In bed, at night, she was sometimes disturbed as he relived a match in his sleep, kicking out or shouting to a team-mate.

'Footballers are all alike, darling, card sharps and gamblers,' one wife said. 'A lot of them are snooker players and that sort of thing. I've always said that it's a good life for the man; it's not so good for the woman.'

At their reunions old-time footballers have three common questions: Are you still with the wife? Have you got any grandchildren yet? How's the knee? They stand around and chat with a dry sense of humour. They show dignity, pride and modesty. They play the conversation game in the same way as they did the football game, passing the story-telling ball from one to another, upholding the team ethic while allowing some individual flair. At the end of each story they might nod and show a twitch that passes for a smile.

'My daughter was born the day we played Manchester United in the First Division, believe it or not,' one begins. 'She was born about six o'clock in the morning. I couldn't get in to see her till nine o'clock. Then I said, "I've got to get some sleep because of this game." I woke up about quarter past one. I thought, My God. You were supposed to report at two o'clock. I finished up parking round the cricket ground. I had to run across the pitch. By this time it's five past two and the crowd's there, and they started chanting, "Eee, aye, addio, Joey is a daddyo." Apparently they'd put it over the Tannoy.'

'When we went to Liverpool, we were three–nil down at half-time and I had to go to the Kop end second half. Good grief. The second half I only let two in. I remember St John heading the ball. I was in mid-air juggling it. I landed on the line. My thought was the ball bouncing out of my hands, over the line. I took a deep breath, and I remember now, seeing the Kop coming down the terracing.'

'People say you must have been on at least £100 per week in the First Division days, and I say, "You must be joking." We were on, like, £35. That was 1966. All right, that was a good wage for then, a good wage.'

The role of memory is crucial in all our lives. The past continues to exist in the present. In the case of retired players, their memories of professional football can either destroy them or help them get on with their present lives. How you tell the story of the past may be more important than the content. You may portray yourself as a victim, a hero or an observer. Memories may fade, disappear or become distorted. When one retired player read a book on the history of his club he was surprised to discover that his memory of a crucial sequence of fixtures – Stoke City one week, Sunderland the next – was actually wrong. There had been two games in between these critical contests. Similarly he read that he'd scored a great goal in one particular match. He didn't score many goals but he couldn't remember that one. He couldn't even remember playing in the game. He didn't know whether this dissonance was caused by *his* bad memory or whether it was just the way everyone's mind operated.

'With football, there's not a follow-on, there's not a continued togetherness,' says seventy-year-old Ben. 'The football club now, they're a completely different regime to what was there when I was playing. People soon forget. Life is like a book. As one chapter opens, another one closes.'

39

'THIRTY THOOSAND ON THE WAITING LIST'

M ICK IS A FORTY-YEAR-OLD BUS driver. At one time he never missed a Newcastle United match. The last few years he's been missing them all.

'It's cost, and yer cannae get a ticket,' Mick says. 'The one time, you could queue up. You were more or less guaranteed to get in. You were queuing for hours. Now it's all bonds, it's all season tickets, it's all money stumped up front. You could save all week and get yer money from yer father and get away to matches on a Saturday and queue up and be sure of getting in. Since Newcastle started to take off, it's all big business and lads like us cannae get there.'

The scene is a pub in Newcastle upon Tyne on a wintry evening in 1998. Nine lifelong local Newcastle United fans are talking about football. The strange thing is that none of them go to St James' Park any more. Most Newcastle United home matches are now pre-sold to bond holders and season-ticket holders. If these men watch their team it is on television, either on Sky Sports or else illegally on a Norwegian cable channel in a Newcastle bar. They are facing something of a mid-life fandom crisis. They feel excluded from the ground they once called their own.

'Even for the games yer can get a ticket for, yer stumping up twenty-four quid for a ticket to gan an' watch them play some third-rate team,' says Paul. He stopped going three years ago, after more than twenty years of regular attendance, including European matches. 'Yer wanna see yer Liverpools and yer Man Uniteds, not Wimbledon or Luton or that, not those kinds of teams. Think back to the Fairs Cup and you were getting a full hoose, sixty odd thoosand, and everyone was getting in. Yer could see all the games. Now you cannot. You just don't want to see one game because if yer get the buzz again yer'll want to gan to all the games and yer cannae see all the games now.'

Most of these men miss the atmosphere of St James' Park acutely. They still want to go, although they would prefer to stand on terraces rather than sit down (as everyone now has to do in the new Premier League version of the sport).

'I mean, like, up there now you start shooting [shouting] and it's a ban,' continues Paul, who has a regular job as a turner. 'A few year gan, I were sitting with wor mates and we're all jumping up, Newcastle had scored. The stewards were in telling wor to stop 'cos we were "over-celebrating". We were over-celebrating a goal! We were just in wor seats jumpin' up an' doon, arms roond each other. "Sit down and get back in yer seats." "Yer kiddin', aren't yer?" And yer cannae argue 'cos yer just straight oot. They've got thirty thoosand on the waiting list for tickets so there's plenty to take wor's place. The way it is now, all people are mixed in together. You can be sittin' there and you'll have a six-year-old laddie on yer right-hand side and a little lassie there. And you swear at the match, like. There ought to be a family enclosure.'

'Something's definitely been lost in the ground when the all-seater stadium came in,' says Kevin, a forty-year-old shipwright who hasn't been to St James' Park for six years. 'I don't think they should bring back the whole standing capacity which was there, but at least some part of the ground where people can go in and pay on the day and stand and recreate some of the passion and intensity that's gone. A lot of these people that have got season tickets and platinum-bond holders are not true supporters that have followed the team for a long time. They are sort of middle-class people with plenty o' dosh, like. It's following on like America. I've seen it over there, I've coached there. It's just the same to a large extent. Football, as we knew it, has disappeared.'

This is a typical setting for football talk, around a couple of pub tables with glasses perched on beer mats, but these Geordies are not talking about the matches they have seen. They are talking about what they don't have any more.

'When we used to go to the match, when we were kids, the match day would start aboot eleven o'clock in the morning,' says Mick, the bus driver, thinking back twenty years. 'A few pints, then you gradually started to make yer way to the groond to get in the queue. Now [in 1998], the queue dinna start going in till quarter past two, 'cos they've all got the tickets. I think you lose some of the atmosphere. 'Cos yer singing and chantin', waiting to get in. If you've been in Keegan's day it were great, man. The whole build-up was a lot longer. Plus now people are leaving the game fifteen or twenty minutes before the end. They all wanna get in their big flash cars and drive home, make sure they're not late, y'know. You even need to buy tickets in advance here for *reserve* team games!'

These nine ex-attenders talk a lot about the cost of tickets. In the 1930s, when there was mass unemployment in this area, the locals still found their match money somehow. Now platinum club tickets are advertised for £6,000. Only three of these nine Geordies are unemployed, but the experience and cost is beyond them all.

'The club doesn't give a toss,' says Lee, a thirty-year-old electrician who went with his father until four years ago. 'It's football, it's money. When the match is on Sky, even though I've got Sky, I'll still gan out to watch it if Newcastle are on. It's a better atmosphere, like. Go in the pub, chock-a-block, big atmosphere, exciting. It gets yer into it. Kicks off at four o'clock so you get out at half past twelve, make sure you've got good seats. You probably have a better laugh in the bar, 'cos if you try to have a laugh at St James' now you've got stewards comin' in saying, "Sit doon and shut up." The bar's packed and yers all standing. The beer gans all over the place. Yer can swear yer head off, do what you want. Yer can jump up and doon. There's no poxy steward tellin' yer to sit doon. It's like what it used to be like at the match.'

Six of the nine men have Sky Sports. It costs them £29 a month.

'You'd pay that for a week at the match,' one of them says.

'It will be the same as everything – start off cheap and then gan crazy,' another one adds.

'When I gan up town with me mates who are ganning to the match, I stay in the bar and wait for them comin' in,' says Paul. 'They gan up the ground around quarter to three. I just wait till around five o'clock. Have a couple of pints, get a paper. I'd watch whatever match is on that Norwegian channel.'

'You get season-ticket holders saying, "Yer don't know fuck-all because yer nay ganning to the match," ' says Mick. 'But some season-ticket holders now dinnae know what they're talking about. They've got no in-depth knowledge of the game. They're there just for the deal. They don't know who's a good player and who's not. It's just fashionable to have a season ticket. Most of them season-ticket holders couldn't sit down and have a conversation wi' anybody here, like, wi' footba'. They'd just be blasted out o' the water. Basically what you have here [in this group] are true Newcastle supporters. The majority of supporters now are corporate, business people.'

'It's business-run, isn't it?' says Lee, the electrician. 'Obviously, if you're gonna get fifty thousand people paying money up front before

June, you're gonna do that. The ground's never gonna be big enough for people like us.'

'Still, a lot of the original ones [fans] are ganning [to matches],' says David, who is thirty-six and unemployed. 'But you've got to be working and if you've got a young family try telling yer kids that yer ganning to the match but you cannae take them. Your lass would string you up. If you have a young family coming up, where are you gonna get the tickets for them? They're gonna lose generations of supporters because parents cannae take 'em to the match. I've said it before, like, my kids will probably never see Newcastle United play. And that's sad. Yer get seventeen-, eighteen-, nineteen-year-olds in Newcastle now who've never ever been to the game. Obviously they're not as passionate 'cos they don't know what it's like.'

'Bank managers and stuff go now, that's how it looks to me,' says Alun, a 44-year-old mental-health nurse. 'More professional people go. The bond scheme, the cost of the season ticket, who can afford that? And that's just for nineteen matches – yer Cup games are extra. There's not many normal people, working-class people with kids, who've got four hundred pound to splash oot on a season ticket. That's why you can pay over twelve months now with interest, like. There's a lot more new people now. We're a victim of wor success to join the elite, the Manchester Uniteds and that. But at what cost?'

'I don't think the new fans are as passionate as us,' says Mick, the bus driver. 'Yer sitting there watching the game in the [working men's] club, like. Newcastle score and we're all over the club, jumping around hugging each other, like. We watch them [fans at the game] on the telly. They're all, "Well done, sir, good goal." *We're* all falling over. We get the same buzz out of Newcastle scoring as you would winning the lottery.'

'There's a lot of people have got tickets for a day oot,' mumbles one of the others. 'Everyone else's got one, so I better get one.'

'Family ticket for those who want to be nice and relaxed,' another adds.

'It's not fair,' Alun says. 'We should be able to go. Up here, it's part of life, we're brought up on it. It's part of the culture. There are so many true supporters here who went for years and years and years, who now cannae go. You feel like you've been pushed to one side to allow the club to go a little further. It's like: "All right, we've had you for long enough now but you cannae afford it; he's got a lot more right now to watch Newcastle because he's got a bigger bank balance, he can afford the tickets."'

*   *   *

Fans in other English cities had similar stories. In London, for instance, the excluded Arsenal fans included Paul, a 46-year-old sales representative. He felt that football got into your blood once you had been a regular attender for a couple of seasons. It didn't matter whether you continued to go or not, football still coursed through your body. If you watched football on the telly the passion would still be there. You couldn't drain all the blood from your body. You couldn't get a sport transfusion. Football stayed in your blood.

'Do you know what the waiting list is at Highbury for a season ticket?' Paul said. 'It's five years.'

What chance have I got, he thought. There was even a waiting list for the £10 loyalty cards that allowed you to apply for other tickets. OK, the standard of football had got better through the 1990s, with Sky pumping all the money in and top players coming from abroad, but they've made the grounds smaller. Arsenal's Highbury Stadium only held 38,000 spectators. There weren't enough tickets. Only 13,000 or 14,000 up for sale for home games, and you've got 20,000 registered supporters, all paying £20 to be a registered supporter.

Paul remembered a time when there were a lot of floating supporters in London. They would go to the game that appealed to them the most on the Saturday. That's all stopped. You just can't do it.

What kind of people go now?

'Lucky ones,' said Paul.

In Sheffield, Dave was a 38-year-old joiner supporting Sheffield Wednesday. His interest in the club was fired from the moment Derek Dooley walked into his uncle's sweet shop. Dave went to Hillsborough regularly until the 1998–9 season.

He found it cost too much to take his two daughters to matches. You could get free tickets for children at some lesser matches. An adult and two kids for £17 wasn't too bad, Dave thought, but the normal costs were prohibitive. You pay to go in, each kid wants a £2 programme, they both want a drink, and they charge you £1 for a Mars bar at Hillsborough. Then you have to take the kids to the souvenir shop. By the time you leave it's cost you £60 for the family. What happened to the days when fathers used to lift kids over the turnstiles? It was no problem to get tickets at Sheffield Wednesday but *the whole package* was too expensive. And it wasn't as though the team was playing well.

Dave's main bugbear was the amount of money paid to the players. It was ridiculous. And what about the arrogance of players? In the past, if a young player was kicked he'd get up. It's not the same game now. Clubs can afford £1 million for transfers but they can't afford the wages. Clubs have cocked it up for other clubs.

What about that man he met the other night? The man came straight up and said, 'I've just been to see Wednesday, it cost forty-three quid for me and our two young uns and it was absolute crap.'

Dave couldn't remember people using that argument in the old days. They might say that Wednesday played crap but they wouldn't bring ticket money into the conversation.

All this research was conducted for the Football Task Force, a body set up in July 1997 by Tony Blair's new Labour government. The Task Force members were generally people from within the game, and the chair was David Mellor, a former Conservative Minister of Sport and presenter of Radio Five Live's *6.06* programme.

One of the Task Force remits was to 'encourage ticketing and pricing policies that are geared to reflect the needs of all, on an equitable basis, including for cup and international matches'. Mellor's group collected compelling evidence to show that many traditional football fans were excluded by price or ticketing methods. But the Task Force had no statutory powers. Moreover, the Task Force was unlikely to make recommendations that could damage its own members. Nothing changed in Newcastle, except that 'the Toon' began to play worse.

The new Blair government had no intention of regulating the game. The top clubs had moved from a *supporter* era into a *customer* era, and customer credit-card details were more important than memories of FA Cup ties. Football was financed by television contracts, merchandise revenue and tickets sold at market prices to people who could afford to pay. Clubs developed corporate images to attract further customers, and problems were dealt with through 'customer services' rather than regulation. Market forces meant that prices went up when demand outstripped supply. Some of the old ideas about 'local clubs for local people' and 'special relationships with supporters' had broken down. The alienated fans' only contact with their clubs came via television, community schemes and club shops. In an era when, nationally, about 17 per cent of attending fans spent over £100 a year on official club merchandise, excluded fans could still buy replica shirts and club scarves. Newcastle United fans spent more on merchandise than any other club – £159 per head in 1996–7 – and they became known as 'the barcode army'.

Something else was happening too. As we have seen, satellite television deals were creating an alternative football experience that allowed fans to watch football collectively in bars. In some ways this pub experience was more real than the real thing, because fans could stand up, jump up and down, swear and sing, just like they had done in old stadiums. For a Geordie electrician called Lee the old and new cultural experiences were not too dissimilar. But his kids will probably only ever watch the Toon on TV.

40

THE TUTORIAL

T HE SCENE IS A ROOM on the first floor of a Victorian-built university in England in 1999. Six people sit around two tables in a Sociology of Football seminar. Sam, a male student in his mid-twenties, wearing a traditional cotton football shirt, reads from a collection of papers. He is summing up his class presentation on the differences between professional footballers in the 1950s and the 1990s.

SAM: . . . so, as I've been trying to show, football today has just become 'buy and sell' like everything else. It has lost its cultural meaning for people. Look at the way you can get Man United replica shirts in Hong Kong. The Premier League and its partners have this whole global division-of-labour thing. They can produce all these products incredibly cheaply in the Far East and Pakistan, and then sell them at ridiculous prices in Britain. Stanley Matthews was an authentic working-class hero in the 1950s. Today's players are celebrities.

LECTURER (*after a pause*): Thanks, Sam. I can see where you are coming from. You're saying that the game's all business now, and it's lost its community spirit. It's all about profit. It's gone from being played by local people *for* local people to being a tradable commodity and a global enterprise. You think it's all to do with neo-liberal economics. Football changed when the market came in, the big clubs were allowed to keep their own gate money, directors could take salaries and so on.

SAM: You can see this just by reading fanzines.

LECTURER: That was quite a telling moment for me when you put those black-and-white pictures of Finney and Matthews up on the screen and no one else in the class knew who they were. At least most of you recognised George Best.

LISA: Why should I have heard of a 1950s plumber from Preston? I was only born in 1980.

LECTURER (*eyes raised*): Do people agree with Sam's analysis?

JONATHAN: I don't. I think all this local-rooted, 'people's game' stuff is a crude, one-dimensional political analysis.

RAJ: I remember what you said in one of your lectures – about how we've had globalisation before. Britain had that whole empire in the nineteenth century. That was globalisation too.

JONATHAN: And professional football has never been totally local. What about that English club with all the Scottish players a hundred years ago?

LECTURER: Yes, Preston North End won the League and Cup double in 1889 with a lot of Scottish players. Accrington Stanley fielded a whole team of Scots in the 1950s.

LISA: You don't have to have generations of football in your blood to get excited by the game, Sam. None of our family watched football until recently. My parents just decided that we needed a hobby. I don't see what's wrong with that. I wouldn't have wanted to be at matches in the eighties. They are proper events now and the stadiums are much safer. What's wrong with today's football being like going to the theatre?

SAM: How come you get to go to Old Trafford, Lisa?

LISA: My uncle has had two Man United season tickets for years. He lets us go to a few games because my aunt doesn't want to go every week.

SAM: The Queen's a Man United supporter, you know.

LISA: Is she?

SAM: Yeah, she lives in London, doesn't know much about football and always seems to get a ticket to the Cup Final.

(*Laughter and groans*)

LECTURER: OK, let's get back to Sam's thesis.

LISA: I don't see why everyone should go through this test of loyalty. Football's an entertainment, and it's a really good entertainment because you don't know what the ending's going to be.

SAM: But these days you *do* know the ending. It'll be the same few top teams in the Premiership and the recently promoted teams will be relegation fodder.

LECTURER: Jonathan, were you going to say something?

JONATHAN: Yeah. Football has to be entertainment today because television is the key promoter of the sport.

SAM: You're not going to say that television has rescued football, are you?

LECTURER: Let him speak, Sam.

JONATHAN: No, I wouldn't go that far. I can see how television seduces us and doesn't give us the whole story. I agree with you on that. But I also think that football can't rely on the old ways. It has to recruit new people like Lisa, and it's doing a good job. The product is obviously better. When we watched that old footage of the 1950s, the players all looked like plodders. They looked so slow. You can just imagine them smoking fags at half-time. Look at Bergkamp today. Some of his touches are breathtaking. He's an athlete.

SAM: Yeah, but there were more goals in the fifties.

JONATHAN: Only because the defenders trained on beer and fish and chips.

RAJ: I want to know where I fit into this. Sam's football seems to be all about white, working-class men. What about me? I'm an England football fan and an India cricket fan. I'd like to support my local football club but they don't make me feel comfortable there. I'd rather support a big club that I can watch on TV. That's why I'm an Arsenal fan. Tell me why that's so terrible, Sam. That's the way I have to connect with football.

LECTURER (*after a pause*): Raj is not unusual in this sense. The research shows that plenty of British people with Asian backgrounds know a lot about football but they don't go to matches. You can learn a lot about the game by watching on TV.

RAJ: And we don't have many professional players either. The few Asians who have played League football have often lived in white communities from an early age. The ones rooted in strong Asian communities are kept out or are too intent on working hard and studying.

(*The door opens. Richard walks in. They all stare at him.*)

RICHARD: Sorry, I couldn't find the room.

LECTURER: Richard, it's week *seven* of term. You couldn't find the room? What's happened to your mate Darren today?

RICHARD: I saw him in the bar last night. I don't think he'll be coming.

LISA (*looking at the lecturer*): What about that quote you told us about, the one about music, comedy and football . . . how did that go?

LECTURER: That was Martin Jacques. He said that music as a cultural form defined the sixties, comedy defined the eighties and football defined the nineties, and football is the biggest of the three. It's a highly contentious argument.

SAM: I don't get it.

JONATHAN: It means that football culture in the nineties began to be seen as less tribal, less gendered, more democratic and more influential.

SAM: Democratic?

JONATHAN: Yeah. Look at the football fanzines, supporters' trusts, Independent Supporters' Associations. Fans have much more of a say today. Football is shedding some of those Victorian values in a positive way. We wouldn't be sitting here talking about the sociology of football if it weren't for the expansion of intellectual interest in the game in the nineties.

SAM: All you're saying is that football has been stolen by the middle classes.

LECTURER: Sonia, you're very quiet. What's your view on this?

SONIA: Well, I like football, but I don't like these top footballers. It's true what Sam says about them being completely divorced from the community. I was in this pricey bar in the vacation and everybody was pointing out this Premiership player. I had no idea who he was, but he was a real git. When I walked past him, he just asked me straight off if I wanted a shag, and he wouldn't take no for an answer. I didn't like him. He was so full of himself.

RICHARD and SAM (*together*): Who was it?

SONIA: There, you see. You need to know his name. You've fallen for all that celebrity culture. People want to be recognised and to be talked about, and other people want to talk about them.

LECTURER: It's difficult for these top young players because they don't fit in anywhere. They have too much money to go back to their own areas. The only safe places for them are hotel rooms and their only safe girlfriends are high-class escorts. They can't go out to nightclubs like other people. They probably feel threatened by women. They feel they should have great girlfriends and great relationships but they often don't. But they also have hard cash and power, and they feel that they have to use their power in those social situations.

SONIA: This one was just arrogant.

RICHARD: It could be a way of funding yourself through college, Sonia.

RAJ: Yellow card for that, Ref.

SONIA: Red.

LECTURER: Footballers have to be confident people on the pitch. The problem comes when they try to take that confidence into other areas of their life. They are raised in a world where they are increasingly told that money – rather than education and knowledge – can solve any problem, and the successful players have a lot of money.

SAM: That's one of my points. If there is so much money involved in football, you are bound to get corruption. You'll get referees being bought off, and pressure for particular results. Everybody chases the money. You get all these spin-offs like Fantasy Football, the betting industry and footballers used to advertise products. Pizza for penalty misses. 'Do I not like this?' They'll soon be selling Lisa footage of Man United goals for her mobile phone.

(*Laughter*)

LECTURER: Anything to add, Richard, even though you didn't hear Sam's presentation?

RICHARD: I bet he didn't say much about the financial revolution in grassroots soccer.

SONIA: How does that work?

RICHARD: My Saturday-club chairman wouldn't mind if we got relegated this season because we can't afford to pay a referee and two assistants any more. In the league below we only need a referee. We have to lock up the ground ourselves to save paying someone from the council.

LECTURER: Do you want to say something about your dissertation at this point?

RICHARD: Oh, yeah, it's on grassroots football. I've been going through the minutes of the Trowbridge and District Junior League.

LECTURER: Any conclusions yet?

RICHARD: Well, there were lots of complaints about poor facilities in the 1990s. Grass eight inches long at Steeple Ashton. Only one bucket of lukewarm water at Deverills. No water at all at Rowde Cross Keys. Unsatisfactory referees' changing facilities at Woolpack Wasps. Problems with dogs fouling pitches. Certain other things have come up repeatedly over the years – fines for late starts or no linesman, players playing under assumed names, all that sort of thing. The referees' secretary is always under pressure, especially when some referees are injured or there's a general shortage. And the committee-meeting minutes often show that flowers or fruit have been sent to some old fart who is in hospital.

LECTURER: By 'some old fart' I presume you mean someone who has devoted forty years of their life to sorting out the squabbles in local football for a small honorarium or nothing at all?

RICHARD: Yeah, that sort of thing.

SONIA: What's the size of this league?

RICHARD: Fairly constant – about forty-five teams in three divisions, all within a radius of ten miles of Trowbridge. There were 1,133 registered players in 1991.

JONATHAN: That's a lot of activity when you add it up around the country. (*Pause for thought*)

LECTURER: OK. Now I also asked you to read some sections of the Pete Davies book, *All Played Out*. Can you start us off, Sonia?

(*Sonia shuffles in her seat, stares at the floor.*)

SONIA: Well, I haven't actually done the reading.

LECTURER: Slacking again, Sonia? Raj?

RAJ: Yeah. Well, you said that the 1990 World Cup tournament was the last time that a journalist or writer had real access to England players in an independent way. Davies wasn't ghosting a book for any of the players, and he wasn't involved with their agents. It was a different world in those days. It stopped after that, partly because of the type of book he wrote.

LECTURER: What did you make of it?

RAJ: When I started reading I thought the book would be about how great the England team were, World Cup semi-finalists and all that. But it was more complicated than that. It was about how a writer could have access to the England players and now they can't. I can see why publicity is *managed* by the FA now – especially after that paragraph about FA Councillors saying that there were too many black fellows in the England team.

LISA: Why was his book called *All Played Out*?

SAM: I thought it was because the players gave everything for their country at that tournament.

RAJ: No, it wasn't. Davies set off to write a book about how white, English working-class culture was spent and all played out. He thought it had degenerated into hooliganism and the oafish behaviour of the likes of Gascoigne. I mean, Gascoigne was like a cartoon of working-class life – drinking, burping and farting.

SONIA: Like Richard here.

RICHARD: Eh?

JONATHAN: Gascoigne is what the French call an *enfant sauvage*. But he also had fantastic skills. Perhaps the sort of skills you saw in English players back in the fifties, eh, Sam?

LECTURER: Go on, Raj.

RAJ: Davies found that he couldn't write that sort of book any more – about the rubbish English – because that 1990 England team, with Gazza running the midfield, became something more beautiful in the second half of the tournament.

LECTURER: Yeah, well done, Raj. Davies thought this tournament would be the last hurrah for an outmoded, in-bred sense of Englishness. You must remember that English club teams had been banned from Europe for five years after Heysel, but fans could still follow the England national team in major championships. That 1990 team had traditional English players such as Pearce and Butcher, who wore their hearts on their sleeves. But it also had the likes of Barnes, Waddle and Gascoigne. England played like a continental team at the end.

LISA: And Gazza cried.

SAM: Yeah, he showed his feminine side all right. He realised that he couldn't play in the final. He couldn't go to the party. He didn't have a dress to wear.

LECTURER: So, suddenly this wasn't a culture that was 'all played out'; it was a culture that was finding itself again. The whole of English football has been reconfigured since then, partly through Euro 96 being held in England. There was a synergy between politics, Britpop and football through the whole commercial development and marketing of the Premier League. After that, football became trendy.

LISA: I liked that *Fever Pitch* book. I liked the way it dealt with identity and masculinity, about being a man and being a fan. His relationship with Arsenal outlasted his other relationships. That bit about agonising over sharing his season ticket with his girlfriend was fascinating.

SAM: Yeah, but Nick Hornby's book wouldn't have been published if it hadn't been about Arsenal and written by a Cambridge graduate. If I wrote one about Crewe Alexandra it wouldn't get picked up.

LISA (*serious*): I didn't know you were a Crewe supporter.

SAM: I'm not. I was giving you a 'for instance'.

LISA: Oh, and I thought you were going to ask me to go to Crewe with you. I can imagine that's the sort of date you offer girls.

RICHARD (*wistful*): I thought I'd picked up a woman in Worcester last year. She was a Torquay fan, up for an FA Cup match. I showed her to the ground. She was working in London and her brother was coming up from Torquay. I thought I'd watch the game with them.

SAM: What was the game like?

RICHARD: I don't know, I couldn't get in. It was all-ticket and I didn't have one, and they weren't selling any on the day.

SONIA: Did you wait for her to come out after the match?

RICHARD: I couldn't be bothered. I was too pissed off. There were empty spaces in the ground and they wouldn't let me in.

SONIA: I think it would have been romantic had you waited for her.

SAM: Hey, Lisa, fancy going to see Crewe play on Saturday?

LISA: Do I not like that?

SAM: Come on, they say football's sexy these days . . .

LISA: It will be if Manchester United win the treble.

SAM: Oh yeah, and where's your French kung-fu man these days?

LISA: Eric Cantona?

SAM: Is he filming a Jackie Chan movie? Or in prison?

LISA: He was provoked by racist comments. Anyway, Sam, you could learn something from Eric – *he* certainly made new football sexy.

LECTURER: OK, enough, we need to get out of here. There's another class waiting.

PART SIX

INTRODUCTION TO PART SIX

Football helped to revive the nation in the late 1940s and provided some hope, stability and community through the fifties. In the sixties and seventies the game symbolised key aspects of social and generational change, but this also brought some negative consequences. Football suffered terrible traumas in the eighties. Then the game was reborn again in the 1990s, although not without its new contradictions and difficulties. After the launch of the immensely successful Premier League the professional game became ubiquitous, no longer contained by the parameters of sport. Football clubs became properties for businessmen to own and exploit, rather than simply community assets. The game's finances became increasingly complex.

Football will always survive. There is something intrinsic that assures the game's longevity. It offers the thrill of playing with a ball or watching others perform, the adrenalin and camaraderie of the dressing-room or the stadium concourse, shared stories and community, family connections, the responsibility of running a club, the dedication of referees and FA officials, and so much more. Stripped of the headlines – money, stardom, stadiums, celebrity, television contracts, scandal, internationalism – football still has enduring attractions. Add in the headlines and the sport becomes an engaging soap opera that helps to sell newspapers and magazines, commits television and radio companies, sells merchandise, attracts oligarchs and billionaires and stimulates millions of conversations.

Arthur Hopcraft, author of *The Football Man*, once pointed out that football had been more than a game since the 1870s, when the working classes first saw it as an escape from drudgery. 'What happens on the football field matters,' Hopcraft wrote, 'not in the way that food matters but as poetry does to some people and alcohol does to others; it engages the personality.'

In England the game has survived its extraordinary post-war journey because of what it means to so many people of so many different backgrounds.

The English game has also been one of the great symbols for football around
the world. The international governing body of football, FIFA, has more
countries in its ranks than the United Nations, and England has often been
a launch pad for that global diffusion. Historically and culturally, England
and Brazil have offered the world two distinctive global brands. England has
history, togetherness, team spirit and hard work; Brazil has flair, imagination
and religious belief. But football in England has also helped to define
relations with countries closer to home. The Scotland–England relationship,
for instance, has been riddled with political, cultural and football baggage.

In this final part we look at how football gives meaning to people's lives
by stimulating basic enthusiasms. We also recognise that there are still
threatening aspects to the game: the lack of respect for referees; certain
styles of spectating; the corrosive effects of too much money; and forms of
exclusion and discrimination. Perhaps the greatest threat, though, is a lack
of knowledge of the impact that the game has on its people. It was this type
of ignorance that contributed to the Hillsborough disaster only forty-three
years after the Bolton disaster.

41

A FAMILY SPORT

INTERVIEWER: This interview is for a research project on family football fans. How did you begin watching football?

PETER: I went to Bournemouth. I was taken by my uncle as my Dad used to work Saturday afternoons. I watched them pretty regularly from when I was about five until I was about twenty. When I was about nine or ten my father changed his job. I went with my Dad then. Either with him or with my friends.

INTERVIEWER: At what age did you start going with your friends?

PETER: Twelve, thirteen. It would have been called Boscombe if you were a local. Yeah, the old blokes behind us used to chant, 'Come on, Boscombe.' I went north to university and started watching Leeds, and it was the crowds at Leeds that put me off football. I didn't go for years. It was racist actually. The last time I went they played West Ham with Clyde Best [1970s]. Ugh, it was terrible and it put me off and I didn't go for ages then. Not until the nineties, with Emma, to Arsenal. A long break. When we started going to Arsenal again it was completely different from fifteen years before. Much nicer.

INTERVIEWER: Why did you start going again?

PETER (*to his daughter*): Why was it?

EMMA (aged thirteen): Because all my friends went and my best friend used to go and then I wanted to go. My best friend was Arsenal, because her brother was Arsenal, and everyone was Arsenal.

INTERVIEWER: Even the girls?

EMMA: Yes.

PETER: Spurs is probably three miles up the road, and Arsenal is about two miles. William Hatton was an Arsenal school so we kind of picked it up, and Emma and I went.

INTERVIEWER: How long did the Arsenal thing last for?

EMMA: It lasted for a season, didn't it? Then it stopped for two years and then Michael went.

PETER: But it kind of fell away because we couldn't get tickets. I couldn't afford *three* season tickets. I could afford two but we couldn't agree on alternating. We go to Arsenal for European matches, or if something comes up through the soccer school, but otherwise we go to [Leyton] Orient. We have just finished our fourth season.

EMMA: We went with the [Orient] checked shirt.

PETER: I know. The Scunthorpe play-off was the second season, wasn't it [1998–9]?

INTERVIEWER: So you are Arsenal supporters in some ways, but Leyton Orient *attenders*?

PETER: I think we are Leyton Orient now, yes.

EMMA: Yes. No one at school had ever heard of them. They have only heard of the big clubs like Arsenal, Man United.

INTERVIEWER: What do you particularly like about supporting Orient compared to supporting a club like Arsenal?

MICHAEL (aged eleven): Easy to get tickets. Some of my friends go and it's a really good atmosphere. Once we went to a match, some people were doing really bad, and the man behind us was shouting stuff like 'I could piss straighter than that.' You can hear everyone shouting at Orient.

EMMA: It's just easier to go to Orient. Arsenal is a bit of a faff. You have to go all dressed up and everyone is so far away [from the pitch] whereas at Orient there is only one tier. It is more like a community spirit and everyone's, like, 'Come on, Orient' even though they are really rubbish. At Arsenal you don't count – if you went to another club they wouldn't miss you as a supporter – but Orient really need their supporters.

MICHAEL: You can see more at Orient.

EMMA: Better visibility.

MICHAEL: All my friends go. Well, most of my friends. We have got season tickets with them.

PETER: I wouldn't mind if they [his children] didn't want to go, although I would probably go on my own. When we lost in Cardiff [in the play-off final] I thought the whole match was a high, and it was a terrific atmosphere. And then dealing with losing, with Blackpool [supporters] outnumbering us. I thought it was a really good thing, (a) to get to, and (b) just to have to deal with it. With football you just don't know what's going to happen and just dealing with the crowd and the anxiety and feeling good and feeling bad, it's just good really. Handling being beaten.

MICHAEL: We wanted to win so we could go up to the Second Division and drive up the motorway with our flag out the window.

PETER: We have strong views on people who are cheats, or lazy, time-wasters. Orient are quite a decent team. They are hard-working and they're not boring. They try. If Orient had one or two players I thought were really shitty, I'm not sure what we'd do. (*To his children*) We like them, don't we? I don't like the lazy ones. I did bridle at Sol Campbell wanting £130,000 a week . . . it does seem obscene. Sometimes going to Arsenal is a real waste of money. They give up sometimes. I never think it's a waste of money at Orient.

MICHAEL: If a team cheats, it makes you want to beat them even more.

EMMA: We like players with a good personality on the pitch.

PETER: I went to football when I was little and it sort of feels like what you do. I *do* know a bit about going to football matches, and it feels like I'm passing something on to them. I think it's a nice thing to do. What is different about it is that you're *talking* about it as you're going along, and these two are very funny – ha, ha funny – and it's very nice.

Many fans have similar tales to tell about the period at the turn of the century. Peter's interest in football had returned, but his daughter and son were new to the game. In the previous fifteen years more and more spectators had been lured to matches in England, thanks to stadium modernisation (as demanded by the Taylor Report), the new FA Premier League, safety measures to counter hooliganism and a better-behaved fan subculture. Aggregate League attendances rose every season from 1986 to reach 25.3 million by 2001, a significant increase on the 19.5 million who watched in 1990–1 but still nowhere near the record 1948–9 level of forty-one million.

By 2001 top-level English football was something of a fashion accessory. It was generally recognised that around five or six million people attended at least one football match in England and Wales each year, although it was difficult to get exact figures. The match-goers included an increasing number of female fans, many of whom, like Emma, were knowledgeable about football and confident around football grounds. In 1995 females comprised 13 per cent of Premier League crowds on average and their numbers continued to rise (to 15 per cent in 2007). Surveys showed that half of hardcore male fans approved of the new stadium comforts and only

20 per cent resented losing the right to stand. But the *cost* of sitting was another matter. A few top-club fans moaned about the number of private boxes and about people 'with their suits and their ties on having their fancy meals' but most loved the buzz of seeing great stars at work (without having to peer through steel fences or watch out for flying missiles).

Football had transformed itself into a family sport that was no longer quite so dominated by a beery machismo, tribalism and violent rivalries. By 2001 all of these still had a place in the game but football was undoubtedly more inclusive of the whole community, with more acceptance of ethnic communities – 'I'm Asian at home but at City I'm just another football supporter,' said one Leicester City fan – and improved facilities for disabled fans. Parents now saw stadiums as safe and trusted places that offered the whole family a break from domestic issues and tensions. Football had been re-established as a central focus for specific forms of consumption, community solidarity and community identity. But there was one drawback – some families were excluded from the entertainment because of cost and restricted access. In fact, as Peter says, children sometimes had to take turns to attend matches because of the cost.

By 2001 'the family' meant all kinds of things. The stereotypical family of man, wife and two children was rare. While the father was still the dominating influence on which club a child supported, there were other influential figures, and family members were more likely to support different clubs. Some children inducted their single mothers. A foster carer in Leicester inaugurated her five foster children at an affordable reserve-team match. Step-parents accompanied their stepchildren. Andy Tilson bonded with his stepson through attending Leicester City matches. It gave them a shared activity and something to talk about, and it took away some of the awkwardness of their relationship. Through football Tilson learned more about what made his stepson tick.

Football can open up conversations with normally uncommunicative teenagers. One great thing about the game is that its basic issues don't change much from one generation to another. While musical tastes, clothes and technology may shift radically every few years, Manchester City v Manchester United maintains its place as a local derby fashionable with all generations.

Michael, Emma and Peter were family fans. But there were many other types of fans. There were committed home-town fans who had the accent and supported the club ('I'm Newcastle born and bred, I bleed black and white');

fans who consciously chose a televised club ('I supported Oxford United but I had to find a respectable team as well so I picked Leeds United'); fans whose second team was in Scotland ('I always liked Dick Barton on the radio so I chose Dumbarton'); fans whose fate was decided by their street location ('Where we lived we had to be Bristol Rovers rather than City'); and fans who abided by family allegiance ('My Dad would have killed me if I'd brought a Spurs supporter home').

The sight of FA Cup Final teams on television seduced many a young child. Sometimes a family holiday determined a fan's second club ('We usually went to Blackpool for a week in August and we always watched a game') or an interest in a bigger club was stimulated by the transfer of a local player. Simon Farmer was originally a Tranmere Rovers fan from Merseyside. Then, when he moved to Shrewsbury, he went native. His whole family hooked up with Shrewsbury Town. Farmer saw following the Town as his civic duty. For him it was location, location, location.

Some supporters are obsessive. Take the Aston Villa fan who really liked the new club badge even though it now meant that his tattoo was out of date. Or the 35-year-old Bristol City fan who gave up his IT job to cycle to every City match in the 2003–4 season (and went to Grimsby twice because the first fixture was postponed when he was thirty miles away). Or the Methodist minister whose children's names included Edson (after Pelé), Jessie (after a female footballer in a book by Brian McLaren) and Dalglish and Paisley (after Liverpool FC managers).

Another category is the disabled fan. There are reckoned to be about 30,000 of them regularly watching professional football in England. Traditionally wheelchair users watched matches for free in uncovered areas at ground level behind the goals. Theirs was a poor view, often made worse by parading policemen. Wheelchair users were allowed one helper but were separated from other family and friends (and from their own club's fans at away matches), and more than a quarter of them left early to avoid the crowds. When the Taylor Report highlighted the need for improved facilities, some clubs worked hard at creating more appropriate areas, appointing contact officers and, in a few cases, providing Red Cross support. But many clubs still failed to take advice from the disabled supporters themselves. The National Association of Disabled Supporters was formed in 1998, but problems remained. At the Millennium Stadium in 2001, disabled fans were unable to see much of a crucial penalty shoot-out because fans around them were standing.

It is rare for any fan to watch a match with a completely blank slate. Perhaps the nearest to neutrality are the ground-hoppers who add as many League and non-League grounds as possible to their card, enjoying football wherever it is played. Most fans form opinions of other clubs, and different clubs have different supporter profiles. Surveys showed that 51 per cent of Sunderland-supporting parents usually brought their kids to the match in 2001, but only 19 per cent of Newcastle United's parents did the same.

It is dangerous to label fans in any one way. At Cambridge City in the early 1990s two fans chatted at the sidelines.

'The referee's an idiot,' said one.

'Tell him,' the other replied. 'Shout at him.'

'No, that's more your line. You're the one with qualifications. You do the shouting.'

Fans can be university-educated or illiterate, single or married, quiet or rowdy. There are moaners ('I've seen Subbuteo men more lively') or loyal backers ('We still love yah, City'), repetitive chanters ('You don't know what you're doing') or masters of the occasional one-liner ('Don't just stand there while he gets treatment – PRACTISE'), drinkers who create a carnival atmosphere or drinkers who cause trouble. There are frequent attenders or irregular attenders who have commitments or live too far away. During their 'supporting careers' fans acquire knowledge about clubs (especially their own). They can define matches by specific incidents and results. They read the sports press and check websites. They exchange news of transfer dealings and playing styles. True fans know exactly how to pronounce a player's name, his origins, his previous clubs and his current (and past) squad numbers. Fans can recognise distant players by their gait, running-style or latest hairstyle. Often the kids know more than the parents, and they have better eyesight. Fans are also curious people. What will happen? Who will I see at the match? Will our injured players be fit? What will the new man be like? Who will win? What odds can I get? Who will score for us?

Some people clearly don't have the knowledge. One day two teenage girls stood by a barrier near the front of a crowded terrace. The men around them gave them as much room as they could. The girls spent the first fifteen minutes of the game looking bemused. Then one girl turned to the other and said, in a serious voice, 'When are they going to let the little man in black have a kick?' Several of the men went pale. These two young girls weren't fit to wear the replica shirt.

True fans want to influence. They try to affect the outcome by shouting, chanting, singing and generally supporting. They feel personally flattered when a player or manager says, 'The crowd were like a twelfth man,' or 'The fans sucked in our equaliser.' Fans try to tell the referee to favour their own team, and they try to help their heroes by wearing lucky clothes, carrying lucky cuddly toys and eating a lucky pre-match meal. They may even try to use their own visualisation techniques from the touchline. Other fans try to influence more formally by joining the club's board of directors or helping to form a supporters' trust. Some write for one of the many fanzines that sprung up in frustration at the way football was run and written about. Others talk on a radio phone-in:

'Mick is a Fulham fan in Kilburn. Hi, Mick. You're on Radio Soccerspeak.'

'How's it going?'

'All right, mate. You're on Radio Soccerspeak. What have you got for us?'

'My main point is that when clubs go up to the Premiership they get this different attitude. I've been a Fulham supporter for a long, long time. I remember going to Fulham when there was thirteen hundred there and you had to shout to the person next to you. In their last season in the old First Division, before they came up to the Premiership, my ticket to sit in the Riverside Stand was thirteen pounds and my son's was six-fifty. Now I have to pay a lot of dough to see how they're playing.'

'Thanks, Mick. I've got a few more of your texts here. We asked you to define real football for us. Andy of Northampton says, "Real football is watching your team at three o'clock on a Saturday afternoon." Here's one from Billy of Birmingham: "Real football is getting up early on a Sunday morning, getting the boots out, scraping the ice off your windscreen, leaving to play the game and not knowing whether the game's on or off." And Lee from Luton says, "I define real football as watching English players in an English league." Keep those calls and texts coming in. Or email us for free. This is Radio Soccerspeak. Let us know what you think about foreign owners and foreign players in English football. We've got John in London on the line. John, you're on Radio Soccerspeak.'

'Afternoon, John, how you doing?'

'Hello, mate, love the show.'

'Thanks very much.'

'I just want to say that this strap-line of "real football" is bandied about by small-town morons with lower-league teams that are trying to make out that they are more loyal than the rest of us. Give me my comfy seat and top-class foreign footballers any day.'

'Yeah, the game's moved on, hasn't it, John?'

'Yeah, it certainly has. There's some pathetic comments from these idiots who try to raise the profile of their lower-league teams.'

'Now we've got Rob in Lincolnshire. Fire away, Rob, you're on Radio Soccerspeak.'

'I knew we'd lost real football when I heard business predators talking about "leveraging the football-club brand" and "maximising the yield from the global brand".'

'What's your point, Rob?'

'My point is that I go to watch Spalding United. There's some romance in that. You know the players. These Premier League players disappear for a week like they've been kept in a fridge . . .'

'OK, Rob . . .'

Click.

Fandom changed with the arrival of the Premier League and globalisation. The world was now awash with 'virtual fans' who supported top English clubs via satellite television, the internet and merchandise trails. Domestic broadcasting fees provided top-league clubs with 32 per cent of their income on average in 2003–4 (compared with only 15 per cent in 1990–1). Television fans now warranted serious consideration; they had particular merchandise fancies and their viewing-hour preferences disrupted the traditional Saturday 3pm kick-off routine.

At grounds football moved more up-market in the early days of the Premier League. In 1995 42 per cent of spectators were earning over £21,000 (compared with 34 per cent in 1992). These fans spent more money on merchandise. In 1994–5 48 per cent purchased a replica shirt and over 50 per cent bought the club 'highlights of the season' video. But national supporter surveys showed that fans objected to traditional club colours being replaced by fashionable blacks and strange hues, and 78 per cent thought that replica shirts were too expensive. The Premier League increasingly directed its marketing at family fans and more affluent customers, but lots of traditional fans also stayed and paid the higher prices. By 2003–4 the League's average income per attendee was £30 (€44), double that of Germany's Bundesliga and almost triple that of France's Ligue 1.

Supporters were kept interested by the various mini-leagues within the Premier League – title contenders, European aspirants, safety-zone teams and the relegation-challenged. Paradoxically these new consumer fans could be more loyal than old-time supporters; Sunderland averaged 33,904 in 2005–6 despite winning only one home Premier League match all season. Top-division crowds rose steadily from 9.99 million in 1991–2 (in the old First Division) to 13.47 million in 2002–3 (in the Premier League). But the loyalty of fans didn't matter as much to the balance sheets as it had in previous eras. Income was now more dependent on sponsorship, merchandising, television contracts and personal fortunes (e.g. Jack Walker at Blackburn Rovers and Roman Abramovich at Chelsea). Clubs relegated from the Premier League could retain most of their fans and yet suffer severe financial problems (e.g. Leicester City and Leeds United).

Some parents incorporated football into their family life because they sensed that football in the twenty-first century could help their kids. At the ground kids could discover independence as they went off alone to buy a drink, visit the toilet or buy a programme. More than anything parents wanted their children to learn the lesson of teamwork above selfishness. One father loved it when his son complained that a particular player 'should have passed it' rather than shot for goal.

At the match the family was on neutral ground and their relationships grew more equal. Children got the chance to see parents when they were off-duty, in public, more relaxed – or more het up. Football offered time together after a week when Mum and Dad may have been working long hours. The travel to and from the match offered chances to chat, but parents had to be careful not to bond too much with a football-going child at the expense of their other children.

Some parents worried that top players were not good role models.

'I think modesty and low profile, in a very high-profile sport, is a very clever thing,' said one Premier League fan. 'I do think the players should be better role models, if I am honest. I think the enormous contracts are part of the entertainment and the excitement but it's not really. It's not one of my values to be flash and irresponsible.'

'It's entertainment now as much as it is sport,' added his wife. 'Pop stars are role models, actors and actresses, they're all role models. And they are all divorced, they all sleep around and they all do stupid things. There's always somebody around who's a role model. But, hopefully, our two get their role models from their parents.'

'I don't have footballers as my role models,' said one thirteen-year-old girl who watched Leicester City regularly. 'David Beckham and Michael Owen get very up themselves. They get very mardy when they lose or a decision is given against them. They really don't know what to do with the money they have, do they? Mardy and spoilt.'

Some parents felt that supporting successful clubs didn't prepare children for the uncertainties of life. Life wasn't like winning all your home matches. Life was more 'win some, lose some'. Peter thought it was better to follow a club like Leyton Orient, where fans learned how to cope with adversity, often using droll humour as a coping mechanism ('Wonderful man-to-man football, red to blue, blue to red, red to blue'). Peter was a new type of fan, but he and other parents were using the game in a traditional way – as family fun and to give their kids the right attitude.

42

'CUP OF TEA, REF?'

D URING THE HALF-TIME INTERVAL AT a local football match
the referee, wearing the traditional black uniform, walks slowly across
the muddy pitch, replacing divots with his foot as he goes. The home-team
secretary carries a mug of tea towards him.

'Cup of tea, Ref?' the secretary asks.

'Thank you very much,' says the referee, taking the mug. 'Have you peed
in it?'

The two men's faces barely change. Maybe, if you look closely, there is a
twitch of a smile as a moment's humanity shines through. Players and club
officials too often see referees as rule-book automatons.

Referees are taught to be unbiased and to be seen to be unbiased. A
referee won't accept a lift from a player or club official. A referee must not
do anything that can be misconstrued as being partisan. A cup of tea is just
about acceptable . . . as long as there is no artificial sweetener on offer.

A 1993 study of West Midlands referees found that 69.5 per cent of
experienced referees reckoned that the least enjoyable thing about the job
was 'abuse from players or fans'.

'In the [local] Premier Division the players get to know you – and give
their respect, once they see you know your job,' said one referee. 'Lower
leagues seem to think "Just another referee to shout and bawl at." '

'The influence of football on TV has been remarkable,' said another
referee. 'Constant instant replays from six different camera angles of difficult
decisions do not help, with a panel of so-called experts passing comments
about the laws of the game and refereeing decisions when they have never
refereed a match of that kind. Come Sunday morning they are all at it!'

Persistent abuse causes about half of newly trained referees to leave
refereeing in the first two years after qualifying. This retention problem

is a big threat to the sport. But the remaining referees gain enough satisfaction.

Why do referees do the job when they could be doing so many other things instead? Why don't they exercise by playing over-age football for Arthritic Bilbao or running around the park? Why aren't they watching a top-class match or getting their fresh air by nurturing prize-winning leeks? Why do they put themselves in this position of eternal outsider? Almost all referees have no great ambition to referee at the highest level, so why do it at all? Why do they subject themselves to abuse and criticism?

The research provides a few answers: referees love the game; they want to be involved; they want to put something back; it is a good substitute for playing; it keeps them fit; it brings in a little money; they want to help other people enjoy themselves; they get a great feeling of satisfaction when a game goes well; and they like to be in charge.

Occasionally they are thanked and their hands are shaken. Sometimes they get a cup of tea.

All the world's inequality can be dismissed when two teams of players step on to the football pitch. That is one aim of the International Football Association Board, the ultimate authority on the laws of the game. One of football's great qualities, which helps send it round the world, is that it is policed and controlled very well when compared with other aspects of society – warfare, car travel, business dealings and so on – and that ethic is safeguarded in the laws. Referees are the agents of the lawmakers. They make equality happen.

In his book *Association Football and Match Control* (1978) Stanley Lover divided the concept of 'spirit of the game' into three main issues: (i) equality; (ii) safety (outlawing dangerous play); and (iii) enjoyment.

Everyone needs to be treated fairly and *equally* – by race or creed, size or stardom, amateur or professional. The referee is a major representative of neutrality, but the competition organisers also have a crucial role to play. Teams should be matched and both sides should be treated the same. Possible outcomes should be anticipated and fair principles should be laid down in advance.

The *safety*-first principle is behind many of the laws. Goalposts should be safe. Temporary stoppages for thunder and lightning are permitted. Pitches should be inspected for anything dangerous. Players should tape up or remove jewellery. Footwear should conform to regulations. And referees should err on the side of caution if a player is injured. Red cards are issued for challenges using excessive force, and yellow cards for recklessness.

Football is for everyone's *enjoyment*. It is for the enjoyment of players (especially in amateur soccer) and the enjoyment of spectators (especially in the professional game). The aim is to keep the game flowing and to make it as entertaining as possible. This is the spirit of playing the advantage, the backpass law, quick free-kicks and cautions for delaying a restart. The enjoyment takes many forms. Football is a lifelong interest, a way to stay fit, a collection of stories and anecdotes, a bunch of mates and characters, a spirit of camaraderie and belonging.

The spirit of the game is also its proven past. It is the preservation of past laws that work and the introduction of new laws that have proved themselves in experiments. The laws must retain the essence of equality, safety and enjoyment. And the participants must remember that it's only a game.

Occasionally an incident threatens the spirit of the game. One example, deeply rooted in the English psyche, occurred at 9.37pm on Thursday 26 June 2004. In the final minute of a Euro 2004 quarter-final, England drawing 1–1 with Portugal in Lisbon, a header by England's Sol Campbell hit the crossbar and Campbell followed up to head the ball into the net. Players and fans began to celebrate but England's John Terry had illegally put his arm on goalkeeper Ricardo's shoulder. The referee, Urs Meier of Switzerland, was close enough to see the incident clearly and far enough away not to interfere with the play. He decided to give Portugal a free-kick, even before the ball reached the net.

To Meier and other elite referees, this was a fairly routine decision. Almost all referees could justify Meier's stance, providing that they saw the incident and maintained their impartiality. Meier didn't hesitate. He was an experienced professional. He had been refereeing for nearly thirty years and had taken charge of over a hundred internationals.

But television pundits in England abused the referee.

'The grocer from Zurich didn't balance the scales very fairly to England there.'

'We have definitely been cheated.'

'There were times when it looked like we were playing against twelve men and one of them was Swiss.'

And the English newspaper headlines were blistering:

'What an Urs Hole.'

'We've Been Robbed.'

'You Swiss Banker.'

'Idiot Ref Robs Beck's Heroes.'

The *Sun* published Meier's telephone number and email address. The Swiss referee later claimed that he received 16,000 emails and 5,000 abusive telephone calls, and many more tried to make contact after blocks were put in place.

The *Sun* sent reporters to Meier's home town. Reporters offered money to his ex-wife and quoted her (even though she said later that she hadn't talked to the press), and attempted to bribe his fourteen-year-old son. England fans in Zurich came at Meier with glass bottles, his internet site was hacked and culture-jammed, and he had nightmares. Meier felt that the FA and UEFA should have acted more quickly in support of him. Instead a *Sun* reporter showed Meier a red card in his hotel lobby the morning after the match and the hate campaign was under way. Giving the correct decision no longer mattered. When Meier's life was threatened he arranged for armed protection.

Of football's many paradoxes, one stands out above all: the referee is the most essential person on the football field and yet the referee is often the most reviled, most abused and most unappreciated person on the park. There are a number of reasons why referees are not respected as much as they should be. Let us look at them (in no particular order).

One reason is simply that the referee is an authority figure. Referees have to be decisive, no-nonsense men with conviction, inner strength and self-belief. They have to be confident, cocksure of their decisions and capable of forgetting mistakes and moving on to the next decision. According to research by Nick Neave and Sandy Wolfson, the profile of senior referees resembles that of police officers, politicians and military leaders. This type of person is not likely to be popular with footballers.

Football is a low-scoring game and football referees make many decisions. Certain refereeing decisions, like a penalty-kick or a sending-off, can seriously affect the match result. One goal may make all the difference. Football is very different from sports such as basketball and lacrosse, where scoring is more frequent, and very different from games such as tennis and golf, where the referee is in the background. In football it is too easy to say, 'We lost the match because of the referee.'

Football's team ethic means that it is easier to blame the referee than a colleague or the manager. Players have self-belief: We are the best team in this league; we haven't won the match, so it must have been the referee who cost us the game. Psychologists call this syndrome cognitive dissonance. Two incompatible thoughts – We're the best team but we've lost – are best resolved by a rationalisation, like blaming the referee.

This combination of tight results, key refereeing decisions and self-belief conjures up some fantastic rationalisations and discussion points. No match is immune. Take England's 9-3 victory over Scotland in April 1961. Over twenty years later Scotland manager Ian McColl recalled how Scotland might have won the game but for the referee. After being 3–0 down at half-time, Scotland pulled back to 3–2. Then, according to McColl, the referee made four errors in the prelude to England's fourth goal. 'The goal was an injustice as we were getting back into the game, and it took the heart out of the lads,' McColl said. 'That was the turning-point.'

Another anti-referee perspective arises from ignorance of the laws. The laws of soccer are nowhere near as complex as, say, banking law, but the referee is often the only expert on the pitch. Very few people read *The Laws of Association Football*. Even fewer discuss interpretations of key phrases with experts. As the philosopher Wittgenstein implied, everything revolves around the *interpretation* of a law. Or, to quote a famous phrase of refereeing guru Ken Aston, 'a referee cannot be a law book on legs'.

In football rumours spread very quickly. After the incident in Portugal in 2004 the media quickly spread the word that the referee had erred. And referees rarely answer back in order to counter rumours. They don't have to explain a decision to players or fans, and they generally don't talk to the media.

In the 1950s top-class referees often trained with part-time professionals at their local club. Some of that generation adapted to other roles in football. Jimmy Jewell became a radio commentator, Jack Topliss was a professional club's chief scout, Jim Finney became a football-club secretary. But that informal contact between referees and other football people began to disappear from the game. The relationship between referees and other football people became distant and weak. Managers have better relationships with rival managers than they do with referees.

Here is a famous England international explaining a view common among professional players: 'We get very frustrated with referees because they're like a totally separate body from us and they shouldn't be. There should be more integration. What they view as possibly a bad tackle wouldn't be viewed as one by professional players, yet the one that is a bad tackle the referees don't even recognise it half the time. They need to get together with us, or with somebody, and say, "We're all going to do the same." ' Paradoxically players call for both robotic consistency and situational common sense from referees.

Referees have never quite belonged in the bigger picture. It is as though they are grafted on to the game from the outside. It is hard to achieve complete independence *and* a sense of belonging. It is hard to say, 'Let's embrace referees and see them as part of the game' *and* also say, 'Referees must be completely impartial and beyond complaint by either team.' The football authorities have always taken the latter option.

Referees are a symbol of neutrality, and you have to go a long way to discover neutrality in football. On the pitch football can be a muddy, unkempt and overly physical game – far removed from the starched whiteness of, say, bowls, cricket and croquet – and it provokes strong emotions and involvement. It is almost axiomatic that every football follower must have a club they want to support, a team they want to win. On the pitch the referee is the sole representative of neutrality. Referees value their integrity above everything. Being called a cheat is an inexcusable insult, punishable by a red card. English referees are much respected throughout the world for their calm, level-headed, unbiased manner.

One way of bringing referees closer to the grassroots community would be to compel all local clubs to nominate a referee. This candidate would officiate in leagues unconnected with the sponsoring club. In that way the club would take some responsibility for the future of the game. Also, players would realise that referees are part of the football community, and not some unfortunate and unwanted distraction.

Players often think that referees are officiating because 'they can't play the game and therefore they don't understand the game'. In fact the referee is usually the only person who does understand the game. About 42 per cent of the sample of West Midlands referees officiated at a lower level than they had played. But, if a referee doesn't have an athletic body that advertises some sporting connection (not necessarily to football), or a real air of authority, that referee may get abused or disrespected.

A final reason returns us to the media. TV pundits may show their prejudices above their analysis, especially for England matches. When it comes to the recruitment of such analysts the criteria are more likely to be outspokenness, charisma, good looks, tactical nous, newsworthiness, celebrity status and topical value rather than knowledge of the laws, refereeing experience and an apprenticeship in journalism. The main quality shared by pundits and referees is a conviction of their views. Some referees would argue that top administrators secretly condone the scapegoating of referees because controversy helps to maintain interest in the game.

Football has always had this paradox where referees are vital but treated unkindly. History is full of tales of referees being chased to a railway station or dunked in a duck pond, but the English game of shouting derisively at the whistle-blower became more popular from the 1960s onwards. The 1971 television trial of referee Ray Tinkler was unquestionably a turning-point in the attitudes to referees in England. By 2004 the disrespect shown to them was engraved in the football world (as it was communicated through television and the press).

'I can see that England, the English newspapers, need a scapegoat when the side loses,' Urs Meier said after the Portugal–England match. 'It can be Beckham missing a penalty or getting sent off, it can be another player, it can be the manager. People didn't *want* to see the truth. Always they need a scapegoat. There is more pressure on referees than ever and I have told the FA, FIFA and UEFA that they must give more protection. You cannot allow the tabloids to destroy them.'

Referees are indispensable to football. Referees are the neutrons you don't see, the spaces between the words in a sentence, the reason why the game works. If referees become extinct, so will the game.

43

FRANCHISE FC

Barry Pearson was in his forties, working as a school caretaker, when he got the bug of being a Dons fan. As a youngster he had watched Spurs for a while, in the Alan Gilzean and Martin Chivers days, before drifting away. For years he didn't give football a second thought. Then came a Cup tie between the Dons and Tottenham Hotspur. He set off to buy a ticket, turned it into a season ticket, and his life changed.

Barry, his wife Karen and son Terry started attending home and away games. Before long they knew most people at the club. They met the chairman, directors, lottery ladies, programme sellers, grounds people, stewards, players and many spectators. Barry Pearson wore a red wig to honour his favourite player. 'Don't get too attached to your wig,' the player told him. 'I might change my hair colour next year.'

The Pearson family reckoned that the football club brought people together and boosted the community. When people discussed the Dons, others joined in. If you wore a Dons shirt, people stopped and talked to you about the club. A postman had 'POSTIE' on the back of his replica shirt. An old lady had 'GRANNY 65' on hers. The Pearsons met some good friends through football.

One New Year's Day Barry drove to the ground for a Dons match.

'I've got pains in my chest,' he told Karen when they arrived. He recognised the symptoms of angina. 'I'll have to go to hospital. Don't you miss the match.'

In the ambulance he talked about football.

'I'm a Dons supporter,' the paramedic said. 'I've got to get you to hospital, book you in and get back for the match.'

The match had started by the time Barry saw the consultant.

'What's the score?' the consultant asked him.

'I don't know, I'm waiting for the phone call.'

This is a wonderful thing, Barry thought. I've never met these people before and we're all talking about the Dons. He meant the MK Dons.

The title of Niall Cooper's book, *The Spirit of Wimbledon*, is repeated many times when former players and current supporters tell their stories of the Dons. Supporter Sis Martin explains about the ecological spirit of the 1920s ('If you were part of Wimbledon community, you were part of Wimbledon Football Club'). The three Wallis brothers played together for Wimbledon during the 1940s and 1950s ('We loved the spirit and the community aspect of the club'). Goalkeeper Dickie Guy talks about the club's inner belief back in the 1960s and 1970s ('The spirit at the club has always been fantastic'). Full back Wally Downes became a founder member of the so-called Crazy Gang in the 1980s ('Those guys had a spirit about them and I just fed off it').

Wimbledon FC replaced Workington in the Football League in 1977. Over the next ten years the south London club grew and grew. They employed *full-time* professional players for the first time (1978), yo-yoed between Divisions Four and Three (1978–82), suddenly rose through all the divisions (1983–6) and won the FA Cup (1988). Wimbledon's great achievements of the 1980s came when many fans and ex-players could still remember the club's local amateur roots and some astonishing FA Cup achievements as a non-League club. Part of the Wimbledon spirit was to accept the underdog tag but not give the opposition much respect.

The term 'Crazy Gang' was first used in the press by *Daily Mirror* reporter Tony Stenson in March 1985. Activity within the camp was wild. Perhaps the craziness first started when cocky teenager Wally Downes played for the Reserves and the players were allowed a free hand in the name of team spirit. The reserve-team bus driver resigned on the spot when Downes put an empty cardboard box over his head. The bus was speeding along a major road at the time.

The initiation ceremonies for new Wimbledon players bordered on lunacy. Players were stripped and rolled around in the snow or thrown into huge puddles. New players had their clothes cut into shreds, or stolen so that they had to drive home with only a towel as protection. One had his kit-bag set on fire in the dressing-room while the other players danced around it and a fire engine rushed to the scene. Another had his genitals daubed with black shoe polish. A player was injured in a training-ground fight and another chased his assailant around with a baseball bat. Even chairman Sam Hamman joined in; he once scrawled obscene graffiti on the dressing-room walls at West Ham's ground.

Wimbledon's style of play often offended aficionados who believed in the beautiful game. Wimbledon were high on gamesmanship, poor on discipline and physically intimidating. The main tactic was known as Route One, after the direct option in the 1970s television show *Quizball*. On the field Route One meant whacking the ball into the channels and scrapping for possession, well-rehearsed set-plays (which brought five out of every six Wimbledon goals), the goalkeeper taking all the free-kicks in his own half, and getting the ball into the opponents' penalty area with long, high crosses. 'I've asked them to take the roof off the stand so we can see some of Wimbledon's best passes,' said one grumpy opposition fan.

At Wimbledon's rudimentary Plough Lane ground the players mixed easily with the fans. Having a nightclub, Nelson's, attached to the ground helped. After a match there could be ten Wimbledon players in Nelson's at midnight. On the eve of the 1988 FA Cup Final against League Champions Liverpool the whole squad ended up at the Fox & Grapes pub, the club's birthplace. On the day of the Final the Wimbledon team made Liverpool players wait in the tunnel and repeatedly yelled the 'Yidaho' war cry to intimidate their opponents. Lawrie Sanchez scored the only goal of the match, following a typical Wimbledon set-piece, goalkeeper Dave Beasant saved an Aldridge penalty-kick, and Wimbledon followers thought it was the last of football's fairy-tales – from non-League to FA Cup winners in only eleven years (with average attendances of below 8,000). But the sporting media was divided on the extraordinary result. Was this a classic romantic achievement for the English underdog or was it an ugly triumph for an up-and-at-'em bunch of nasties?

Wimbledon fans were a mix of a few loyal locals who remembered the amateur days and tourist-fans who had rejected other London clubs. In 2000 only 12 per cent of Wimbledon season-ticket holders were following their father's club, the lowest of any Premier League club, and only 56 per cent were locally born (the second lowest). Some might have been Spurs or Arsenal fans at heart but they felt that Premier League football was safe and cheap at Wimbledon, and they could take their relatives. Wimbledon crowds had more females and children than any other top club.

The spirit of Wimbledon had to be strong because it was severely tested. On 2 August 2001 every season-ticket holder and club member received a letter from Wimbledon FC saying that the club planned a sixty-mile move to Milton Keynes in Buckinghamshire.

*   *   *

Before the announcement the identity of 'little Wimbledon' had already been challenged. Talk of possible mergers with Crystal Palace or a move to Cardiff or Dublin was punctuated by the reality of a ground-share at Crystal Palace's Selhurst Park. In the summer of 1997 came another big change. Two Norwegians, Kjell Inge Roekke and Bjorn Rune Gjelsten, bought up an 80 per cent stake in Wimbledon FC for £30 million. The 1998–9 season brought excellent playing results but the bubble burst when popular manager Joe Kinnear suffered a heart attack. Wimbledon began the next season with a Norwegian manager, Egil Olsen, who didn't fit the club's persona. The Crazy Gang antics disappeared and so did some of the spirit. It led to relegation.

Sam Hamman left, Charles Koppel was appointed chief executive and the new Wimbledon owners planned the move to Milton Keynes. They pointed out that the club couldn't survive on current gate receipts, even though they had done more than most clubs to attract visiting fans. The club owners hoped that Wimbledon fans would travel to matches in Milton Keynes, but that was a forlorn prospect.

When news of the plan broke in August 2001 many members of the Wimbledon Independent Supporters' Association (WISA) wrongly assumed that Football League or FA rules would cut the move dead. Transporting a sports club from one town to another only happened in US sports, didn't it? It was one more example of the American influence. Already football-club executives talked about 'ball-park figures', 'touching base' and 'a whole new ball game'. Team colours were chosen for commercial rather than traditional reasons, and lots of American-style middlemen were trying 'to make a buck or two'. 'The only agent back then was double-oh-seven,' said Brian Clough, reflecting on the 1960s, 'and he just shagged women, not entire football clubs.'

The threat to Wimbledon FC's existing community seemed to symbolise three fears that fans had about the modern game: (i) clubs were distancing themselves from their local communities; (ii) American-style franchise moves were possible; and (iii) owners were in the game to asset-strip and make money. Wimbledon owner Sam Hamman had made millions by selling the Plough Lane ground to a supermarket chain (in 1994) and the club to Norwegians (in 1997).

Wimbledon fans protested vehemently during the 2001–2 season – black balloons at the first match, a merchandise boycott, a march from Wimbledon to Selhurst and five minutes of fans turning their backs on play at the last match of the season. Here was a surprisingly resourceful fan base. Any group of supporters faced with such a move would have fought back, but the Wimbledon fans were particularly capable. They had people with media skills, organisational talent, financial nous and technological know-how. Twenty-three per cent of Wimbledon season-ticket holders earned over £50,000 a year, the second-highest behind Chelsea (33 per cent).

An alternative Wimbledon match programme, *Yellow and Blue*, was launched – it eventually outsold the official programme by three to one – and the word was spread via websites. A supporters' trust was formed, ready to take over the club if it went into administration, and Charlton Athletic fans' successful campaign to return to the Valley was an inspiration. Suddenly Wimbledon switched from being disliked by outsiders to being lauded for its heroic fans.

The Football League turned down the proposed move to Milton Keynes, but a three-man FA committee ruled two to one in favour. The supporters' trust moved into action. Ivor Heller found an office at his factory and Kris Stewart spoke convincingly at public meetings. By mid-June 2002 a new club, AFC Wimbledon, had been formed by angry fans.

The Combined Counties League accepted AFC Wimbledon, Terry Eames was appointed manager, trials were held for prospective players and pre-season friendly matches were arranged. The first match, at Sutton United, drew a 4,657 crowd. The first home league match attracted 4,262 spectators. Crowds compared favourably with Wimbledon FC's 2,786 average in their last season in London. After the first season AFC Wimbledon took control of their own future by buying the lease at Kingsmeadow.

Meanwhile the remnants of Wimbledon FC finally moved to Milton Keynes in September 2003. The blue-and-yellows soon became the all-whites, and Wimbledon FC became the MK Dons (or Franchise FC to its critics). Keeping Wimbledon's original nickname angered traditional Wimbledon fans, who now felt disenfranchised. But the warnings had been there for years. In his 1968 report on the condition of English football Norman Chester wrote with prescience: 'New communities have developed, particularly in southern England, but also, for instance, in the Midlands, which lack clubs in League membership. Amalgamations of old clubs would provide vacancies for new clubs to enter the League. Alternatively the movement of established clubs to new communities could provide a way both of saving old clubs and at the same time bringing League football to new and growing areas.'

Milton Keynes was a new community. The town was known to outsiders for its shopping centre, American-style layout, Open University and concrete cows.

When Barry Pearson moved to Milton Keynes in 1997 it didn't bother him that the town had no Football League club. When MK Dons started up, six years later, Barry showed little immediate interest and there was a lot of bad press about the move from Wimbledon. Then came the MK Dons v Spurs Cup tie. Barry bought two season tickets and was hooked. He wanted to support his local club.

Barry and his wife Karen saw that the Dons chairman, Peter Winkelman, had a dream. A new stadium was built at Denbigh, five miles from the centre of Milton Keynes. In honour of the concrete cows two football-club mascots dressed up as cows called Mooey and Donny. Karen loved the cows and wore 'lucky socks' with cow designs to matches. The new stadium was built in a bowl, in the manner of Barcelona's Nou Camp. You entered at street level and dropped down thirty rows of seating to the pitch. The official stadium name was stadiummk but its popular name was the Moo Camp. Here was a new club with Premier League ambitions in a decent catchment area. Barry Pearson felt excited about following a club that was just beginning.

Barry occasionally noticed a few traditional Wimbledon scarves at MK Dons matches. He reckoned that these old fans were an integral part of MK Dons. When a legal battle decided that the Wimbledon FC trophies should go to AFC Wimbledon rather than MK Dons, Barry agreed with the decision. He understood that a club's history belonged to the fans. He wanted his club, MK Dons, to create their own history.

The Pearson family's first away trip was to Walsall. At Farsley Celtic, in the FA Cup, they were close enough to take throw-ins. At Shrewsbury the home fans threw coins at them. But the rewards were greater at away matches. When the players scored goals they came up close to the fans. Barry was also impressed with his son's observational talent. Terry could remember the detail of grounds, games and the kiosk food.

At ten years old Terry Pearson was both a Dons supporter and a Man United fan. Two players in his junior football team said, 'You should support Man United – they're a good club and they play good football.' Terry watched them on the TV and thought, Yeah, they're good, so he went out and bought a shirt. At that time he was one of only two kids in his class who also supported Dons. But the interest grew in the next two years. Terry's mum noticed more and more kids wearing Dons shirts to school. That was becoming their school uniform.

The club quickly collected local crowd characters. 'Wolfman' was a homeless man in his mid-forties. He wore a leopard-pattern jacket and trousers, a Dons scarf and hat and a wig. He sold *The Big Issue* in central Milton Keynes and watched matches at the National Hockey Stadium from near the invalid cars. He would run up and down with a big music-box, recording all the songs sung in the Cow Shed. When MK Dons moved to their purpose-built new stadium there was no obvious place for Wolfman. But a collection bucket was sent round the ground and the fans bought him a season ticket. It was part of the spirit of the club.

At times the Pearsons noticed the antagonism of rival fans. A lot of people wanted Dons to go down into the Conference League and AFC Wimbledon to come up. Luton Town fans were very anti-Dons. Rivalries built up with Peterborough and Wycombe Wanderers. Relegation to League Two in 2006 felt like a punishment for the move and for being called Dons. Soon, though, a positive identity was constructed. The fans chanted 'MK Army' and responded to taunts with pride. When Stockport County fans chanted, 'You've got no history', Dons fans replied cheerfully, 'We've got no history.' Other songs in the Dons' repertoire were 'You're Getting Beat by the Franchise' and 'No One Likes Us – We Don't Care' (an old Millwall favourite). Dons fans embraced the hostility, just like Wimbledon FC fans had in the past.

MK Dons fans also had a siege mentality to match Wimbledon's. Everybody was against them. They were banned from some supporters' organisations, frozen out of some radio phone-ins, made outcasts by football publications such as *When Saturday Comes* and felt targeted by referees. AFC Wimbledon fans had no objection to a club in Milton Keynes per se; they just didn't want it to be *their* club in *their* League. But it all helped to create another Wimbledon spirit – in Milton Keynes.

Barry and Karen Pearson talked about the spirit of the Dons growing into a 'mass community feel'. Their seventeen-year-old daughter Lucy, having originally shown little interest, suddenly converted, and the Pearsons could talk about the Dons at the dinner-table. Outsiders saw MK Dons as a brand-new plastic club with a privileged start, but it didn't feel that way to the Pearson family. Fans of England's newest professional club had developed their own sense of belonging and community integration.

44

AN A-Z OF THE NEW PROFESSIONAL GAME

ABRAMOVICH, Roman An oil tycoon who bought Chelsea FC for £140 million in August 2003, when he was thirty-seven, Abramovich was reckoned to be worth £11.7 billion in the 2008 *Sunday Times* Rich List. Having become a billionaire almost overnight by buying state-owned Russian assets relatively cheaply in the mid-1990s, Abramovich set the standard for Premier League clubs with European ambitions by investing over £500 million in Chelsea. Helped by the appointment of José Mourinho as coach, Chelsea won League titles in 2004–5 and 2005–6, their first since the 1954–5 season.

BECKHAM, David Born in May 1975, Beckham grew up in north-east London and signed for Manchester United at fourteen. His career developed in parallel to professional football's rebirth after the Hillsborough disaster. At twenty-one Beckham had an advertising deal with Brylcreem (£1 million) and a four-year Adidas contract (£800,000 a year). His image could sell products to a global market in an unprecedented way. He became a pop star's husband, a clothing model, a gay icon, a party animal, a tattoo-and-jewellery trendsetter, a hairstyle pacesetter and, from 2003 to 2007, a Real Madrid *Galáctico*. The 2007 *Sunday Times* Rich List estimated he was worth £125 million. In the next year he earned £38.6 million, including £23.3 million from promotional contracts, shares of LA Galaxy's income and his £3.6 million salary.

CELEBRITY Football was no longer contained by football issues. It was also about glamour and consumption. The public was obsessed by what was going on *around* the game. People were hooked into football via celebrities who dated footballers, or through celebrity shows which recruited footballers as dancers, pundits, hosts or guests. Images of top-class professional footballers could be used to sell anything from hair gel to helicopters. Footballers appeared in popular magazines (*OK, Hello!*, etc.), on supermarket displays, on mainstream TV programmes, across billboards and on internet sites. Cristiano Ronaldo (Manchester United) registered 14.5 million Google hits in December 2008. But even fans could be football celebrities through internet sites such as YouTube.

DEBT Many clubs took on such great debts that they risked bankruptcy. Between 1996 and 2008 over half the clubs in the lower two divisions of the Football League went into administration. The Premier League introduced 'parachute payments' – £20 million over two years – to safeguard relegated clubs, but this irked second-tier clubs, who felt that ex-Premier League clubs were unfairly advantaged. When clubs went into administration a League rule stipulated that all *football* debts – to players, staff and other clubs – had to be settled in full for the club to stay in the League. This often meant that less than 10 per cent of tax and National Insurance debts could be paid. In 2008 one insider claimed that football clubs owed about £50 million in aggregate to Her Majesty's Revenue and Customs (HMRC). Points penalties were introduced for clubs going into administration or failing to agree a Company Voluntary Agreement (CVA).

EXECUTIVE BOXES Corporate season-ticket deals offered viewing facilities, meals, hostess service, half-time refreshments, match programmes, parking spaces, private bar, television facilities and the use of boxes on non-match days. Corporate fans were a good reason for moving stadiums if the original stadium had development restrictions. After 2006 Arsenal's 9,000 premium seats at the Emirates Stadium brought in the same revenue as the whole of Highbury Stadium, their previous home. In 2006 Manchester United's annual income was around £169 million – 36 per cent from match-day revenues, 37 per cent from media revenues and 27 per cent from commercial services (sponsorship deals, conferences and catering, financial services and museum and stadium tours).

FA CUP The FA resisted FA Cup sponsorship until 1994, when the competition was backed by Littlewoods. Top clubs began to field weakened teams in early rounds, but the trophy was usually won by an elite club. Fans were stunned, though, when FA Cup holders Manchester United withdrew from the 1999–2000 competition in order to compete in the FIFA Club World Championship in Brazil, thus supporting England's bid to host the

2006 World Cup Finals. But the romance of the FA Cup was kept alive, and the distribution of gate receipts was far more egalitarian than for League matches. Burton Albion and Manchester United each took 45 per cent of the net receipts from two matches in 2006. This third-round tie also brought Burton Albion televised fees (£300,000), increased merchandising sales and sponsorship. The FA Cup helped the club's turnover rise from £587,000 in one year to £2.25 million the next.

GAMBLING After the launch of the National Lottery football-pools companies suffered a rapid decline – from ten million customers in 1994 to 700,000 in 2007 – but bookmakers benefited from increased betting on football matches. Punters could bet on results, half-time score, first and last goalscorers, time of first goal, number of throw-ins, number of free-kicks, the added time on the fourth official's board and a multitude of other matters. Global gambling opened the possibility of corruption. In August 1999 a plot was uncovered to halt English professional matches, via floodlight failure, in order to aid betting syndicates in Malaysia. In 2008 Vietnamese government officials were sacked for gambling millions of pounds of public funds on Premier League matches, and the FA opened investigations that a top player had agreed to get sent off in a match in order to square a £50,000 debt with a bookmaker.

HYPE According to some analysts, media companies' football investments helped to skew coverage of the sport towards advertising and promotion rather than critical analysis and journalism. The media was rife with exaggerated excitement, constant chatter and hyperbole ('That's a massive result and they have some big, big, big matches coming up'). With the rise of the internet, designated sports TV channels and radio stations, plus 24-hour sports news, there was plenty of airtime to fill. Phone-ins proliferated, often encouraging fans to phone and moan ('Let us know your view'). Football-club managers complained about media people exaggerating the prospects of sackings, dwelling on controversial incidents and forcing up transfer fees.

ITV DIGITAL In 2001 lower-league English clubs signed up with the fledgling ITV Digital for a television deal worth £315 million over three years. But there was chaos from the start. Subscription forecasts were overoptimistic, advertising slowed down and ITV Digital went into administration in March

2002. The Football League brought a futile court case. By August 2002 there were over 300 out-of-work professional footballers.

JOURNEYMAN PROFESSIONAL PLAYERS In *The Work of Professional Football* Martin Roderick offered a realistic view of the professional game that contrasted sharply with the media's glamorous picture. Roderick showed that lower-league journeymen players began with an idealised view of the sport and soon learned that it was a brutal world of tough physical work and conformity. These journeymen players were always on the brink of ending their professional careers. If an injury didn't get them, then the competition did. In 2006 there was a big gulf between the average wages of Premier League players (£676,000 a year) and League Two professionals (£49,600), with those in the second and third tiers averaging £195,750 and £67,850 respectively.

KICK-OFF TIMES In the 2002–03 season only five of Manchester United's twenty-two Premier League and FA Cup matches kicked off at the traditional time of 3pm on a Saturday. Kick-offs were staggered at the request of either the police or television companies. On Saturday 6 October 2007, following Thursday-night UEFA Cup matches, only one Premier League match kicked off at 3pm. Fans had to continually check kick-off times and it could be difficult to plan a month ahead if television schedules hadn't been released or were changed. Some spectators lost the rhythm of Saturday spectating. Fixtures were no longer fixtures.

LITIGATION In *Condon v Bari* (1985) the judge awarded the plaintiff £4,900 damages after a foul tackle by Gurdever Bari (Khalsa FC) broke the right leg of James Condon (Whittle Wanderers) in a match in 1980. In the professional game Gordon Watson (Bradford City) was awarded over £900,000 in damages after Kevin Gray's challenge in February 1997 caused a double fracture of 25-year-old Watson's leg. The award covered medical care costs and loss of earnings. Sports law became a growth area. Cases were brought for racial discrimination, unfair dismissal, compensation for injuries while on international duty and many other issues.

MURDOCH, Rupert Football was changed irrevocably when Murdoch's Sky Sports company attained the television rights to live Premier League matches – for £191 million for five seasons (1992–7), £670 million for four seasons (1997–2001), £1.1 billion for three seasons (2001–4), £1.024 billion (2004–7) and £1.3 billion (2007–10). Ninety per cent of the last sum went to Premier League clubs, whereas ninety-two clubs had shared television money equally only fifteen years previously. (The total figure for 2007 Premier League rights was estimated at £2.7 billion when rights for overseas broadcasters, internet, mobile phones, etc., were included.) Meanwhile the highlights rights were bought by the BBC for £22.5 million in 1992 and £73 million in 1997, ITV for £183 million in 2001 and the BBC for £105 million in 2004 and £171.6 million in 2007. Rupert Murdoch's bid for Manchester United was blocked by the Monopolies and Mergers Commission in 1999.

NEW LABOUR The Labour government of 1997 saw football as a gateway for garnering public support. Prime Minister Tony Blair posed with England managers Glenn Hoddle and Kevin Keegan. It became cool for politicians to support a club, whether it be Raith Rovers (Gordon Brown), Burnley (Alistair Campbell) or Chelsea (Tony Banks). New Labour politicians saw football as a free market, and they supported foreign investors. But paradoxically they also sought greater self-regulation for football. The government sponsored the Independent Football Commission, a football watchdog that was largely ignored, and in 1998 launched the Football Task Force, which investigated the sport's commercial and community functions, racism in football and ticket prices. The government (via Sport England), the FA and the Premier League each contributed one third of an annual £45 million, in order to develop the Football Foundation for grassroots football projects.

OWNERSHIP OF CLUBS In the 1990s a number of established businessmen invested self-made millions in clubs they had followed since boyhood, e.g. Steve Gibson (Middlesbrough), Jack Hayward (Wolverhampton Wanderers), Lionel Pickering (Derby County), Jack Walker (Blackburn Rovers) and Dave Whelan (Wigan Athletic). Then came British or foreign owners who had no prior association with their clubs. By 2008 the twenty-club Premier League had four American owners, two Russians, one Irish consortium, an Icelander, an Egyptian and a deposed Prime Minister of Thailand. Monitoring football-club owners was difficult and costly, but the 'fit and proper person's test' excluded those who had already experienced two football-club insolvencies. Clubs could now be money-making ventures – Bradford City directors were paid £7.2 million in dividends in the late 1990s and the club was insolvent soon afterwards – or asset-stripping opportunities. An alternative model was that of supporters' trusts. By 2005 thirteen clubs were in supporters' trust ownership or control. The trend towards public ownership and Stock Exchange listings was eventually reversed, especially after an American businessman, Malcolm Glazer, paid £790 million for a hostile takeover of Manchester United, largely through borrowed money, in May 2005.

PLAYERS' AGENTS In 1967 Harry Brown, editor of the *Football League Review*, bemoaned a new trend for leading professional players to use agents. Forty years later about £150 million a year of English football money went to agents. Most of this was through legal means, but there were accusations of 'bungs' – secret financial incentives to ensure a transfer. In 1995 Arsenal manager George Graham was banned for a year and sacked by his club for receiving an estimated £425,000 from a Norwegian agent. In 2006 Luton Town manager Mike Newell claimed publicly that agents had offered him money. The Stevens Committee, set up to study the integrity of transfers, found that thirty-nine of the 362 Premier League transfers (in the two years from January 2004) needed further examination. Accusations about unscrupulous agents led to counter-accusations of unscrupulous managers, chairmen and chief executives.

QUALIFICATION FOR MAJOR TOURNAMENTS A study commissioned by Mastercard estimated that the Euro 2008 football tournament would boost the European economy by €1.4 billion, and Adidas predicted that its global sales would rise by 12 per cent because of its role as a sponsor. But the marketing power of football was shown most clearly when the England team *failed* to qualify for Euro 2008. The retail sector was hit by substantially reduced sales of replica shirts, T-shirts, St George flags, new television sets, memorabilia, barbecue equipment and alcohol. UK beer sales dropped by an estimated £100 million in the summer of 2008. The England team's absence cost the FA a £4-million qualification sum, the chance of £16 million for winning the tournament and hope of major sponsorship deals. England's absence also brought down global television audiences from Euro 2004's average of ninety million per match.

REFEREES The Professional Game Match Officials Ltd (PGMOL) was formed in 2001 in order to provide officials for professional matches in England, and a cadre of full-time referees was introduced. This brought improved fitness levels, more time to study tactics and decision-making, better pay for top referees, easier arrangements for disciplinary hearings and a career goal for all referees. The disadvantages were the costs of full-time salaries, an enforced early retirement age of forty-seven or forty-eight and concerns that full-timers might be too willing to keep in favour so as not to lose their jobs.

SHIRT SPONSORSHIP 'Footballers are nothing but glorified sandwich board men,' moaned one traditionalist when shirt sponsorship began in the early 1980s. 'Would Margot Fonteyn [the ballerina] have worn a leotard marked Guinness?' asked another. By 2005 shirt sponsorship was commonplace. In the Premier League deals were worth between £5 million and £12 million a year to top clubs and under £1 million to clubs lower down. In 2006 American International Group (AIG) paid a record £56.5 million for a four-year shirt deal with Manchester United, a deal that survived when the company was bailed out by the US government during the 2008 financial meltdown. But West Ham United suffered losses in 2008 when their sponsor, XL Holidays, collapsed halfway through a £7.5-million three-year contract. Thomas Cook, shirt sponsor of Manchester City from 2003, found that Manchester City fans were four and a half times more likely to use Cook than fans of other clubs.

TRANSFER SYSTEM When Jean-Marc Bosman's contract at RC Liège ended in 1990 the Belgian player wished to transfer to US Dunkerque. Liège demanded a transfer fee and Dunkerque refused to pay one. Five years later the Court of Justice of the European Communities (CJEC) ruled that transfer fees were incompatible with the EC Treaty if a player was out of contract. After the Bosman Case transfers were sealed by higher wages rather than higher transfer fees. Transfer windows were introduced to British football in 2002, restricting all transfers to two separate periods: (i) between mid-May and the end of August; and (ii) during January. This was designed to restrict the movement of footballers who were under contract and prevent too much rumour-mongering. A further change came with the 2008 Webster Case. Andy Webster, the Scotland defender, walked out on Heart of Midlothian for Wigan Athletic with a year of his contract to run. The Court of Arbitration for Sport (CAS) ordered him to pay only £150,000 compensation to Hearts, proving that players could terminate contracts under certain conditions.

* * *

UEFA CHAMPIONS LEAGUE The European Cup, a two-legged knock-out competition, was replaced by the UEFA Champions League in 1992 (after a year's pilot). England generally had four entrants rather than one. The new group structure guaranteed more income for European club giants and opened up major financial divisions within the domestic league. The conflict between domestic leagues and European competitions continued, with some clubs criticising the timing and location of national fixtures during weeks of European club competition.

VICE Top-level football became a dystopian soap opera. Footballers received publicity through marital break-ups, bad driving, brawling, gambling, drinking, womanising, drug-taking and their associations with lap-dancers, betting rings and criminals. Lee Hughes (West Brom) served three years of a six-year sentence after his Mercedes caused the death of a married couple who had four children. High-profile England international players, such as Paul Merson and Tony Adams, publicly acknowledged addiction problems, and Chelsea's Adrian Mutu was suspended for seven months after testing positive for cocaine in November 2004. There were tales of players 'roasting' (i.e. sexually sharing) eager young women, and sometimes rape accusations followed. But the footballers themselves could be preyed upon. Their wealth and fame made them targets for burglary, false rape accusations, 'kiss and tell' newspaper stories and blackmail.

WAGES In his book *My Defence* England's Ashley Cole admitted that footballers were always on a 'sticky wicket' discussing cash when there were 'nurses, policemen and firemen doing more important jobs'. However, Cole also described how he was 'trembling with anger' when he learned that Arsenal could offer him only £55,000 a week rather than the £60,000 he had wanted. Cole tried to justify his worth by comparing his wages with those of team-mates rather than those of essential workers. While many Premier League clubs were paying huge wages to stars, they were also paying the minimum hourly wage to programme sellers, cleaners and catering staff.

XENOPHOBIA During the 1970s and 1980s England supporters routinely booed the national anthems of other countries and attacked and abused fans from around Europe. Many black players in England were targeted by banana-throwers, monkey chanters and other racists. This endemic problem was addressed by a 'Let's Kick Out Racism' (later 'Kick It Out') campaign that led to definite improvements. When black England international players suffered abuse abroad – Emile Heskey in Yugoslavia (November 2000) and Shaun Wright-Phillips and Ashley Cole in Spain (November 2004), for instance – the English authorities were able to take the moral high ground. However, there were still unsavoury incidents in England, such as the 'I'd rather be a Paki than a Turk' chorus at an England–Turkey match at Sunderland (April 2003). Overall, though, English fans became remarkably accepting of foreign players, unless they perceived them as 'divers' or 'whingers'.

YOUNG PLAYERS AND ACADEMIES Until youth academies were introduced in the 1990s, allowing clubs access to youngsters aged nine and above, English professional clubs could work only with teenagers and then only for a maximum of four hours per week. Traditionally the education authorities tried to protect the child's schooling and morals from the ravages of football. After all, only 25–35 per cent of England schoolboy internationals stayed in professional football past eighteen. The Premier League required its member clubs to follow a set of guidelines for academies, but top clubs started to attract more youngsters from abroad. UEFA president Michel Platini accused some managers of trafficking players as young as thirteen.

ZOLA, ZENDON, ZAKI, etc. In the Premier League's first season, 1992–3, only eleven non-British players featured in starting line-ups. But far more foreign players were soon enchanting the public. One prime example was Gianfranco Zola, an Italian who became Chelsea's most popular player ever after being signed by Dutchman Ruud Gullit in November 1996. By 2008 more than 75 per cent of players in the top four teams were non-English, and pundits argued that this shortage of English players was affecting the national team. The assimilation of foreigners was best demonstrated by the remarkable case of Watford first-teamer Alhassan Bangura, a talented teenaged asylum-seeker from Sierra Leone. The Watford community successfully campaigned to keep Bangura in Britain.

45

FOOTBALL AND ENGLISHNESS

Marcos Alvito is living in Oxford for a year. He is fascinated by his topic of study – English football culture – and finds it relatively easy to collect information. He can walk up to partisan club fans in England and chat to them without too much fear of reprisal. His passport allows him respect around the football world. He is Brazilian.

The Brazilians are very interested in English football. They can see Premier League matches on cable TV, and some Brazilian players are based at English clubs. On Brazilian television they even show a selection of the goals scored by Brazilians in Europe that week. But older, middle-class Brazilians such as Alvito are also lured to English football because of its strong traditions. From a distance there is a unique charm and mystique about the English game and its stadiums. Alvito has followed up his long-standing interest in the sport by becoming a football anthropologist and historian.

Alvito is forty-seven. In his childhood, when he played table football in Brazil, his team was England with Kevin Keegan as number seven. He knew that England had won the World Cup in 1966, and he watched the amazing 1970 England–Brazil World Cup group match on television. He had heard of Stanley Matthews and Bobby Moore, and he liked Leeds United when they were at their peak. Sometimes, when Alvito and his friends played table football, someone would say, 'Let's make the English championship' and each player would choose a team. He has heard many Brazilians argue that the English might have invented the game but the Brazilians have taken it to a new height; the English don't have such great technique – they are too stiff – but their game has such amazing roots. He thinks that English people sometimes take those roots too much for granted.

In England Alvito has seen hard-up working-class men, veteran season-ticket holders, drive for three hours to a place such as Doncaster or Yeovil. Well, you wouldn't see that kind of attachment and club loyalty in Brazil, where fans concentrate on the top teams and rarely commit themselves to season tickets. Brazilians watch football when they want to. They go to see a winning team; they don't religiously follow small clubs. In Brazil thirty-five million of the nation's 190 million support one club, Flamenco, and 80 per cent of the fans support only thirteen clubs.

Alvito also sees that English football is so much better organised than the Brazilian game. There is a stronger code of discipline in England, the referees are trusted more and England has thousands more small clubs. English football has a better infrastructure. One day Alvito visited Leamington Spa and talked to two men who worked voluntarily for a small, non-League club. The men were very proud of what they were building. Alvito shook his head; that just doesn't happen in Brazil. Very few Brazilian local teams are based around neighbourhoods, villages, pubs or workplaces. Where there are such teams, supporting them is more like charity work and owning those clubs is more like business opportunism. He often thinks about one particular football field in his home province. Some 40,000 people used that one pitch, but the local council didn't improve the facilities. Instead they sold the land for more houses.

Alvito saw that the two countries had very different political structures. Civil society in Brazil was still weak, whereas it had existed in England since the Magna Carta. Brazil was part of Portugal's empire for a long time, and then came a brief period as an undemocratic republic (1889–1930). In Brazil there is more poverty, misery and autocracy. In England there is more participation and better planning. Alvito reckoned that the English formed clubs for everything. If people like chess, they make a chess club. If people like books, they make a book club.

The Brazilians look for excitement in football, or so Alvito thought. That was why they generally supported the big clubs, the potential champions. The English must be looking for something else. Otherwise why would so many people have supported Birmingham City for over 130 years without their club ever getting near to a League Championship? Alvito thought the English tradition had more to do with identity, ethics and morals. English fans weren't really having fun and most expected their team to muddle along, but the fans seemed happy within themselves because they were being loyal. Ethically they were born with that club and they are going to die with that club. And that was the right thing to do.

Alvito thought that the spirit of fair play still existed in England. Take an incident at Celtic Park in 2007. AC Milan's Brazilian goalkeeper Dida faked an injury to try to get the match abandoned when a spectator ran on to the field and brushed against him. In Brazil this sort of deception was an acceptable strategy because Brazilians rarely trusted officials or politicians. But the English were furious at Dida's obvious play-acting. Yes, fair play is still deeply rooted in English football.

England international players usually accept that their continental counterparts show more skill, but they argue that this isn't necessarily because of innate ability. It could be because continentals have more *time* to show their skills in their national leagues. English players feel they are just as good as foreign players. The traditional English game just happens to be more robust and more physical than that played by other nationalities. It displays typical working-class traits of hard work, courage, masculinity and a strong team ethic. English managers have usually looked for bravery, loyalty and commitment from their players. Back in the 1940s and 1950s foreigners found the physical British game intimidating, especially its sliding tackles and heavy shoulder-charging. In return English players blamed foreigners for spitting, cynically blocking players off the ball, shirt-pulling, diving and feigning injury.

Yet somehow, since the original statement of the laws of the game, in England in 1863, football has been successfully adopted by very different cultures. 'The English are unaware that among their supreme achievements in the transmission of culture, something not forced upon foreigners but sought out by them, is association football,' said Sir Ernest Butler, author of *Britain and the British People*.

The coach John Cartwright is both an insider and an outsider to the English game. An Englishman himself, he has worked with elite English players in his role as a youth coach, but he is not an Establishment figure. Cartwright concluded that young elite English players lagged behind the progress of youngsters in other countries. When he coached at Lilleshall, the National Sports Centre, between 1989 and 1991, he was shocked at the poor technical skills of some fourteen-year-olds who were supposedly the country's most talented players. Cartwright had long felt that skills were best developed between the ages of seven and fourteen, and yet at Lilleshall he was coaching elite youngsters who lacked basic skills. There were too many one-footed players with no variety in their kicking. The boys were very experienced eleven-a-side players but they lacked an understanding of the game as a whole. They were one-dimensional in terms of their concepts of play. It was basically about knocking the ball forward and scrapping for it in midfield. It was as though these young players saw football as a kind of combat sport.

'We are a fierce sort of nation, but at the same time we have shown the world that we can have a lot of grace and art and culture,' Cartwright once said. 'Unfortunately we tend to disregard this when it comes to football. We tend to take the art and grace away from the game and to rely on the physical aspects of the game. I think that's important to have, but it's not more important than having the skill and grace to play the game.'

The problem, as Cartwright saw it, was that young English footballers were too focused on *winning* organised matches. The trial-and-error methods of street football had given way to competitive matches where managers and parents emphasised negative parts of the game – the offside trap, squeezing up, physical commitment and so on – at the expense of imaginative and experimental play. Parents and managers had also come through a system where winning was all-important. Crucially junior football's need to win caused physically developed children to be selected instead of smaller players who had more technical competence.

The development of young English footballers went down a narrow corridor. In other countries, especially Brazil, youngsters were encouraged to 'go out and try it'. In England people said, 'Don't do this' and 'Don't do that.' One outcome, according to Cartwright, was a succession of England international defenders who were courageous and patriotic, strong headers of the ball and fierce tacklers, but not as comfortable as continentals in passing the ball around. These ill-equipped players have the ball for long periods in international football, so English football gained a reputation for ugliness and awkwardness. The dominant coaching ethic (direct play at a high tempo) and the pressure to satisfy an impatient crowd meant that English players sacrificed ball possession too easily at the highest levels. The more physical effort you put into a game, the more tired you get, the more concentration levels drop, the more injuries you get. That began to detract from England team performances.

'We tend in England to be having to play at 100 miles an hour and at 100 per cent all the time,' said Cartwright. 'This is one of the problems about our senior players being tired. One of our games would probably represent three games abroad. They don't expend so much energy in a particular game in such a fierce way. Their game is more of a controlled, thoughtful approach, whereas ours is a fierce, fighting approach.'

Cartwright thought that England players were not foxy enough. They were like poker players who showed their hands. And you couldn't expect England players to change their style for an international match. The work had to be done through the system, concentrating on children between the ages of seven and fourteen. An England training camp was too late. The last thing learned was the first thing forgotten.

'Football is athleticism with a ball,' said Cartwright, 'so we need to produce good athletes who have high technical quality, and if we can produce that on a regular basis, we'll be going along the right lines. Whether or not you are a defender, you should look like an athlete and not like something that gets wedged in a barn door.'

By the early 1990s overseas players were matching England players for guts, fight and physical presence, especially in those countries where there had been recent wars. But England continued to lag behind in technical ability. 'Outfought, out-played, out-thought,' was how one television pundit described England's crucial 2007 European Championship home defeat to Croatia.

Let us canvass another knowledgeable outsider's view of the English. Professor Raymond Boyle is a Scotsman based in the Centre for Cultural Research at the University of Glasgow. The co-author (with Richard Haynes) of *Football in the New Media Age*, Boyle is an astute observer of football both sides of the border. He explains that in some ways the new English Premier League sits separately from traditional England–Scotland rivalry. He asks, 'How English is the English game today?' and notes that the English Premier League is full of foreign players and dominated by foreign managers. As the top English league became a United Nations league, it became more popular with the Scots.

A much more traditional source of conflict is the bias of the British media towards the England national team and Englishness. The BBC is the *British* Broadcasting Corporation but you wouldn't know that if you were watching *Match of the Day* in Glasgow on a Saturday night. The anchorman and his cohort rarely talk to viewers north of Newcastle, and this can anger the Scots, especially when it is accompanied by Premier League hype and English jingoism. Too often BBC reporters will ignore Rangers and Celtic matches on European nights. Too often, according to the Scots, BBC commentators are England supporters with microphones.

The rivalry between England and Scotland has always been intense, whether it be centuries of territorial battles, Margaret Thatcher's choice of Scotland for the poll-tax experiment (in 1989), the exodus of Scottish footballers to England or the world's oldest series of football international matches. In 1977, after Scotland had won 2-0 in England, Scottish fans wrecked the Wembley pitch, destroyed goal-frames and caused £150,000 worth of damage. Scottish journalists have traditionally referred to England as 'the Auld Enemy'.

Until the late 1950s, when national football associations began to be seduced by the glory of the world game, the England team's major competitive focus was Northern Ireland, Scotland and Wales in the British Home Championship. That tournament continued until 1984. After the 1980s England–Scotland clashes were limited to the luck of the draw. They met in a group match at the Euro 96 finals and again, in a two-match play-off, for a place in the Euro 2000 finals.

Ray Boyle sees an attitude difference between supporters of Scotland's Old Firm clubs (Rangers and Celtic) and fans of other Scottish clubs. The Old Firm fans think their clubs are as big as any English club, but they know they cannot compete because the television money is different. (The 1998 Scottish Premier League television contract was worth £45 million over four seasons whereas the 1997 English Premier League deal was worth £670 million over four seasons.) Rangers and Celtic notwithstanding, supporters in Scotland recognise that they live in a smaller country with a smaller league. While they might like more money to bolster the clubs and achieve past European glories, they have no delusions of grandeur.

Television ensured that the English elite game was watched in around 200 countries, including Scotland. *Match of the Day* highlights of English Premier League matches reached Scottish homes at the same time as they reached English homes. European Champions League matches, English FA Cup matches and England international matches were all shown on terrestrial channels in Scotland (whereas Scotland's home fixtures were only available on satellite channels). Young Scottish children could see more of Manchester United's stars than the Old Firm's.

About 8 per cent of the five million people in Scotland are English-born and some of them will support Premier League clubs. The Scots themselves might be attracted by interesting-looking English matches, or an English Premier League decider, but very few would habitually seek out a sports bar to watch two Premier League also-rans on a satellite channel. England has followed Scotland's lead by skewing its Premier League titles towards very few clubs. Manchester United, Arsenal and Chelsea became the Rangers and Celtic of the English game.

According to Boyle, the Scottish reaction to the English Premier League has been mixed. On the upside there is the thrill of seeing stars from around the world. On the downside there is a tremendous churn of playing staffs. The constant recruitment brings instability and discontinuity. Only the top managers became reliably familiar. Men like Alex Ferguson (Manchester United), Arsène Wenger (Arsenal), David Moyes (Everton) and Rafael Benítez (Liverpool) became integral to the brand identity of their clubs.

The Scots view the English professional culture with a mixture of admiration and disdain. They admire the quality at the top but are contemptuous of the crazy logic that accompanies some profit-making schemes. Have you heard the one about a thirty-ninth Premier League fixture to be played somewhere else in the world? Ha, ha, ha! On such occasions the Scots scratch their heads and say, 'They must be all mad down there.'

The Scots admire lasting iconic figures, such as Henry at Arsenal and Gerrard at Liverpool, but they are disdainful about the way top clubs gobble up the talent and count the revenue from what Boyle calls 'blow-in' spectators. Scots also dislike the way players show their wealth ostentatiously. They are particularly scornful of the 'bling' culture of stars in England, because the Scots reckon that their kin are better at keeping their feet on the ground than the English. Money has distorted the game at the iconic level. Even Old Firm fans wouldn't want their clubs to become a corporate entity, because Rangers and Celtic are so rooted in cultural and religious heritage. The Scots reckon that they have a stronger sense of tradition, continuity and history than the English, and they think well of English clubs that have kept that ethic. Scots could still identify with Manchester United, for example, for retaining British players in their team – and a brilliant, successful Scottish manager – during the first fifteen years of the Premier League. But otherwise the Scots feel that the English *lost* their top league during that period.

England's military history has provided plenty of enemies – Scotland, Germany, France, Spain and Argentina, among others – and the English have sustained aspects of this global enmity through football. Taking on foreign nations, with blood coursing through your body and fight in your belly, can apply to English spectators and players alike. Yet, in one of the many paradoxes of Englishness, it is a stiff upper lip and a cool head that make English referees popular around the world for their poise and neutrality.

And stoicism in the face of injury is a traditional English trait, from Derek Dooley's amputated leg to Terry Butcher's bloodied bandaged head when playing for England in Sweden over three decades later. Englishness can be either expressed passion or repressed passion.

The strong class delineators (amateurs and professionals) of the early 1950s have slowly turned into the quicksand of the commercial marketplace. Indeed the spirit of entrepreneurship, capitalism and expansion is also part of the English character, from Walter Raleigh to the FA Premier League, via Jimmy Hill. The English are good at taking initiatives, even though their innovations are not always fully thought through (e.g. the first English all-seater stadium or the Football Membership Bill). The English tradition is full of strong, avuncular, older rulers who think they know best but sometimes lack an understanding of grassroots youth culture, diversity in English communities and working-class behaviour patterns. Ethnic minorities are under-represented in football's positions of authority (as administrators, club managers and referees), even though black players have established themselves in the Premier League. Top decision-makers and local leaders trust their English heritage, their own experience and the belief that they are in a position of power because they know best. They distrust the advice of outsiders, even when they commission the wisdom of a Sir Norman Chester. A lack of identification with the lumpen rank and file sours the local game, and a lack of concern for spectators proved disastrous at Bolton (1946), Bradford (1985) and Sheffield (1989).

Englishness is full of contrasts and paradoxes. The English are undoubtedly brave, but they are also fearful. They particularly fear strangers – immigrants, foreign teams, foreign countries, foreign ways and so on – and they can be racist under the slightest pressure. But football also provides a route for foreigners to be accepted. England's first professional footballer was a Scot, and English clubs have always recruited heavily from Wales, Ireland and Scotland. In the 1950s Albert Uytenbogardt, Bert Trautmann, Alec Eisentrager, Felix Starocsik and John Ostergaard played in the Football League, and Dietmar Bruck was a Coventry City stalwart during the 1960s. Foreign players were assimilated if they fit the culture of the club, whether it be the Bulgarian Berbatov at Tottenham (a throwback to Scotsman Alan Gilzean) or the traditional workaday skills of a Hamman or a Hyypia at Liverpool. Local African-Caribbean football clubs such as Highfield Rangers made a place for themselves in the 1970s and 1980s as England slowly became a more open society, and the establishment of the European

Community increased geographical mobility. During major national football championships English sporting patriotism now includes women and the middle classes.

On the one hand Englishness is about mates and neighbourhoods and community. On the other hand it's about taking over the world, winning the 1966 World Cup, sending Premier League television pictures around the globe, kids wearing David Beckham shirts in an otherwise closed country such as Bhutan, and Manchester United claiming over 300 million fans worldwide. England has built a football empire to rival its Victorian empire. But English football is also a morality tale. It is about showing your support, sticking by your club and your friends, and even boycotting Wimbledon FC (aka MK Dons) or Manchester United (for FC United) if the club isn't loyal in return. Local support is wonderful for the building of strong communities, but it can easily become a way of excluding people who don't fit the English model, and it can lead to intense rivalries and inward vision. The English are essentially non-cosmopolitan in their identity. They distance themselves from global football parties. When the Mexican wave first began to travel around stadiums in the mid-1980s English fans didn't join in. They stayed seated and aggressively aloof. The English don't identify easily with fans from other countries. The English are separate and singular.

England has a long history of spreading the game around the world, albeit with no conscious intent. This means that many other countries still value a victory over England more than any other. But there has also been a reversal here. In the 1980s the football world started coming to England. Foreign players became entrenched at top clubs. Bolton Wanderers, a club fielding nine Lancastrians in the 1953 FA Cup Final, had players from fifteen different football nations fifty years later (including Muslims, Jews and Rastafarians). Whereas two-thirds of Barnsley's players were locally recruited during the 1950s, the club's 2007–8 squad included men from Brazil, Spain, Portugal, Jamaica, Trinidad, Nigeria, Hungary, the Netherlands and Germany. English club academies began to recruit *foreign* youth players to the exclusion of local youngsters, giving rise to a debate that English players were not given the space to develop. And even grassroots clubs had a more worldly feel with names such as FC Poland (Southampton), All Nations FC (Asylum Welcome), Barnsley International FC and Sonali Othit FC (London). In Leicester, Highfield Rangers, traditionally an African-Caribbean club, worked to settle new arrivals from Africa and Eastern Europe.

But nothing is more demonstrative of the world coming to England than a study of the recent ownership of England's top professional clubs. Local businessmen have given way to regional businessmen, to national businessmen, to international entrepreneurs, to global moguls from Russia, Thailand, the USA and elsewhere. And the owners have hired managers and coaches from outside England. The FA even appointed a Swede, Sven-Göran Eriksson, and later an Italian, Fabio Capello, to coach the England team.

Football is England's national winter sport, but it is not always the regional sport. The South-West has its rugby union and the M62 corridor has its rugby league. In the South-West rugby union is played by middle-class *and* working-class males. When Cornwall reached the Rugby Football Union county final in 1989 and 1991 some 25,000 fans went to Twickenham bearing Cornish flags as a symbol of Celtic nationhood. The press dubbed them 'Trelawny's Army'. 'The lusting spirit of national independence is alive and flourishing in the undeclared republic of Cornwall,' wrote the *Guardian*'s reporter. Cornwall doesn't easily engage with either football or the English.

There are lots of negatives about England's national stereotype, but it also has something residually admirable and dignified. The English reject the fripperies of foreigners and continental football. They get stuck in with a no-nonsense, direct, up-and-at-'em approach, rejecting the niceties and unseen authority. The English will do what they want. What's the point of showing off like the foreigners do? Englishness is about belonging, camaraderie, sticking up for your mates, being a bit crazy and enjoying telling crazy stories about crazy behaviour. There is something satisfyingly rebellious and potentially victorious about being seen as 'mad' in a competitive world. Other nationalities are a bit wary of how brave and mad they might have to be to compete with the English.

Above all else, the English are participants. The grassroots story of English football may be the real story of Englishness. It's about playing with your friends or forming a club. There is something very resourceful about a bunch of people setting up a team out of nothing, as English women players did in the 1960s, and playing at a level of informality that few other comparable countries would accept. You don't worry about the surrounding paraphernalia, you just get on with it. English football is about participation rather than membership, subscriptions or matching kit. It is about the bus driver playing in his driving boots, or a team playing with their shirts inside out to avoid a colour clash. Ideally it is about being ill-prepared and yet beating better-resourced opponents. A glance at the 2008 list of Cheltenham's Bentham five-a-side teams shows a plethora of ironic and self-deprecating names that are chosen to demonstrate drinking, junk food and incompetence – Midtable Obscurity, Beercelona, Zimmerframe Zidane's, Can't Score Won't Score, Chronically Fatigued, Real Ale Madrid and Athletico Fried Chicken. The fantasy, rooted in community and class traditions, is to have a handicap and then win your league through courage, togetherness and bloody-mindedness. Historically this is one of the great motifs of Englishness.

A lot of what makes English football identifiably English goes back to the rhetoric of amateurism. You don't prepare too well for football matches because to do so is almost like cheating. According to this English ethic, sport should be left to the liminal and visceral components of life. This ethos is celebrated by the emotive language used by the tabloid press, a distinctly English institution that both reflects the culture and shapes it. A rush of blood must never be far away. But then, if a player does get sent off (or if a referee is labelled a cheat), it sets up the quintessential English battle – an outnumbered, indignant underdog team against the rest of the world. This English approach intrigues middle-class Brazilians, frustrates modernising English coaches and draws grudging respect from Scottish neighbours. Eventually, of course, it means that the English may be out-thought or beaten by science. But all that scientific stuff is a bit against the raw spirit of the game as it was first played in England, isn't it?

Such is Englishness.

Such is English football.

APPENDIX

Introduction

Here we supplement the human interest short stories from football's post-war period with some selected statistical data. We include these to add some wider context to our account. After all, association football draws its meaning partly from a popular scrutiny of playing records, league tables, crowd sizes, financial data and disciplinary trends. However, longitudinal data-sets can vary in their statistical definitions, the periods they cover, the collection methods used and their presentation. In short, figures can often obscure as much as they reveal. In the words of an old adage, most people use statistics like a drunken man uses a lamppost – for support rather than illumination.

Table 1: *Aggregate League attendances 1946–7 to 2006–7*

1946–7	35,604,606	1964–5	27,641,168
1947–8	40,259,130	1965–6	27,206,980
1948–9	41,271,414	1966–7	28,902,596
1949–50	40,517,865	1967–8	30,107,298
1950–1	39,584,967	1968–9	29,382,172
1951–2	39,015,866	1969–70	29,600,972
1952–3	37,149,966	1970–1	28,194,146
1953–4	36,174,590	1971–2	28,700,729
1954–5	34,133,103	1972–3	25,448,642
1955–6	33,150,809	1973–4	24,982,203
1956–7	32,744,405	1974–5	25,577,977
1957–8	33,562,208	1975–6	24,896,053
1958–9	33,610,985	1976–7	26,182,800
1959–60	32,538,611	1977–8	25,392,872
1960–1	26,619,754	1978–9	24,540,627
1961–2	27,979,902	1979–80	24,623,975
1962–3	28,885,852	1980–1	21,907,569
1963–4	28,535,022	1981–2	20,006,961

1982–3	18,766,158	1995–6	21,844,416
1983–4	18,358,631	1996–7	22,783,163
1984–5	17,849,835	1997–8	24,692,608
1985–6	16,488,577	1998–9	25,435,542
1986–7	17,379,218	1999–2000	25,341,090
1987–8	17,959,732	2000–1	26,030,167
1988–9	18,464,192	2001–2	27,756,977
1989–90	19,445,442	2002–3	28,343,386
1990–1	19,508,202	2003–4	29,197,510
1991–2	20,487,273	2004–5	29,245,870
1992–3	20,657,327	2005–6	29,089,084
1993–4	21,683,381	2006–7	29,541,949
1994–5	21,856,020		

(Source: *Sky Sports Football Yearbook, 2007–8*)

Post-war aggregate English League attendances peaked at 41.27 million in the 1948–9 season (for 1,848 matches). Despite the increase in the number of matches to 2,028 in 1950, the trend was then downwards, dramatically so in 1960–1 when almost 4 million were lost. But some of that fall was taken up by attendances elsewhere – at European matches (after 1956) and in the new League Cup competition, introduced in 1960–1 and established with a Wembley Final by 1967. England's 1966 World Cup win boosted League attendances for a few seasons, but hooliganism and changing leisure patterns provoked a continuing decline. A post-war low was reached in the 1985–6 season, following the disasters at the Heysel Stadium and Valley Parade, Bradford. The English professional game then began a slow revival, aided by stadia modernisation and the arrival in 1992 of the FA Premier League.

Table 2: *Size of County Football Associations 1948–67 (no. of registered clubs)*

	1948	1967
Bedfordshire	186	323
Berks. and Bucks.	430	739
Birmingham	1,174	2,375
Cambridgeshire	115	210
Cheshire	512	1,032
Cornwall	220	318
Cumberland	136	183
Derbyshire	376	533
Devon	367	465
Dorset	178	189
Durham	631	990
East Riding of Yorkshire	224	344

Essex	703	1,379
Gloucestershire	563	711
Hampshire	497	1,020
Herefordshire	82	131
Hertfordshire	257	624
Huntingdonshire	58	80
Kent	660	1,153
Lancashire	873	1,495
Leicestershire and Rutland	323	484
Lincolnshire	555	664
Liverpool	683	1,030
London	1,580	2,982
Manchester	582	1,118
Middlesex	577	755
Norfolk	370	650
Northamptonshire	169	453
North Riding of Yorkshire	250	446
Northumberland	303	459
Nottinghamshire	366	771
Oxfordshire	188	265
Sheffield and Hallamshire	650	1,031
Shropshire	130	198
Somerset	280	441
Staffordshire	375	849
Suffolk	268	381
Surrey	560	985
Sussex	413	779
West Riding of Yorkshire	680	1,193
Wiltshire	190	341
Worcestershire	213	252
Westmorland	26	41

(Source: Norman Chester, *Report of the Committee of Football* HMSO, 1968)

As Britain recovered from the war, football was in the vanguard of men's communal weekend activity. The number of affiliated clubs around Birmingham doubled between 1948 and 1967, and many other regions showed rapid rises. The administration of local football associations relied on volunteers; an FA survey in 1967 found that 75 per cent of county FAs paid their secretaries honoraria of between £200 and £250 per annum, including expenses. The figures reported above refer to men's clubs of course; women's clubs were not recognised at all by the FA during this period.

Figure 1: *Real match admission prices 1946–95*

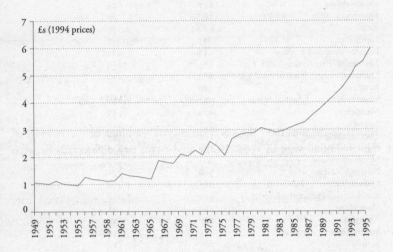

(Source: Stefan Szymanski and Tim Kuypers, *Winners & Losers*, Viking, 1999)

Stefan Szymanski and Tim Kuypers show that ticket prices remained
stable in real terms between 1949 and the mid-sixties. After England's
1966 World Cup win real prices climbed as the sport sought to capitalise
on new fans attracted by the television coverage. Prices began to climb
again in the mid-1980s as crowds fell and professional clubs fought
their financial crises. In the 1990s the real cost of match tickets rose
rather more rapidly, producing new forms of exclusion for previously
committed supporters, many of whom resorted to televised football at
home or in pubs.

Table 3: *Average earnings of first-team players, 1955–64 (£)*

	Div 1	Div 2	Div 3*	Div 4**
1955	800	769	720	671
1956	832	800	731	682
1957	872	842	784	740
1958	1,030	960	863	820

1959	1,150	1,093	918	875
1960	1,173	1,132	1,034	937
1961	1,540	1,205	1,130	965
1962	2,200	1,500	1,300	1,085
1963	2,640	1,970	1,450	1,290
1964	2,680	2,003	1,475	1,304
% increase	235	160	105	94

* Division Three (South) until 1958–9
** Division Three (North) until 1958–9

(Source: Norman Chester, *Report of the Committee of Football*, HMSO, 1968)

This table demonstrates the effect on players' earnings of the removal of the maximum wage in 1961. In the mid-1950s pay differentials between professional footballers at different levels of the League game were incredibly small. Slowly, starting in the 1960s, the elite players began to place themselves in a different business to their fellow union members. Later, after the arrival of satellite television contracts in the 1990s, this early pay gap grew astronomically.

Table 4: *League championship dominance: some European comparisons, 1940–99 (%)*

ENGLAND	FRANCE	GERMANY	ITALY	SPAIN
Liverpool 19.5	St. Etienne 11.7	B. Munich 27.3	Juventus 26.2	Real Madrid 30.6
Man United 17.9	Nantes 11.4	B. Monchen'bach 11.1	AC Milan 22.4	Barcelona 26.9
Arsenal 8.2	Marseille 11.1	Werder Bremen 9.7	Inter Milan 16.1	Atletico Madrid 14.2
Leeds U. 6.3	Monaco 10.2	Hamburg 8.8	Fiorentina 6.3	Athletic Bilbao 7.4
Tottenham 6.3	Bordeaux 9.6	Koln 8.3	Torino 6.3	Valencia 6.8
Wolves 6.0	Stade Reims 8.6	B. Dortmund 6.0	Napoli 6.0	Real Sociodad 3.4
Everton 5.3	Nice 5.6	Stuttgart 5.1	Roma 4.1	Deportivo 2.5
Nottm, Forest 3.5	Paris SG 5.2	Kaiserslauten 4.2	Lazio 3.2	Sevilla 2.5
Ipswich T. 3.1	Lille 4.6	B. Laverkusen 2.8	Bologna 1.6	Real Zaragoza 1.9
Burnley 2.5	Lens 3.4	Hertha Berlin 2.8	Cagliari 1.6	Espanol 0.9
Others 21.4	Others 18.6	Others 13.9	Others 6.2	Others 2.9

Points totals have been converted to percentages.

(Source: adapted from Stephen Dobson and John Goddard, *The Economics of Football*, Cambridge University Press, 2001)

Dobson and Goddard's interesting comparison of top European divisions shows that success in England has traditionally been less easy to predict than in other countries. The advent of the new FA Premier League in

1992 changed this position somewhat. The table is based on three points for a title win, two for second place and one for third place. Only France has shown no obviously dominant cluster of elite clubs – though recently Lyons have reigned supreme. Spanish football has survived in reasonable health despite the overwhelming superiority of Barcelona and Real Madrid.

Table 5: *Demographic data on convicted football hooligans (1968)*

Age		Previous Convictions		Occupation	
Under 15	6	Nil	182	School/apprentice	79
15–19	164	One	69	Unskilled/labourer	206
20–24	129	Two	53	Semi-skilled	112
24–29	92	Three	36	Skilled	50
30–34	53	Four	32	Salesman/clerical	19
35–39	23	Five	29	Professional/managerial	2
40–44	16	Six–ten	51	Not known/unemployed	29
44–49	5	Eleven–fifteen	13		
50 plus	9	Over fifteen	13	Total	497
		Not known	19		
Total	497	Total	497		

(Source: J Harrington, *Soccer Hooliganism: A Preliminary Report*, John Wright & Sons, 1968)

In 1968, Denis Howell, the Labour Minister for Sport, invited social psychologist John Harrington to analyse the growing problem of football hooliganism. Harrington produced some early statistical data on the subject. According to these figures, a large proportion of those involved were youngsters, but hooligans could also be middle-aged; by the 1980s some very committed hooligans were older men rather than rampaging teenagers. Harrington's data suggested that 1960s hooligans were typically lower working-class males with previous convictions. But twenty years later this was less clear cut as some key hooligan organisers had disposable income and were from stable lower-middle class backgrounds.

Table 6: *Causes of professional footballers' injuries during training and matches in the 1980s (%)*

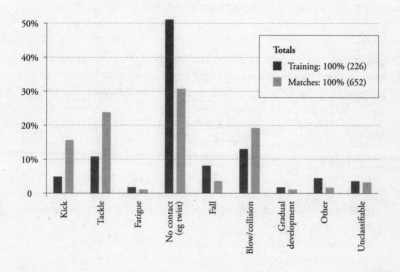

(Source: K. Macpherson, 'Injuries to Professional Football Players' Report for the Football Trust)

After first becoming involved with football research in 1966, the Oxford academic and Manchester United supporter Sir Norman Chester tried to improve the general quality of research data in the sport. This elegant study was the first national audit of football injuries and was produced with Chester's encouragement after a first conference on football injuries organised by the Football Trust in 1982. Soon after, the Football Trust began to publish the *Digest of Football Statistics*, the first series of data collated and presented about the non-playing side of the sport.

Table 7: *Number of sendings off in the four top English professional divisions, 1979–80 to 2000–01*

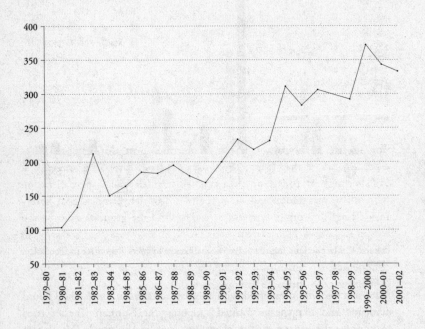

(Source: Tony Brown, *Red – Missed: Sendings Off in English Football*, Tony Brown publications, 2001)

The English game has always prided itself on toughness and discipline. Tony Brown's figures seem to suggest that football has become more violent, but many players from the 1960s would argue that the game was rougher in their day (before the closer scrutiny of television). Reactions to an increase in gamesmanship, from the late-1960s, led to a rise in the number of sendings off. Then the authorities cracked down on the professional foul (in 1982) and a new sending-off offence of 'denying an obvious goalscoring opportunity' was also introduced (in 1990). In a period of 74 years between 1892 and 1966 Manchester City had only seven players sent off in total.

Table 8: *Arrests at League football matches, all Divisions, 1986–7 to 1998–9*

1986–7	5,502
1987–8	6,147
1988–9	6,185
1989–90	5,945
1990–1	4,119
1991–2	5,006
1992–3	4,588
1993–4	4,227
1994–5	3,850
1995–6	3,441
1996–7	3,307
1998–9	3,341

(Source: National Criminal Intelligence Service)

The spectre of hooliganism hung over the sport during the 1980s, especially after the Heysel Stadium disaster. After the tragedy at Hillsborough in 1989, top-class English football took a new direction with all-seater stadia and new regimes for delivering crowd safety inside English grounds. Arrests in and around the grounds were halved within a decade. Figures remained lower in the years that followed as crowd disturbances moved further away from major grounds. Some commentators even talked about the 'post-hooligan era' but football's difficulties never fully disappeared.

Table 9: *The most and least enjoyable things about being a local referee in 1995 (%)*

Most Enjoyable		Least Enjoyable	
Involvement in the game	52.5	Abuse from players/fans	69.5
Putting something back	20.3	Isolation	8.1
All aspects	11.5	Weather	5.2
Keeping fit	10.5	Inhospitable clubs	3.5
Other	5.2	Travel	2.8
		Other	10.9

(Source: John Williams, *The 'Lords of Truth'? Local Refereeing in England and International Trends*, Sir Norman Chester Centre for Football Research, University of Leicester, 1995)

This 1995 survey of West Midlands Football Association referees incurred the wrath of the Football Association, an organisation that generally prefers referees not to speak out. The survey highlighted the lonely aspects of the job in the local leagues and the constant abuse involved. Local referees complained that not only was such abuse unpleasant but that much of it was also ill-informed, as players and spectators often had only a partial understanding of the laws of football. In 2008 the FA launched a 'Respect' campaign to re-affirm the authority of the referee at local and professional levels.

Table 10: *Supporters' views of the most serious problems facing the professional game in 2000 (%)*

Ticket prices	64
Changing kick-off times and dates	60
The power of big clubs	57
Too much 'big business'	56
Bad behaviour of some players	33
Lack of atmosphere at matches	32
Hooliganism at football	28
Racism at Football	28
Bad language among some fans	24
Increase in European football	23
Problems bringing kids/friends	15
Too much football on TV	14

(Source: FA Premier League National Fan Survey, 2000, Sir Norman Chester Centre for Football Research, University of Leicester)

In the 1990s, in line with its new customer-service ethic, the Premier League began collecting data on fan demographics and supporters' views via independent means. In 2000, almost 30,000 club supporters were asked which of a number of issues they considered the most serious problems facing top level football. However, club chairmen soon demanded that this type of independent data should be more tightly controlled, giving way to more of a public-relations projection of the Premier League. These sorts of issues continued to niggle fans however and, in 2009, even the British Government questioned the Premier League's internal imbalance and its approach to finances.

Table 11: *Square centimetres of fame:*
British newspaper coverage of celebrities in 2002 (sq. cm.)

1. David Beckham	200,090
2. Prince William	189,974
3. Victoria Beckham	110,040
4. Prince Harry	94,685
5. Kylie Minogue	86,309
6. Michael Jackson	75,729
7. JK Rowling	69,920
8. Liz Hurley	66,332
9. Catherine Zeta-Jones	61,444
10. Zoe Ball	61,000

(Source: survey for BBC3 programme Celebdaq, quoted in the Guardian, 4 July 2003)

In the 1990s, top-class English football became part of the celebrity business. This survey of total annual column inches of British press coverage devoted to celebrities in 2002 showed how the world was changing. A footballer and his pop-singer wife could create more national newspaper interest than two Royal Princes, top pop singers (Minogue and Jackson), star actresses (Hurley and Zeta-Jones), Harry Potter writer JK Rowling and television presenter Zoe Ball.

LIST OF ILLUSTRATIONS

Derby County's Leon Leuty (left) and Jack Nicholas (with FA Cup), 1946 *(Hulton Archive / Getty Images)*

Young children passed overhead to safety at Chelsea's Stamford Bridge, 1947 *(Harry Shepherd / Getty Images)*

FA Cup Finals were national celebrations: Aston Villa fans at Wembley, 1957 *(Popperfoto / Getty Images)*

Spectators at Millwall supporting 'the Lions', 1957 *(Terry Fincher / Getty Images)*

An enthusiastic fan shows her allegiance to Banstead Athletic, a Surrey League team near Epsom, 1955 *(Getty Images)*

Aerial view of 111 football pitches, Hackney Marshes, London, 1962 *(Popperfoto / Getty Images)*

The inner chamber: Manchester City's dressing-room, 1951 *(Getty Images)*

Orderly, respectable fans watching Wolverhampton Wanderers, 1949 *(Picture Post / Getty Images)*

A Sheffield & Hallamshire county FA fixture at Worksop, 1950s *(Courtesy of Nottingham City Council and www.picturethepast.org.uk)*

An early floodlit match intrigues Arsenal fans at Highbury's Clock End, 1951 *(Hulton Archive / Getty Images)*

FA Cup winners Nottingham Forest at Canning Circus, Nottingham, 1959 *(Courtesy of Nottingham City Council and www.picturethepast.org.uk)*

Players' union chairman Jimmy Hill, Minister of Labour John Hare and Football League president Joseph Richards after resolving the players' dispute, 1961 *(Hulton Archive / Getty Images)*

Tom Finney, Preston plumber and England footballer, meets George Best, a celebrity player of the next generation, 1969 *(Popperfoto / Getty Images)*

England women's international Sue Lopez playing in Italy, 1971 *(Photographer unknown)*

Arsenal physiotherapist Bertie Mee applies science to his profession, 1961 *(Courtesy of Press Association Images)*

Derby County manager and media pundit Brian Clough with his son Nigel, 1968 *(Courtesy of Raymond's Press Agency)*

The singing sixties: Wolverhampton Wanderers' fans in a Kop choir *(Courtesy of Press Association Images)*

A boot up the backside wouldn't always be enough, Blackpool, 1970 *(Courtesy of Press Association Images)*

African-Caribbean pioneers Highfield Rangers in the Leicestershire Youth League, 1971–2 *(Photographer unknown)*

Two members of England's 'Task Force' camp in Spain during the 1982 World Cup Finals *(Bob Thomas / Getty Images)*

The Bradford City fire, 11 May 1985 *(Hulton Archive / Getty Images)*

The dressing-room: A place for banter, speeches and fears, Stevenage Borough, 1998 *(Getty Images)*

SOURCES

Our essential books for checking timelines were Barry Hugman, *Football League Players' Records* (Tony Williams Publications, 1992), Gordon Smailes, *The Breedon Book of Football League Records* (Breedon, 1992), Dennis Turner and Alex White, *The Breedon Book of Football Managers* (Breedon, 1993), the *Rothman's Football Yearbook* annuals (Queen Anne Press, 1970–1 to 2002–3) and *Sky Sports Football Yearbook* annuals (Headline, from 2003–4). Another indispensable source was Peter Seddon, *A Football Compendium* (British Library, 1995).

The abbreviation 'K & S' is used to indicate data obtained from the BBC's *Kicking and Screaming* project. Over 300 K & S interviews were conducted during 1993–4 by Alan Brown, Harry Lansdown, Rogan Taylor and Shelley Webb, and the six-part BBC2 series began on 16 October 1995. The series producer was Jean-Claude Bragard, and Rogan Taylor and Andrew Ward wrote the accompanying book, *Kicking and Screaming* (Robson, 1995).

In the sources below, 'AW' refers to Andrew Ward and 'JW' to John Williams. Names are spelled out in full for book titles.

Introduction

We acknowledge our debt to classic works on football and English society, including Nicholas Fishwick, *English Football and Society, 1910–1950* (Manchester University Press, 1989), Richard Holt, *Sport and the British* (Clarendon, 1989), Tony Mason, *Association Football and English Society, 1863–1915* (Harvester, 1980), Dave Russell, *Football and the English* (Carnegie, 1997) and Matthew Taylor, *The Association Game* (Pearson Longman, 2003). Much of the introduction comes from our own observations. Examples of 'something new' were Bristol City manager Gary Johnson's promise to reveal all if Liam Fontaine ever scored, which he did at Wolverhampton Wanderers (3 November 2007), John Dalton's five goals for Brimscombe & Thrupp against Cheltenham Civil Service (20 September 2008) and the sprinkler at the Pirelli Stadium, Burton upon Trent (27 September 2008).

Introduction to Part One

For a detailed description of the events and issues of the 1946–7 start-up season, see Thomas Taw, *Football's War and Peace* (Desert Island Books, 2003). Analysis of *The Times* was between January 1956 and March 1956.

1. Don't Mention the War

The Bobby Daniel story came from Ray Daniel (K & S), the Dennis Herod interview from Anton Rippon, *Gas Masks for Goal Posts* (Sutton, 2005) and AW interviewed Henry Walters for Ian Alister and Andrew Ward, *Barnsley: A Study in Football, 1953–59* (Crowberry, 1981 and 1997). George Shaw was interviewed by Ashley Franklin for the BBC Radio Derby series *The Derby County Story* (1984). Data on the Glikstens and Charlton Athletic came from an interview with Michael Gliksten (K & S), Anthony Bristowe, *Charlton Athletic Football Club* (Convoy, 1951), Colin Cameron, *Home and Away with Charlton Athletic 1920–1992* (Colin Cameron, 1992) and accounts in contemporary newspapers, especially the *Kentish Mercury*. Tales of Sam Bartram came mainly from *Sam Bartram, His Autobiography* (Burke, 1956). Leon Leuty's story was from interviews (Wendy Baker, Tim Leuty and Leon Leuty's Derby County contemporaries) and the Leuty family scrapbooks, including Leuty's own story in the *Nottingham Evening Post*. Other Derby County details were from Anton Rippon and Andrew Ward, *The Derby County Story* (Breedon, 1991 and 1998), Andrew Ward, *Armed with a Football* (Crowberry, 1994) and the *Derby Evening Telegraph* (January–April 1946).

2. 'Surely They'd Fainted'

In 1995 John Harding began work on a projected fiftieth-anniversary book about the Burnden Park disaster. After writing to the *Bolton Evening News Football Pink*, to request people's memories, he received twenty-three replies. He also collected cuttings from the *Bolton Evening News* (March and April 1946 and 16 November 1994), the *Weekly News* (28 December 1957) and *Weekend Mail* (2–6 June 1955). The book did not materialise but Harding kindly handed over his material for the writing of this chapter. Other essential sources were Ronw Moelwyn Hughes, *Enquiry into the Disaster at the Bolton Wanderers' Football Ground on the 9th March 1946* (His Majesty's Stationery Office, 1946) and K & S interviews with Bert Gregory and Audrey Nicholls. We also consulted Percy Young, *Bolton Wanderers* (Stanley Paul, 1961), Stanley Matthews, *Feet First Again* (Kaye, 1952), Nat Lofthouse, *Goals Galore* (Stanley Paul, 1954) and Neil Franklin, *Soccer at Home and Abroad* (Stanley Paul, 1956).

3. Abide with Me

This chapter used the same sources as for Chapter 1. Also, Peter Blake was interviewed for K & S, Harold Miller and Walter Bates were interviewed by Ashley Franklin for BBC Radio Derby's *The Derby County Story* (1984) and Anton Rippon interviewed seven of the Derby County Cup Final team for the same series. AW talked to Rosemary Annable, Raich Carter, Peter Doherty and Tim Ward. Tom Phillips's *Daily Mirror* story appeared on 28 January 1946. Information on Geordie Ridley came from W Tynemouth, *Blaydon Races* (Newcastle upon Tyne City Libraries, 1962).

4. Never Have So Many Attended

The story of Winsford United v Macclesfield Town came from the *Winsford Chronicle*, the *Macclesfield Times* and the *Macclesfield Courier* (February and March 1948). Also important was Graham Phythian, *Saga of the Silkmen* (Carnegie, 2001). To portray a feel for the era we called on many interviews and conversations with fans and players. The Yorkshire colliery statistic on bonuses came from Ferdynand Zweig, *Labour, Life and Poverty* (Victor Gollancz, 1948) and aggregate attendance figures came from Simon Inglis, *League Football and the Men Who Made It* (Willow, 1988). Queuing tales came from *The Times* (7 April 1947 and 23 February 1948). Figures on crowd trouble came from *English Football and Society, 1910–1950* (op. cit.). Eddie McMorran was interviewed for *Barnsley: A Study in Football, 1953–59* (op. cit.). Newcastle United details came from Paul Joannou, *United: The First 100 Years* (ACL Colour Print & Polar, 1991). Barnsley home-comfort figures came from the 1951 census. The Lucas story appeared in *The Times* (18 January 1949 and 22 January 1949). Details of grassroots football came from minutes of the Trowbridge & District Junior Football League (Wiltshire & Swindon History Centre) and Brian Weekes, *The Herefordshire Football League: The First 100 Years* (Lugg Vale Press, 1999). The Leuty story used the same sources as for Chapter 1.

5. The Flying Horse at Wembley

Our story of Pegasus drew from Ken Shearwood, *Pegasus* (Oxford Illustrated Press, 1975), Ken Shearwood, *Hardly a Scholar* (Tiger & Tyger, 1999), Dilwyn Porter, 'Amateur Football in England, 1948–63: The Pegasus Phenomenon', in Adrian Smith and Dilwyn Porter (eds.), *Amateurs and Professionals in Post-war British Sport* (Cass, 2000), Colin Weir, *The History of Oxford University AFC* (Yore, 1999) and AW's interview with Ken Shearwood (December 2006). The interview with Alf Jefferies was by Geron Swann and AW for BBC Radio Oxford's *White House to Wembley* (1996), presented by Hedley Feast. Swann interviewed Pegasus supporters for another BBC Radio Oxford programme (21 April 1987). The *Oxford Mail* sports editor wrote about Oxford people being 'chary of anything new' (*Sports Mail*, 5 February 1949). Interviews with Vic Morris, Edmund Gibbs and Jimmy Smith were by Geron Swann and AW for BBC Radio Oxford's *Village Club to Wembley Winners* (1993) and Geron Swann and Andrew Ward, *The Boys from up the Hill: An Oral History of Oxford United* (Crowberry, 1996). Extra detail came from the *Oxford Mail* (April 1951).

6. 'Run it Off, Son'

Information on Derek Dooley's career came from Derek Dooley and Keith Farnsworth, *Dooley: The Autobiography of a Soccer Legend* (The Hallamshire Press, 2000), Keith Farnsworth, *Wednesday!* (Sheffield City Libraries, 1982), Arthur Hopcraft, *The Football Man* (Collins, 1968), Arthur Ellis, *The Final Whistle* (Stanley Paul, 1962), the *Lancashire Evening Post* (February 1953), the *Sheffield Star* (February 1953) and interviews with Dooley's contemporaries. Detail about Ledger Ritson, who, like Dooley, later had a leg amputated, came from the *Leyton, Leytonstone, Wanstead and Eastern Mercury, Woodford and Chingford Post* (September 1948). The quirks of Harry Cooke and Bob Paisley were explained by Everton and Liverpool players for Rogan Taylor, Andrew Ward and John Williams, *Three Sides of the Mersey* (Robson, 1993). The 1953 Cup Final story came from the BBC match video, plus Martin Johnes and Gavin Mellor, 'The 1953 FA Cup Final' (*Contemporary British History*, June 2006). Leuty's story used the same sources as for Chapter 1.

7. Shine a Light on Stanley

The major sources were Tom Booth (ed.), *The Best Season Ever: The Story of Accrington Stanley Football Club in the Season 1954–55* (Accrington Stanley Football Co. [1921] Ltd, 1955), Phil Whalley, *Accrington Stanley FC* (The History Press, 2001), Phil Whalley, *Accrington Stanley: The Club That Wouldn't Die* (Sportsbooks, 2006), Mike Jackman and Garth Dykes, *Accrington Stanley: A Complete Record* (Breedon, 1991), contemporary reports from the *Accrington Observer & Times*, and K & S interviews with Mike Ferguson and Joe Devlin. *The Index to The Times* for 1954 contained nearly a hundred references to football clubs and the 1934 Betting and Lotteries Act. The *Soccer Star* article on television viewing appeared on 23 April 1955. Sources for the Wolves floodlit matches include Geoffrey Green (*The Times*, 17 October 1954 and 14 December 1954), Richard Whitehead (*The Times*, 7 December 2004) and Michael Peirce, *Blinded by the Lights: A History of Night Football in England* (Desert Island Books, 2006). The four quirky stories came from Ian Addis, *A Passing Game: Fifty Years of Northampton Football (Part 1)* (Jema Publications, 1995), *Soccer Star* (13 November 1954), *The League Paper* (29 October 2006) and Jeff Kent, *Port Vale Tales* (Witan Books, 1991).

8. On the Road

Joe Thorpe was eighty-two when he was visited by AW on 15 November 1979. Thorpe was spending his retirement baking cakes and enjoying his five children, eleven grandchildren and sixteen great-grandchildren. The club's other bus driver, Alma Bell, was interviewed a month later. Between September 1979 and March 1980 Ian Alister and AW interviewed ninety-seven people associated with Barnsley FC in the 1950s (including fifty-nine ex-professional players) for *Barnsley: A Study in Football, 1953–59* (op. cit.). These Barnsley interviews were important here and for other chapters in this book. Barry Barber died on 17 April 1960 and the Sheffield Wednesday accident happened on Boxing Day 1960 (see *The Times*, 28 December 1960). These were only two of many accidents during this period. For instance, Harry Bamford, a Bristol Rovers player, died after a scooter crash on 28 October 1958 when he was on his way to coach schoolboys, and two Willington players died in a car crash after a Northern League match in 1956 (see *The Times*, 12 September 1956). National migration figures came from A. Harris and R. Clausen, *Labour Mobility in Great Britain, 1953–1963* (HMSO, 1967). Macmillan's famous quotation ('most of our people have never had it so good') was delivered at Bedford's football ground on 20 July 1957, according to Peter Hennessy, *Having It So Good* (Allen Lane, 2006), and Harold Macmillan, *Riding the Storm, 1956–1959* (Macmillan, 1971). See also *The Times* (22 July 1957).

Introduction to Part Two

Statistics on the number of teams came from Norman Chester, *Report of the Committee of Football* (HMSO, 1968).

9. 'If This Is Death . . .'

Our main sources were Jack Cox, *Don Davies: an Old International* (Stanley Paul, 1962) and obituaries of journalists who died in the Munich disaster. Relevant material was found elsewhere: David Rayvern Allen, *Arlott: The Authorised Biography* (HarperCollins, 1994); Neil Berry, *Johnny the Forgotten Babe* (Brampton Manor, 2007); Matt Busby, *Soccer at the Top* (Weidenfeld & Nicolson, 1973); Roy Cavanagh and Brian Hughes, *Viollet* (Empire, 2001); Bobby Charlton, *My Soccer Life* (Pelham, 1964); Sir Bobby Charlton, *My Manchester United Years: The Autobiography* (Headline, 2007); Jeff Connor, *The Lost Babes* (HarperSport, 2006); Bill Foulkes, *Back at the Top* (Pelham, 1965); Geoffrey Green, *There's Only One United* (Hodder, 1978); Geoffrey Green, *Pardon Me for Living* (George Allen & Unwin, 1985); Harry Gregg, *Wild About Football* (Souvenir, 1961); Harry Gregg (with Roger Anderson), *Harry's Game* (Mainstream, 2002); Brian Hughes, *The Tommy Taylor Story* (Empire, 1996); Iain McCartney, *Duncan Edwards* (Britespot, 2001); Iain McCartney, *Roger Byrne* (Empire, 2004); Stephen Morrin, *The Munich Air Disaster* (Gill and Macmillan, 2007); Jimmy Murphy, *Matt, United and Me* (Souvenir, 1968); John Roberts, *The Team That Wouldn't Die* (Arthur Barker, 1975); and Frank Taylor, *The Day a Team Died* (Stanley Paul, 1960). Ray Wood's wife was interviewed by Bill Wilson for 'Waiting for news from Munich' (BBC News, 4 February 2008), and the fiftieth anniversary of Munich brought much coverage, e.g. the *Guardian* supplement (2 February 2008). AW's interview with Johnny Morris revealed the importance of MUJACS (February 1991). The 'unsportsmanlike' quotation, allegedly translated from *Politika*, appeared in a number of British newspapers. H. E. Bates wrote 'Manchester United' in *The Official FA Year Book, 1958–59* (William Heinemann/Naldrett Press, 1958). Gavin Mellor wrote 'The Genesis of Manchester United as a National and International "Super Club", 1958–1968' (*Soccer and Society*, summer 2000) and ' "The Flowers of Manchester": The Munich Disaster and the Discursive Creation of Manchester United Football Club' (*Soccer and Society*, summer 2004). The antagonism at Burnley was also described in David Hall, *Manchester's Finest* (Transworld, 2008), and the Dennis Evans story was recorded by Tom Watt, *The End* (Mainstream, 1993). *The Times* covered the pelting of Bolton players (6 May 1958) and Maurer's complaints (7 May 1958).

10. On the Production Line

Geron Swann and AW interviewed fifty-three Oxford United people in a project that produced a BBC Radio Oxford documentary, *Oxford United: Village Club to Wembley Winners* (January 1993), an exhibition at the Museum of Oxford, a BBC Radio Oxford series called *United Memories* (January 1994 to May 1994) and *The Boys from up the Hill* (op. cit.). The interviews pertinent to this chapter – with Harry Thompson, Geoff Denial, Arthur Turner, Ron Atkinson, Ken Fish, Vic Morris, Colin Harrington and Harold Kimber – were all conducted between June 1992 and July 1994. Vic Couling listed Oxford United's Football League potential in a letter to Football League secretary Alan Hardaker (8 March 1961). See also Vic Couling, *Anatomy of a Football Club* (New Horizon, 1983). Figures on the vehicle industry are from Teresa Hayter and David Harvey, *The Factory and the City* (Mansell, 1993). Nicholas Phelps studied the link between Portsmouth FC and its locality for 'The Southern Football Hero and the Shaping of Local and Regional Identity in the South of England' (*Soccer and Society*, autumn 2001) and 'Professional Football and Local Identity in the "Golden Age" ' (*Urban History*, 2005).

11. A Bit of a Flutter

Background about the class, gender and extent of pools participation came from Mark Clapson, *A Bit of a Flutter: Popular Gambling and English Society c1823–1961* (Manchester University Press, 1992), Ferdynand Zweig, *Women's Life and Labour* (Victor Gollancz, 1952) and Keith Laybourn, *Working-class Gambling in Britain, c1906–1960s* (The Edwin Mellon Press, 2007). 'Football Pools' by Ray Galton and Alan Simpson was first broadcast in *Hancock's Half Hour* (November 1959). *Sporting Life Guide* (27 August 1965) gave the advice on pitch size and result. Evocative descriptions of the Saturday tea-time scene came from Michael Palin, 'The Saturday Afternoon

Football Results', in John Mitchinson (ed.), *British Greats* (Cassell & Co, 2000), and the introduction to Lady Henrietta Ross (ed.), *The Ossie Clark Diaries* (Bloomsbury, 1998). Data on big winners came from Macdonald Hastings, 'After winning a fortune' (*The Times*, 17 May 1967), Penny Hunter Symon, 'Things money can do' (*The Times*, 18 January 1971), various other 'News in Brief' items from *The Times*, and Stephen Smith and Peter Razzell, *The Pools Winners* (Caliban, 1975). The Nicholson story came from Phil Reed (ed.), *Football & Fortunes: The Inside Story of Littlewoods Football Pools, 1923–2003* (Brahm, 2003) and Vivian Nicholson and Stephen Smith, *Spend, Spend, Spend* (Jonathan Cape, 1977). See also 'Spend, Spend, Spend' in Jack Rosenthal, *Three Award-winning Television Plays* (Penguin, 1978). The Littlewoods story is told in *Football & Fortunes* (op. cit.) and the company's finances were reported annually in *The Times*.

12. 'Mr Football'

Detail on Sir Joseph Richards came from a *Barnsley Chronicle* obituary (June 1968), interviews with Barnsley players and officials and interviews with Leslie Richards (son) and Mary Sheridan (wife of Richards's chauffeur). Some material was used in *Barnsley: A Study in Football, 1953–59* (op. cit.). K & S interviewees provided extra data on under-the-counter payments. The Sunderland case can be followed via *The Times* in 1957 (e.g. 15 January, 31 January, 11 April, 18 April, 26 April, 9 May, 18 May, 23 May, 11 July, 19 October and 25 October). Background information for this chapter came from *League Football and the Men Who Made It* (op. cit.), John Harding, *For the Good of the Game* (Robson, 1991), Jimmy Hill, *Striking for Soccer* (Peter Davies, 1961), *The Football Man* (op. cit.), Alan Tomlinson, 'North and South: The Rivalry of the Football League and the Football Association', in John Williams and Stephen Wagg (eds.), *English Football and Social Change: Getting into Europe* (University of Leicester Press, 1991), and a court transcript of the Wilberforce judgement. *The Times* covered the 1957 Football League AGM (3 June 1957). Bryon Butler's study of Alan Hardaker appeared in *FA Today*, spring 1980.

13. Saturday Afternoon and Sunday Morning

The main sources here were Peter Smith (K & S interview), Martyn Percy and Rogan Taylor, 'Something for the Weekend, Sir? Leisure, Ecstasy and Identity in Football and Contemporary Religion' (*Leisure Studies*, 1997) and AW's and

JW's own notes on playing and watching Sunday football. The second section relies on *The Times* in 1955 (22 February and 7 June) and 1960 (10 February, 23 February, 7 May, 28 May, 3 June and 12 July). Some background material was taken from *Report of the Committee of Football* (op. cit.), Tony Stephens, *The Sunday Footballer* (Roks Publishing, 1982), an interview with Canon Reg Smith in Brian Radford, *Through Open Doors* (Harrap, 1984), Peter Lupson, *Thank God for Football* (Society for Promoting Christian Knowledge, 2006) and Jeffrey Heskins and Matt Baker, *Footballing Lives* (Canterbury Press, 2006). The Lol Hammett story came from *Port Vale Tales* (op. cit.) and the NOP survey was conducted in January 1967 for the *Daily Mail*.

14. Football, Yeah, Yeah, Yeah

The conversation between Bill Shankly and Harold Wilson was first broadcast on Radio City, Merseyside's commercial radio station, on 1 November 1975. The text has also been transcribed by John Keith for *Shanks for the Memory* (Robson, 1998). Other books on Shankly include Bernard Bale, *The Shankly Legacy* (Breedon, 1996), Dave Bowler, *Shanks* (Orion, 1996), Tom Darby, *Talking Shankly* (Mainstream, 1998), Karen Gill, *The Real Bill Shankly* (Trinity Mirror Sport Media, 2006), Stephen Kelly, *Bill Shankly* (Virgin, 1999), Bill Shankly, *Shankly* (Arthur Barker, 1976) and Phil Thompson, *Shankly* (The Bluecoat Press, 1993). The St John story drew on Ian St John, *Boom at the Kop* (Pelham, 1966), Ian St John, *The Saint: My Autobiography* (Hodder & Stoughton, 2005) and a K & S interview. The history of the Anfield Kop came from interviews for *Three Sides of the Mersey* (op. cit.) and interviews by Rogan Taylor for BBC Radio Merseyside's *On The Kop* (March 1994). The section on spontaneous chanting benefited from conversations and correspondence between AW and Nigel Tattersfield in the early 1980s.

15. Wembley 1966 and After

World Cup details came from Jimmy Armfield, *Right Back to the Beginning: My Autobiography* (Headline, 2004), Bobby Charlton, *Forward for England* (Pelham, 1967), Matt Dickinson, 'Rattín's role in feud chain will never be lost in translation' (*The Times*, 9 November 2005), Geoff Hurst, *My Autobiography: 1966 and All That* (Headline, 2001), Hugh McIlvanney, *McIlvanney on Football* (Mainstream, 1996),

Harold Mayes, *World Cup Report* (William Heinemann, 1967), Martin
Peters, *The Ghost of '66* (Orion, 2006), Nobby Stiles, *After the Ball:
My Autobiography* (Coronet, 2003), David Thomson, *4–2* (Bloomsbury,
1996) and K & S interviews with Alan Ball, Bobby Charlton, Geoff
Hurst and Nobby Stiles. The rest of this story was based around JW's
interview with Sue Lopez (August 2007), Sue Lopez, *Women on the
Ball* (Scarlet Press, 1997) and Wendy Owen, *Kicking Against Tradition*
(Tempus, 2005). The early history of the women's game was covered by
Barbara Jacobs, *The Dick, Kerr Ladies* (Robinson, 2004), Gail Newsham,
In a League of Their Own (Scarlet, 1997), Jean Williams, *A Game for
Rough Girls* (Routledge, 2002) and David Williamson, *Belles of the Ball*
(R & D Associates, 1991). The WFA history came from WFA minutes
and David Marlowe, *Legs Eleven: The Women's Football Association, 1969–
1993* (unpublished). AW interviewed a former Manchester Corinthians
player (November 1984).

16. Chester's XI Takes the Field

This story was based on Sir Norman Chester's football papers, kept in the
Department of Sociology at the University of Leicester. They included
Chester's own handwritten notes, his letters, a collection of cuttings and
articles, a copy of his *Report of the Committee of Football* (op. cit.) and a small
collection of football programmes.

Introduction to Part Three

The opening quotation came from Stephen Wagg, *The Football World*
(Harvester, 1984). The source for television methods during the 1974 World
Cup Finals was Edward Buscombe (ed.), *Football on Television* (British Film
Institute, 1975).

17. The Boss and His Bosses

AW's many interview-conversations with his father, Tim Ward, formed the
basis for *Armed with a Football* (op. cit.) and sections of *The Derby County
Story* (op. cit.). Sam Longson was interviewed by Anton Rippon and Brian
Clough by Ashley Franklin for BBC Radio Derby's *The Derby County Story*.
The discussion on football relationships is from Rogan Taylor and Andrew

Ward, 'Kicking and Screaming: Broadcasting Football's Oral Histories' (*Oral History*, spring 1997). The sources for Clough's life included Brian Clough, *Clough: The Autobiography* (Partridge, 1994), Brian Clough, *Cloughie* (Headline, 2002), George Edwards, *Right Place Right Time* (Stadia, 2007), Tony Francis, *Clough: A Biography* (Stanley Paul, 1987), Duncan Hamilton, *Provided You Don't Kiss Me: 20 Years with Brian Clough* (Fourth Estate, 2007), Brian Moore, *The Final Score* (Hodder & Stoughton, 1999), Gerald Mortimer, *Are the Fixtures Out?* (Breedon, 2003), Patrick Murphy, *His Way: The Brian Clough Story* (Robson, 1993), David Peace, *The Damned Utd* (Faber & Faber, 2006) and Peter Taylor (with Mike Langley), *With Clough by Taylor* (Sidgwick & Jackson, 1980). Other useful learned sources on the changing role and status of the football manager included Stephen Wagg, *The Football World* (op. cit.) and Neil Carter, *The Football Manager* (Routledge, 2006).

18. The Referee Said, 'Play on'

Italicised sections show Barry Davies's commentary for the BBC's *Match of the Day* (17 April 1971). Jack Charlton, George Best, John Giles, Norman Hunter and the ex-referee were K & S interviewees. Details of the match incident were taken from the *Evening Post* (Leeds), the *Birmingham Evening Mail* and Chapter 4 of Stanley Lover, *Soccer Match Control* (Pelham, 1978). Much of Lover's chapter was based on Tinkler's account. Crowd detail came from the two local newspapers and our observations of television footage. IFAB AGM agenda and minutes were consulted. *Match of the Day* viewing statistics came from the BBC Written Archives in Caversham. Tinkler's words were from secondary sources, in particular the *Evening Post* (Leeds).

19. 'Mum, They Haven't Got Tails'

This story was dominated by the voices of people connected to Highfield Rangers during the club's first twenty years (1970–90). Twenty-five of them were interviewed by Laurence Redmond and JW for a Living History Unit project – *Highfield Rangers: an Oral History* (Leicester City Council, 1993). Additional sources were minutes of meetings, reports, *Leicester Mercury* accounts and an obituary of Charlie Williams (*The Times*, 4 September 2004). See also Phil Vasili, *The First Black Footballer* (Cass, 1998) and Phil Vasili, *Colouring Over the White Line* (Mainstream, 2000).

20. 'Never in My Life . . .'

The BBC radio commentary on the match is in italics. We studied footage of the incident and relied heavily on reports in the *Nottingham Evening Post* and *Newcastle Evening Chronicle* (March 1974). Sunderland's economic improvement was studied by E. Derrick and J. McRory, *Cup in Hand: Sunderland's Self Image after the Cup* (University of Birmingham Centre for Urban and Regional Studies, 1973). AW and Geron Swann interviewed Jim Barron for *The Boys from up the Hill* (op. cit.) and JW interviewed Alan Kennedy for Alan Kennedy and John Williams, *Kennedy's Way* (Mainstream, 2004). Ian Jones wrote to Sir Norman Chester (1 November 1982). General information on hooliganism between 1970 and 1976, including punishments and letters of response, came from Sir Harold Thompson's papers at the Royal Society. Relevant club histories included John Lawson, *Forest, 1865–1978* (Wensum Books, 1978) and *United: The First 100 Years* (op. cit.).

21. Don't Call Us, We'll Call You

This chapter is based on Tim Ward's letters to and conversations with AW, who occasionally accompanied him on scouting expeditions. The other main sources were Alan Jenkins and Andrew Ward, 'On the ball about talent spotting' (*Times Higher Education Supplement*, 5 April 1996), Fred O'Donaghue, *Scouting for Glory* (F. O'Donaghue, 1996), John Harding, *Living to Play* (Robson, 2003) and the interview with a scout called Bill Stewart in Robin Daniels, *Blackpool Football* (Robert Hale, 1972).

22. Jimmy Hill Will Fix It

The crux of this chapter was John Williams, Eric Dunning and Patrick Murphy, *All Sit Down: A Report on the Coventry City All-seated Stadium, 1982–83* (Sir Norman Chester Centre for Football Research, University of Leicester, 1984) and John Williams, Eric Dunning and Patrick Murphy, *All Seated Football Grounds and Hooliganism: The Coventry City Experience, 1981–84* (Department of Sociology, University of Leicester, 1984). JW interviewed the 74-year-old Coventry City fan. The story also called on Jimmy Hill, *Striking for Soccer* (Peter Davies, 1961), Jimmy Hill, *The Jimmy Hill Story* (Hodder & Stoughton, 1998) and K & S interviews with Charles Harrold, Eddie Plumley and Jimmy Hill. The summary of the late 1970s was aided by the *Rothman's Yearbook* diary sections. The Lang Report referred to John Lang, *Report of the Working Party on Crowd Behaviour at Football Matches 1969* (HMSO, 1969). Details of the Coventry economy were collected by JW from a range of local sources. The November 1982 survey of Coventry City fans was conducted by JW.

23. If You Think You're Hard Enough

The conversation in the Britannia pub was based on transcripts of interviews with West Ham United fans, most of whom were interviewed by Ian Stuttard for a Thames Television documentary, *Hooligan* (1984). JW was out and about with the Dodge City boys between 1979 and 1982. More detailed accounts appeared in Patrick Murphy, John Williams and Eric Dunning, *Football on Trial* (Routledge, 1991) and Eric Dunning, Patrick Murphy and John Williams, *The Roots of Football Hooliganism* (Routledge and Kegan Paul, 1988). The Middlewich story appeared in a historical chapter in *Football on Trial* (op. cit.).

24. Dodgy Knees, Groin Strains and Metatarsals

The Sir Norman Chester papers contained a complete transcript of the Football Injuries conference (17 February 1982) and contemporary survey data on injuries. During his first Enquiry, in April 1967, Chester had penned questions to his committee: 'Can we make out a case for an inquiry/research centre and medical service for football? Should not this be provided under the National Health and Hospital Service? Could research on injuries be confined to footballers?'

Introduction to Part Four

Analysis of disasters came from Rhona Flin, Paul O'Connor and Margaret Crichton, *Safety at the Sharp End* (Ashgate, 2008). The *Sunday Times* quotation appeared on Sunday 19 May 1985.

25. The Club v Country Show

This chapter may have a fictional setting, but the words were taken from interviewees familiar with the roles indicated. In some cases the character is a composite. The words were adapted from K & S interviewees, an Oxford United manager and Nicholas Allt, *The Boys from the Mersey* (Milo, 2004).

26. Task Force

The opening section reprised interviews with West Ham fans (see Chapter 23). The rest was taken from JW's observational notes from the 1982 World Cup finals and the match in Paris on 29 February 1984. A more complete account of fans at the 1982 finals appeared in John Williams, Eric Dunning and Patrick Murphy, *Hooligans Abroad* (Routledge and Kegan Paul, 1984). The mortality figures were official ones, but veterans' organisations claim that the number of Falklands-related suicides is now greater than the number of deaths during the conflict.

27. Chester's Six-a-side Team

As with Chapters 16 and 24, this story relied on the Sir Norman Chester papers at the University of Leicester's Department of Sociology. The 1983 report was Sir Norman Chester, *Report of the Committee of Enquiry into Structure and Finance* (The Football League, 1983). The Chester papers used here included letters received from club chairmen and members of the public. In addition Martin Spencer was interviewed for a BBC Radio Four *File on Four* programme (1982) and figures on players' incomes came from *Labour Research* (September 1983). Among the books written in the midst of the financial crisis were *Through Open Doors* (op. cit.) and Anton Rippon, *Soccer: The Road to Crisis* (Moorland, 1983). The Dooley information came from *Dooley: The Autobiography of a Soccer Legend* (op. cit.).

28. Fire and Rain

JW observed Leeds United fans during the 1984–5 season and was present at Birmingham on the season's final day. The story was bolstered by accounts from the *Birmingham Evening Mail* and Paul Firth, *Four Minutes to Hell: the Story of the Bradford City Fire* (Parrs Wood, 2005). The Inglis quotation came from Simon Inglis, 'Cause of Death? Complacency . . .' (*The Times*, 9 May 2005). The Tony Delahunte commentary was played on BBC Radio Four's *The Archive Hour* (20 January 2007).

29. 'Corrupt to the Point of Murder'

Alan Kennedy and Keith Kennedy were interviewed by JW for *Kennedy's*

Way (op. cit.). Alan Kennedy was also interviewed by Rogan Taylor for *Three Sides of the Mersey* (op. cit.). Rogan Taylor told the FSA story to AW (December 2007). The extracts from children's essays came from a 1985–6 Liverpool City Council project directed by JW; with the support of the director of education, students aged between ten and sixteen in twenty-one schools were asked to write unsigned essays describing their experiences of, or views on, association football. This led to John Williams, Eric Dunning and Patrick Murphy, *Young People's Images of Attending Football: A Preliminary Analysis of Essays by Liverpool Schoolchildren* (Sir Norman Chester Centre for Football Research, University of Leicester, 1987). The *Financial Times* editorial appeared on 31 May 1985. The inquiry report was Oliver Popplewell, *Committee of Inquiry into Crowd Safety and Control at Sports Grounds* (HMSO, 1985). See also Oliver Popplewell, *Benchmark* (IB Tauris, 2003). The Popplewell Inquiry papers are held at the University of Bradford.

30. 'What Studs Will it Take?'

The cleaner story was told to AW (in different forms) by two professional players of the 1950s and 1960s. Dressing-room team-talks were based on our observations as players and spectators, our interviews with players and YouTube footage. The concept of flow was developed by Mihály Csíkszentmihályi, *Flow: The Psychology of Optimal Experience* (Harper and Row, 1990). The teacher's words came from Mary Chamberlain, *Fenwomen* (Quartet, 1975).

31. Members Only

This chapter's centrepiece was research conducted by JW for inclusion in John Williams, Eric Dunning and Patrick Murphy, *The Luton Home-only Members Plan: Final Report* (Sir Norman Chester Centre for Football Research, University of Leicester, 1987) and John Williams, Eric Dunning and Patrick Murphy, *The Luton Town Members Scheme: Final Report* (Sir Norman Chester Centre for Football Research, University of Leicester, 1989). The chapter also calls on editions of the *Luton News* and *The Times* during March 1985. Some of the discussion about a club's 'rough position in the League hierarchy' was based on *The Football Manager* (op. cit.) and Stephen Dobson and John Goddard, 'Performance, Revenue and Cross Subsidisation in the Football League, 1927 to 1994' (*Economic History Review*, November 1998).

32. 'Soccer on the Rates'

During 1987 JW spent a day a week in Halifax, observing, interviewing and compiling the cuttings file which formed the basis for this story. In that year he interviewed David Helliwell, Billy Ayre, Carol Bell, Gerrie Norrie and Mike Blanch, and regularly talked with Helliwell in the White Swan Hotel. JW also did a follow-up interview with Helliwell (May 2008). Sadly Billy Ayre died in April 2002. Johnny Meynell, *The Definitive Halifax Town AFC* (Tony Brown, 2005) provided excellent background, and Meynell also kindly answered our queries. Halifax Town went into extinction in May 2008 after failing to exit administration correctly. A new club, FC Halifax Town, was formed.

Introduction to Part Five

This part calls on *The Hillsborough Stadium Disaster, 15 April 1989: Inquiry by Rt Hon Lord Justice Taylor, final report* (HMSO, 1990), also known as 'The Taylor Report', Ian Taylor, 'English Football in the 1990s: Taking Hillsborough Seriously' in *British Football and Social Change: Getting into Europe* (op. cit.), and Nick Hornby, *Fever Pitch* (Gollancz, 1992).

33. 'Amen to the Kop'

Jim was interviewed by Rogan Taylor for *On The Kop* (op. cit.). Other sources for this story were Rogan Taylor, Andrew Ward and Tim Newburn, *The Day of the Hillsborough Disaster* (Liverpool University Press, 1995), *The Hillsborough Stadium Disaster, 15 April 1989* (op. cit.), Neil Middleton and John Williams, *Policing Football Matches* (Sir Norman Chester Centre for Football Research, University of Leicester, 1993) and *Three Sides of the Mersey* (op. cit.). Bryan Drew and Trevor Hicks were K & S interviewees, the Lord Hatch letter came from the Sir Norman Chester papers and Mike Brennan wrote 'Mourning and Loss: Finding Meaning in the Mourning for Hillsborough' (*Mortality*, February 2008). Stories about compensation were taken from 'Paying for Blame' (*Police Review*, 10 February 1995).

34. Don't Trust the Press

Fifteen current England players were interviewed by Rogan Taylor and JW between December 1991 and April 1992. The Sir Norman Chester Centre for Football Research was commissioned by the FA to conduct the research, and they were much aided by the then England manager Graham Taylor. Anonymity was assured and therefore the players are not named here. Drawing on this material, John Williams wrote 'Ordinary Heroes: England International Football Players in the 1990s' (*Innovation*, no. 4, 1992). In addition JW saved eight weeks of World Cup national-newspaper cuttings (beginning in mid-May 1990). Seven K & S interviews were relevant too.

35. A Whole New Ball Game

This story was constructed from JW's interviews with Graham Kelly (August 2007) and Rick Parry (May 2002), Graham Kelly, *Sweet FA* (Collins Willow, 1999), Alex Fynn and Lynton Guest, *Out of Time: Why Football isn't Working* (Pocket, 1994), Ted Croker, *And the First Voice You Hear Is –* (Collins, 1987), Greg Dyke, *Inside Story* (HarperCollins, 2004) and a K & S interview with Greg Dyke. Statistics on home ownership and central heating came from *The Blueprint for the Future of Football* (The FA, 1991). Also, JW attended FA meetings and wrote the chapter on fans for *The Blueprint for the Future of Football* (op. cit.).

36. Looking After the Locals

In 1993 and 1994 JW worked with Rogan Taylor on *The National Football and the Community Programme: A Research Report*, funded by the Professional Footballers' Association and completed in September 1994. Billy, Alan, Josh and the London-club community officer were among the interviewees. Flashback information came from K & S interviews with Graham Taylor, Eddie Plumley and Denis Howell, JW's observations at Watford, a talk by Micky Burns and Roger Reade, 'The Community Programme in Professional Football', at the *Football into the 1990s* conference (University of Leicester, September 1988), and Roger Ingham, *Football and the Community Monitoring Project: Phase Two, Summary and Recommendations* (unpublished, 1981).

37. Moving Grounds

Stuart Clarke's story was based on discussions with Clarke, information on his website, Stuart Clarke, *The Homes of Football: The Passion of a Nation* (Little, Brown, 1999), Stuart Clarke, *Football in Our Time: A Photographic Record of Our National Game* (Mainstream, 2003) and 'Grounds for Optimism' (*East*

Cumbrian Gazette, 4 March 1993). Topophilia and topophobia are discussed in John Bale, *Sport and Place* (Hurst, 1983) and John Bale, *Landscapes of Modern Sport* (Leicester University Press, 1994). The average age of stadiums came from *The Economist* (18 April 1993). The meaning of stadiums stemmed from our countless interviews with fans, Simon Inglis, *The Football Grounds of England and Wales* (Willow, 1983), Simon Inglis, *Football Grounds of Britain* (CollinsWillow, 1996) and Stuart Clarke's work. Eric Cantona was quoted in the *Without Walls* television documentary (Channel 4, November 1992). Chris Lightbown described Rootes Hall (*The Sunday Times*, 26 August 1989). Sources on finance include John Major, *John Major: the Autobiography* (HarperCollins, 1999) and *Declining Income and Implementing Taylor* (The Football Trust, November 1996). Various newspapers covered Arsenal's 'move to Wembley' (19 January 1998 and 13 March 1998), Wimbledon's 'move to Ireland' (30 November 1997) and the idea of Leicester City using Coventry City's 'new 100,000-capacity stadium' (15 April 1993). Alf Jefferies was interviewed by Geron Swann and AW in 1996. Millwall leaving the Den was captured by the *Independent* (27 May 1993) and the funding of the New Den by the *Observer* (15 August 1993). Peter Corrigan's Reebok joke was in the *Independent on Sunday* (4 May 1997) and the discussion on atmosphere in the mid-1990s owed a lot to Steve Frosdick and Mel Highmore, 'Ewood Effect' (*Football Decision*, August 1997). Details on the various Wembley schemes appeared in, for example, *The Times* (16 September 1996) and the *Guardian* (9 July 1997 and 3 April 1998). The national-venue preferences of fans came from John Williams and Sam Neatrour, *A National Fan Survey on the New National Stadium: Fans' Responses to the Birmingham and Wembley Bids* (Sir Norman Chester Centre for Football Research, University of Leicester, October 2001). AW spoke to John Gausted in 1990.

38. Where Have All the Players Gone?

This story owes almost everything to Brian Gearing, who interviewed twenty-three former footballers between January 1996 and March 1999. Gearing's original intention was to write a PhD on the subject of retirement from professional and amateur football, but he retired from his own job as Senior Lecturer at the Open University. Gearing's papers on the topic included 'More Than a Game' (*Oral History*, spring 1997) and 'Narratives of Identity Among Professional Footballers in the United Kingdom' (*Journal of Ageing Studies*, spring 1999). Gearing kindly handed over his raw material, discussed his findings and allowed this story to be written. We agreed to maintain the anonymity of the players and the club. Figures on the average length of a career were taken from Gordon Taylor, chief executive of the Professional Footballers' Association, speaking at a Football Injuries conference (17 February 1982). The 'three questions' were attributed to Derek Dougan in Andy Gray, *Gray Matters* (Pan Books, 2004). Additional information on players' wives came from Shelley Webb, *Footballers' Wives* (Yellow Jersey, 1998) and Becky Tallentire, *Real Footballers' Wives* (Mainstream, 2004). We also drew on our own observations from attending reunions of professional players.

39. 'Thirty Thoosand on the Waiting List'

This story was based on research commissioned by the Football Task Force, conducted during November and December 1998, and published as John Williams and Sean Perkins, *Ticket Pricing, Football Business and Excluded Football Fans: Research on the 'New Economics' of Football Match Attendance in England* (Sir Norman Chester Centre for Football Research, University of Leicester, 1998). We also used the original transcripts of focus groups held in Newcastle, Sheffield and north London. Names had been changed. Figures on 'the barcode army' came from Stephen Morrow, *The New Business of Football* (Macmillan Business, 1999).

40. The Tutorial

As with Chapter 25, this story was a composite of interview material and observations, but we have constructed the setting and the flow of the tutorial. The Martin Jacques quotation was taken from the *Observer* (13 July 1997) and discussed in John Williams, *Is It All Over: Can Football Survive the FA Premier League?* (South Street Press, 1999). Minutes of the Trowbridge & District Junior Football League were consulted at Wiltshire & Swindon History Centre (Chippenham). Pete Davies wrote *All Played Out* (Heinemann, 1990) and Nick Hornby wrote *Fever Pitch* (op. cit.). Torquay United won 1–0 at Worcester City (14 November 1998) and Eric Cantona, sent off at Crystal Palace, reacted to a fan's taunts with a feet-first attack on 25 January 1995.

Introduction to Part Six

The Hopcraft quotation came from Arthur Hopcraft, *The Football Man* (Penguin, 1971).

41. A Family Sport

Most of the interviewee data in this chapter came from John Williams and Sam Neatrour, *Football and Families* (Sir Norman Chester Centre for Football Research, University of Leicester, 2001). Peter, Emma, Michael, Andy Tilson, Simon Farmer and others were all interviewees. (In some cases the names have been changed on request.) The 'football and families' data was augmented by interviews with fans from Andrew Ward's and John Williams's other projects. Detail on obsessive fans came from the *Birmingham Evening Mail* (4 May 2007), Jeremy Boon's blog during his 2003–4 bicycle odyssey and the *Stroud News and Journal* (16 January 2008). Information on disabled fans was from John Williams, *Fans at the Trackside* (Sir Norman Chester Centre for Football Research, University of Leicester, June 1992) and John Williams and Sean Perkins, *Leaving the Trackside* (Sir Norman Chester Centre for Football Research, University of Leicester, 1997). The story about the two girls came from a K & S interviewee. Other data on fans was from surveys directed by JW for the FA Premier League in the late 1990s and early 2000s. Also important was John Williams and Jackie Woodhouse, 'Can Play, Will Play? Women and Football in Britain', in *British Football and Social Change* (op. cit.).

42. 'Cup of Tea, Ref?'

This chapter relied mainly on John Williams, *The 'Lords of Truth'? Local Refereeing in England and International Trends* (Sir Norman Chester Centre for Football Research, University of Leicester, 1995), and Andrew Ward, *Ward's Soccerpedia: The Lore and Laws of the Beautiful Game* (Robson, 2006). The cup-of-tea incident was observed by AW at a Gloucestershire Northern Senior League match in 2007. Other general points on refereeing came from Stanley Lover, *Soccer Match Control* (Pelham, 1978 and 1986), Julian Carosi's website, John Baker, *Basic Refereeing* (Hodder & Stoughton, 2004), Robert Evans and Edward Bellion, *The Art of Refereeing* (A & C Black, 2005), Jeffrey Caminsky, *The Referees' Survival Guide* (New Alexandria, 2007), autobiographies of referees, and Nick Neave and Sandy Wolfson, 'Soccer Referees' Perceptions and Coping Mechanisms' (Keynote Address at the Third International Congress of Science Applied to Football, University of Costa Rica, 2002). Ian McColl was interviewed by AW (1984). The unnamed England international was interviewed by Rogan Taylor and JW during their England project (see Chapter 34). The Urs Meier quotation was taken from Jon Henley, ' "It was absolutely the right decision" ' (*Guardian*, 13 October 2004).

43. Franchise FC

The Pearsons were interviewed by AW and JW (March 2008). Other sections rely heavily on Niall Cooper, *The Spirit of Wimbledon* (Cherry Red Books, 2003). Also useful were Michael Lidbury, *Wimbledon Football Club: the First 100 Years* (Wimbledon Football Club, 1991), an MA thesis by Mike Collingwood at the University of Leicester, and Dennis Wise, *Dennis Wise: The Autobiography* (Boxtree, 1999). Clough's view on agents came from *Provided You Don't Kiss Me* (op. cit.). Statistics were from national fans surveys conducted by JW for the FA Premier League. Sir Norman Chester's foresight was demonstrated in *Report of the Committee of Football* (op. cit.).

44. An A–Z of the New Professional Game

Background detail came from Simon Banks, *Going Down: Football in Crisis* (Mainstream, 2002), Tom Bower, *Broken Dreams* (Pocket Books, 2003), David Conn, *The Football Business* (Mainstream, 1997), Sean Hamil, Jonathan Michie and Christine Oughton (eds.), *A Game of Two Halves* (Mainstream, 1999), *The New Business of Football* (op. cit.), Stephen Morrow, *The People's Game: Football, Finance and Society* (Palgrave Macmillan, 2003) and Stefan Szymanski and Tim Kuypers, *Winners & Losers* (Viking, 1999). Books on Beckham included Julie Burchill, *Burchill on Beckham* (Yellow Jersey, 2001), Andy Milligan, *Brand it Like Beckham* (Cyan Books, 2004) and Andrew Morton, *Posh and Becks* (Michael O'Mara, 2003). Beckham's LA Galaxy earnings were from the *Mail on Sunday* (23 November 2008). The section on debt was helped by BBC Radio Four's *File on Four* (11 November 2008), reported by Simon Cox and produced by Paul Grant. Figures on Arsenal's corporate hospitality came from Simon Ellery, 'Corporate Hospitality: The battle of the stadiums' (*PR Week UK*, 28 February 2007). Burton Albion finances came from Nick Harris, 'FA Cup Countdown' (*Independent*, 4 January 2007). Details on gambling were from 'FA launches investigation into £50,000 thrown match' (*Independent*, 5 April 2008), 'UK bad bets and blown lights' (*BBC Online*, 20 August 1999), Helen Pidd, 'Web gambling scam clue to murders of Chinese pair' (*Guardian*, 16 August 2008) and Paul Smith, 'Football: gambling epidemic' (*Sunday Mirror*, 19 February 2006). The ITV Digital story was summarised from Raymond Boyle and Richard Haynes, *Football in the New Media Age* (Routledge, 2004). Journeymen players were studied by Martin Roderick, *The Work of Professional Football: A Labour of Love?* (Routledge, 2006). Kick-off times were discussed by Vicki Hodges, 'Crazy kick-off times and TV guide' (*Daily Telegraph*, 22 November 2008) and Simon Stone, 'United fans protest over kick-off times' (*Independent*, 21 March 2003). Details on players' agents and bungs came from 'Keep out the ten per cent gents' (*Football League Review*, 18 November 1967), Nick Harris, 'What are "bungs" and are they widespread in British football?' (*Independent*, 3 October 2006), Oliver Kay, 'Evil empire? The agents hit back' (*The Times*, 24 January 2005), Kaveh Solhekol, 'Colchester lead the way as clubs strive to cut out middlemen' (*The Times*, 27 July 2007) and the BBC's *Panorama* (19 September 2006). Qualification finances relied on D. Owen, 'The big prize for fans and business' (*Financial Times*, 30 November 2007) and a report by Credit Suisse Global Research (21 May 2008). Stan Hey reviewed the onset of shirt sponsorship (*The Listener*, 25 August 1983) and the Margot Fonteyn analogy came from a letter to Sir Norman Chester (23 December 1982). The Bosman case was outlined in *The New Business of Football* (op. cit.) and Andrew Warshaw, 'No regrets for Bosman' (*UEFA Champions Magazine*, no. 10, 2005). The Webster case was covered by Graham Spiers, 'Webster ruling set to herald a revolution to rival Bosman' (*The Times*, 31 January 2008) and Scott Rutherford, 'Webster sees case paving the way for players to up and leave' (*The Times*, 21 February 2008). The wages story was from Ashley Cole, *My Defence* (Headline, 2006) and part-time staff were studied by David Conn, 'Football's plutocrats resist call for living wage for staff' (*Guardian*, 29 October 2008). The 'young players' section called on Andrew Hussey, 'This man can save English football' (*Guardian*, 26 October 2008) and Martin Samuel, 'English football at risk from French revolution' (*The Times*, 19 November 2008). Alhassan Bangura was featured by Simon Hattenstone, 'The Ultimate Penalty' (*Guardian Weekend*, 15 December 2007).

45. Football and Englishness

JW conducted interviews with Marcos Alvito (March 2008) and Raymond Boyle (February 2008) and John Cartwright was interviewed for K & S. Background information came from *Football in the New Media Age* (op. cit.) and Andrew Ward, *Scotland the Team* (Breedon, 1987). The *Guardian* reporter's observations on Cornwall appeared on 3 April 1989 and other details on the county came from Philip Payton, *The Making of Modern Cornwall* (Dyllansow Truran, 1992). Bentham five-a-side teams were listed in the *Gloucestershire Echo* (19 November 2007).

AUTHORS' NOTE AND ACKNOWLEDGEMENTS

We discussed this book idea for nearly a decade before deciding that the time was right for our project. By then we had independently researched football for over thirty years and between us we had an array of original research material. We had access to nearly a thousand interviews with football-related folk, results from numerous questionnaire surveys, focus-group transcriptions, letters, scrapbooks, statistics, the Sir Norman Chester papers and enough newspaper cuttings and books to block a goal-mouth. We could also draw on our own observations and experiences. One of us was fifty yards from a young Leeds United fan who died at Birmingham City's ground in 1985, present at the 1989 Hillsborough disaster, and helped to write a revolutionary FA document, *The Blueprint for the Future of Football*, in 1991. The other, a football-club manager's son, grew up inside the professional game and watched one of Keith Nicholson's eight draws in 1961.

We particularly acknowledge those who have contributed substantially to this project. Brian Gearing and John Harding generously provided the considerable data on which two chapters are based. Rogan Taylor was our colleague on a number of projects and five chapters of this book are as much a testimony to his work as ours. We thank those who were kind enough to read sections of the manuscript and offer valuable comments: Marcos Alvito, Karen Annesen, Ray Boyle, Stuart Clarke, Winston Heard-White, Richard Holt, Steve Hopkins, Alan Jenkins, Graham Kelly, Sue Lopez, Stanley Lover, Alec McAuley, Chris Moore, Barry Pearson, Anton Rippon, Rajnish Sharma, Ken Shearwood, Geron Swann and Graham Taylor. Thanks also to Ian Blake, Giancarlo Gemin, Julie Highmore, Pete Wood, all the other alleged readers of *The Top Flat Picayune* and our work colleagues over the years. Special thanks to David Kynaston for his advice, inspiration and vision, and to those in Leicester who provided convivial atmosphere: Millie

Banwait, Joy Drinkwater, Alison Langham, Sylvia Langham, Erin Langham, Seb Langham, Arnold Yanovich, Sasha Yanovich and Zelda Yanovich.

Many thanks to all at Bloomsbury who worked on the project, especially our editor Bill Swainson, his assistant Nick Humphrey and managing editor Anna Simpson.

INDEX

A NOTE ON THE AUTHORS

Andrew Ward is a freelance writer. His football books include *Kicking and Screaming* (with Rogan Taylor), *Football's Strangest Matches*, *Ward's Soccerpedia* and *Barnsley: A Study in Football, 1953–59* (with Ian Alister). He lives in Stroud, Gloucestershire.

John Williams is an academic researcher and lecturer in the sociology of sport at the University of Leicester. He has pioneered football research since his studies of hooliganism in the late-1970s and has written twelve books on football and fan culture, the most recent being *The Miracle of Istanbul* (with Stephen Hopkins) and *Groove Armada: Benítez, Anfield and the New Spanish Fury* (with Ramon Llopis). He lives in Leicester.

A NOTE ON THE TYPE

The text of this book is set Adobe Garamond. It is one of several versions of Garamond based on the designs of Claude Garamond. It is thought that Garamond based his font on Bembo, cut in 1495 by Francesco Griffo in collaboration with the Italian printer Aldus Manutius. Garamond types were first used in books printed in Paris around 1532. Many of the present-day versions of this type are based on the *Typi Academiae* of Jean Jannon cut in Sedan in 1615.

Claude Garamond was born in Paris in 1480. He learned how to cut type from his father and by the age of fifteen he was able to fashion steel punches the size of a pica with great precision. At the age of sixty he was commissioned by King Francis I to design a Greek alphabet, for this he was given the honourable title of royal type founder. He died in 1561.